SEDUCTION

SEDUCTION

A HISTORY
FROM THE ENLIGHTENMENT
TO THE PRESENT

CLEMENT KNOX

PEGASUS BOOKS
NEW YORK LONDON

SEDUCTION

Pegasus Books, Ltd.
West 37th Street, 13th Floor
New York, NY 10018

Copyright © 2020 by Clement Knox

First Pegasus Books hardcover edition February 2020

Interior design by Sabrina Plomitallo-González, Pegasus Books

ISBN: 978-1-64313-199-3

10 9 8 7 6 5 4 3 2 1

Printed in the United States of America
Distributed by W. W. Norton & Company

To My Parents

When we behold two males fighting for the possession of the female, or several male birds displaying their gorgeous plumage, and performing strange antics before an assembled body of females, we cannot doubt that, though led by instinct, they know what they are about, and consciously exert their mental and bodily powers.

—Charles Darwin, *The Descent of Man*, Chapter VIII

CONTENTS

INTRODUCTION
1

CHAPTER ONE
Rake Culture   13

CHAPTER TWO
The Transit of Venus   80

CHAPTER THREE
An Unsentimental Education   143

CHAPTER FOUR
Circling Mary Shelley   197

CHAPTER FIVE
Of Mann and Men   251

CHAPTER SIX
Blood Out   320

CHAPTER SEVEN
Seduction Remains   374

AFTERWORD
418

ACKNOWLEDGMENTS
433

ENDNOTES
434

INDEX
473

INTRODUCTION

In 1873, a Georgia court heard the appeal of Myron Wood against his earlier conviction in a seduction case involving Emma Chivers. Wood was a reverend, schoolmaster, and Civil War veteran, a pillar of the community in Decatur, the seat of DeKalb County, in northeast Georgia. Chivers was fifteen when she first met Wood, who was her teacher at school and her pastor at church. She was the daughter of a destitute widow, so poor that Wood took the family into his own home to help relieve their poverty. But Wood had other motives. His own wife was terminally ill, and he seduced Chivers, promising her that he would marry her once his sick spouse died. Chivers trusted him, respected him, and probably somewhat feared him, and she submitted to his advances, the first time she had ever done so. A child was born, whereupon Wood went back on his word and denied all responsibility. This was the background to Chivers's initial, successful lawsuit. On appeal Wood adopted a new strategy. He did not deny that the affair took place, simply that Chivers was ineligible for protection under the seduction statute as she was a lascivious girl, sluttish, and primed for sin. Wood's lawyers marshaled an array of witnesses willing to testify to Chivers's low morals and lustful nature. The sins of the mother were visited upon the daughter. A spinster was found who claimed that Chivers's mother was rumored to have consorted with black men and may have even run a brothel in Atlanta. Classmates took to the stand. They revealed that Chivers was not in the habit of concealing her legs as a good Christian girl was expected to do. Some had seen her hug and kiss young men. Others noted her penchant for unfruitful fruit-picking expeditions with local boys. Was it not true, the counsel for the defense asked her, that she was known to go "black-berry hunting with young men and [bring] no blackberries back?"

The state supreme court sided with Wood. Emma Chivers, the justices ruled, was not a seducible woman.[1]

Seduction is normally conceived of as something that happens between individuals. The case of Myron Wood and Emma Chivers is one example among countless available that this is not the case. A casual survey of modern Western history reveals that as long as sex has been considered a private matter, seduction has been considered a public concern. For centuries, seduction had a legal dimension and today remains a perennial problem for human resource professionals in corporations and administrators at universities. For just as long, writers, dramatists, and film-makers have relied upon the tales of seduction to titillate and provoke their audiences. The rise of seduction as a popular literary genre was simultaneous with the birth of modernity. Widely considered the first novel in English, *Pamela* (1740), is about the trials faced by a precari-ously employed young woman working for a wealthy and sexually rapa-cious young man. An absurd conceit for a book, one might say, though the immense popularity of this tale in its day is better understood when one considers its elements as being essentially indistinguishable from one of the great bestsellers of our own time, *Fifty Shades of Grey* (2011). Fic-tional seduction narratives entertain us in equal measure as they disturb us. Seduction draws into its dragnets a whole range of sensitive issues. To think about seduction as a social concern is to engage with matters of morality, philosophy, politics, class, race, and gender. If these sub-jects fascinate in fiction, then they scandalize in fact. Factual instances of seduction—broadly defined—have dominated the attention of head-lines, courtrooms, and legislative bodies from the eighteenth century to the twenty-first. All this to say, seduction very clearly has a social and cultural existence that can be charted, yet its history has never been written. There seems to be no clear reason why that should continue to be the case.

Every aspect of human experience has its history; the problem is identifying how best to measure it. The unit of measurement for the history of seduction is that strange and powerful thing, the seduction narrative. The basic claim of this book is that the seduction narrative is a product of the modern world and serves as a vehicle for the exploration of modern values, modern experiences, and modern concerns.

This is not to say that seduction *never* existed in fact or fiction before the onset of modernity. The moons of Jupiter are named for four of Zeus's most celebrated seductions. The nymph Io he enshrouded in darkness and then turned into a snow-white heifer to conceal her from his jealous wife. Callisto, the "Arcadian virgin [who] suddenly caught his fancy and fired his heart with a deep-felt passion," he approached in the guise of her mistress, the goddess Diana, before taking her in his arms and revealing his identity. To win the Phoenician princess Europa, he "discarded his mighty sceptre and clothed himself in the form of a bull." Once he had lured her to sit on his back, he swam out to sea, taking her all the way to Crete, where they eventually had three children together. To secure the Trojan youth Ganymede, Zeus took the form of an enormous eagle and swooped down from the skies and carried him away to Mount Olympus. All these stories are recorded in the *Metamorphoses*, written by the Roman poet Ovid, who is arguably more famous for authoring the first-ever seduction manual, the *Ars Amatoria*, in the second century BC. Ovid's frank treatment of seduction scandalized the emperor Augustus, and Ovid was sent into exile on the Black Sea. Whatever tribulations he experienced in his own lifetime, Ovid's legacy endured. In the premodern world he was the paradigmatic writer on seduction, name-checked by Chaucer and Shakespeare and avidly read by every educated young man. Indeed,

Ovid's influence was so great that it became an inspiration for perhaps the first proto-feminist analysis of seduction. Writing in the early fifteenth century, Christine de Pizan mocked the clerks who lived by Ovid's sexual commandments while lamenting that the sexual culture his writings had helped forged made life impossible for women. For a beautiful woman to keep herself chaste, de Pizan wrote, is "like being in the midst of flames without getting burnt" on account of her having "to fend off the attentions of young men and courtiers who are eager to have affairs."[2]

Classical writers aside, the other major influence on how premoderns thought about seduction was Christianity. In the Christian tradition, the problem of seduction had begun not with Ovid but with Eve in the Garden of Eden. From the earliest days of the Christian faith, theologians had identified the first woman, Eve, and consequently *all* women, with lust. Saint Augustine had claimed that mankind's original sin was the lustfulness uncovered in Eve after she ate the apple at the serpent's urging. Augustine believed that the "legacy of Eve" was the "sorrow she brought into the world" through her discovery of her sexuality. As a result of this mythology, early Christian culture was astonishingly misogynistic. Saint Jerome was so aghast at the carnality he associated with women that he counseled chastity for men wherever possible. Indeed, he identified men with sexual restraint (with "the virtue of continence"), whereas women were marked with the "command to increase and multiply" associated with the expulsion from Eden and with "the nakedness and the fig-leaves which speak of sexual passion." The writer and apologist Tertullian described women as "each an Eve . . . You are the devil's gateway: you are the unsealer of that forbidden tree: you are the first deserter of divine law." For the eleventh-century Benedictine monk Saint Peter Damian women were "bitches, sows, screech-owls, night owls, she-wolves, blood suckers . . . harlots, prostitutes, with your lascivious kisses, you wallowing places for fat pigs, couches for unclean spirits, demi-goddesses, sirens, witches."[3]

The consequence of theological misogyny was a literary tradition in which the dominant seduction narrative was that of a woman seducing a man. In "The Wife of Bath's Tale" in Chaucer's *The Canterbury Tales*, this trope was mocked by the female narrator who describes how men, drunk on Ovid, Jerome, Tertullian, and all the rest, came to believe that women were intrinsically licentious and that they "cannot keep the vow of marriage." When at the end of the fourteenth-century romance *Sir Gawain and the Green Knight*, Gawain discovers that the witch Morgan Le Fay has been toying with him throughout the tale, he gives vent to his frustrations concerning male powerlessness in the face of female manipulation:

> But it's no wonder a fool should lose his senses and be brought to
> his downfall through the wiles of women. For Adam in this world
> was misled by one, and Solomon by several, and Samson after
> him—Delilah was his ruin—and David afterwards, was blinded
> by Bathsheba and suffered much misery. Since all of these were
> deluded, it would be a fine thing to love them well without trusting,
> if a man could do it.[4]

Many of these concerns spilled over into the popular fear about witches. "All witchcraft comes from carnal lust," intoned the *Malleus Maleficarum*, the classic treatise on the subject, "which in women is insatiable."[5]

In the sixteenth and seventeenth centuries these attitudes began to soften. The continental tradition of courtliness popularized by writers like Baldassare Castiglione and Philip Sidney encouraged socializing among the sexes—at least at an elite level—and emphasized that courtship could be an aesthetic pleasure and not a moral hazard. This attitude is certainly in evidence in Shakespeare's comedies, where the game of love is played out in an endless carnival of disguise, gender confusion, and enchantment. In figures like Richard III, who as the Duke of Gloucester seeks to seduce the widow Lady Anne, gloating that he will triumph though he has "nothing to back my suit at all, But the plain devil and dissembling looks," Shakespeare also looks forward to more modern conceptions of the seduction narrative, where men are predators and women are prey.

⸻ ⊰✦⊱ ⸻

These precursors are interesting, but they feel intellectually apart from our modern conceptions of sexual morality and sexual experience. The cause of that distance—and the reason that this book begins at the start of the eighteenth century and not before—is the Enlightenment. The seduction narrative was made possible by a series of intellectual developments and value shifts that arose out of this period. Specifically, three new modes of thought gave rise to the modern seduction narrative: liberalism, materialism, and feminism. All three had an interconnected influence on one another. A theological conception of the world (one where the devil was abroad in society, witches met in covens, saints worked miracles, and angels intervened in the lives of men) was replaced with a material understanding of reality based on our perceptions of measurable phenomena. This in turn led to the development of liberal political theories that invested individuals with rights, responsibilities, and autonomy over their own lives. Taken together, these two developments undermined millennia of reflexive misogyny and put what was long known as "the woman question," now known as feminism, at the center of public debate.

This can all sound quite abstract, but there were real-world consequences. Take the example of marriage. Between 1600 and 1800 there was a revolution in marriage norms. At the beginning of the period, arranged marriages were a common and unremarked-upon feature of daily life. By the turn of the nineteenth century, it was considered barbaric to coerce anyone into marriage. The ideal was now companionate marriage where man and woman met, bonded, and freely chose to enter into wedlock. Writing in the *Spectator* (the magazine he co-founded) in 1711, liberal essayist Joseph Addison declared that "those marriages generally abound most with love and constancy that are preceded by a long courtship. The passion should strike root and gather strength before marriage be grafted on to it." This attitude was basically unchallenged by the end of the eighteenth century—but it raised a raft of issues. If marriage was now a private choice, then individuals, especially women, had to be trusted to make their own decisions. But could they be trusted to make the right ones? What if they were deceived? If they were misled, were they owed any special sympathies or even particular legal protections? Conversely, if men were judged to have behaved in a deceptive or exploitative manner, how were they to be dealt with? Should they be punished? Should they be reformed? Or, as the hackneyed saying goes, is all fair in love and war? As we shall see, these questions occupied the attention of some of the most celebrated minds of the past. They still concern us now.

Underpinning all these debates is a more fundamental question. The Enlightenment is sometimes referred to as the Age of Reason—a time when rational thought supplanted superstition and ignorance and the world was metaphorically illuminated by the light of logical thinking. This is not the entire story. While it is true that most Enlightenment thinkers rejected theology in favor of empiricism, systematic investigation, and the scientific method—in other words, in favor of materialism—this did not lead all of them to a dogmatic faith in the power of reason. When they studied themselves, some philosophers found that they were far from logical. Observing his own brain trying to make sense of the world, philosopher David Hume concluded that his mind was "a kind of theatre, where several perceptions successively make their appearance; pass, repass, glide away, and mingle in an infinite variety of postures and situations." Hume believed that these fleeting sensations and momentary impulses—what he called the passions—influenced human behavior more than rational thought. Hume was not alone in reaching this conclusion. The question as to whether reason or passion exerts greater sway on human decision-making was one of the foundational debates of the Enlightenment. And it is with us to this day.[6]

The argument of this book is that this debate has survived in the seduction narrative. This finds expression in the fact that seduction narratives come in two forms. Each takes a different side of this debate. Each tells a complementary story about the modern world. In the classic seduction narrative—what we might call the "Villainous" kind—the seducer uses guile, deception, and mental games to overcome their target's resistance. It implies a psychological vulnerability on the part of seduced—a fact reflected in the etymology of the word: *se + ducere*, to lead away. Seduction assumes one person is manipulating another, leading them away from their true preferences. This was the basis for the crucial legal distinction between rape and seduction. Whereas rape was coercive, seduction admitted consent while assuming that consent had somehow been degraded by the techniques of the seducer. As one New York court put it in 1896, "to constitute seduction, the defendant must use insinuating arts to overcome the opposition of the seduced and must by wiles, without force, debauch her."[7] In common law the classic example of seduction was a woman who agreed to sex after accepting a disingenuous marriage proposal. This, in the eyes of society and the law, was a species of fraud, as consent had been obtained by a lie. Early-nineteenth-century feminists campaigning for increased legal protections for women and girls understood the threat of seduction as being pervasive. In a pamphlet from 1910, one wrote that

> *Every human atom is endowed with some primeval instinct of self-preservation, and it is this instinct which must be relied upon to give its danger signal. Yet it cannot be expected to do its work, if hampered by the toils of unreasoning and prejudiced ignorance.*[8]

Seduction—the "ultimate inferno"—was brought about by the assault on the rational mind "by the toils of unreasoning and prejudiced ignorance." Nowadays the language used to describe such scenarios tends to focus on structures of power and patterns of grooming and assault. The common feature is that the seduction narrative dramatizes powerlessness. This is why from *Clarissa* (1748) to *Cruel Intentions* (1999), the victims of seducers are portrayed as naive, unworldly women. This is not to say that there have not been seduction narratives featuring women seducing men—as we shall see, this has been a recurring countercurrent from the eighteenth century to the twenty-first—simply that they rely on the premise that men are the powerless playthings of predatory, powerful women, a contention that has lacked credibility for almost all recorded history. This speaks to the political, feminist dimension of these seduction narratives. They tell a story about women's place in society. They allegorize their oppression.

If the villainous seduction narrative dwells on psychological vulnerability, the other kind of seduction narrative focuses on the power of reason. Enlightenment philosophers believed that individuals were endowed with reason and could use it to make decisions in their own best interests. In one of the foundational manifestos of the Enlightenment, the

Declaration of Independence, the founding fathers of the United States declared that among the "unalienable Rights" of free men were "Life, Liberty, and the Pursuit of Happiness." The other kind of seduction narrative—the one that portrays the seducer as a hero, not a villain—is intensely interested in that pursuit. Throughout this book we shall meet writers and intellectuals who believed that the rational pursuit of sexual pleasure was an endeavor characteristic to the enlightened individual. In England, one of the earliest champions of this position was the writer and dramatist Henry Fielding, who considered men and women's desires natural "and productive not only of corporeal delight, but of the most rational felicity." In continental Europe, philosophers like Voltaire and Casanova argued much the same. Nor was it just men who trumpeted the virtues of sexual freedom. The pursuit of what she called "rational desires" was central to the intellectual project of Mary Wollstonecraft. Among the Romantics, Free Love was embraced in theory and practice by women such as Mary Shelley and Claire Clairmont as much as it was by men like Percy Shelley and Lord Byron. In the latter half of the twentieth century, this view of human sexuality became basically unchallenged. From James Bond to Brigitte Bardot, seducers were celebrated in the culture as symbols of sexual freedom, free agents who had unburdened themselves of the irrational prejudices of custom, religion, and taboo. In the twenty-first century, the rise of algorithmic online dating represents the triumph of seduction as a logical exercise.

These rival traditions in the seduction narrative—reason versus passion; the seducer as hero versus the seducer as villain—coexist. They are, in fact, deeply intertwined. This book covers a period of three centuries, and both kinds of narrative exist in every time and in every place that is studied. Indeed, the foundational conflict between reason and passion that is at the heart of this history is often found within seduction narratives themselves. For example, in the eighteenth-century novel *The*

Man of Feeling, the seduced and betrayed Emily Atkins contrasts her passionate abandon with her seducer's cold, calculating nature:

> *It was gratitude, it was pride, it was love! Love which had made*
> *too fatal a progress in my heart, before any declaration on his*
> *part should have warranted a return: but I interpreted every look*
> *of attention, every expression of compliment, to the passion I*
> *imagined him inspired with, and imputed to his sensibility that*
> *silence which was the effect of art and design.*

This dynamic tension between reason and passion also accounts for another recurrent theme in this book: the use of hypnosis as a metaphor for seduction. As we shall see in the chapters on Mary Shelley and Bram Stoker, hypnotism was a potent symbol of seduction, as it was a transitional psychological state that bridged the worlds of reason and passion. Seduction is bewildering, exciting, and dangerous because it occupies this gray zone of agency. It is also precisely for this reason that seduction has repeatedly been the subject of legal interest. As we shall see in the later chapters of this book, the legal principles that brought Emma Chivers to the courtroom in the 1870s were born of passionate public debates about the limits of rational sexual decision-making and consequently with the limits of consent.

This tension creates paradoxes—contradictions that will surface again and again in this narrative. Those who believe that individuals are prone to violent passions and vulnerable to manipulation tend to argue for the creation of laws and rules that will try to rationally regulate sexual desire. As we shall see, the successful campaigns on both sides of the Atlantic in the nineteenth and early twentieth centuries to bring about a body of law to police seduction mobilized these "Villainous" seduction narratives to achieve their goals. Out of the chaos of the passionate mind was born the need for a set of logical legal codes. Yet these supposedly rational laws were quickly revealed to be capricious themselves. As the example of Emma Chivers showed, far from being impartial, seduction laws were used to police arbitrary boundaries of class, race, and gender.

Conversely, the "Heroic" seduction narrative uses the claim of rationality to advance a culture of sensual revelry. From the hedonism of Enlightenment London, Paris, and Venice, to the Free Love doctrines of the Romantics, to the Sexual Revolution of the 1960s and 1970s, sexual rationalism has been used to justify a culture of pleasure, permissiveness, and emotional authenticity. Yet time and again, the promise of sexual freedom in theory has run up against the problem of sexual freedom in practice. The dream of emotional authenticity underpinned by a model of rational decision-making has all too often led to a reality of sexual exploitation motivated by an unfeeling transactionalism that conceals itself within a masque of sexual liberation. At the height of the Sexual Revolution, Germaine Greer observed as much when she wrote in *The Female Eunuch* that "sex for many has become a sorry business, a mechanical release involving neither discovery nor triumph, stressing human isolation more dishearteningly than ever before."[9]

These paradoxes, these brawling contradictions, are the engine of this book. But what follows is not an attempt to endlessly restate the arguments made in this introduction. These are intended to function only as the poles, pegs, and guy ropes that give structure to the marquee of the book. Crowded under the canopy are a dozen or so major figures, and a selection of minor figures, through whose lives and relationships and writings the history of seduction will be explored.

CHAPTER ONE

─◦─ ≡◦≡ ─◦─

RAKE CULTURE

He could not fidget—as a man well might, standing in the dock of the Old Bailey, charged with a capital offense—because his thumbs were bound together with twine. This seemed to be the end of the road for Colonel Francis Charteris. After a long and infamous career as Britain's most notorious rake, Charteris, now in his late sixties, stood accused of the rape of his onetime maidservant Anne Bond. Standing before a judge and jury in February 1730, he had little hope of obtaining an acquittal. He was one of London's most renowned sexual predators, so detested for his lechery and his abusive methods that his house in Hanover Square had been attacked by angry mobs on more than one occasion. He had a previous conviction for rape that he had only managed to have annulled through generous bribery (what was then known as a *"Golden Nol. Pros."*). His trial took place amid a blizzard of Grub Street pamphlets that chronicled his misdeeds, real and fictional, and denounced him as "the Rape Master General of Great Britain." In taverns, coffeehouses, and salons throughout the capital the most scandalous rumors were spread about him, including allegations that he had raped his own grandmother.[1]

When he was found duly guilty the courtroom erupted in cheers. A few days later he was summoned to the same place for sentencing. Dressed in a cavalry officer's uniform, attended to by a brace of footmen, Charteris was sentenced to hang at Tyburn along with nine other common criminals brought before the magistrate in the same session. His carriage back to Newgate Prison was followed by a large crowd of happy Londoners, eager to advertise and celebrate the imminent demise of the nation's most prolific and unprincipled sexual adventurer. "The most popular Whore-master in the three Kingdoms," as one contemporary account had it, "said to have lured as many Women into his toils as would set up a *Sultan*."

Charteris had been born in Edinburgh at some point in the 1660s. His father was a wealthy landowner in Dumfriesshire, and the Charterises were a family with ancient ties to the Scottish aristocratic elite. His youth was almost exactly coterminous with the reign of the restored Charles II, the Merry Monarch, whose priapic rule signaled a dramatic end to the Puritanism of Cromwell's Protectorate. The libidinism of Charles's court was without parallel in English history. The king very much led by example. "His scepter and his prick are of a length," the Earl of Rochester reported, "and she may sway the one who plays with th' other." St. James's was a long way from the Charteris family seat in Amisfield. Nevertheless, the cyprian spirit of the age made itself felt on the young man and would find morbid expression in him in his later years.

Charteris's devilish ways first became matters of public record in the 1690s, when he joined the army of the Duke of Marlborough in Flanders. It is unclear how much, if any, combat Charteris saw. What is known is that he soon became a figure of general loathing for his ill-treatment of his brother officers. Charteris had become an inveterate card cheat as well as a ruthless loan shark. It seems that he used his skills in one arena to create customers for the other. These demoralizing activities, combined with various unspecified abuses of the local population, secured his expulsion from the army twice, the second occasion shortly before the Battle of Blenheim in 1704. Thereupon Charteris returned to Scotland, where he paid his way back into the army, came into his inheritance following his father's death, and, to general amazement, managed to marry. The details of this union, like so much about his earlier life, are unknown, but it yielded a daughter, Janet Charteris, who would later do no service to the cause of British women through her loyalty to her villainous father.

Rich and married, Charteris now embarked on a phenomenal spree. He invested his income at the card table, where he systematically bilked the Scottish elite of their wealth. The master of the marked card and the loaded die, he had soon multiplied his net worth. In one particularly scandalous occasion he managed to inveigle his way into the Edinburgh salon of the Duchess of Queensbury and, with the aid of a strategically situated mirror, rob his hostess blind during a card game in her own living room. This enraged her husband the Duke so much that he lobbied Parliament to change the law concerning the amount of money one could wager while gaming.

This incident and many others like it served to make him a persona non grata in Scottish society. But ostracism could little restrain a man with Charteris's capacity for roguery, nor did it hinder the indulgence of his other appetites: women and property. Acquiring the latter was fairly straightforward. As for the former, Charteris used money, force, and fraud to obtain sex and traveled far and wide to do so. His preference was for working-class women, "strong, lusty, fresh Country Wenches," one account records, "of the first Size, their B—tt—cks as hard as Cheshire Cheeses, that should make a Dint in a Wooden Chair and work like a Parish Engine at a Conflagration." The accumulation of a substantial property portfolio created the need for large permanent staffs upon whom Charteris could prey. In 1713 he purchased Hornby Lodge in Lancashire, a place that became host to any number of proto-Sadean scenes as Charteris remodeled the house for his own debauched purposes—including the installation of secret passages that led to trapdoors in the servants' bedrooms—and then sent his agents out into the neighboring countryside to find victims for his orgies. Soon the residents of the surrounding villages knew better than to send their wives and daughters to work for Charteris, and his panders had to search farther afield for suitable targets.

On one famous occasion, Charteris's valet John Gourley found a girl looking for work as a maidservant but who was only willing to enter the service of either an unmarried woman or a widow. Gourley lured her to Hornby Lodge on the promise of work with his benign and virtuous mistress. Upon arrival she was told her potential new employer would interview her from her bed. Halfway through the conversation her would-be mistress sprang from bed and disrobed to reveal the degenerate form of Francis Charteris, struggling to free himself from his disguise. He presently tried to seduce the shocked girl and, when that failed, drew a pistol and demanded sex. She pretended to comply, and when Charteris laid down the gun in preparation for his ministrations, she seized it, turned it upon her attacker, and "swore by all that was sacred, she would discharge it into his Body, if he did not return instantly to his Bed." Charteris obliged, and the girl made her way safely out of the building, gun in hand[2].

The great number of properties Charteris owned necessitated a considerable amount of travel between them, and it was during these sojourns that much of his most despicable business was carried on. On one such occasion Charteris was traveling between Musselburgh and Edinburgh, when he came across a solitary woman carrying a sack of corn. Charteris solicited her, and when she refused both his advances and his money, he raped her at pistol point. After she escaped, she told her husband, who sought personal revenge, and when that was not coming, legal redress. Charteris's customary attempts to bribe his way out of trouble failed, and an Edinburgh court summoned him to appear before it and charged him with rape. Fearing that justice would be done Charteris fled south to England and made his way to London.

London in the early eighteenth century, according to one jaundiced contemporary, was "like the Ocean, that receives the muddy and dirty Brooks, as well as the clear and rapid Rivers, swallows up all the *Scum* and *Filth*, not only of our own, but of other Countries: *Wagons, Coaches, and Carrivans; Pack-Horses, Ships,* and *Wooden-Shoes; French, Dutch, German,* and *Italian* tattered Garments, being constantly emptying and discharging themselves into this *Reservoir*, or *Common-Sewer* of the World." With a population of over half a million it was the largest city in Europe and the largest conurbation by far in the United Kingdom, accounting for a tenth of the total population and dwarfing the next largest city, Bristol, which was home to a mere thirty-thousand people.

London was dirty, crowded, and dangerous. There were innumerable ways to die. Highwaymen worked the roads between the built-up center and the nearby villages and market towns of Kensington, Camberwell, Hampstead, and Islington. Swords were worn in public and used in street fights, tavern brawls, and confrontations in the theatre. Smallpox was the terror of every citizen; the sexually indulgent, or even just the unlucky, faced an agonizing death from the venereal diseases that claimed several thousand lives each year. The poor died of gin-drinking and starvation and upon the ravenous scaffolds at Tyburn. The old wooden houses in Covent Garden and Drury Lane came cheap—as little as twopence a night—but collapsed with regularity and were at perpetual risk of fire. "Here malice, rapine, accident, conspire," Samuel Johnson wrote in "London, A Poem":

> *And now a rabble rages, now a fire;*
> *Their ambush here relentless ruffians lay,*
> *And here the fell attorney prowls for prey;*
> *Here falling houses thunder on your head,*
> *And here a female atheist talks you dead.*

The city's capacity to kill was offset by the enormous quantity of sexual activity going on among its populace. To read the London press of the day is to enter a world seemingly exclusively populated by coquettes, coxcombs, cuckolds, and prudes engaged in a permanent carnival of amorous intrigue. "I confess," wrote one despairing Londoner to a country friend, "if you have a Design to make your self a good Proficient in the Arts of *Whoring*, and *Drunkenness*, or to understand exactly the Methods of *Debauchery* and *Profaneness*, this is indeed the Place of the World." Sexual profligacy was then the fashion and the men of London competed with one another to prove their seductive powers. The mania for sexual adventure and amorous expertise found innumerable expression. A whole new vocabulary sprang to life to describe the mores of the day. Seemingly every man aspired "to keep cully," the more prodigious were known as "Whore-mongers"; for those with limited resources a couple of shillings could afford a visit to a "Vaulting School" kept by an "Abbess" or "Mother," though doing so brought with it the risk of contracting the "Drury-Lane Ague" or the "Covent Garden Gout." Among the Quality, "Whoring, Drinking and Gaming, are reckon'd among the Qualifications of a fine Gentleman." These well-born, moneyed sybarites were the rakes who either as individuals or gathered together in clubs—the Mohocks, the Hell-Fire Club, and many more—roved the city searching for trouble and pleasure. One ballad recorded in print in 1719 records the sexual escapades of these leisured men:

> *But the Town's his* Seraglio, *and still he lives free;*
> *Sometimes she's a Lady, but as he must range,*
> Black *Betty, or* Oyster *Moll serve for a Change:*

As he varies his Sports his whole Life is a Feast,
He thinks him that is soberest is most like a Beast:
All Houses of Pleasure, breaks Windows and Doors,
Kicks Bullies and Cullies, then lies with their Whores:
Rare work for the Surgeon and Midwife he makes,
What Life can Compare with the jolly Town-Rakes.

Such behavior was by no means limited to the wealthy elite. Scandalized observers recorded the democratic nature of the phenomenon. One complained of the *"Suburbs gallant Fop that takes delight in Roaring, / He spends his time in Huffing, Swearing, Drinking, and in Whoring."* A Portuguese visitor singled out for criticism the legal clerks who "are under no manner of government; before their times are half out, they set up for gentlemen; they dress, they drink, they game, frequent the playhouses, and intrigue with the women." In London, even the humblest apprentice could don his finest clothes and go to the theatre or to the Vauxhall Leisure Gardens for a shilling and mingle, unobserved with other young men and women looking for adventure. For this was not exclusively a man's world. Women were active and perceptive participants in the London frolics. There were, in the first instance, the thousands—perhaps tens of thousands—of active sex workers: "*The* Sisterhood *of* Nightingale-lane, Ratcliff-high-way, Tower-Ditch, Rose-mary-lane, Hatton-Wall, Saffron-hill, Wetstone's-Park, Lutener's-lane," the women of Bankside, known as the Stewes Bank for its great quantities of prostitution, and, of course, the wealth of formal, informal, and opportunistic sex work going on amid the storied "Hundreds of Drury Lane"—the vast and murky warren of back alleys, dim courtyards, and precarious tenements that ran between Drury Lane and the Piazza of Covent Garden. These women were understood as tempters as much as temptations,

and it became almost a matter of form to warn young men to steer
well clear of their siren call:

> *Of Drury's mazy courts, and dark abodes,*
> *The harlot's guileful paths, who nightly stand,*
> *Where* Katherine-street *descends into the* Strand.
> *Say, vagrant Muse, their wiles and subtil arts,*
> *To lure the strangers unsuspecting hearts;*
> *So shall our youth on healthful sinews tread,*
> *And city cheeks grow warm with rural red.*

Prostitution was not then understood in as clear terms as it is now.
Language was used loosely, and who or what was a "whore" and what
their motives were in any one moment was always in flux. Biographer
James Boswell recorded picking up two girls in Covent Garden with
nothing more than the promise of "a glass of wine and my company."
Even the doubtlessly hardened regulars of the trade often understood
their position as being essentially a gamble on social mobility, preferable to a lifetime as a domestic servant. Author Jacob Ilive, confined in
Clerkenwell Prison, vividly recalled the imprisoned prostitutes trading
stories of jaunts down to Bath, nights out at the theatre, and days out at
the races with their "Gallants," as they beat hemp together.

To be sure, the opportunities of social mobility on offer for those
who chose a life as a courtesan operated at the vertiginous extremes—
but there were those who made it. Lavinia Fenton, the first woman to
play the female lead in *The Beggar's Opera*, wound up as the Duchess
of Bolton. Fanny Murray came to London after being seduced by the
Duke of Marlborough's grandson and worked her way up from Covent
Garden to be the mistress of the Earl of Sandwich before ending up
happily married to the actor David Ross. In the next generation, Soho

native Kitty Fisher became one of the most famous women in the country, charming her way to the top through a deft manipulation of men, the media, and her own potent sexual allure. These are just some of the most famous examples. That the average female Londoner could be just as sexually adventurous as any man was attested to by the immense literature that worried about the morality of modern women. One pamphleteer complained in the 1730s that women were running riot "on account of the promiscuous liberty allowed both Sexes" and that consequently even "the best Husbands are often hornified, as well as bad ones." The specter of the seductress loomed large in the consciences of god-fearing Englishmen:

> 'tis a deplorable Truth, that our young ladies . . . are wise, and
> more, knowing in the Arts of Coquetry, Galantry [sic], and others
> Matters relating to the Differences of Sexes, &c. before they come
> to be Twenty, than our Great-Grandmothers were all their lives.[3]

More equanimous observers of the London scene agreed with the famous and oft-repeated lines from Alexander Pope's *Moral Essays*: "Men, some to Bus'ness, some to Pleasure take; But ev'ry Woman is at heart a Rake."

It was into this world that Francis Charteris entered at some time around 1720, living first in Poland Street, Soho, before moving to Great George Street, near Hanover Square, by 1729. He was soon immersed in the sexual demimonde of Georgian London. With the help of his faithful deputy John Gourley and the assistance of the West End's many bawds and procuresses—Mother Needham of Park Place, St. James's, emerged as his preferred intermediary—Charteris was soon well supplied with women. His methods remained much the same as they had in the provinces. In 1724 Isabella Cranston applied for poor relief in St. Margaret's

Parish, Westminster, following her seduction by Charteris. She reported that she had been ruined by him after she was lured to the house of one Mrs. Jolly in Suffolk Street under the promise of domestic service. Many more girls would share Cranston's fate. One victim who departed from the typical profile was a young widow in Marylebone who Charteris wooed while disguised as a foreign nobleman. Charteris extorted her out of her jewels, causing her such torment in the process that she went mad and had to be committed to an asylum. On another occasion Charteris was drawn to an actress at Lincoln's Inn Theatre. After the performance ended he found her backstage and when his advances failed raped her at pistol point in the greenroom while four of his lackeys guarded the door with their swords drawn. Some of his more egregious transgressions— such as this assault at the theatre—did not go unanswered, and Charteris was not infrequently obliged to bribe victims, judges, and husbands to forget about his crimes. But for the most part justice was not forthcoming.[4] Then came Anne Bond. Tricked into working for "Colonel Harvey" of Hanover Square, Bond was raped by Charteris before being beaten his servants and thrown out onto the street. Bond found a friend, one Mrs. Parsons, and together they went to court to file a suit against Charteris. A Middlesex jury agreed to indict the colonel—a fact made retrospectively inevitable when it emerged that Charteris had once attempted to seduce the sister of one of the jurors—and in a matter of months he had been sentenced to hang.

Charteris's life was saved through the intervention of his daughter Janet. In 1720, she had married the eldest son of the Earl of Wemyss, a preeminent Scottish peer. George II relied upon such men to keep the peace in Scotland, where the prospect of Jacobite rebellion still lurked just beneath surface of daily life. When Janet, operating through influential Scottish intermediaries in London, sought her scoundrel father's pardon, the king had little choice but to comply. In April 1730, a pardon

was issued through the Privy Council, and Charteris was released from
Newgate. He was obliged to pay damages to Anne Bond, and, all told,
the price of his freedom was £15,000—an immense amount for the time.
But freedom did not buy security. London was no longer safe for him.
In a reversal of his previous fortunes, he now fled up north[5]—doubtless
encouraged in his decision when he was pulled from his carriage and
beaten by an angry mob as he swept through Chelsea. He was now
an old and ravaged man, and he died two years later in Edinburgh.
His estate was valued at a plumb[6] (or two, depending on whether one
believed his lawyers or his Grub Street obituarists), the awesome gains
of a lifetime of fraud, larceny, and extortion. He left the bulk of his
estate to his grandson, the future 7th Earl of Wemyss, whose grateful
descendants have borne the name of Charteris ever since.[7] His burial
in Edinburgh was as turbulent as his life. Enraged crowds repeatedly
attacked the constables present to keep the peace in an attempt to seize
and destroy Charteris's body. They failed to do so but succeeded in
pelting the service from afar, and so Colonel Francis Charteris's coffin
was lowered into the ground accompanied by a hail of dead dogs, dead
cats, living cats, and offal.

　　Charteris's was a uniquely eighteenth-century life. His was the era of
the rake, and he was the rake nonpareil. His ignominious achievements
in this field secured him lasting recognition as the great sexual villain of
his time. He passed directly from life into art. Alexander Pope paired
him with the Devil in the third of his *Moral Essays* (1733); Jonathan
Swift did likewise on more than one occasion. Charteris, his henchman
Gourley, and his bawd of choice, Mother Needham, all appear together
in the first plate of William Hogarth's *The Harlot's Progress*, the fantastically popular 1732 series of etchings that made the young artist's name.
Most significantly, Charteris, the class of rakes he exemplified, and the
problem he posed to women, morals, and society found their clearest

and most enduring expression in a trilogy of books by a man who, more than any other individual, codified and popularized the modern concern with seduction: Samuel Richardson.

——◆━◈━◆——

Samuel Richardson was born in 1689, on the cusp of two worlds. The year before his birth the Dutch king William of Orange and his English wife, Mary Stuart, were invited to take the throne from Mary's father, James II, in the so-called Glorious Revolution. This bloodless handover of power was accompanied by a new constitutional settlement embodied by two acts of Parliament instituted in the year of Richardson's birth. The Bill of Rights codified the rights and liberties of English subjects and confirmed Parliament's sovereignty. The Act of Toleration granted religious freedom to dissenting Protestants (though not to Catholics) and so ended the attempt to impose religious uniformity on the nation from above. In the spirit of the new, liberty-infused age, the Printing Act was allowed to lapse in 1695, bringing an end to pre-publication censorship; marking England's arrival as a pragmatic, mercantile power, the Bank of England was established in 1694. These bureaucratic landmarks did not intend to transform the moral worlds of regular Englishmen and -women but the second order effects of the upheavals of late-seventeenth century were to inaugurate a revolution in social conduct and sexual attitudes. The celebration of individual political liberty opened the door to libertinism. The toleration of religious minorities implied a willingness to turn a blind eye to private peccadilloes. A Swiss visitor in the early eighteenth century was in awe, like so many Continental visitors, of English freedoms but was appalled at the permissiveness it had unleashed in society at large. "They cherish their liberty to such an extent," he wrote, "that they often let both their religious opinions and their morals degenerate into licentiousness. . . . Debauch runs riot with an unblushing countenance."[8]

In one of the few extant autobiographical accounts of his early life, Richardson made a conscious effort to link his own family to the events of 1688. His father was a humble London joiner who, he claimed, enjoyed the patronage of the Duke of Monmouth. In 1685, Monmouth staged an ill-fated uprising against the rule of James II. When it failed, Richardson's father, in his son's telling, "he thought proper, on the Decollation of the first-named unhappy Nobleman, to quit his London Business & to retire to Derbyshire; tho' to his great Detriment; & there I, & three other Children out of Nine, were born." Richardson Sr., however, was on the right side of history, and after the Glorious Revolution, he and his family returned to London and had his remaining sons baptized in his native parish of St. Botolph's in Aldgate. The family lived initially in Tower Hill, a poor neighborhood just outside the eastern limit of the City of London on a street called Mouse Alley, which sat in the shadow of the Tower of London, connecting the city's commercial center to the docks. Later the family would move a short distance north, to Rosemary Lane just inside the City. In neither location were the family considered rich, or even prosperous, but in both the young Richardson would have been exposed to the hectic realities of daily life in the capital. Given his silence on his youth it is hard to accurately reconstruct what he absorbed from the city in these years. One likes to think that as a child he would have been privileged to live so close to the Tower of London, known then not just for its prison but for the menagerie of exotic animals that were kept on public displays in its precincts, including its famous pride of lions. More prosaically, it seems likely that Richardson's lifelong fascination with clothing and the details of fashionable dress must have begun in the thronged streets of the City, where the parvenu "Cits" (the merchants and tradesmen made good) mixed with apprentices, journeymen,

foreign businessmen, off-duty servants, clerks, molls, vendors, and ped-
dlers eager to display themselves and their finery. The City was still a
distinct entity from Westminster and had its own fashions, typically
more democratic (some would say garish) than those that prevailed in
the haughtier neighborhoods that surrounded St. James's. The "mix'd
Crouds of saucy Fops and *City* Gentry" that thrived in the streets of
Richardson's childhood were ripe targets for social satire.

The vibrancy of London life attracted the concern of moralists as well
as the condescension of snobs. The neighborhoods around the Tower,
the aptly named Tower Hamlets, were the epicenter of the movement to
transform English manners. The freedoms enshrined in the post-1688
settlement were extended only grudgingly to the common people. The
recognition that the state could no longer prescribe moral and religious
conformity from the top-down was balanced out by a countervailing
belief that individuals were amenable to suasion, instruction, and shame
from the bottom-up. Encouraged by Queen Mary, citizens in Tower
Hamlets set up a Society for the Reformation of Manners in 1690 to
suppress brothels and to stymie immoral behavior in their community.
Over a dozen companion societies were active elsewhere in the city by
the mid-1690s and would remain as features of London life until the
1730s, when they finally abandoned their Sisyphean task. Even if their
mission was ultimately in vain, the attempt at moral reformation made
a great impression on Richardson. Their animating ideal—the notion
that individuals were moral agents susceptible to reason, whose better
impulses could be cultivated by instruction and example—was to shape
his entire worldview. One of the first glimpses we get of the young Richardson is his admission that as a teenager he sent anonymous letters to
dissipated members of his community, urging them to reform their ways.
This was an early manifestation of his lifelong love of letter writing. A
shy boy, Richardson immersed himself in books and was known in his

neighborhood for his literary abilities. His bashfulness and his way with words made him a favorite of the local women, who had him read to them while they sat at their needlework and, later, recruited him to help manage their correspondence with their suitors:

> *I was not more that thirteen when three of these young women,*
> *unknown to each other, having an high opinion of my taciturnity,*
> *revealed to me their love secrets, in order to induce me to give them*
> *copies to write after, or correct, for answers to their lovers letters:*
> *Nor did any of them ever know, that I was the secretary to the*
> *others. I have been directed to chide, and even repulse, when an*
> *offence was either taken or given, at the very time that the heart*
> *of the chider or repulser was open before me, overflowing with*
> *esteem and affection; and the fair Repulser dreading to be taken at*
> *her Word; directing this word, or that expression, to be softened*
> *or changed. One, highly gratified with her lover's fervor, and vows*
> *of everlasting love, has said, when I have asked her direction: "I*
> *cannot tell what to write; But (her heart on her lips) you cannot*
> *write too kindly." All her fear only, that she should incur slight for*
> *her kindness.*

Better training for an epistolary novelist can scarcely be imagined.

Richardson's obvious intelligence and eagerness to learn put him on the path to train as a clergyman, and one can glimpse an alternative reality where Richardson joined the ranks of the great Georgian scribbler-divines: Jonathan Swift, Laurence Sterne, and Charles Churchill. But this would have required a university education, and his family's poverty forswore that possibility. Unable to afford an education, in July 1706, Richardson was bound as an apprentice to John Wilde, a London printer. At any one time London had a floating population of around

ten thousand apprentices paying their dues in trades as diverse as twee-
zer-making, bridle-cutting, and calico-printing. Bound to their respective
masters for seven years and taken into their homes and families to live,
work, and learn, apprentices, aside from actual criminals, constituted
the most suspect London demographic. "The Blood runs warm in their
young veins," one commentator observed in one the innumerable tracts
decrying the moral threat these rampant young men posed, "against this
Evil the young Apprentice must exert all the Force of Reason, Interest,
and Religion." Morality and the urges of young manhood aside, apprentices were also trapped in an economic bind: there were far more apprentices than masters. In the printing industry there were only a hundred or
so master printers, with each employing at any one time between four
and ten apprentices on top of a regular staff of journeymen printers. With
only faint prospects of ever matching the prosperity of their masters, the
loyalty of apprentices to their masters and their commitment to society
as a whole was always contingent. The vast cultural effort that went into
preaching to apprentices on matters of morals, manners, and work ethic
was symptomatic of this fear of a social group not yet integrated into the
order of things. In this respect, male apprentices were the counterparts
to that other group that the Georgians worried so much about: young,
single women.

The most enduring artifact of this culture of suspicion toward apprentices is William Hogarth's great cycle of etchings, *Industry and Idleness*.
It depicts the divergent life paths of two apprentices bound at the same
time to the same London weaver. The Good Apprentice, Francis Good-
child, works hard, goes to Church, marries the master's daughter, and
so inherits his business, and ends up a prosperous merchant who in the
final scene parades through London in a carriage, having recently been
made Lord Mayor. The Bad Apprentice, Thomas Idle, shirks his duties
as an employee and a Christian, finally runs away to sea before returning

to London to whore and carouse and, ultimately, murder, for which he is
hung at Tyburn in the penultimate plate.

Samuel Richardson was ever the Good Apprentice. "I served a seven
diligent years to it, to a master who grudged every hour to me." He
recalled of his apprenticeship. "I took care, that even my candle was
of my own purchasing, that I might not in the most trifling instance
make my master a sufferer (and who used to call me The Pillar of his
House)." His apprenticeship to Wilde ended in July 1713. Two years
later he became a freeman of the Stationer's Company. Moving from
printer to printer, Richardson accrued experience as an overseer, com-
positor, and corrector while searching for a patron. One of the printers
he worked for was John Leake, and when Leake died in 1720, he took
over his printing business in Salisbury Court, off Fleet Street. A year
later, in 1721, he married his former master John Wilde's daughter,
Martha. Richardson was now thirty-two and was finally established as
a husband and businessman.

Salisbury Court was to be the base of Richardson's operations for
the next four decades of his life. Situated between Fleet Street and the
Thames, Richardson's business was at almost the exact midway point
between the old center of London around St. Paul's and the fashionable purlieus of St. James's. His immediate world was bounded, to the
west, by the Temple Bar, the gateway that marked the boundary between
Fleet Street and the Strand, between London and Westminster, and
whose elaborate facade was, as occasion required, decorated with the
heads of Jacobite traitors. To the east, Fleet Street was separated from
Ludgate Hill and the City proper by Fleet Ditch and the New Canal,
the artificial tributaries that drained much of the human and industrial
effluvium of the City into the Thames, whose stench did little to hinder
the brisk business done by the countless stalls selling fresh oysters that
lined their banks.[9] In between these limits thrived a neighborhood of

tailors, lawyers, clerks, doctors, and tavern owners. There were also a significant number of printers and booksellers.[10] Conveniently for Richardson, Salisbury Court was equidistant between the booksellers of West London, like Andrew Millar, the greatest literary dealmaker of the day, based on the Strand, and those in the east, on and about Paternoster Row, such as Richardson's great friends and boosters, Charles Rivington and John Osborn.

Richardson's timing was as propitious as his location. England in the 1720s was on the verge of a great explosion of printing activity. Literacy rates were approximately 60 percent for men and 40 percent for women. Rising education standards combined with economic prosperity and, for the most part, social stability created a ready market for the printed word. On the supply side, a bare minimum of government intervention in printing, improving legal protections for intellectual property, and an efficient postal service, all nourished the growth of the industry. Printers were kept busy by the three thousand unique titles being published each year by the 1740s—two-thirds of which were printed in London—and by the dozens of daily, weekly, thrice weekly newspapers, journals, and gossip sheets, not to mention the sleet of Grub Street pamphleteering that ever rained down upon the capital.

The first big break in business came in 1733, when he was awarded a contract to print bills for the House of Commons. A decade later he won a second, considerably more lucrative, contract to print the Journals of the House of Commons. In between these two coups he continued to accumulate experience and trust in the book trade, his presses at Salisbury Court producing respectable tomes on history, geography, and various religious and moral matters. He engaged through his publications with some of the great intellectual debates and problems of the English Enlightenment. His presses took both sides of the fractious public discussion over Deism and demonstrated, through works like

Daniel Defoe's *Religious Courtship*, an emergent interest in problems of love, romance, and marriage. Many of his publications, such as the *Weekly Miscellany* and the *Daily Journal*, were fantastically dull and his authors were little better. They did, however, provide Richardson with entrees into literary London—the author Aaron Hill became his great friend and supporter—and his correspondence with other, lesser figures provide us with crucial insights into his life in this period. In the mid-1730s he became a friend and correspondent with Dr. George Cheyne, a quack doctor and nutritionist from Bath whose books on dieting and nutrition Richardson published.[11] It is largely through his letters with Cheyne that we get our first idea of what Richardson may have looked like. Cheyne, who had been extraordinarily fat and who detailed his obesity and its consequences in horrifying detail in his letters to Richardson (he wrote on one occasion of his "putrified overgrown body . . . regularly the gout all over six months of the year, perpetual [retching], anxiety, giddiness, fitts and startings. Vomits were my only relief.") and extolled the merits of his "strict milk, seed, and vegetable diet" and "the necessity of frequent gentle vomits that cleanse the glands."

Richardson, it emerges, was sorely in need of this course of treatment. Cheyne berated him for his girth and prolific appetite, and his cowed friend agreed to slim down and would boast of his progress in letters to him. By the time the first images of Richardson emerge in the 1740s, we see a man who, if not vastly overweight, generously fills his breeches, with a pink, round, complacent face—like a ham—and a simple white wig. Richardson's struggles with his weight may have concealed a deeper personal torment. He was frequently ill throughout this period and at times hinted at psychological and physical exhaustion. Overwork likely accounted for some of this, but familial tragedy also haunted Richardson. His marriage to Martha had produced six children—including three Samuels—none of whom survived infancy. Martha died in January 1731;

four months later their last surviving daughter died, too.[12] The next year he married Elizabeth Leake, the daughter of his former employer. Their marriage produced four daughters Mary (Polly), Martha (Patty), Anne (Nancy), and Sarah (Sally), all born between 1735 and 1740. Richardson never had the son he had hoped for, and it is quite possible that the profusion of women in his life sharpened his interest in the dynamics of courtship.

Richardson's failure to produce a male heir indirectly led to his first outing as an author. In the summer of 1732, he took as his apprentice his nephew Thomas Verren Richardson, perhaps with an end to one day handing his business over to him. Worried for the young man's morals, Richardson took the occasion of Thomas's apprenticeship to set down his own thoughts on how an apprentice should conduct himself. The result was *The Apprentice's Vade Mecum*, printed from his own press in 1734. In its tone, content, and rambling form the *Vade Mecum* did little to depart from the conventions of the instruction manual. Beginning with the customary decrying of "the degeneracy of the times, and the profaneness and immorality, and even the open infidelity that is everywhere propagated with impunity," it proceeded through the normal list of moral threats that the pious apprentice would have to circumvent in the city (women, the theatre, the tavern). One of the few moments in which Richardson reveals his considerable descriptive powers come during a critique of modern fashions, which he considered "one of the epidemick evils of the present age," an especial threat to the young apprentice as it "lifts up the young man's mind far above his condition." What follows is an inadvertently hilarious description of the various modish affectations in dress that Richardson has observed in the streets of London ("fine wrought buckles, near as big as those of a coach-horse, covering his instep and half his foot") before ending with a prayer that the "ingenious Mr. Hogarth would finish the portrait" and "shame such Foplings into Reformation." There is a hard edge to Richardson's criticism of such pretensions. The dangers of material ambition haunt all his novels. The idea that status could be purchased rather than earned through moral example was repugnant to him and he saw in that notion's prevalence the route by which men would be made work-shy and women would be sexually ruined.

The *Vade Mecum* never sold much, despite being supported by his bookseller friends and celebrated in various magazines and journals that Richardson had a hand in. His book's commercial failure figured little in his larger fortunes. Richardson was prospering by this point, and in 1738 he began to rent a country home in Fulham, a pile with three floors, a cellar, and a garden with a grotto. While he retained his quarters in Salisbury Court, Richardson now had the perfect writer's retreat in the countryside just west of London. No sooner had he taken up the lease than he was approached by his bookseller associates Rivington and Osborn with a commission to write a book of familiar letters. The concept—which conformed to a long-standing form—was a book of letters sent from various stock characters (Mother to Daughter, Master to Servant, etc.) that doubled as a guide to letter writing and as an exercise in moral instruction. Richardson agreed and set to work on these letters to be written "in a common style" for the use of rural readers. The first couple he wrote were "letters to instruct handsome girls, who were obliged to go out to service, as we phrase it, how to avoid the snares that might be laid against their virtue." In the writing, Richardson recalled a story he had been told decades before. It was about a beautiful girl from a respectable but financially ruined family who was obliged as a teenager to go into the service of an aristocratic family. She faithfully served her mistress until she died and she was transferred into the service of her libertine son,

who, on her lady's death, attempted, by all manner of temptations and devices, to seduce her. That she had recourse to as many

innocent stratagems to escape the snares laid for her virtue; once,
however, in despair, having been near drowning; that at last, her
noble resistance, watchfulness, and excellent qualities, subdued
him, and he thought fit to make her his wife, that she behaved
herself with so much dignity, sweetness, and humility, that she made
herself beloved of every body, and even by her relations, who, at
first despised her; and now had the blessings both of rich and poor,
and the love of her husband.

In a fit of inspiration Richardson laid aside the first project and began
writing at speed. The product, finished in January 1740 after fewer than
three months labor, was a novel, *Pamela*.

⸻ ❖ ⸻

The basic narrative of *Pamela; or, Virtue Rewarded* departs little from
Richardson's account of its supposed real-life model. Pamela Andrews
is the beautiful, virtuous, and literate girl from a recently impoverished
family who is taken into the service of a wealthy landowning family.
When her kindly mistress dies, Pamela's services are assumed by her
late mistress's libertine son, Mr. B—, who proceeds to pursue her with
avidity. His predations drive her to the point of suicide. Finally, Mr. B.—
comes to recognize Pamela's great moral character and, inspired by her
example, undergoes a moral reformation. Thus transformed, he asks her
to marry him and she, ludicrously, accepts.

The plot of *Pamela* needs no embellishment—it does, indeed, resist
it—but the novel's place in the history of seduction is better grasped
with some additional context. First, *Pamela* helpfully demonstrates what
behavior constituted "seduction" at the dawn of the modern age. The
first half of the book consists of Mr. B—'s escalating attempts to claim

his servant's body. Initially, his actions are relatively innocent. He gifts her books, clothes, and other small objects; he offers her additional sums of money to send home to her poor parents; he showers her with attention above and beyond what her lowly status in his household warrants; he flirts with her in private. When these gambits fail, Mr. B— becomes more aggressive: he kisses her against her will; he gropes her bosom; he harangues her as a "sauce-box," a "bold-face," an "artful young baggage," a "little slut [with] the power of witchcraft." Her resistance holds, and his methods become truly Charterisian.[13] He hides in her room at night and surprises her while she sleeps. He kidnaps her and takes her to a private home where Mrs. Jewkes, a London procuress, endeavors to corrupt her. Disguised as an elderly female servant, Mr. B— enters the room Jewkes and Pamela share and tries to ravish her while his bawd holds her down. His rape frustrated (Pamela faints and Mr. B— desists), he tries to arrange a sham marriage to trick her into believing that they can now legitimately have sex.[14] This, too, fails, and in a final throw of the dice Mr. B— offers her a contract to become his kept mistress in exchange for 500 guineas, property in Kent, the use of all his servants, and "two diamond rings, and two pair of ear-rings, and a diamond necklace." The variety, ingenuity, and rapacity of Mr. B—'s attempts on her leave Pamela rightfully despondent. "This plot is laid too deep," she laments at one point, "and has been too long hatching, to be baffled, I fear." It is also clear, though, that all this behavior was tolerated if not celebrated as actions that a well-born man might undertake in pursuit of a comely woman from a lower social class. Mr. B— approaches but never crosses the line of actual rape, which was a capital offense, albeit a rarely prosecuted one. As such, all his behavior up to that point fell within the capacious eighteenth-century definition of "seduction."

In this context what is remarkable is that Pamela is able to hold out at all. All the forces of English society are arrayed against her, and yet still she, a simple serving girl, is able to maintain her resolve. What guides her is a monomaniacal interest in maintaining her chastity, a duty that is buttressed by her parents in their letters to her. In their correspondence they impress upon her the impassable divide between the world of material wealth and that of priceless moral precepts. When they learn early on of Mr. B—'s favors to her, they immediately warn her to be on her guard against him and remind her of the immeasurable value of "that jewel, your virtue, which no riches, nor favor, nor any thing in this life, can make up to you." Her parents ask her not only that she return to them to live in honest poverty rather than risk her virtue but further that she prefer death to the loss of her chastity.

Pamela completely internalizes these ideas. When Mr. B— first kisses her and fondles her breasts she writes that she "would have given my life for a farthing" rather than succumb to his advances. There is an abiding significance to her refusal to sell or exchange her chastity. In an avowedly commercial age that celebrated and encouraged material wealth and accumulation, Pamela makes the claim that her virtue exists on a plane apart from the market economy. In the founding text of the modern literature of seduction, Richardson—no critic of the capitalist ethos—declares that questions of sex will not be subsumed by the rising tide of mercantile morality. The seduction narrative becomes the place where older Christian values survive the otherwise general triumph of the new values of the market and the merchant. There is a trap here, too. The elevation of virtue heightens the drama of its menace by a seducer. Things placed on pedestals have a tendency to fall from them, and the higher the column, the more devastating the impact. The counterpoint to the celebration of virtue was the loathing of its loss. "Moral" men were as comfortable in venerating the virtuous as they were in slandering the fallen. "A Woman discarded of Modesty," one book of manners advised, "ought to be gaz'd upon as a Monster."[15] Another author observed that

if any man of worth and substance learned that the object of his affections had been previously seduced, then she underwent an immediate
and irreversible transformation: "her beauty fades in his eyes, her wit
becomes nauseous, and her air disagreeable."[16]

Consequently, virtue was a tightrope that all chaste women walked,
ever aware of the chasm all about them. Henry Fielding's Amelia would
later decry the bind that the cult of virtue put women in. "Let her
remember," she tells her innocent female reader, that "she walks on a
precipice, and the bottomless pit is to receive her if she slips; nay, if she
makes but one false step."[17]

Richardson was well aware of the public fascination with the drama
of that false step. From the outset he made it clear that his aim was to
bait the hook of moral instruction with the worm of titillation.[18] He
could not know how successful that formula would be. The first hint
of his imminent success came from his wife. She read his proofs as he
wrote them and after a few weeks' work on *Pamela* she would start to
come to his study each evening and ask, "Have you any more Pamela,
Mr. R.?" It emerged upon publication that Mrs. Richardson was not
alone in her hunger for more of Pamela Andrews. First published in
November 1740, *Pamela* went through an astonishing five editions in
ten months. French and Italian translations were rapidly commissioned
and were circulating on the continent within two years of the English
publication.[19] [20] In London, Horace Walpole recorded that "the late singular novel is the universal, and only theme—Pamela is like snow, she
covers every thing with her whiteness." *Pamela* was originally published
anonymously and as a nominally "true" story. Only years later would
Richardson coyly list himself as the "editor" of the work. Upon publication only a handful of close friends knew that Richardson was the
author, though word soon spread through gossipy literary London. The
rest of the public had to content themselves with open letters to the

author published in magazines and periodicals or directed to the book's printer, who was, naturally enough, Richardson himself.

Named or unnamed, the rapturous reception of *Pamela* propelled Richardson to the front line of English literary life. His friends, perhaps predictably, showered superlatives on his novel, and their letters to him strain the norms of acceptable flattery. More revealing of the general adulation that the book received was the praise that ordinary people, either unknown to Richardson or ignorant of his identity as the author, laid upon *Pamela*. Clergymen wrote that his book would do more good for national morals than any number of sermons; writer and editor Ralph Courteville declared that "if all the Books in England were to be burnt, this Book, next to the Bible, ought to be preserved." Members of the public told how the novel had inspired them to seek the reformation of the rakes among their acquaintances; some even claimed success in this endeavor. Theatrical adaptions were written and performed; Hogarth, whom a few years before Richardson had praised from afar, was commissioned to create a series of etchings depicting scenes from the novel.[21] *Pamela* was a cultural event that touched all classes. London society ladies proudly displayed their copies in public while the villagers of Slough gathered at the blacksmith to hear the book read aloud and ran off to ring the church bells when their heroine finally married Mr. B—.

Literary success seldom comes without controversy; *Pamela* bred critics as well as fans. These critics can be loosely divided into the satirists and the moralists. The former consisted of the writers, critics, and readers who were skeptical of *Pamela*'s claim to realism. They saw in Pamela's rise from servant to lady of the manor a tale of canny social climbing, not the triumph of morality. Surely, they argued, if moral values were distinct from, and superior to, material values then rewarding the first with the second—which was what the book's subtitle seemed to celebrate—made nonsense of the novel's value system. The result was a chorus of scabrous criticism emanating from the capital's pleasure districts. Eliza Haywood, the best-selling female novelist of the age, published *Anti-Pamela; or Feign'd Innocence Detected* in June 1741, which recounted in the original's epistolary format the rapid social ascent of Syrena Tricksy. Haywood's work came a few months after the more complete parody of Richardson's moralizing, Henry Fielding's *Shamela,* whose anti-heroine is a courtesan on the make until she realizes she can dupe Mr. Booby into marriage instead. "I thought once of making a little fortune by my person," she writes to her bawdy mother. "I now intend to make a great one by my vartue."

Shamela and *Anti-Pamela* are but two examples among many. The satirical attacks on *Pamela* probed the holes in Richardson's worldview. They also demonstrated how opposing views of morality can cohabit in the same period. Richardson's morality, as we shall see, may have been ascendant, but it still had to contend with the more permissive attitudes of Fielding and Haywood and their Covent Garden milieu. Any one sexual ideology rarely attains hegemonic status. The question is not which one triumphs but who attains cultural top billing. The rivalry between *Pamela* and *Shamela* is not simply an episode from English literary history but a permanent feature of the history of seduction.

As a printer and a long-standing participant of the London literary scene, Richardson could not have been surprised by the satirical attacks that came his way. Friends wrote to console him of the barbs hurled his way—the ever-faithful Aaron Hill prayed that some higher power might "Deliver Pamela from these cold, *Killers,* who assume a Merit in destroying her!"[22] Richardson's occupation of the moral high ground was, however, impregnable, and he could readily shrug off such attacks. More worrying were the criticisms of his work that came from fellow moralists. In works like *Pamela Censur'd* and *The Virgin in Eden,* Richardson was attacked by conservatives for writing little better than pornography. *Pamela*, they argued (and not without reason), was needlessly salacious and possessed of a wholly perverse moral lesson. It would doubtless corrupt more youths than it would save. They scorned the notion that this was suitable reading material for their daughters. The anonymous author of *Pamela Censur'd* went further and declared that *Pamela* functioned as incitement to seduction. "The Advances are regular, and the amorous Conflicts so agreeably and warmly depicted," he wrote,

> that the young Gentleman Reader will at the best be tempted
> to rehearse some of the same Scenes with some Pamela or other
> in the Family, and the Modest Young Lady can never read the
> Description of Naked Breasts being run over with the Hand, and
> Kisses given with such Eagerness that they cling to the Lips; but
> her own soft Breasts must heave at the Idea and secretly sigh for
> the same Pressure; what then can she do when she comes to the
> closer Struggles of the Bed, where the tender Virgin lies panting and
> exposed, if not to the last Conquest . . . at least to all the Liberties
> which ungoverned Hands of a determined Lover must be supposed
> to take?[23]

The passage inadvertently demonstrates the author's own criticism of *Pamela*. Writing about seduction, even for moral or instructive purposes, brings with it the unavoidable risk that the realistic portrayal of sexual collision will tip into salaciousness and pornography. The charge stung Richardson, and he quietly modified the text in response to such criticisms.[24]

The controversies surrounding *Pamela* add to the sense that if Richardson's novel cannot be confirmed as the first novel of the English language, then its publication must surely be considered the first great literary event in the history of the form. Its local and international popularity, the fervid debates it triggered, the parodies it spawned, the conversations and correspondences it informed, the sheer quantity of copies it sold, all militate toward the view that this was the moment that the Western world fell in love with the novel. Richardson courted his readers no less assiduously than Mr. B— pursued Pamela and in so doing acknowledged how the strategies of fiction mimicked the stratagems of the seducer. The novelist spins fictions to win an audience just as the seducer contrives to win his intended—and with much the same artistry. Richardson seems to nod to this symbiosis between real and fictional worlds in a brilliant passage put into the unlikely mouth of Mr. B— shortly before he marries Pamela. Seeing his fiancée writing away, he expresses an interest in reading her letters and journals, and puns upon the similarities between reading, writing, and courting:

> *I long to see the particulars of your plot, and your disappointment, where your papers leave off: for you have so beautiful a manner, that it is partly that, and partly my love for you, that has made me desirous of reading all you write; though a great deal of it is against myself; for which you must expect to suffer a little: and as I have furnished you with the subject, I have a title to see the fruits of your pen.*

The passage could act as epigraph for *Pamela*'s enduring cultural resonance. Its publication was the moment that the fiction of seduction proved the seduction of fiction.

Before the publication of *Pamela*, Richardson was prospering; after it he was on his way toward being rich. In Georgian England, wealth brought with it obligations to the poor and needy in one's extended social group, and a man in or above Richardson's position could expect a steady stream of petitioners and supplicants making their way to his door. Early in 1743, one such indigent was directed to his offices at Salisbury Court by one of his clients, Dr. Patrick Delany, an Irish cleric. Her name was Laetitia Pilkington, and her life and career captured some the vagaries of womanhood at the dawn of the modern age.

Born Laetitia van Lewen in either Cork or Dublin around 1710, Pilkington was the daughter of a Dutch doctor and and a (Protestant) Irish mother. After a bookish childhood in Dublin, she was married in her mid-teens to Matthew Pilkington, a young clergyman with literary ambitions. Their courtship had been defined by mutual dissimulation as to the wealth and status of each family on the part of Matthew and Mr. and Mrs. van Lewen, and an understandable naivety, not to mention powerlessness, on the part of Pilkington, matched by her husband-to-be's cynical persistence in an affair of the heart that would not long detain him. The precarious prospects for the newlyweds were reflected in the material belongings he bought to their new home: a harpsichord, a cat, and an owl, which "were all his worldly goods" at the age of twenty-five. Both Pilkingtons sought literary recognition, a fact that might have given them common cause and certainly gave them such social access—Jonathan Swift became a great friend to the couple and an enthusiastic supporter of Matthew's work—but it also seems to have driven a wedge between them, largely on account of Matthew's vanity. "And if a man cannot bear his friend should write," Pilkington would later write, apropos of literary jealousy,

> *much less can he endure it in his wife; it seems to set them too*
> *much upon a level with our lords and masters; and this I take to*
> *be the true reason why even men of sense discountenance learning*

in women, and commonly choose for mates the most illiterate and
stupid of the sex, and then bless their stars their wife is not a wit.
But if a remark be true which I have somewhere read, that a foolish
woman never brought forth a wise son, I think the gentleman
should have some regard to the intellects of those they espouse.

Her husband's true feelings toward her were revealed in 1732 when he obtained a year's posting in London to be supplemented by a commission from Swift to act as his agent in the capital.[25] Laetitia was desperate to accompany him, but that September, as Matthew prepared to leave, he told her quite frankly that "he did not want such an Incumbrance as a Wife, that he did not intend to pass there for a married Man, and that in short he could not taste any Pleasure where I was." Pilkington was shocked; this admission was only the beginning of her marital woes.

Soon after his arrival in London Matthew began neglecting his clerical duties and was instead devoting himself to the pleasures of the West End. In Covent Garden he went to the theatre daily after work and spent the night carousing with the fast set. Among his new rakish acquaintances was James Worsdale, a painter, poet, musician, wit, and libertine with at least four illegitimate children, possessed of an immense and indefatigable charm, who moved easily among the liberal-living aristocracy. Pilkington was soon to know all about Worsdale's charms. In 1733 she joined her husband in London, where she found him immersed in the nightlife: drinking, theatre-going, and in hot pursuit of a Drury Lane actress, one Mrs. Heron. "I thought this but an odd manner of Life for a Clergyman," she recalled. Matthew was by now convinced that he had to rid himself of the burden of a wife and set about trying to lure Laetitia into adultery. His first port of call was Worsdale, who was soon seducing his friend's wife. "He did everything in his power to afford and encourage an amour between his friend and me," Pilkington wrote. This included the organization of a romantic weekend trip to Windsor—the party consisting solely of Laetitia and Worsdale. After fending off her companion's hands for much of the coach ride there, Pilkington then had to barricade herself in the hotel bedroom at night to keep her suitor out. The evening's shenanigans made for a frosty morning's sightseeing. Pilkington made it back to London, assailed but unconquered.

Pilkington was as frank as any of her female contemporaries about the existence of her own desires and used the language and literary stylings of moral outrage more as a satirical device than as an actual expression of her private beliefs. She wanted love; she wanted intimacy. As an educated woman she knew that the costs of seeking either were infinitely greater than those men faced. She was instantly aware that her husband's inducements to adultery could be lethal to her life fortunes. Women lost more in sexual adventure than men. They risked pregnancy and death and, at a minimum, pariahdom. "'Tis play to you, 'tis but death to us," Lady Mary Wortley Montagu had said of seduction. This was a double standard embedded in the law. Male infidelity within marriage was not apt cause for divorce; female infidelity was—and Matthew Pilkington well knew it.

At the end of 1733, the unhappy couple returned to Dublin. They were joined there by Worsdale, who became a leading figure in the Dublin Hell-Fire Club, an outfit that far exceeded its English model in its transgressions. Its members dined at a table with a seat left spare for the devil. Their mascot was a black cat who was served first at supper. Their womanizing, drinking, and harassment of the subject local population soon passed into lore. As a divine, Matthew could not easily associate himself with such a group and had to content himself on its fringes. But he remained committed to losing his wife. Pilkington had to fend off the advances of a young poet named William Hammond, from whom she later extracted the confession that:

Mr Pilkington described you to me, as a Lady very liberal of your
Favours, and begged I would be so kind as to make him a Cuckold,
so that he might be able to prove it, in order to [get] a Separation
from you; promising to give me Time and Opportunity for it: he
assur'd me, it would be no difficult Task; that I need but throw
myself at your Feet, whine out some tragedy, and you would
quickly yield.

After several years of such antics, Pilkington was by 1737 understandably fed up with her husband's behavior and admitted in her poems that she considered herself free of her marital vows. That summer she fell in love with a young surgeon named Robert Adair. An affair began, and later in the year the two were disturbed in bed by Matthew Pilkington, with posse concomitant, who, having finally succeeded in proving his wife's infidelity, broke out the wine, toasted their freedom, and kicked her out the house at two in the morning. A divorce was granted by a Dublin court in February 1738; Adair vanished from her life soon afterward. Unmarried, unsupported, and terrifyingly free, Pilkington made her way back to London at the end of the year.

Pilkington's journey to London was a taste of things to come. On the crossing from Ireland a wealthy rake propositioned her to be his kept woman. She refused. In the stagecoach from Chester to London a Welsh parson bought her food and then "began to offer a little more of his civility then I was willing to accept of." Spurned but not embittered, he "made me a present of a ginger-bread-nut, curiously wrapped up in white paper." This scene so amused their fellow passengers that they invited her to dine with them at a tavern in Barnet. There another man swooped down upon on her, insisting that this "little Hibernian nymph should dine with him," regaling her while she ate with tales of his wealth. She finally made it to London, with three guineas to her name.

There her chief patron and support was Colley Cibber, actor and poet laureate, who set her up in St. James's as the in-house wit and writer for the moneyed men of White's, the exclusive club (originally a coffeehouse) in St. James's. Pilkington lived for a period directly across from the site and played host to its members, who came to enjoy her humor, partake of her conversation, or have her write love letters or political pamphlets on their behalf. This in turn funded her own literary outings, including the 1739 poem "The Statues: or, The Trial of Constancy. A Tale for the Ladies," which bemoaned the "changeful" male sex, who

> *in perfidy delight,*
> *Despise perfection, and fair virtue slight;*
> *False, fickle, base, tyrannick, and unkind,*
> *Whose hearts nor vows can chain, nor honour bind,*
> *Mad to possess, by passion blindly led,*
> *And then as mad, to stain the nuptial bed.*

For all the outward glamour, Pilkington still existed from commission to commission and was always only a misstep from calamity. This calamity came in 1742, when an unscrupulous landlady lured her into accepting a trifling loan—forty shillings—and then had her arrested for debt. In October she began a three-month stint at the Marshalsea, where the costs of survival in prison only exacerbated her financial crisis. Half-starved, she wrote to everyone and anyone for help. Cibber secured a guinea each from sixteen dukes. Her Irish acquaintance Dr. Delany sent her twelve guineas, to be collected from his printer, Samuel Richardson of Salisbury Court.

Shortly after her release, Pilkington presented herself with some trepidation at the home and office of the author of the "incomparable

Pamela"—a work she had read and admired. She was impressed by
Richardson's obvious wealth (his house, she reported, was "of a very
grand outward appearance") and his unfailing generosity. Richardson
introduced her to his wife and children and invited her to stay for lunch
and dinner. That evening he gave her the twelve guineas from Delany as
well as two of his own and sent her on her way with an encouragement
to write to him. This she did, though only her portion of the correspondence survives. Over the next few years Pilkington would continue to
experience setbacks and would return again and again to Richardson's
generosity. When she needed a letter of credit to establish a print and
pamphlet store, she wrote to him. When her store was robbed, her home
burgled, and her daughter Betty arrived on her doorstep penniless and
heavily pregnant, Richardson sent money, linen, and clothing. When her
prodigal son appeared back from sea in rags, Richardson sent money to
clothe him. When at length, she decided to return to Ireland in 1747,
once more it was Richardson who conveyed the money to make her final
departure from London possible.

Richardson was a great collector of women and of their stories, which
he needed as the raw material for his books. In supporting Pilkington he
was doing his duty as a man of wealth and Christian charity, but he was
also accessing a world he would otherwise have known next to nothing
about. But the literary transaction—though he did not know it—went
both ways. For back in Dublin, Pilkington did something both very
novel and very of her time: she wrote her autobiography. *The Memoirs
of Laetitia Pilkington*, published in three volumes from 1748, first in
Dublin and then in London, was Pilkington's magnum opus, and the
work that, after a lifetime of impoverished scribbling, made her famous
and financially stable.

The tone and style of the *Memoirs* is Swiftian, but the content matter
is Richardsonian. Pilkington's life in her telling was one long battle

against the cruelties of a male world made manifest time and again in the license men displayed toward her body. She had seen "the world from the palace to the prison" and the one constant was male rapacity. Clergymen were "generally the first seducers of innocence"; one swinish aristocrat she met had "devoted himself entirely to Belial" and then had "the cruelty to attempt his virgin daughters"; the rakes of White's boasted to her of their conquests of girls' chastity ("a loss," she knew, "never to be retrieved"), others lived lives of Caligulan debauch, like her acquaintance and client General Ligonier, who kept four adolescent mistresses in a single house in Mayfair. At the end of it all women were discarded by their exploiters and shunned by wider society. The injustice was outrageous, Pilkington declared:

> *Of all things in nature, I most wonder why men should be severe in their censures on our sex, for a failure in point of chastity: is it not monstrous that our seducers should be our accusers? Will they not employ fraud, nay, often force to gain us? What various arts, what stratagems, what wiles will they use for our destruction? But that once accomplished, every opprobrious term with which our language so plentifully abounds, shall be bestowed on us, even by the very villains who have wronged us.*

Pilkington was far from alone in her diagnosis. The middle of the century saw an explosion in women's writing, and a recurring theme was of the sexual wrongs women endured at the hands of licentious men. Memoirs likes Teresia Constantia Phillips's *Apology* (1748) and Charlotte Charke's (the daughter of Colley Cibber) *A Narrative of the Life of Mrs. Charlotte Charke* (1755) told of women's real-life struggles and were met with enormous public success. Veteran female writer Eliza Haywood established *The Female Spectator* in 1744, the first publication of its kind aimed at women and written by women, and one whose early issues almost entirely consisted of tales of sexual entrapment. Many of the new female writers were friends, correspondents, or clients of Samuel Richardson. His long-standing correspondent Sarah Chapone wrote a proto-feminist critique of English marital laws. His printers produced some of the later editions of Charlotte Lennox's brilliant burlesque of sentimental culture, *The Female Quixote* (1752), and supported satirical essayist Jane Collier's work from the outset. His dear friend Sarah Fielding (sister to Henry) published a long essay on Richardson's work, and he encouraged and mentored a whole raft of aspiring female writers through his prodigious daily regimen of letter writing.

The 1740s and 1750s were the period when women discovered and rejoiced in what Thomas Seward (himself the father of a prominent female belle-lettrist, Anna Seward) called "the female right to literature" in a poem of the same name in 1748. Male writers and moralists understood the right of women to enter the literary space as of a piece with the expanding work of Enlightenment and as a hallmark of England's generous and farsighted civilization. The new chorus of female voices and the tales of suffering and adversity they related also inspired a revolution in sexual ideology. For centuries it had been taken for granted that men were morally superior than women. The Bible and the church fathers had said as much. In eighteenth-century England the exact reverse came to be widely believed. Namely, that women were the moral betters and that men were vicious, predatory, and lustful. Seduction narratives proselytized this new paradigm. Richardson had done his part with *Pamela*, but the long war to change perceptions and win new sympathy and respect for women could not have been won without the legion of new female voices. Male control of the cultural means of production, Samuel Johnson wrote in a typically perspicacious *Rambler* essay in 1750, had been a constant since antiquity, and as a consequence, "the reproach of making the world miserable has been always thrown upon the women." But that stranglehold had now been broken. "The pleas of the ladies appeal to passions of more forcible operation than the reverence of antiquity," he wrote, and they were likely to win the day, he concluded, for "they have stronger arguments."

The arrival in some numbers of female writers with lived experience of womanhood might have been Richardson's cue to leave the literary field to those who knew better than he whereof they wrote. This, however, was not Richardson's way. No sooner had the final revisions to *Pamela* been completed than he plunged into a new and more ambitious work, ultimately published in installments between 1747 and 1748 as *Clarissa: or, the History of a Young Lady.*

Clarissa and *Pamela* share much in common. Richardson claimed his second novel was based on the same real-life tale of seduction that had inspired *Pamela*. Their basic literary and dramatic structures are very similar. Both are epistolary novels. Both involve pursuit, abduction, deception, and assault on the part of their male characters and virtue, eloquence, and sublime forbearance on the part of their female ones. Where they part ways is in their endings. *Pamela*, for all its moralizing, is essentially a comedy that ends, in the Shakespearean mode, in marriage. *Clarissa* is a tragedy that ends in the death of its titular heroine. These conflicting finales reveal a major departure in Richardson's moral message. As its subtitle explained, the story of Pamela Andrews is one of virtue rewarded. The humble servant is elevated in stature and ultimately in station by her unerring commitment to her moral principles. In practical terms Mr. B—'s attempted "seduction" of Pamela amounts to little more than severe workplace harassment. The disparity in power between seducer and seduced is so great as to deny the novel any great psychological depth. Richardson's decision to have *Pamela* end with Mr. B—'s moral reformation and his marriage was probably necessary to make the book at all readable. If *Pamela* ended with Mr. B—'s raping of his servant and her subsequent death, then his novel would be little more than an exercise in literary sadism.

Rape and death, however, are exactly what befall the heroine of his second novel. The first quarter of *Clarissa* follows Clarissa Harlowe's desperate attempts to avoid marrying Roger Solmes, a doltish local squire, whom her family insist she wed for his money. Her steadfast refusal to marry a man she loathes drives her into the arms of Robert Lovelace, a rakish aristocrat with designs on her heart and body. Lovelace engineers her escape from the Harlowe home and then sets about his epic attempt on her virtue. His pursuit ends neither with her capitulation nor in his reformation. Instead, after close to a million words of text, Lovelace transports Clarissa to a Hampstead bordello, where he drugs and rapes her. Despoiled but not ruined, Clarissa is transformed by Lovelace's rape into a martyr for virtue. She spends the rest of the novel dying, and in the process of her death becomes a kind of secular saint whose example illuminates the lives of those around her and succeeds in bringing about the reformation of Lovelace's best friend and fellow voluptuary, Jack Belford, who records her death and eulogizes her

> *unblemished virtue, exemplary piety, sweetness of manners, discreet generosity, and true Christian charity: and these all set off by the most graceful modesty and humility; yet on all proper occasions, manifesting a noble presence of mind, and true magnanimity: so that she may be said to have been not only an ornament to her sex, but to human nature.*

Lovelace himself is driven close to madness when he realizes what he has wrought. He flees to Italy, where he is tracked down by one of Clarissa's relations and slain in a duel.

Clarissa's darker turn is legitimized by the relative social parity that exists between the Lovelaces and the Harlowes. The families are not perfectly equal—the Lovelaces are nobles and the Harlowes are not—but they are close enough in wealth and lifestyle to remove from the novel the tawdry class drama that underpins *Pamela*. Richardson was now free to explore the topic of seduction with more nuance. Lovelace and Clarissa are, in terms of breeding, education, and social sophistication, peers. The drama of her seduction is not therefore one of power but of free will—a fact that Richardson helpfully (if somewhat elliptically) alludes to in the preface to the novel. There he writes that the goal of his novel is twofold:

> *to caution parents against the undue exertion of their natural authority over their children in the great article of marriage: and children against preferring a man of pleasure to a man of probity, upon that too commonly received notion, that a reformed rake makes the best husband.*

The Harlowes' refusal to allow their daughter to marry a man of her choosing[26] had channeled her toward Lovelace,[27] a man she would have safely avoided if left to her own devices. Once in his hands, her capacity to act rationally for her own benefit was further compromised by a social belief that a woman's mission was to rescue and reform wayward libertines. One of the many threads of *Clarissa* is the heroine's internal debate as to if and how Lovelace can be reformed. In Clarissa's mind, the prospect that Lovelace "might be reclaimed by a woman of virtue and prudence" becomes her "secret pleasure," a moral adventure analogous to the sexual adventure of seduction that Lovelace is bent on. For his part, Lovelace recognizes from the outset that fostering the illusion that Clarissa's benign presence is bringing about his reformation is the key to winning her trust, her love, and, finally, her body. "Reformation shall be my stalking-horse," he gloats to Belford. Again, Clarissa's free will has been imperiled by the false belief that her mission as a woman was to edify dissolute men.[28]

The roots of this belief were tangled up in one of the core concerns of the English Enlightenment. In *An Essay Concerning Human Understanding* (1690), John Locke had asserted that at birth the mind was like an empty room. His mission was to discover how it came to be furnished. The answer, he believed, lay "in one word, from EXPERIENCE. All our knowledge," he continued,

> *is founded; and from that it ultimately derives itself. Our observation employed either, about external sensible objects, or about the internal operations of our minds perceived and reflected on by ourselves, is that which supplies our understandings with all the materials of thinking.*[29]

The key word is "sensible." Man was endowed with "sensibility"— the capacity to perceive the world, which, through cultivation, education, and moral effort, could be expanded into a larger project of empathy, intellectual refinement, and social sophistication. At a physiological level, Locke and his disciples (including Richardson's friend and client Dr. George Cheyne) believed that sensibility operated through the nervous system. Medical research seemed to have demonstrated that women had more sensitive nervous systems and so had an innately superior capacity for sensibility compared to men. In a complete reversal of the ancient Christian belief that identified women with carnality, chaos, and nature, the Georgians now understood women as the agents of a process of moral and social amelioration. Men were now cast as coarse and brutish, and those denied regular contact with women (sailors, scholars, backcountry squires) were deemed doubly so.[30] Men were encouraged to socialize with women in the hope that women's natural delicacy would rub off on them.[31] This so-called Cult of Sensibility encouraged just the kind of risky heterosocial behavior that could trap women like Clarissa Harlowe in perilous situations. Moreover, women with a surfeit of sensibility—as was thought to be rife among the educated middle and upper classes—were vulnerable to manipulation. Locke had warned in his *Essay* that humans were readily fooled by rhetoric and counseled that eloquent words "are for nothing else but to insinuate wrong ideas, move the passions, and thereby mislead the judgment."[32] In the next generation, David Hume embellished the quandary. In *A Treatise of Human Nature* (1739–40), he famously claimed that each individual's experience of life was "but a bundle or collection of different perceptions, which succeed each other with an inconceivable rapidity, and are in a perpetual flux and movement." Reality was chaos. Resorting to reason was no guarantee, as it was "and ought only to be the slave of the passions, and can never pretend to any other office than to serve and obey them." Passions were primary to reason, in Hume's view, but they too could be "founded on false suppositions" and so lead to fallacious beliefs and foolish actions. Locke and Hume moved our understanding of what guided human action away from old, inflexible theological categories of good and evil, sin and virtue, and toward a highly subjective, highly unstable vision of how humans interacted with their environment and with one another. The explosion of seduction narratives in the same period situated sexual conflict in the same new perceptual framework—and none did so with more care and psychological realism than Samuel Richardson's *Clarissa*.[33]

Seduction fascinates because it dramatizes this conflict between reason and passion. Clarissa keenly feels within her the tussle between these rival forces. She proudly claims the "right to a heart"—the freedom to feel and to love—while equally stating her pride in her powers of reason and perception. Her best friend and endlessly entertaining correspondent, Anne Howe, observes from afar the exact same contest, writing suggestively of how the "throbs and the glows" of passion contrive to weaken women's resolve in the face of hardened seducers "practised in deceit." The philosophical opposition between logic and emotion is brilliantly illustrated in a small but revealing episode that occurs while Clarissa is still held hostage at her parents' home. As they will not allow her to communicate with Lovelace, he has organized a dead drop at a wall at the end of the garden where the two can deliver and retrieve the letters they write to each other. One morning she goes to the wall with a letter for Lovelace. No sooner has she left it in the designated place than she changes her mind and decides she would rather not send the letter after all. She returns to the wall, but her note is no longer there:

> How diligent is this man! It is plain he was in waiting: for I
> had walked but a few paces, after I had deposited it, when, my
> heart misgiving me, I returned, to have taken it back, in order to
> reconsider it as I walked, and whether I should or should not let it
> go. But I found it gone.
>
> In all probability, there was but a brick wall, of a few inches
> thick, between Mr. Lovelace and me, at the very time I put the
> letter under the brick![34]

Clarissa's internal conflict between the diktats of reason and the urgings of an illicit desire are temporarily displaced by the erotic thrill at recognizing that the exact same drama is playing out within Lovelace, too. His eagerness to propel their romance onward has led him to lurk behind a crumbling country wall, meters from a family who openly despise him and now only inches from the woman he lusts after. The vignette at the wall encapsulates the sexual danger that is the appeal and the peril of seduction. The contest between wooer and wooed, seducer and seduced, is in its preliminaries an attempt by both to assert emotional control over the other. Even in the eighteenth century, men had no clear advantage in this game. Anne Howe, for instance, delights in toying with her male suitors. "Our courtship-days, they say, are our best days," she writes to Clarissa. "To see how familiar these men-wretches grow upon a smile, what an awe they are struck into when we frown; who would not make them stand off? Who would not enjoy a power, that is to be short-lived?" Clarissa's deepening tragedy is the realization that she has emphatically lost this contest to Lovelace. She comes to realize that her own delicacy—her heightened sensibility—has led her into disaster. She fluctuates between emotional states, arrives at and discards any number of "logical" conclusions, and is confused by competing passions toward her tormentor. Her own unstable personality—a word Richardson was the first to use in its modern sense in the novel that bore her name—is her greatest enemy. "What strange imperfect beings!" she writes to Anne. "But *self* here, which is at the bottom of all we do, and of all we wish, is the grand misleader."

Lovelace has no such problems. A cold logician, totally amoral, totally without sensibility ("What *sensibilities* must thou have suppressed!" Clarissa exclaims at one point), he expertly stage-manages his shifting personas and her correspondent responses to them. "Ovid was not a greater master of metamorphoses than thy friend," he boasts to Jack Belford, his confederate. Lovelace does not, in the end, succeed in technically seducing Clarissa—hence his need to resort to rape. Richardson, however, did succeed in articulating the dilemma at the heart

of all post-Enlightenment seduction narratives. An examination of con-
stellations of power in society at large can go only so far in explaining
interactions among individuals. More pertinent, and infinitely more
ambiguous, is the struggle between reason and passion that rages within
and between individuals. These are finally questions of free will and
its limits, ones that go unresolved from generation to generation even
if each has its own prescriptions. Richardson's remedy was invariably
some mixture of reformation for men and sequestration for women, as
well as the generous admonition that all readers concerned for the virtue
of the young ought to purchase his book, which had been written "to
warn the inconsiderate and thoughtless of one of the sex against the base
arts and designs of specious contrivers of the other."

Debut authors write in obscurity, untroubled by public interest; successful
ones must perform their duties in the spotlight, burdened by expectation. After the astounding success of *Pamela*, *Clarissa* was written under
fierce scrutiny. Richardson's exertions were made all the more trying
by the book's protracted gestation and long birth. *Clarissa* was begun
shortly after the final editions of *Pamela* were released into the world.
It was largely finished by the end of 1746, but even before the final
manuscript was completed, suggestions and complaints were pouring in
from his various correspondents, many of whom demanded to see the
proofs of the work he was laboring on. Consequently, well before the
publication of the first two volumes in December 1747, Richardson was
already being harried by critics. The interludes between the release of
the third and fourth volumes in April 1748 and then the fifth, sixth, and
seventh in December of the same year provided yet more opportunities
for a now enlarged critical community to probe his plot, his characters,

and his parable. Rarely has an author had to defend a work before and during publication with such energy.

Given its now canonical position in English literature, it is easy to forget that *Clarissa* never sold as well as *Pamela*. It did, however, spark a debate as equally intense as its forbear and won Richardson new respect from the literary community. Lady Mary Wortley Montagu, who had damned *Pamela* as cheap trash fit only for her scullery maids, recorded how she "eagerly read" *Clarissa*, sobbing over it and felt transported by his art back to her own courting days.[35] Henry Fielding,[36] who had gleefully mocked *Pamela*, was another convert to Richardson's work, writing at some length to him of his own emotional reactions to the novel, praising Richardson's artistry and moral force, before concluding warmly: "I heartily wish you Success. That I sincerely think you in the highest manner deserve it."[37] Edward Young, a literary tastemaker almost as esteemed as Johnson, declared that the book's power confirmed the arrival of the novelist as an arbiter of moral norms and that "the Bench of Bishops might go to School to the Writer of a Romance."[38] Richardson accomplished in *Clarissa* what he had not with *Pamela*: he had become a writer's writer.

Few, then, doubted Richardson's achievement. What was endlessly debated was his characters and the moral message they performed. Many questioned the need for Clarissa to die and interceded on her behalf. When Colley Cibber, an early reader of the manuscript, learned from Laetitia Pilkington that Richardson had decided Clarissa was to perish at the novel's end, he could not contain his outrage: "G—d d—n him, if she should,"

My heart suffers as strongly for her as if word was brought to me that his house was on fire, and himself, his wife, and little ones, likely to perish in the flame. I cannot bear it! had Lovelace ten

thousands souls and bodies, I could wish to see them all tortured,
stretched on the rack: no punishment can be too bad for him.[39]

Others took the opposite tack and chose to blame Clarissa's behavior
for her demise. Richardson displayed rare genius when he received in
the same mailbag one letter declaring Clarissa a prude and another a
coquette and replied by sending each the other's argument.[40]

Inevitably, much of the criticism focused on the character of Lovelace.
As early as the autumn of 1746, when the novel was still circulating
among a coterie of close friends, Richardson was having to defend his
depiction of Lovelace to Aaron Hill, who thought it unrealistic that a
character as evidently wicked as Lovelace would be able to ensnare the
saintly Clarissa Harlowe. In a robust rebuttal of his creative decisions,
Richardson claimed that he had made Lovelace as dislikable as possible
to ensure that he would not inadvertently make him attractive in the
eyes of impressionable young ladies. "I once read to a young Lady part
of his Character," he explained to Hill, "and then to his End; and upon
her pitying him . . . I made him still more and more odious."[41] Richardson was wise to stress the cruelty of his creation. Lovelace is easily
the most enticing of his characters, something that was both a triumph
and a quandary. Richardson was alive to accusations that he was of the
devil's party without knowing it. This was one of the lessons learned
from the moral clamor surrounding *Pamela*. He sought to make Lovelace irredeemable and consequently impossible to love.

He did not succeed. In October 1748, while he prepared for the publication of the final three volumes, he received a remarkable letter from
a female fan, who signed off as Belfour, a play on his fictional Jack
Belford. After explaining at length why she believed the author should
spare Clarissa, his anonymous correspondent made a frank declaration
of interest in his great villain:

If I was to die for it, I cannot help being fond of Lovelace. A sad
dog! Why would you make him so wicked, and yet so agreeable?
He says, sometime or other he designs beings a good man, from
which words I have great hopes; and, in excuse for my liking
him, I must say, I have made him so, up to my own heart's wish;
a faultless husband have I made him, even without danger of
a relapse. A foolish rake may die one; but a sensible rake must
reform, at least in the hands of a sensible author it ought to be so,
and will I hope.[42]

The letter continued in this vein, by turns chiding and winsome, before concluding with the promise of a curse on the author should he see fit to deny his characters a happy ending. "Now," she concluded, "make Lovelace and Clarissa unhappy if you dare."

This was the beginning of a brilliant friendship. Richardson would respond and respond again, and his correspondence with "Belfour" would turn into a friendship that would last until the end of his life. For close to two years he and his circle would refer to this unnamed correspondent at his "Incognita." Her real name was Lady Dorothy Bradshaigh, the leisured wife of a baronet (and fellow Richardson enthusiast), Sir Roger Bradshaigh. Richardson was almost sixty; Bradshaigh was in her mid-thirties. He would not know her identity until February 1850, a full eighteen months after their first exchange of letters, and then only through the indiscretion of his friend, the artist Joseph Highmore. They would meet for the first time in Bird-Cage Walk, in St. James's, a few weeks after her unveiling, but this was one of relatively few meetings given the length and depth of their relationship. Theirs would never be a friendship of shared experience. Like his characters, they consumed themselves in writing to each other, and those first, crucial exchanges focused on the person of Lovelace.[43]

Richardson maintained to Bradshaigh that his fictional villain had to be an incurable case to prevent his becoming an excuse for male abandonment in the real world. If Clarissa had reformed Lovelace after all his wickedness, Richardson reasoned, then what would the lesson be to the everyday rake of Georgian England? He would conclude, Richardson reasoned, entering deftly into the mind of the debauchees he impersonated so well, that

> I [might] pass the Flower and Prime of my Youth, informing
> and pursuing the most insidious Enterprizes . . . As many of the
> Daughters and Sisters of worthy Families, as I can seduce, may
> I seduce, Scores perhaps in different Climates—And on their
> Weakness build my profligate Notions of the whole Sex.

Such a view was the logical outcome of giving Lovelace an opportunity to atone. Clarissa's death was not Richardson punishing her, but punishing him, and her parents. "Whence my double Moral," he finished grandly, "extending to tyranical [sic] Parents, as well as to Profligate Men; and laying down from her the Duty of Children, and that whether Parents do theirs or not."[44] Shortly afterward, Richardson sent Bradshaigh an advance copy of Volume V, which contained the infamous scene where Lovelace rapes Clarissa in Hampstead. The reading of it shook Bradshaigh's perception of Lovelace ("You have drawn a villain above nature," she wrote) but did not break it. "Blot out but one night, and the villainous laudanum, and all may be well again."[45] By now the book was only weeks away from publication and her prayers fell on ears deafened by the clatter of printers at work. At the beginning of the new year she wrote again, shortly after reading the final volumes of his novel. "You will hardly believe what Pains I have taken to reconcile myself to the Death of Clarissa, and to your Catastrophe," she wrote, and then proceeded to give a dramatic account of her reading of the last moments of Clarissa Harlowe's life:

> *Had you seen me, I surely should have moved your Pity, When alone in Agonies would I lay down the Book, take it up again, walk about the Room, let fall a Flood of Tears, wipe my Eyes, read again, perhaps not three Lines, throw away Book crying out Excuse me good Mr. Richardson, I cannot go on.*
>
> . . .
>
> *Seeing me so moved, [my husband] beg'd for God's Sake I would read no more, kindly threatened to take the Book from me, but upon my pleasing my Promise, suffered me to go on. That promise is now fulfilled, and am thankful the heavy Task is over, tho' the Effects are not. . . . My Spirits are strangely seized, my Sleep is disturbed, waking in the Night I burst into a Passion of crying, so I did at Breakfast this Morning, and just now again. God be merciful to me, what can it mean?*

It meant that she was proving her sensibility, her delicacy, her worthiness as a woman fit to inhabit Richardson's worlds—fictional, moral, and material. The letter signaled her submission to Richardson's fictional designs and also to the exigencies of his moral outlook. No more would she champion Lovelace. Instead, Bradshaigh would go out of her way to demonstrate to Richardson how his art had transformed her own life. One sign of this came near the end of 1749, when Bradshaigh related how she had set out on an adventure of moral redemption of her own. She had come to know of a Cornish girl in her neighborhood who had been "artfully seduced, and ruined" by her brother-in-law. She was now shunned by her family and the wider community; he had gone unpunished. Having learned of the sorry case, and inspired by the

morals contained within Richardson's fiction, Bradshaigh determined
to do something about it. She set about finding her ward honorable
employment among good Christians, and harbored hopes for her long-
term reclamation despite the loss of her virtue. Richardson encouraged her in these efforts, and joined her in execrating "the inhospitable
wretch, who could ensnare and ruin so young a creature."[46] Bradshaigh
and Richardson both used the same word to describe this young woman:
"Magdalen." Taken from the Biblical figure of Mary Magdalen, a Magdalen was literally a reformed prostitute but was more generally a fallen
but meritorious woman, like Bradshaigh's "poor unfortunate"—or,
indeed, Richardson's Clarissa—who had at no point prostituted herself
but was no longer a virgin. The conflation of the two meanings in a
single word is revealing. In stating an equivalence between former sex
workers and unchaste women, moralists like Richardson and Bradshaigh merged together economies of virtue with economies of value.[47]
By drawing a parallel between the condition of prostitutes and the condition of seduced women, they were identifying a community of women
that shared a common feature: exploitation by men. This was one (of
many) necessary and important precursors to recognizing women as a
group who needed special protections. It was a prototypical example of
the feminist tactic of consciousness raising. Though as with many of the
moral messages of the pre-feminist era, it cut both ways. If prostitutes
were like seduced women, then seduced women were like prostitutes.
The campaigning language of rescue and reform also doubled as a device
to police and constrain the behavior of unmarried young women.

The example of the Magdalen shows how Richardson's fiction altered
the lives of his readers. This was as he intended. Less predictable and, as
it turned out, less palatable to Richardson, was the influence his readers
would have on his fiction. Bradshaigh had been urging Richardson to
write another novel from the very beginning of their correspondence. In

November 1749, Richardson gave the first hint of what his new project
might look like. Noting somewhat coolly "the warm solicitude you so
repeatedly express for my resuming my pen with a view to publication,"
he alluded in passing to the notion that he should write about "a good
man—a man who needs not repentance" before seeming to dismiss the
idea and move on to other matters. His impetuous correspondent seized
on these crumbs in her next letter, reminding Richardson what a service
he would be performing for the cause of male reformation and noting in
addition that his pursuit of such a project would "let me have to brag,
that I was instrumental in persuading you to do it."[48] By March the following year, Richardson had committed to the new book, which would
in time become his third and final novel, *The History of Sir Charles
Grandison* (1753–54), and, as with *Clarissa*, his work would be hurried
along by the exhortations of his correspondents in England, but also
of those in France and Germany. Richardson needed their support, for
the novel did not come easily to him.[49] He complicated his own work
by setting a decent portion of the action overseas, in Italy, where his
titular hero goes to pay court to Clementina della Porretta in Bologna.
Richardson had, of course, never left the British Isles, and had barely
left a five-mile radius in the preceding decades. He compensated for his
total ignorance of Italy through diligent research and consultation with
those who had traveled there—but the fundamental issue remained.
More prosaically, he had the deceptively challenging job of getting his
character there and back in a manner that made narrative sense. This
perennial writer's problem was compounded by his usual ill health. He
wrote miserably to Bradshaigh that "this is the worst of all my tasks,
and what I most dreaded. Vast it the fabric; and here I am under a kind
of necessity to grab it all, as I may say; to cut off, to connect; to rescind
again, and reconnect." He persevered. By the summer of 1753, he had
written much of the book and began to look ahead to publication.

Even in his own time, *Grandison* was not considered Richardson's finest work. But whatever its literary shortcomings, it fascinates because it reveals what Richardson thought an ideal man should look like—how he should behave, how he should talk, even how he should dress. The composition of such a man caused him as much trouble as any other part of the book. He wrote in April 1750 of the "Difficulty of drawing a good Man, that the Ladies will not despise, and the Gentleman laugh at." (He was, by the latter measure, at least, not wholly successful. Colley Cibber laughed out loud when he was told that Grandison was a virgin upon marriage.) After three years of labor, the final product was a man worthy of the new English civilization. Civility, manners, politeness—these are the words endlessly associated with Sir Charles Grandison. The emblematic episode is when he talks the rakish Sir Hargrave Pollexfen—from whose clutches he has rescued Harriet Byron, his future wife—out of a duel. Grandison rejects dueling, as did many enlightened Englishmen, on the grounds that it was harmful to society and unbecoming of a man at ease with himself. Harriet understands Grandison's rejection of the feudal code of honor as a sign of his embrace of "goodness, piety, religion; and to every thing that is or ought to be sacred among men." Grandison has arrived at civility because he has allowed his coarse masculinity to be curbed by feminine delicacy. Grandison is thoughtful, empathetic, in touch with his emotions. His admirers note his "feeling heart" and his endless capacity to "speak feelingly" on any number of issues. He is, in other words, the ideal male product of the feminine culture of sensibility. His adaption to feminine mores does not, however, render him foppish, unmanly, or—that fatal word—unsexed. Grandison is decisive, plain-speaking, and a man of action. He has simply internalized the merits of sensibility to just the right degree. Richardson's most well-traveled male character is consequently and paradoxically his most domestic one. "I live not to the world," he declares at one point. "I live to myself; to the monitor within me."

What Richardson was trying to achieve with *Grandison* can be best understood by reference to what he was writing against. It is no coincidence that the composition of his third novel was almost exactly coextensive with his bitter campaign against Henry Fielding. The two men's literary fortunes were intimately connected—*Pamela* had effectively launched Fielding's careers as a novelist by inspiring him to write *Shamela* and then *Joseph Andrews*—but their personalities were poles apart. Fielding was an Old Etonian, a master of Greek and Latin responsible for a suspiciously didactic translation of Ovid's *Ars Amatoria*, and a bawdy writer who had made his name as a Drury Lane playwright. Spendthrift, genial, and subversive, Fielding was a habitué of the Covent Garden scene and embodied its easy values. In a curious echo of Richardson's first novel, he had even married his former servant, Mary Daniel, following the death of his first wife. He was everything Richardson was not. This did not necessarily mean that the two men were obliged to feud. After all, Fielding's sister was close friends with Richardson, and Fielding's glowing letter in praise of *Clarissa* could have been the start of an amicable correspondence. Richardson, however, chose to go to war. A year after Fielding wrote in admiration of *Clarissa*, Richardson savaged Fielding's masterpiece, *Tom Jones*, in a long and invidious letter to Lady Bradshaigh. "Nothing but a shorter life than I wish him," he wrote,

> *can hinder him from writing himself out of date. The Pamela,*
> *which he abused in his Shamela, taught him how to write to please,*
> *tho' his manners are so different. Before his Joseph Andrews . . .*
> *the poor man wrote without being read, except when his Pasquins,*
> *&c, roused party attention and legislature at the same time.*

Elsewhere in his correspondence he described *Tom Jones* as a "dissolute book" and a "profligate performance" and expressed satisfaction when he learned it had been (temporarily) banned in France. His friends rushed to confirm his opinions. Aaron Hill's daughters referred to the book as a "rambling Collection of Waking Dreams." David Graham wrote cloyingly that "they who can listen to the dissonant jingle of Tom Jones, wou'd for ever be deaf to the Music of *your Charmer* [Clarissa]." Richardson maintained a posture of carefully curated scorn toward Fielding over the next few years. He reveled in the dismal reception to *Amelia* (1751), joking sourly to Bradshaigh that had Fielding "been born in a stable, or been a runner at a sponging-house, we should have thought him a genius" for composing such a book, "but it is beyond my conception, that a man of family, and who had some learning . . . should descend so excessively low."[50] In "A Concluding Note By The EDITOR," appended to *Grandison*, Richardson stated that his book was a riposte to the "many modern fictitious pieces in which authors have given success (and happiness, as it is called) to their heroes of vicious, if not of profligate, characters . . . The God of nature," he continued magniloquently, "intended not human nature for a vile and contemptible thing" and so he had written the book to show "that characters may be good, without being unnatural." This was widely viewed as an attack on Fielding, who was by then near death—his body broken by gout, cirrhosis, and other ailments, the fruits of a lifetime of hard living—and who was obliged to leave England for Portugal in 1754 in a bid to improve his health. Fielding certainly regarded it as such. In his final work, *Journal of a Voyage to Lisbon*, he referred to *Grandison* as a "tedious tale of a dull fellow" and then went on to call out Richardson by name and mock his oft-proclaimed belief that novels existed to instruct and that entertainment was "but a secondary consideration in romances."[51] He died shortly afterward, but death brought him no respite. Thomas Edwards, a member of Richardson's circle, wrote to him apropos of the *Journal* of his surprise that "a man who had led such a life as he had . . . should trifle in that manner when immediate death was before his eyes."[52] Richardson himself had the last word on their rivalry two years after Fielding's passing. In a letter to Sarah Fielding, he declared her brother a "fine writer" before stating that "His was but the knowledge of the outside of a clock-work machine, while your's was that of all the finer springs and movements of the inside."

Ostensibly Richardson was referring to the difference between Henry Fielding's and Sarah Fielding's writing. In reality, he was describing the difference between Henry Fielding's writing and his own. The literary difference matters because the opposition between Fielding's fiction and Richardson's is inextricable from Richardson's conception of their opposition in moral outlook. Fielding's characters go out into the world and find adventure. Richardson's characters go out into the world and find disaster. The deep message of all of Richardson's writings is that all would be good if women simply stayed at home. The internal nature of Richardson's writings—the endless inner monologues, the endless examination of selves, the endless, endless writing of letters in rooms—reflects his belief in the merits of domestic values, which are the values of delicate, domestic women. When women stray from this norm they meet with catastrophe. This is why Clarissa on her deathbed blames herself for what has happened. "Who was most to blame?" she asks. "The brute, or the lady? The lady, surely! For what she did was out of nature, out of character, at least: what it did was in its own nature." Women can avoid seduction by staying at home as women should. Not only that, but by being totally domesticated, women can impart some of their domesticity to men, making them, like Sir Charles Grandison, men of feeling who will no longer contrive on women's virtue. Adherence to the moral code of domesticity created an actual virtuous cycle, the cost of which—and it was a cost, in Richardson's mind, well worth incurring—was that women had to retreat from the public world of men into the private world of the home.[53]

In praising Sarah Fielding for writing of the inside of human experience, he was praising her for living up to this ideal of womanhood. This was in contrast to another group of women whom he judged to have abandoned their sex's norms—both in writing and so in life. In the same period that he was inveighing against Fielding, he was also busy slandering the reputations of certain female writers whom he believed were a discredit to the virtues he espoused. He singled out Constantia Phillips, Lady Frances Vane, and Laetitia Pilkington. In a 1750 letter to Sarah Chapone, he notoriously referred to the trio as "a Set of Wretches" and compared them to a previous generation of female authors (such as Eliza Heywood and Aphra Behn) who had also incurred his displeasure. It was the role of virtuous women, he told Chapone, to write against "the same injured, disgraced, profaned Sex." A few weeks, later he repeated the message. "Ladies, as I have said, should antidote the Poison shed by the vile of their Sex."[54] The critical attacks on Pilkington and the others were premised on the same set of beliefs that inspired his attacks on Fielding. The adventurous spirit had to be stamped out. Literature had to turn inward, and so did women. It was the only way to save virtue from seduction and to bring about the general reformation of men.[55]

Richardson's moral system was by then heavily fortified, and his faith in it unassailable. Even in his own lifetime, it was obvious that his ideas were on the rise. The values he evangelized in his books and in his private writings were increasingly the values of the ascendant middle class. His novels were landmarks in the culture of sensibility and vital reference points for the resolutely dimorphic conception of gender roles that flowed from it. His was the vision of the proper sexual identities for men and women that would predominate in Britain until the end of the

Victorian period. Nonetheless, it cannot be repeated enough that for all its influence, it was never an outlook without critics. Sexual ideology, like any ideology, is always a work in the making, an aspiration striven toward in a world marred by refusal, resistance, and chaos. Richardson's triumphal march through the drawing rooms of the English mind was resisted every step of the way by satirists, pamphleteers, and hacks eager to put his preening worldview in the Grub Street pillory.

One of the most substantive demolitions of Richardson's oeuvre came in the spring of 1754, exactly halfway through the publication of *Grandison*. Written anonymously but addressed directly to the author, *Critical Remarks on Sir Charles Grandison, Clarissa, and Pamela* was a gloriously unrestrained assault on Richardson's work and influence. Rambling, imprecise, and unabashedly ad hominem ("Your success has farther corrupted our taste"[56]), the *Critical Remarks* nevertheless score some direct hits upon the citadel of Richardson's Weltanschauung. Women, he argues, are not the asexual figures that Richardson wishes them to be but individuals with the same range of desires, ambitions, and appetites as men—and with the same capacity for profligacy. "Every woman is at heart a rake," he writes, quoting Alexander Pope, and if they suppress their inner rake, then they will seek to inhabit him vicariously.[57] This makes nonsense of Richardson's claim that his books exist to instruct the youth in Christian morality. However he rationalized it to himself, Richardson's singular focus on seduction resulted in novels that functioned to titillate rather than to castigate. His purported moral pedagogy was in practice a kind of primitive sexual education.

Approaching the apex of his argument, the author continues with brilliant sarcasm that the literary preoccupation with matters of the heart that Richardson popularized would be more a spur to sexual activity than a bridle. A casual reader of the sentimental literature Richardson wrote himself and inspired in others "would be apt to imagine, that the propagation of the species was at a stand,"

> *and that, not to talk of marrying and giving in marriage, there was hardly any such thing as fornication going forward among us, and that therefore our publick-spirited penmen, to prevent the world from coming to an end, employ'd all their art and eloquence to keep people in remembrance, that they were composed of different sexes.*[58]

Such work, he noted dryly, was not only antithetical to the propagation of virtue but served to compound the existing work of "provident nature" who had already "implanted too many allurements, and has affixed too great a variety of pleasures to the intercourse between the sexes."

The pamphlet, like so many others, made a passing impression in Richardson's world, arousing the righteous anger of his correspondents and occasioning a few harrumphs from the great man himself. Richardson had seen off far worse, and by this point, well into his seventh decade, he could afford a certain diffidence toward lowly attacks on his celebrated body of work.

By the mid-1750s Richardson had arrived at the apex of his career as a printer-writer. His private business was flourishing. He continued to invest in his site at Salisbury Court, and his printers were kept busy by lucrative government contracts as well as the steady work of printing his own writings. Success brought recognition within his profession. In 1753 he completed his decades-long ascent of the Stationer's Company, when he was appointed master of that body. Like Hogarth's Good Apprentice, he had scaled the heights of his profession from base to summit. His parallel conquest of the London literary scene brought him

into the innermost circle of the cultural elite and won him the friendship
of Hogarth himself, who was an occasional attendee at the salons held
at Richardson's Fulham pile.

James Boswell records a memorable incident at one such gathering in
1753. Over tea, Hogarth spoke approvingly to the room of George II's
recent decision to execute a Jacobite, Archibald Cameron, for his participation in the uprising of 1745.

> *While he was talking, he perceived a person standing at a window*
> *in the room, shaking his head, and rolling himself about in a*
> *strange ridiculous manner. He concluded that he was an ideot,*
> *whom his relations had put under the care of Mr. Richardson, as a*
> *very good man. To his great surprise, however, this figure stalked*
> *forwards to where he and Mr. Richardson were sitting, and all*
> *at once took up the argument, and burst out into an invective*
> *against George the Second, as one, who, upon all occasions was*
> *unrelenting and barbarous . . . he displayed such a power of*
> *eloquence, that Hogarth looked at him with astonishment, and*
> *actually imagined that this ideot had been at the moment inspired.*

The "ideot" was, in fact, Samuel Johnson, who was a firm friend and
prolific defender of Richardson's literary project. As Johnson was destined
to become the majestic center of English literary life, Richardson could
not have wished to have a more prestigious critic in his corner. Their alli-
ance blossomed. Johnson savaged Fielding; Richardson bailed Johnson
out of debtors' jail. Friendships with such luminaries by now came easily
to Richardson. Hailed as the "great genius of Salisbury Court,"[59] he now
handled correspondence with some of the great names of his age. His
fame crossed borders, and his fans traveled from far and wide to see him,
as with the German editor who traveled several hundred miles to kiss the

inkwell that gave the world *Clarissa*. Richardson responded to his celebrity with the unembarrassed satisfaction that won and would secure him the bitter resentment of his detractors. "Twenty years ago, I was the most obscure man in Great Britain," he observed, "and now I am admitted to the company of the first characters in the kingdom."[60]

Wealth, fame, and well-publicized moral positions brought Richardson in his final years into the budding world of Georgian philanthropy. Organized private charity was a relatively new phenomenon but one that London's fashionable classes took up with enthusiasm. The rapid growth in number and scale of charitable institutions in these years was fueled by the same trends that drove the obsession with Richardson's novels. The culture of sensibility had fostered an attitude of empathetic concern toward the poor and needy; the culture of moral reformation motivated moneyed (and concerned) elites to intervene in the lives of the working classes. The connection between moral panic and charitable sympathy was captured in the twin careers of William Wilberforce, whose anti-slavery campaign was premised on an identification with the suffering of others (the abolitionist slogan "Am I Not a Man and a Brother?" could never have been arrived at without the advance work performed by cult of sensibility), but who was also the founder of Society for the Suppression of Vice, a resurrection of the extinct Societies for the Reformation of Manners that Richardson grew up with in Tower Hamlets.

Some of the new charities focused on the first- or second-order consequences of sexual immorality, and unsurprisingly they found a willing patron in Samuel Richardson. His first foray into philanthropy was with his association with Thomas Coram's Foundling Hospital, which he donated to for several years and became a governor of in 1754. The Foundling Hospital was an orphanage that served to house and protect the unwanted offspring of fugitive sexual encounters. The children there were the bastard fruits of seduction, and some of the more cynical Londoners believed that the existence of such an institution would only encourage more fornication.[61] The Foundling Hospital was an enormous success and became a model for all future philanthropic empires. It also indirectly inspired the birth of another charity that came to represent in bricks and mortar what Richardson's novels had taught in paper and ink. In March 1751, Samuel Johnson's *The Rambler* contained an article written by a pensive "Amicus." On a recent walk the author had passed the Foundling Hospital, "which I surveyed with pleasure, till, by a natural train of sentiment, I began to reflect on the fate of the mothers." Why, Amicus wondered, did society protect the vulnerable infants spawned by seduction but did not move to protect women from the predations of exploitative men? Prostitution was visible all over the city, and Amicus believed, like a growing number of educated Georgians, that the woman he saw working the streets in rags and misery was a victim of seduction "who, being forsaken by her betrayer, is reduced to the necessity of turning prostitute for bread."[62] Prostitution was the consequence of circumstance, not of irretrievable individual corruption. Institutions existed to punish prostitutes—why did companion institutions not exist to reform them? The question was taken up the next month in *The Gentleman's Magazine* when "Sunderlandensis" wrote a response piece that laid out how such an institution might be run and upon what principles. He referred to the example of convents on the Continent as an imperfect image ("because they withdrew good people from general life") of what the refuge might look like and also stated that while the focus should be on actual sex workers, "the project could be extended to the seduced who had not yet become prostitutes."[63] These discussions in the press dovetailed with what Richardson had been saying in his novels and in his private correspondence for some years.[64] *Grandison* contained repeated disquisitions on the virtues of just such a proposed institution and made the same parallel to existing Catholic institutions.⁶⁵ As we have observed in his correspondence with Bradshaigh, Richardson had also internalized the equivalence between seduced women and established prostitutes.

In 1758 discussion gave way to action. That year the Magdalen House was established in Whitechapel, East London, and accepted its first eight women, or penitents, as they were known. Richardson was soon involved as a donor and later as a governor. In 1759 he offered up his printers in Salisbury Court to produce *The Histories of Some of the Penitents in the Magdalen House*, a book of narrative lives of some of the penitents published with an end of attracting favorable publicity to the new institution. Richardson was skeptical that the book would sell but printed it anyway. "It *must* appear," he declared, "for Virtues sake." The Magdalen House, like many London charities, was open to the public at certain times each week. Just as fashionable citizens went to the Foundling Hospital to see the orphans baptized, and to Bedlam to gawp at the insane, they went to observe the fallen women on their rocky road to reformation. On Sundays, the Magdalen's chapel was open for paying visitors for both the morning and the evening services. These became some of the most sought-after attractions in London, and tickets for them circulated at wildly inflated prices on the secondary market. The evening services, which, for the first eighteen years of the institution's life, showcased the florid preaching style of the notorious Reverend William Dodd,⁶⁶ were a particular draw. Richardson never went, but Bradshaigh did and wrote of her impressions to him. "I was charm'd and mov'd with their behaviour," she wrote, "with their preachers, excellent, proper [illegible] drops of pleasing tears, glad I was, that you and your delicate nerves were at home. In short, I was in Love with the whole management, and regularity of the place, and I must observe, the psalm-singing was the sweetest of melody."⁶⁷ Bradshaigh took from her visit to the Magdalen the same lessons that she took from Richardson's novels. For her, the chapel of the Magdalen House was a place where Richardson's themes—those of seduction, abandonment, reclamation, and repentance—were acted out in real time. The place was a monument to and a buttress for the feminine values of delicacy and sensibility.[68] Her tears were appropriately shed.

Richardson's novels were torn between the rival impulses of moral instruction and prurient entertainment. So, too, were the services at the Magdalen. When the decidedly more rakish Horace Walpole visited in January 1760 (in a party of four coaches, which contained, inter alia, Prince Edward, George II's brother) he provided a vivid account of the scene within the chapel:

> At the west end were enclosed the sisterhood, above an hundred
> and thirty, all in grayish brown stuffs, broad handkerchiefs, and
> flat straw hats, with a blue riband, pulled quite over their faces. As
> soon as we entered the chapel, the organ played, and the Magdalens
> sung a hymn in parts; you cannot imagine how well. The chapel
> was dressed with orange and myrtle, and there wanted nothing but
> a little incense to drive away the devil—or to invite him. Prayers
> then began, psalms, and a sermon: the latter by a young clergyman,
> one Dodd, who contributed to the Popish idea one had imbibed,
> by haranguing entirely in the French style, and very eloquently and
> touchingly. He apostrophized the lost sheep, who sobbed and cried
> from their souls.[69]

Afterward the party went on a tour of the refectory where the Magdalens ate, hatless. "A few were handsome," Walpole noted, "I was struck and pleased with the modesty of two of them, who swooned away with the confusion of being stared at." His account reveals what was driving the great demand for tickets to such occasions. The Magdalen became a safari of seduction, where the rich and powerful could go and gaze upon the sullied but virtuous poor, striving—so publicly—for society's forgiveness. Georgian churches were one of the few places where unmarried women were regularly displayed. Places of worship became spaces of desire.[70] The Magdalen chapel, where the drama of seduction was performed for a paying audience of notables, was perhaps the most erotically charged religious space in the country. The titillation of these services drove the charity's popularity, and by the 1760s it was obliged to move to new lodgings. When it was finally completed, the new Magdalen House, situated in Southwark, just south of the newly constructed Blackfriars Bridge, contained an expanded chapel that could sit five hundred visitors. Here amid the modish crowds, in a room that smelled of warm bodies and cool stone, and which was brilliantly illuminated by the light that flowed in from the high windows, the Sunday visitor, with the sound of the preacher's exhortations ringing in their ears, could ponder their own moral reckoning with the example of the penitents before them.[71]

In the new design, the penitents were placed in the gallery, behind a latticed screen, only the silhouettes of their straw hats and pigeon-gray bodices visible through the woodwork. Invisible but present; secluded but displayed; confined from sexual life but considered as objects of sexual warning. For most of the audience, sitting in the naves and aisles, they were a spectral presence, hovering above the action in the church, heard only when they sang. But some lucky visitors were seated by them in the gallery and could observe them from up close. Glimpsed through the grille, and separated by only a few inches of wood, penitent and tourist beheld each other at an intimate remove, like Clarissa and Lovelace at that crumbling wall, and animated by the same forbidden sexual thrill.[72]

Richardson did not live to see the scene. On July 1, 1761, painter Joseph Highmore visited him at home in Fulham for tea. Highmore had painted a number of works inspired by Richardson's books, including a celebrated series taken from *Pamela* and an iconic depiction of the moment Clarissa elopes with Lovelace. He had also been commissioned to do several portraits of Richardson, including one owned by Lady Bradshaigh that she hung in her closet, out of sight from her husband. He was sitting by Richardson's side when, while taking delivery of his third cup of tea, the author had a massive stroke "and immediately faltered in his speech, and from that time spoke no more articulately."[73] Richardson's condition rapidly declined and very soon he could no longer recognize his own family members. He died a few days later and was buried in St. Bride's on Fleet Street, only meters from his printing shop in Salisbury Court.

Richardson had always insisted on the indivisibility of his moral and literary projects. This is a union that has lost credibility in each successive generation since his death. Richardson is the most consistently (and acceptably) loathed of authors in the canon, largely on account of his overweening commitment to using literature as a vehicle for moral instruction. Most of his critics accept a grudging acceptance of his literary contribution as the admission price to a general attack on his work. Accepting that his literary achievements and moral outlook might be better treated separately might allow a clearer-eyed evaluation of both, then we must nonetheless recognize the major part he played in the development of modern literature. In England his influence was total, and remained so well into the nineteenth century. His celebration in France by Rousseau and Diderot made him one of the most-read foreign novelists of the pre-revolutionary period. It was in French translation that he was read by many Russians, including Alexander Pushkin. When Tatyana in *Eugene Onegin* went to bed with a novel beneath her pillow and dreamt the dream that became the whole of modern Russian literature, it was Richardson's books she laid her head upon. Richardson was translated into Dutch, German, Danish, and Italian in his lifetime. His novels circulated widely in the New World and heavily influenced the first works of American literature. The size of his audience and the pleasure with which he was read was instrumental in popularizing the novel as a format and introducing readers to the literary devices of modern fiction.

As for his moral project, Richardson stands at the head of one of the two great traditions in the history of seduction. One that worries; one that dwells on interiority; one that seeks redress for women and reformation for men. The subsequent chapters will show how far from being particular to his time, Richardson's concerns about seduction, and the language and perceptual framework he drew upon to articulate that concern have served subsequent generations well. Anyone who has ever understood seduction as a problem of power, or as a quandary concerning the limits of free will, or as a social scenario that illuminates the discrepancy in condition between men and women, or as a battleground for competing visions of how enlightened citizens should behave toward one another—anyone who has ever considered such questions has lingered a while in Richardson's world. Seduction was a problem born of modernity, and Richardson was the first modern to recognize it as such.

Richardson's view of seduction was the perfect foil to the other great tradition in its history, one that rejected the conception of seduction as a problem to be pathologized but rejoiced in the possibilities for personal and philosophical emancipation that it harbored. By his death in 1761, Richardson missed by two years the arrival in London of the itinerant Venetian musician, con man, and *saloniste* who exemplified this rival vision of what seduction could be.

CHAPTER TWO

THE TRANSIT OF VENUS

The Grand Tour was the rite of passage for any well-born English rake. At the Tour's height in the mid–eighteenth century, hundreds of boorish young men left Dover each year for the continent. Their traveling schedules conformed to a norm: a sampling of French society, a dutiful survey of some of the westerly German states, then an ascent of the Alps and to Switzerland, before a journey to Italy—the climax of any Englishman's foreign sojourn. Admired for its rich legacy of art, music, and architecture, Italy, and Rome especially, was the place that English parents and English tutors sent their English sons to gain some learning, some philosophy, and some sheen of culture. For the young men on tour, Italy held out other charms. She existed in the English imagination as a place of pleasure and passion, where Northern morals were thawed by Mediterranean seas. Traveling from Switzerland to Italy, James Boswell recorded a metamorphosis in his manners and constitution. "The climate of Italy affects me much," he wrote. "It inflamed my hot desires, and now it keeps my blood so warm that I have all day long such spirits as a man has after having taken a cheerful glass." The very air of Italy was intoxicating. No wonder then that English libertines misbehaved with even more energy on Italian piazzas than they had even on the Piazza of Covent Garden. The effect of their homeland on their English guests did not go unnoticed by the locals. "*Inglese italianizzato*," the proverb went, "*è un diavolo incarnato.*"[1]

The city most intimately associated with the scourge of Englishmen behaving badly was Venice. The Most Serene Republic was a place of pilgrimage for Europe's voluptuaries. Famous for her courtesans, her actresses, her bevies of scandalous nuns, and her expedient attitude toward matters of marital fidelity, Venice was the epicenter of a new sexual culture, her very name a gift to the punning poets of the *settocento*:

> But chief her shrine where naked Venus keeps,
> And Cupids ride the Lyon of the Deeps;
> Where, eas'd of Fleets, the Adriatic main
> Wafts the smooth Eunuch and enamour'd swain.

When the lusty English swain disembarked at Venice, one of his first ports of call was at the British embassy. From 1754 to 1766 the Resident in Venice was John Murray, one of the most notorious libertines in English diplomatic history. The son of a successful Manx merchant, Murray had won his sinecure through high-placed connections in Whitehall.[2] Set-up in Venice, he acted as a paragon of dissolution to those English subjects who passed through his patch. The presence of his wife did not prevent Murray from maintaining high-profile relationships with courtesans nor later from fathering a second Italian family, four children strong, to whom he eventually left all his worldly possessions. Lady Mary Wortley Montagu developed a strong aversion to him, memorializing Murray as a "scandalous fellow, in every sense of that word . . . not to be trusted to change a sequin, despised by this government for his smuggling, which was his original profession, and always surrounded with pimps and brokers, who are his privy councillors."[3] Others were less censorious, with many travelers grateful for his help in navigating that enigmatic city. He was well-liked among a portion of the Venetian population, as well. One local friend recalled him as "a handsome man, full of wit, learned, and a prodigious lover of the fair sex." The same Venetian was well-placed to affirm that last statement, for sometime in the spring of 1755, Murray asked him to accompany him on an errand that lay well outside his consular duties.

For many months Murray had been the principle lover of Ancilla, a celebrated courtesan. Ancilla had been sickly for sometime. Friends suspected she had a venereal disease, though this could not be true, as Murray remained unafflicted. Lately, it had emerged that her body was racked by a cancer that was corroding her throat, her neck, and her beautiful face. She was now lying on her deathbed, and she summoned Murray to love her one last time. In healthier times both of them had been exhibitionists who had welcomed voyeurs to their assignations. This time was no different. And so Murray's Venetian friend was brought along and installed in some secret viewing chamber whence he could glimpse Murray's ministrations and Ancilla's final ecstasies. She died scarcely fifteen minutes afterward. "It was," their secret sharer later wrote, "one of the most striking spectacles I have seen in all my life."

If Venice is the capital city of seduction, it is in large part due to the man on the other side of that spy-hole. There are several ironies to the phenomenon that was Giacomo Casanova, not the least glaring of which is that a man of whom we know so much through his twelve volumes of autobiography has been reduced to a single word, a magical invocation of seductive triumph, and in the process effaced, diminished, and denied a place in the material world that he so delighted in. The conundrum expands when we realize that Casanova, as indomitable a social climber as ever existed, would have rejoiced in this fate, a posthumous victory after life failed to properly reward his ambition. A child of the stage who matured in the stalls and reigned briefly from the boxes, Casanova understood better than anyone alive that the purpose of performance was to turn perishable reality into immortal myth. Actors, like all artists, seek to cheat death. Casanova was not an artist, but, driven by that same impulse to survive beyond his allocated years, he used the devices of art to sculpt his own existence. Casanova's was a life lived as a work of art.

Performance came easily to Casanova; introspection did not. His light touch on matters of ethics, morality, and philosophy all vouch for his candidacy as representative of the second great strain in the history of seduction. If the classic seduction narrative discussed in the previous chapter was grounded internally—in the house, in the letter, in and between the heart and the mind—Casanova embodied the counternarrative that roamed and gossiped and performed, that lived joyfully, carelessly out in the world. These two competing stories of seduction may have tipped in opposite directions—they still do—but they were also connected by a set of shared assumptions. Specifically, both took different sides of the great Enlightenment debate that pitted reason against passion. These were discussions that Casanova eagerly participated in, for, despite his reputation as a fop and a charlatan, he was, as this chapter will demonstrate, shuffled into the deck of the Enlightenment, even if only as a joker or a knave.

━━◆≍◆━━

Giacomo Casanova was born in Venice in April 1725. His parish, where he was baptized and later tonsured, was San Samuele, remembered in a bawdy local ditty as a "*grande bordel*" where "the men are all cuckolds and the women whores."[4] The stereotype held true in the incommodious Casanova family home on Calle Delle Commedia, halfway between the Rialto and St. Mark's Square. Gaetano Casanova, who gave Giacomo his surname though most likely not his genes, was an actor-singer-dancer who some years before had courted Zanetta Farussi, a cobbler's daughter from Burano. The two married in Venice against her family's wishes, and Farussi became an actress. Her career soon outshone that of her husband's. In Venice she was originally attached (as was he) to the Teatro San Samuele, owned by the Grimani family, members of Venice's closed patriciate caste. As the Venetian theatres were closed for half the year, Farussi, like many actors, lived a nomadic life, traveling in Italy, Germany, England, France, and Poland looking for work. Carlo Goldoni, the leading Venetian playwright of the eighteenth century, recalled her fondly as "a very pretty and a very able widow of the name of Zanetta Casanova, who played the part of young lovers in comedy."[5] This description dates from after Gaetano Casanova died in 1733, but all the evidence suggests that Farussi had begun to wander from their marital bed many years before. Giacomo, their first child, believed that he was the actual son of Michele Grimani—and on his deathbed Gaetano formally entrusted him to the Grimani family's care. Francesco Casanova, their second son, was born in London and was reputedly the son of the Prince of Wales, the future George II. The paternity of Casanova's other three siblings (Giovanni, Maria, and Gaetano) is unknown and largely irrelevant given their nominal father's early death.

Farussi herself features only briefly in Casanova's early years as a sportive beauty, well aware of her charms, who embarrassed her son by flirting with his clergyman tutor, and who later worked every angle to get her children ahead in life. From 1737 these machinations were conducted from afar; that was the year Farussi moved to Dresden, where she took up a position as an actress in the court of the Elector of Saxony. She remained there for much of the rest of her life. Giacomo was left in Venice in the care of his beloved grandmother. Farussi did not initially have high hopes for her son. As a young boy, Casanova was sickly, prone to mysterious nosebleeds and periods of inanition where, in his own account, he "was unable to apply myself to anything, and looked like an idiot." Doctors thought the air of Venice was thickening his blood and making him simple. Farussi and Alvisi Grimani (the member of the

Grimani clan deputized to watch over their ward) agreed on a course of action to have him sent to Padua to study.

On his ninth birthday, in April 1734, Casanova boarded a *burchiello* (a capacious barge, something like an outsize punt with two cabins) at midnight, crossed the lagoon in darkness, and woke up as day broke on the Brenta Canal, the stretch of water and post road that connected Venice to Padua. Riding on one of the most dramatic waterways in Italy, Casanova would have glimpsed some of the many palazzi that lined the banks of the canal, with their English gardens, their twee little bridges, their concealed platforms where musicians could invisibly serenade al fresco dining parties. He would have passed the enormous building site that would in his lifetime reorganize itself as the colossal Villa Pisani; he may have passed, unknowably, the Villa Foscarini, where Lord Byron and Teresa Guiccioli would spend a blissful autumn eighty years hence; he was passing numerous sites that would later figure in his wild twenties, places where he dueled, danced, and loved. For now, as a doltish child, he lay in bed watching the tops of the trees troop past one by one by his window and asked his mother why the trees were walking past them. "It is the boat that is moving, not the trees," the despairing mother replied. "Get dressed."

Padua was part of imperial Venice's inland empire—what the seaborne Venetians knew with marine disdain as the Domini di Terraferma—and the crèche for Venice's privileged youth, who were sent to the university there to gain an education and to keep them from causing trouble in the capital. In the summer, all Venetians of any means decamped to Padua and its environs to escape the stench of the baking canals and the spies and the sumptuary laws of the city's much-feared governing body, the Council of Ten. Padua was close to Venice in every respect. Still, the transition was a difficult one for the young Casanova. Adapting to living in a strange home was hard enough; negotiating his way through life in a rowdy student city forced certain realities upon him at a tender age. Under the care of Doctor Gozzi, Casanova was soon recognized as a brilliant student, devouring Latin and Greek, demonstrating a nascent mastery of rhetoric and literature, a great love of medicine and chemistry—though ultimately he was obliged by his mother and guardians to study law—and learned to dance and to play the violin. Padua worked on his health and body, too. Away from the malarial lagoon he regained his appetite, slept well every night, and was soon growing rapidly. If the myth of Casanova centers on an effete courtier, the reality was of a strong, graceful man, over six feet tall, with thick Mediterranean features. He needed this new strength and new learning to survive the bustle of Padua. "I made as many undesirable acquaintances as possible among the notorious students," he recalled.

> *The most notorious cannot but be those who are the greatest libertines, frequenters of places of ill repute, drunkards, debauchees, seducers of decent girls, given to violence, false, and incapable of entertaining the slightest virtuous feeling. It was in the company of fellows of this kind that I began to know the world by studying it in the harsh book of experience.*[6]

It was one of the characteristics of Casanova's world that a familiarity with the bawdy demimonde could aid the ambitious society man on the make. He records with some pleasure in his memoirs his first great success in polite society. It came at a supper in Venice attended by his mother and other friends of the family held shortly before his mother left for Dresden. Among the party was a learned Englishman who decided to test the precocious student with a Latin riddle:

> *Discite grammatici cur mascula nominea cunnus*
> *Et cur femineum mentula nomen habet*

To which Casanova replied, in perfect pentameter:

*Disce quod a domino nomina servus habet**

The room was rocked with surprised laughter. Casanova was awarded with a gold watch from the Englishman and the first taste of approval from his mother. One cannot but help but think that this was the kind of humor a young boy could only have learned among dissolute students. Whatever its provenance, its success made a great impression on him. "It was my first literary exploit," he recalled, "and I can say at this moment that the seeds of my desire for the fame which comes from literature were sown in my soul, for the applause of the company set me on the pinnacle of happiness."

At sixteen, Casanova was awarded a degree in law from Padua University and returned to Venice to pursue what everyone now agreed was a promising career in the clergy. Under the tutelage of Father Tosello in San Samuele he took minor orders, assumed the title of *Abate* (as in Abbot or *Abbé*), and became a regular at mass. Through Tosello he met and impressed with his quick wit a local patrician, Senator Alvise Malipiero. Malipiero took the young man under his wing—no small matter in a society as closed and jealous of its social borders as the Venetian oligarchy—and inducted him into the ways of high society, advising him how to converse, how to hold himself, what boundaries could be tested and which had to be respected. He encouraged the young man to philosophize, to advance himself professionally and socially, to cultivate his mind and his palate. A bachelor well past his active years but prodigious

---

* Roughly translated, the Englishman's question is:
    *Teach us, grammarians, why the vagina is a masculine noun and why
    penis is feminine?*
And Casanova's answer is:
    It is because the slave takes his name from his master.
Casanova, *History of My Life*, Vol. 1, 62.

in his day, Malipiero also taught the young man about women both by instruction and by inadvertent example. This elderly senator, whatever wisdom he dispensed willingly, gave Casanova a more profound lesson than he could ever intended. For Malipiero was in love with Teresa Imer, a seventeen-year-old daughter of an actor,[7] whose parents' home abutted the Malipiero pile. Each day the voluptuous Teresa would appear at her window to practice her singing, and each day Malipiero listened to her song and fell more deeply in love. Learning of the senator's infatuation with her daughter, Teresa's mother began to take her to the senator's palace in the afternoons for closely chaperoned visits. There the senator would plead for her favors, only for the daughter to plead chastity while her mother harangued the pathetic old man with moral advice and dire warnings as to the security of his immortal soul. Once Malipiero was reduced to a state of impotent rage they would leave, and as the shadows grew long in the empty parlor he would philosophize with his young friend for hours at a time. Nested within the otherwise joyful account of Casanova's coming of age, the melancholy remembrance of Malipiero's fading powers points to something larger in Casanova's literary project. Casanova's own memoirs were written in a quiet library in a silent castle in provincial Bohemia in his eighth decade of life, just as he discovered Malipiero's agony for himself. The Malipiero vignette is both a por-tent—a hazard sign tucked away in his heady youth—and the entirety of his condition. The aging senator sought to escape death through com-munion with the young, and now the aging Casanova tries to escape death through immersion in his memories of the grand old man's humil-iations, which were, he realizes, fifty years too late, his own. There is a trail of ink and time and pain that connects Casanova at his desk in sleepy Dux to the young man confounded by the spectacle of an old man immiserated by his own absurd passions.[8] The example of Malipiero is situated *mise en abyme* in the memoirs, inserted not as simply one more incident in a varied life but as a belated recognition that fate had once tipped its hand, that the contours of his own life had been revealed to him in passing in the knowledge that revelation is wasted on the young. The lesson was missed; the headlong charge continued. A few months later Casanova lost his own innocence in bed with Nanetta and Marta, two girls he had met through Father Tosello's niece.

The beginning of Casanova's amorous career at seventeen was marked by a series of rococo sexual escapades (a fumble with the blue-eyed courtesan Giulietta, a thwarted country romance with the maidenly Lucia, an encounter with a newlywed in a rattling carriage in a rumbling storm) and a betrayal. One day after lunch at Malipiero's, the old man went to have his siesta, leaving Casanova and Teresa Imer alone together. In his inimitably elliptic style, Casanova recalls "sitting side by side at a small table with our backs to the door of a room in which we supposed our patron was sleeping, at a certain turn in the conversation it occurred to us in our innocent gaiety to compare the differences between our shapes. We were at the most interesting point of the examination when a violent blow from a cane descended on my neck." Hounded out of the house without his cloak or hat by the wrathful Malipiero, Casanova had both returned to him later that day with a note informing he was no longer welcome at the senator's soirées. Never one to hold a grudge, Casanova took this banishment in his stride and continued on his way. He had taken what Malipiero had to offer him at that stage in his life; he knew there would be other patrons in other palazzi. He remained grateful for his worldly instruction for the rest of his life, warmly recalling him as "M. de Malipiero, my first master in the art of good breeding."

The breach with Malipiero came just as Zanetta Farussi had accomplished what she believed to be a considerable coup on her eldest son's behalf. In Warsaw, the sharp-elbowed Farussi, having charmed her way into circles of influence, had petitioned the Queen of Poland to have her daughter the Queen of Naples appoint Bernardo de Bernardis to the bishopric of Martorano in his native Calabria. She had done so with prior agreement with de Bernardis that the quid pro quo would be that her son would be taken into his service once his appointment was made final. This duly happened in May 1743, and de Bernardis began his thousand-mile journey south, sending instructions to Casanova to meet him along the way. The two men met for the first time in Venice that autumn. Casanova was not overly impressed with de Bernardis and suspected that the feeling was mutual. Nonetheless, this was the man he believed would "guide me to the great stage of the Church" and inwardly he promised to try to win over his new patron.

De Bernardis told him that the two would travel separately to Rome and thence to Martorano via Naples. They then went on their respective ways. What followed was a comedy of errors as Casanova traveled from Venice to Rome in the company of a thoroughly corrupt monk amid a carnival of roguery and misadventure that left him penniless only to discover upon arrival that de Bernardis had already left for Naples. Arriving in Naples, his purse bare, he learned that de Bernardis had gone on ahead without him once more. Pondering what to do, he made the acquaintance of a Greek peddler who was hawking a supply of mercury. Casanova, remembering his chemistry lessons in Padua, had a brainstorm and used some basic chemical knowledge to fool the Greek into believing that he had knowledge of alchemical secrets, belief in which were widespread at the time. With the skill of a con man of greater experience than his eighteen years afforded him, Casanova patiently defrauded the Greek over several days and then made a small fortune selling his "secret" to the credulous man. Such dealings, he hastened to remind his readers, were wholly forgivable in such circumstances and "could be condemned only by a civic morality which has no place in the business of life." "Cheating is a sin," he aphorizes, "but honest cunning is simply prudence." Now in rude financial health and high spirits, the young man bought himself a new wardrobe and set out at last for Martorano. But as his rented carriage penetrated the Calabrian interior his suspicions began to mount. The countryside was dreary and visibly poor. At Martorano the bishop's palace was in a state of disrepair and the food appalling. When Casanova asked if "he had good books, a literary circle, or any good society in which to spend a pleasant hour or two" the old man merely smiled and said he had not so much as a newspaper to read. This was not a tolerable state of affairs. "Without a good library, a circle, a spirit of rivalry, a literary intercourse, was this a country in which I must settle down at the age of eighteen?" The final straw came when Casanova laid eyes on the congregation in church the next day. "I saw nothing but brutes," he wrote, "who seemed to me positively scandalised by my entire appearance. What ugly women!" There was no future for him here. He asked de Bernardis's forgiveness and his release from his service. He received both as well as a letter of introduction. Within three days of arriving in Martorano he was in a carriage to Naples with his eyes set upon Rome.

"I was in Rome, with a good wardrobe, a fair amount of money, some jewelery, and a fair amount of experience, with good letters of recommendation, completely free, and at an age when *a man can count on the help of fortune if he has a spark of courage*." Rome was a city built for the young Casanova, a place where a man "must be a chameleon sensitive to all the colours which the light casts on his surroundings. He must be flexible, insinuating, a great dissimulator, impenetrable, obliging, often base, ostensibly sincere, always pretending to know less than he does."

His youthful optimism was in this case vindicated by his possession of a letter of introduction to Cardinal Acquaviva, a man of much influence in the capital. At his audience with the cardinal he was instructed to learn French, given His Eminence's hand to kiss, and told to report to the Palazzo di Spagna, where he held court, the next day. There he was given a job, a salary, and an apartment. The young man marveled at his good fortune. Thereafter Casanova fell into an easy routine, consisting of French lessons and clerical work for the cardinal. Members of the cardinal's circle occasionally took him into society, where he learned the ways of the famed Roman salons, or *conversazione*. In his own time he was energetically pursuing a romance with Anna Maria d'Antoni Vallati (given the pseudonym Donna Lucrezia in his memoirs), with whom he had shared a carriage from Naples. Anna Maria's husband and sister had been traveling with her, but this had been no barrier to Casanova's initial advances. In Rome he courted her assiduously, with her husband's apparent indifference, but their budding romance was scotched time and again by sisters, mothers-in-law, priests, and rival suitors. Finally, Casanova secured an outing to Frascati, two hours from Rome. There they lost themselves in the sylvan gardens of the Villa Aldobrandini until they found themselves in a secluded spot, bound in shade, and with a prospect of the Roman plains, where they lay down together on a bed of grass. "Here in the garden at Dux," the older man interposes, "I have seen an arbor of the same sort." Then the fantasia continues:

Standing face to face, intensely serious, looking only into each
other's eyes, we unlaced, we unbuttoned, our hearts throbbed,
our hands hurried to calm their impatience. Neither of us having
been slower than the other, our arms opened to clasp the object of
which they were to take possession. . . . At the end of two hours,
enchanted with each other and looking most lovingly into each
other's eyes, we spoke in unison, saying these very words: "Love, I
thank thee!"

Their affair produced a daughter, Leonilda, the first of Casanova's eight recorded love children.

Such frolics were not, however, compatible with the life of a serious young *abate*, and at some point even the genial Cardinal Acquaviva decided that his protégé was not cut out for a life in the Church. Summoned to his rooms, Casanova was informed, not without some regret, that he would have to leave his service and was offered a payoff and letters of recommendation for a city of his choice. Casanova, for reasons he never fully examined (or confessed to), chose Constantinople.

⸻ ❈ ⸻

Constantinople turned out to be a dead end. Casanova's visit to the Sublime Porte was not dull—neither for him nor for the reader of his memoirs—but it was informative in shaping Casanova's cultural orientation. Given the chance to marry into the Ottoman elite by wedding Zelmi, the daughter of a rich old philosopher named Yusuf Ali, Casanova, after some weeks of reflection, declined. His decision reveals the breadth of his horizons at that stage of his life. Later, as a legendarily well-traveled man, Casanova would profess a thorough-going cosmopolitanism. Whether this was merely an affectation of middle age or something he grew genuinely into with time, it was not felt when faced with the prospect of turning his back on his European inheritance and turning Turk for Yusuf Ali and Zelmi. Casanova instead exhibited chauvinist attitudes typical of his day, mocking the idea that he would abandon "fair hope of achieving fame among polished nations" to change his religion, sever his ties with his friends and family, and take up the study of "a barbarous tongue."

After several months in Constantinople Casanova returned to Venice via Corfu, where he presented himself for military service and was assigned the role of adjutant to Signor D. R., the Governor of the Galleasses. His days were spent attending to his superior, his evenings in attendance on the card tables. The latter was immensely profitable, while the former brought him into the orbit of one Signora F., the eighteen-year-old wife of a galley commander, who immediately dazzled him with her beauty. The signora, however, was not an easy conquest. Indeed, she ignored him totally apart from the occasionally contemptuous remark directed his way while he waited on the senior officers and their wives. Ever jealous of his *amour propre*, Casanova was stung by her evident distaste for him. Unable to court her, he adopted "the course of avoiding her, abandoning her to the stale gallantries of Sansonio, who had rotten teeth, a blond wig, a dirty complexion, and a stinking breath. But I remained chagrined and furious."[9] He busied himself with his gambling and made good money playing faro at the local coffeehouses.

A curious and singularly Casanovian event proved to be the pivot upon which his romantic fortunes turned. Upon becoming an adjutant, Casanova had been assigned a French soldier as a servant. La Valeur was an illiterate peasant from Picardy, "a scapegrace, a drunkard and a debauchee" ever at hand with a song or a funny tale.[10] Casanova was fond of the man, if only because he could practice his French with him. Then La Valeur fell ill, so ill that he was taken to hospital and given his final sacraments. Upon his death, the priest delivered a bundle of papers to Casanova, saying he had been told by the dying man to ensure it was passed on to the highest authorities on the island. Opening the package Casanova found a "brass seal bearing a coat of arms surrounded by a ducal mantling, a baptismal certificate, and sheet of paper" upon which was written, in French, a confession that La Valeur's true identity was that of "Francois VI, Charles Philippe, Louis FOUCAULD, Prince of LA ROCHEFOUCAULD." This statement was accompanied by a request that the French ambassador in Venice be contacted so that his illustrious relations in France could be notified and could come and claim his corpse for the family vault. Casanova immediately recognized this to be some variety of posthumous prank on the part of his deceased servant as he had known some members of that family when in Rome serving Cardinal Acquaviva. Nonetheless he delivered the letter to his superiors, who, to his astonishment, believed its authenticity and ordered the body to be accorded the proper respect his rank as an aristocrat demanded. No sooner had the dead La Valeur transformed into the late Prince de la Rochefoucauld than news came from the hospital that the patient had undergone a miraculous recovery and was conscious once again. In no time at all, the revived prince was up and about and was being feted in the small world of the Corfu garrison. He was now a fixture in society, the guest of honor at every supper party, and fawned over by the officers' wives. Casanova was adamant that this man was an imposter but was alone in this view. His refusal to recognize his servant's eleva-tion came to a head at a dinner party where, in response to Casanova's declared assertion that his baptismal certificate was a forgery, the prince cuffed Casanova about the face with the back of his hand. The young man left the house in a dignified fashion, waited in an alleyway for the drunken man to stagger out after dinner, and then had his revenge in the darkness, beating the prince half to death with his cane. His honor restored, Casanova retired to the coffeehouse whence news arrived that he was wanted for assaulting an aristocrat. Rather than face military dis-cipline for what he considered a non-crime, Casanova absconded to the nearby island of Casopo, where he lived the life of a glamorous outlaw, seducing shepherdesses and impressing the local men with various dis-plays of guile. After some weeks of this, an envoy from Corfu arrived. A letter had come from the French ambassador in Venice confirming what Casanova had declared all along, namely, that La Valeur was a fraud. Both the prince and the Picard had since vanished, and the Corfu authorities were much embarrassed by the whole episode. He was now welcome back to Corfu without risk of punishment.

Casanova's vindication in this matter won him the admiration of Signora F. She now showed him signs of her favor, and soon a romantic intrigue was afoot. Their affair is noteworthy not as a demonstration of Casanova's seductive prowess but as an example of a peculiarly Italian institution. For Casanova's entanglement with Signora F. did not conform to the pattern of his regular sexual escapades. At first it all seemed very promising: sentimental dialogues were had, gifts were exchanged, emotional confessions were made. Casanova felt final victory was near when Signor D. R. transferred him into the service of Signor F. and he was installed in her house in a bedroom not far from her own. He now spent his days waiting on her: helping her in and out of carriages, dining with her when her husband was busy with military matters, caring for her when she was poorly. The performance of a sentimental courtship continued, but after a few weeks it became clear that he was little more than her servant. She teased him with displays of passion and promises of future release, but he was always and everywhere confounded. Perhaps out of pride, Casanova does not use the term to describe the position he was in, but as a Venetian and a man well-versed in the ways of polite society, he could not but have known that he was not Signora F.'s lover but merely her cicisbeo.

The culture of *cicisbeismo* flourished in Italy throughout the *settecento*. It was one of the most widely remarked-upon features of Italian high society, and Casanova's reticence on the topic is curious given its ubiquity not only in foreign accounts of Italian society but also in Italian culture itself. The exact nature of *cicisbeismo* is contested, but in essence it was a kind of male concubinage whereby when a woman married, she took a man (in some accounts several men) as her cicisbeo (also referred to as a cavalier servente). This was done with the full

assent of her husband, who, according to custom, was expected to tolerate this situation as a regular part of married life. The origins of *cicisbeismo* are unclear, as is the etymology of the term. The exact parameters and the legal status of such an arrangement were hotly debated
by contemporaries and remain so by historians. What is clear was
that the phenomenon was to be found throughout the Italian peninsula in Casanova's lifetime, and especially in Venice, which, along with
Naples, was considered the seat of *cicisbeismo*. In that city, English
traveler Samuel Sharpe observed in the 1760s, "GALLANTRY is so
epidemical . . . that few of the Ladies escape the contagion. No woman
can go into a public place, but in the company of a Gentleman, called
here, a *Cavaliere Servente*, and in other parts of Italy a *Cicesbeo*."
Sharpe went on to give the canonical description of what a Venetian
cicisbeo's life consisted of:

> *This* Cavaliere *is always the same person; and she not only is
> attached to him, but to him singly for no other woman joins the
> company, but it is usual for them to sit alone in the box,
> at the opera, or play-house, where they must be, in a manner, by
> themselves, as the theatres are so very dark that the spectators can
> hardly be said to be in company with one another. After the Opera,
> the Lady, and her* Cavaliere Servente *retire to her* Casine, *where
> they have a Tete-a-Tete for an hour or two, and then her visitors
> join them for the rest of the evening, or night; for on some festival
> and jolly days, they spend the whole night, and take Mass in their
> way home.*[11]

Sharpe is circumspect, as so many observers were, as to what went on
during that time alone in the *casino* at day's end. The extent to which the
relationship between lady and cicisbeo was sexual has been a subject of

fierce debate for several centuries now, with most reasonable observers reckoning that it would be naive in the extreme to believe that it was not. To be sure, the cicisbeo's duties were not principally carnal. Their main role, which never ceased to appall foreign visitors, was to *serve* their lady. This could involve anything from helping her dress, arranging her hair, playing cards with her, or ensuring she had something to eat and drink while she played cards with someone else. They were to be more uxorious than their actual, absent, and frequently far older, husbands could ever be expected to be.

The most famous cicisbeo, and the one who left the most complete account of the inner workings of this arrangement, was Lord Byron. While living in Venice in 1818, Byron met the eighteen-year-old Teresa Guiccioli, wife of Count Guiccioli, a wily politician from Ravenna well into his fifties. The two met at a Venetian salon and fell tumultuously in love. When Teresa returned to Ravenna and to her husband's house, she summoned Byron to join her there, and he soon found himself set up on a separate floor of the same palazzo as she, communications between the two enabled, Byron caustically noted to a friend, by "the aid of a Priest, a Chambermaid, a young Negro-boy, and a female friend." What followed was a crash course in *cicisbeismo*. Soon Byron was attending to Teresa at the theatre, ensuring her comfort at *conversazione*, and making small talk with Count Guiccioli, who, according to the edicts of *cicisbeismo*, had little choice but to accept the infamous English lord into his household.[12] The arrangement pleased Teresa—and had its upsides for her husband, who was soon borrowing money from the wealthy poet upstairs—but it drove Byron to distraction. "I feel—& I feel it bitterly— that a man should not consume his life at the side and on the bosom of a woman," he wrote to his friend John Hobhouse in August 1819, "and that this Cicisbean existence is to be condemned." He begged Teresa to spare him the humiliation of *cicisbeismo* by eloping with him to some distant place, but she would have none of it and demanded he stay with her in the Romagna, which he did, albeit in a state of growing exasperation. A few months later he vented again to Hobhouse on the subject:

> *I am not tired of Italy—but a man must be a Cicisbeo and a singer*
> *in duets—and a Connoisseur of operas—or nothing—[here] I have*
> *made some progress in all these accomplishments—but can't say*
> *that I don't feel the degradation.—Better be a unskilful planter—an*
> *awkward settler—better be a hunter—or anything, than a flatterer*
> *of fiddlers——and fan-carrier of a woman.—I like women—God*
> *he knows—but the more their system here developes upon me—the*
> *worse it seems—after Turkey too—here the polygamy is all on the*
> *female side.——I have been an whoremonger, intriguer, a husband,*
> *and now I am a Cavalier Servente—by the holy! it is a strange*
> *sensation.*[13]

Byron was not alone among otherwise forward-thinking men in believing that *cicisbeismo* travestied male dignity. Tobias Smollett, who witnessed the practice when in Italy in the 1760s, wrote that he "would rather be condemned for life to the gallies, than exercise the office of a cicisbeo, exposed to the intolerable caprices and dangerous resentment of an Italian virago." Similarly, in his memoirs Carlo Goldoni recorded that he had "long looked with astonishment on those singular beings called cicisbei in Italy, the martyrs of gallantry, and the slaves of the caprices of the fair sex."[14]

The revulsion toward the practice on the part of so many men warrants further consideration. In the classical seduction narrative an unmarried woman was seduced and abandoned by an older, financially secure man. *Cicisbeismo* subverted all this. The woman was married and so financially secure—even more so in Italy than in England, where marriage contracts often stipulated her personal income and the exact division of assets—and also socially secure. Furthermore, her cicisbeo served her—and who knows what more—at her pleasure, and hers alone. As it was not uncommon for girls to marry straight out of a convent, as Teresa Guiccioli did, and to marry a man much older than they, as Teresa did, too, *cicisbeismo* was a humane way of allowing a young wife freedom, companionship, and some experience of the pleasures of sexual exploration without taking any risks as to their short-term respectability or long-term solvency. This was why Teresa rebuked Byron when he begged her to abscond with him: that would have defeated the whole purpose of the arrangement. Byron might have found the system degrading and unsatisfying, but it clearly worked for Teresa. In asking her to elope he was really asking her to prioritize his pride over her security. She was wise to refuse.[15] "I am all for morality now," a defeated Byron wrote ruefully to his friends, "and shall confine myself henceforward to the strictest adultery."[16] Byron and his like were used to a system of moral hypocrisy that served men. They could not abide a system of moral hypocrisy that served women.

Neither, it seemed, could Casanova. After playing cicisbeo to Signora F. for some weeks he was in a state of near madness on account of a potent mixture of perceived humiliation and thwarted desire. After yet another encounter with the signora that left him at a new pinnacle of sexual frustration, his resolve broke and he fled into the arms of Mesulla, a local courtesan. His few hours with her left him with a venereal disease whose existence he was obliged to acknowledge to Signora F., who promptly dismissed him from her affections. Soon afterward his luck at the card table failed and he found himself without "health, money, credit, good humour, consideration, wit, the ability to express myself, and with it, my power of persuasion." Once more he found himself without money, connections, or prospects, and once more he decided to throw himself on fate. "Not having abjured the goddess Fortune," he explains in his memoirs, "I thought that I could still count on her. I knew that she exercises her sway over all mortals without consulting them, provided that they are young; and I was young."[17] He gave up his commission and returned to Venice.

— · — ⊷◆⊷ — · —

Star student, failed cleric, decommissioned officer—by the age of twenty-one Casanova had been all of these things, and now, back in Venice without money or obvious direction, he returned to his roots in the theatre while he awaited Fortune's next play. Playing the violin in the pit of the Teatro San Samuele would, for some young men, have been an adventure in itself, and had he more respect for his parents' vocation he might have found in his new role a fitting tribute to Zanetta and Gaetano, who had walked those very boards he now sat beneath. But for the ambitious Casanova his lot was a deplorable one. He considered himself a failure and hid from Venetian polite society where he was now remembered—if at all—as an also-ran, a youth who had failed to live up to the promise of his precocious boyhood. Exiled from the drawing rooms of the beau monde, he joined a group of hard-drinking pranksters who made merry and made trouble all over the city. He had, by his own measure, gone completely to the dogs.

In the spring of 1746 fate came to his rescue. The scions of two great patrician families were wed in some splendor at the Palazzo Soranzo, and Casanova was one of many musicians hired to provide a soundtrack to the occasion. On the third and final day of the festivities Casanova was making his way out after his shift ended and found himself walking behind a man dressed in the red robe of a Venetian senator. As the cowled figure ahead of him was boarding his gondola he reached for his handkerchief and unwittingly displaced a letter, which fell onto the ground before Casanova's feet. Casanova hurried over to the senator before he could leave and handed him the dropped letter; in gratitude the old man offered him a trip home in his boat, and soon the two men were seated next to each other as his gondoliers picked their way through the packs of departing guests.

What happened next is unclear: the senator seems to have had a stroke of some kind, losing sensation in his arm and leg and experiencing uncontrollable facial contortions. Casanova quickly directed the gondoliers to a coffeehouse, where he obtained the address of a local surgeon. As the gondola hastened back to the senator's palazzo, the surgeon bled him while Casanova tore apart his shirt to make an improvised bandage. He stayed with his new acquaintance while a doctor, and a priest were found, and later, over dinner in the palazzo, learned that he was Senator Matteo Giovanni Bragadin, a member of the patrician class, a well-known statesman, and a man known for the "love affairs which had signalized his stormy youth," now long since past. He was also introduced to the two bachelors who lived with Bragadin, Marco Dandolo and Marco Barbaro, who were both also members of illustrious patrician families. Inspired by either concern or cunning, Casanova stayed by Bragadin's bedside through the night. Before he had left, the doctor had strapped a compress containing a mercury ointment on Bragadin's chest. Seated by the patient, Casanova watched with alarm as Bragadin's eyes fluttered and his breath became shallow. By midnight he was in the grip of a fever, and Casanova, apparently without consultation, decided the compress was doing more harm than good and removed it. Bragadin soon recovered and the next morning thanked the young man for saving his life and fired his physician. In Casanova's telling, Bragadin, Barbaro, and Dandolo identified in his timely appearance in the senator's life something portentous, and they begged him to stay with them. They revealed that they were students of the esoteric and had surmised that Casanova had a gift. After some needling, Casanova confessed that yes, he was indeed well-versed in the ways of the cabala and demonstrated his oracular powers for them. His favored device was a numerological oracle, a system of numbers that, when organized in pyramids, could reveal the future. They informed him grandly that he was in possession of a great gift, at which point Casanova made an astonishing pronouncement. His oracle, he told them, had foreseen their meeting. "If I had not constructed my pyramid three weeks ago," he said, "I should not have had the happiness of knowing Your Excellency."

"How is that?"

"Having asked my oracle, on the second day of the festivities in the Palazzo Soranzo, if I should meet anyone at the ball whom I did not wish to meet, it answered that I must leave the festival at exactly ten o'clock."

Signor Bragadin and his two friends were as if turned to stone.

Casanova proceeded to induct the three men into the mysteries of arcane knowledge, speaking loftily of the philosopher's stone, the universal medicine, magic, spirits, and much more nonsense besides. Thoroughly under his spell, the three men implored him to move into their palace and live with them as an adopted son and an on-call magus. They offered him rooms, a generous monthly allowance, and an instant entrée into high society. Casanova had little compunction with taking advantage of these credulous old men. He was, he wrote, "a young man who needed to live well and to enjoy the pleasures which my constitution demanded." If he did not dupe Bragadin, he reasoned, some other, less scrupulous and less deserving adventurer would do so in his place. Furthermore, it would have been unforgivably poor manners to refuse the generosity of such esteemed men. Consequently, he "took the most creditable course, the noblest, and the only natural course. I decided to put myself in a position where I need no longer go without the necessities of life."

Casanova's account of his incredible transformation from fiddler to aristocrat has not been without its skeptics. The incident of the dropped letter seems to owe more to opera than to life, and his sudden facility with esoterica arrives with little explanation or precedent. Casanovists have also pointed out that the route the two men were taking through Venice when the stroke was alleged to have taken place does not align at all with where Casanova was living at the time. Whatever the truth of the matter, what is known is that Casanova's elevation to the ranks of Venetian nobility was real. It is a matter of documented fact that he lived at the Palazzo Bragadin for much of the next decade and drew an allowance from the senator until the latter's death in 1767. By means fair, foul, or felicitous Casanova had made his way to the top of Venetian society, and his twenties would be spent in exhausting the sensual possibilities that money, rank, and charm afforded a young man in Venice.

The world Casanova now immersed himself in was one bathing in the immediate afterglow of a revolution in sexual manners. Venice had been associated with leisure for centuries, largely because of the state policy of permitting, regulating, and taxing prostitution, which had helped spread the legend of Venice as the Venus of the Adriatic.[18] However, the sexual license she granted to professionals was not extended to the majority of women. On the contrary, Venice was similarly renowned for the virtual captivity in which unmarried girls and married women were kept. Well into the seventeenth century travelers consistently reported on this custom. Englishman Fynes Moryson wrote that Venetian women were "locked up at home, as if in prison."[19] The very bricks of the city served to reinforce this idea that the home was a place of detention.

Expecting to see one of the most splendid cities in Europe, many visitors were taken aback by the grim visages of Venetian houses with the heavy metal bars and the wooden latticework (known as *gelosias*—literally, "jealousy") laid upon the windows. Even when they were allowed out of the home, women were hindered by the requirements of fashion. Venetian *zentildonne* were long famous across Europe for their peculiarities of dress. They wore heavy *zendale*, a kind of all-encompassing shroud that hid their face and figure, and on their feet *zoccoli*, platform shoes so extravagant that they were essentially stilts and so unstable that they required one or more servants to aid with movement.[20]

By the mid–eighteenth century, however, this culture of seclusion and concealment had been swept away. In Casanova's time, Venice was known for the expansive freedom that her women enjoyed. "No women on earth are under so little restraint," one visitor noted, "and the word jealousy is become obsolete." This new freedom was symbolized by new fashions: the *zoccoli* gave way to *scarpe*, infinitely more convenient flat-soled leather slippers, while the *zendale* morphed into something suggestive, so suggestive that a scandalized English visitor complained that "the dress of their modest women is hardly more decent than that of our common prostitutes."[21] Far from being shuttered indoors, Venetian women of means and fashion now maintained their own private apartments, or *casini*, where they could entertain their friends with cards, music, and conversation, and retreat to with their cicisbei or anyone else they so wished to spend time with unobserved. Women were now ubiquitous in public and could be found at the theatre, the opera house, gambling at the Ridotto (the state-run casino), taking chocolate and sorbet on St. Mark's, or promenading around the gardens of the Giudecca. This transformation of the lives of Venetian women unleashed one of the great sexual revolutions of the eighteenth century, and Venice soon vied with Paris in the permissiveness of its sexual culture.

This turn from confinement to libertinism was so sudden and so pronounced that contemporaries, Casanova included, marveled at it while having little understanding—outside of weary clichés concerning corrupted morals—of its origins. Venice is a fascinating case study for a revolution in mores precisely because of the sclerotic nature of the Venetian state. By design, very little changed in the Republic of Venice. The laws and the system of government had gone untouched for centuries. The geographic constraints on the island-state meant that the economy could neither grow nor seriously diversify, and in fact in this period the city was, if anything, depopulating and its economy shrinking. Revolutions in sexual manners are often associated with social, political, and economic upheavals—none of these were present in eighteenth-century Venice, and yet it underwent one nonetheless.

What had changed, of course, was the Enlightenment. Venice was not, like Paris or London, one of the centers of Enlightenment learning and debate, but nor was it isolated from the consequences of the new ideas about man, the mind, and society then circulating in Europe. Venice was the center of the Italian printing industry and played host to some tens of thousands of annual visitors, and so naturally imbibed some portion of the new philosophies. To be sure, the growing discourse surrounding individual liberties, the sustained attack on clericalism and religious superstition, and the nascent discussion of women's rights did influence sexual manners. However, it is easy to overstate the importance of Enlightenment *thought* in changing behavior while understating the importance of Enlightenment *culture* in bringing about the same. For what united the disparate elements of Enlightenment Europe was a shared belief in the importance of sociability. After the horrors of the wars of religion of the seventeenth century, there was a general acceptance that Europeans would be better served by a culture of amiability and leisure than one of confrontation and conflict. This new ideal was fostered in the court culture spawned by Louis XIV at Versailles and in his many imitators around Europe and was simultaneously promoted in the public sphere—that enormous network of salons, academies, coffeehouses, and correspondences that constituted the Republic of Letters—that acted as a counterweight and occasional critic to those same absolutist monarchies.

At the same time European voyages of exploration, trade, and colonization led to encounters with a great variety of non-European, non-Christian peoples that forced a philosophical conversation about what European-ness meant and a new self-consciousness about the distinguishing features of European civilization. One of the consequences of these developments was the creation of a beachhead for female influence in an overwhelmingly male society. The new sociability was one that took its cues from supposedly feminine values and that had women—as *salonnières*, as patrons, as figures of fashion and admiration—as its social arbitrators. Across Europe women came out of the home and assumed a public role as the agents of a new public culture. For thousands of educated and monied Europeans, the experience of Enlightenment was not predominantly one of studying the tomes of the philosophes but of learning civility, politeness, and manners—what Montesquieu referred to as *moeurs douces*—by socializing with women. As social norms softened, social life accelerated, and attitudes liberalized by this new, heterosocial world created plenty of opportunities for carefree sexual adventure, which was understood within this new hyper-social paradigm. Looking back on his youth, Milanese playwright Giuseppe Compagnoni observed in the 1790s that in his lifetime, "society changed completely, and the long custom of staying together refined tastes, and introduced a culture of wit and good manners." Part of this culture was a playful attitude toward sex and courtship:

I regard European gallantry as one of the strongest social bonds:
I attribute to it both the peaceful tranquility which reigns in our

cities, and the esteem, respect, mutual assistance, which families
and citizens have for each other. . . . Gallantry only has, as its
general objective, a series of reciprocal actions, which, by their
nature, are suited to increasing harmony and benevolence.[22]

In Italy, the new sociability collided with a new realism about the severity of the marriage market for women. Whereas in Protestant societies there was a shift toward conjugal marriage inspired by romantic love, in Catholic countries marriage was still frequently brokered by family patriarchs out of dynastic considerations. Many Enlightened Italians regarded the new sexual freedom granted to wives (through, for example, the culture of *cicisbeismo*) as just recompense for the mercurial way they were handled on the marriage market.[23]

Whatever the cause, the fact remained: no other city in eighteenth-century Europe enjoyed life like Venice. Prostitution and gambling were legal, summers were spent in the bucolic estates along the Brenta Canal (where aristocrats kept open houses for months at a time, entertaining dozens of guests at ruinous expense), the masquerade of the carnival reigned for six months of the year, which in turn attracted thousands of tourists. The cramped nature of city living in Venice forced activity out into the *calli* and *campi*, while the necessity of traveling by gondola (with their singing oarsmen, who helpfully doubled and tripled as both procurers and intermediaries between honest lovers) added a glamor to the most prosaic journeys. The city had Europe's first opera house and seven theatres—more than either Paris or London—and a staggering profusion of coffeehouses, wine shops, and street stalls that were open at all hours of the day. The sheer exuberance of Venetian street life had no parallel in Europe. "The spectators are themselves actors," Goethe wrote of his experience of life on the lagoon, *and the multitude is melted into one whole with the stage. All day long the buyer and the seller, the beggar, the sailor, the female gossip, the advocate and his opponent, are living and acting in the square and on the bench, in the gondolas and in the palaces, and make it their business to talk and to asseverate, to cry and to offer for sale, to sing and to play, to curse and to brawl. In the evening they go into the theatre, and see and hear the life of the day artificially put together, prettily set off, interwoven with a story, removed from reality by the masks, and brought near to it by manners. In all this they take a childish delight, and again shout and clap, and make a noise. From day to night, nay, from midnight to midnight, it is always the same.*

The musicologist Charles Burney had a comparable experience, though given his interests his senses were attuned to Venice's particular soundscape:

The people here, at this season seem to begin to live only at midnight. Then the canals are crowded with gondolas, and St. Mark's square with company; the banks too of the canals are all peopled, and harmony prevails in every part. If two of the common people walk together arm in arm, they seem to converse in song; if there is company on the water in a gondola, it is the same; a mere melody, unaccompanied with a second part, is not to be heard in this city: all the ballads in the streets are sung in duo. Luckily for me, this night, a barge, in which there was an excellent band of music, consisting of violins, flutes, horns, bases, and a kettle-drum, with a pretty good tenor voice, was on the great canal, and stopped very near the house where I lodged; it was a piece of gallantry, at the expense of an inamorato in order to serenade his mistress.[24]

The intense sociability of Venetian life accounts for one of the peculiarities of Casanova's own memoir of his tempestuous life there. What
is striking about Casanova's prose style is how visually and sonically
flat it is. Casanova has neither Goethe's eye nor Burney's ear. He has
no interest in taking the reader through the dim and musky back alleys
with him, or in describing the brilliance of a flamingo sunset over the
lagoon. For Casanova the only active ingredient of Venice was its social
life. He forgoes a literary treatment of the sensory experience of Venetian life to absorb the reader in labyrinthine ways of its social existence.
Casanova faithfully records every hand of faro or basset, every scalding
cup of postcoital coffee, every midnight passage across the water from
palazzo to *casino*, every ball, every quip, every dance—for it was in these
seemingly facile episodes that he found the vital essence of his age. For
this was his time—as he recalls with that typical mixture of pride, pain,
and awe—that he was "at no loss for money, endowed by nature with a
striking exterior, a resolute gambler, a spendthrift, a great talker with a
sharp tongue, completely without modesty, fearless, running after pretty
women, supplanting rivals, and thinking no company good except such
as amused me, I could not but be hated."[25]

Venice was a bad place to be hated. For all its outward gaiety, the city
was a police state with powers temporal and spiritual gathered in the
hands of the Council of Ten—the politburo of the city's patrician class—
and total powers of investigation, arrest, and punishment invested in
the Council of Three, the much-feared Inquisition. This secretive body,
peopled by incorruptible old men monomaniacally focused on maintaining their caste's grip on the Republic, retained a huge network of
spies and informers whose task was facilitated by the cramped geography
of the city and the talkativeness of its inhabitants. In Venice, Casanova
remarks in his memoirs, with as much accuracy as hypocrisy, libertinism was substituted for liberalism. His meteoric rise to social eminence

and his cohabitation with Bragadin, Barbaro, and Dandolo immediately marked him out for investigation by the Council of Three. Although it lived among the rest of the population, the patrician class was hermetically sealed off from it by the continuity of its constituents' bloodlines. Every member of every patrician family had his or her name inscribed in the Golden Book, a ledger that contained the names of every Venetian descended from the Republic's founding elite. By Casanova's time the book had been closed to new entrants for centuries. No one could join it. If a patrician made a morganatic marriage, the children produced by it would be forfeit the rights of their patrician parent.[26] Moreover, as the patricians were obliged to govern the city, rule its colonies, and staff its army and navy, they were constantly under surveillance by the Council of Three for signs of corruption or rebellion. The social lives of patricians were closely monitored. At the extreme, the penalty for interacting with any foreign diplomat was death. But even their more casual friendships could be viewed with suspicion in the paranoid chambers of the Ducal Palace. Casanova's magical elevation to the trust and confidence of three of the city's most illustrious men could not be ignored by the Council of Three. His constant gambling, quarreling, and womanizing, not to mention his occasional brushes with the courts, did little to endear him to the authorities. Less than two years after Casanova had entered Bragadin's household, his new guardian advised him that he better flee the city before he was arrested. Casanova went to Milan, and Bragadin got to work smoothing out his young charge's legal problems.

For the next two years, Casanova circulated through the peninsula on the first of his many tours. He visited Milan, Mantua, Cesena, Naples, Parma, Bologna, and Ferrara. His activities were always the same—women, cards, and opera—as was the company he kept—gamblers, noblemen, actors, soldiers, and adventurers. It was in this time that Casanova laid the groundworks for his legend, putting in the anonymous hours of his apprenticeship to seduction, loving freely, passionately, and at times unsuccessfully. His affairs in this period—some of which brought him close to marriage—reveal him to be something more than a cynical libertine, if something less than an honest lover. For Casanova, the pursuit of women was about more than the pursuit of his own pleasure. He was impelled by a boundless love of novelty, which was cruelly counterbalanced by a genuine love of individuals. Unlike many of the rakes and scoundrels he moved among, his earnest courtship of the women who fascinated him was normally devoid of the double-dealing he regularly employed on the rubes he encountered at the card table and elsewhere. Seduction was neither the purely rational exercise in manipulation as practiced by the classic Enlightenment libertine nor the surrender to florid sentiment of the man of sensibility, but a game that both parties played and whose consequences both parties suffered. While he openly admits that he "had no scruples about deceiving nitwits and scoundrels and fools," he argues that in the course of his affairs "this sort of reciprocal deceit cancels itself out, for when love enters in, both parties are usually dupes." Casanova grounded this philosophy in typical Enlightenment precepts, viewing men and women as rational agents who met—romantically or otherwise—on terms of parity. This was a presumption he rarely interrogated, though it is not hard to see how it might be complicated.

In early 1750, Bragadin sent word that Casanova was now free to return to Venice. This he did, although he stayed barely long enough to make some money at cards before he struck out for Paris. Casanova spent eighteen rather unremarkable months in France. In Lyon he became a Freemason, and in Paris he describes himself as "a candidate in the Republic of Letters." He spent an enormous amount of time at the opera learning the code of high-society sociability and a comparable amount of effort perfecting his French—the language he would ultimately write his memoirs in.[27] His first forays into the networks of Enlightened society would stand him in good stead for many years to come, but at the time his eager attempts at penetrating the French court and his occasional lapses from polite norms marked him out as a callow outsider. Eventually, legal woes and financial worries obliged him to return to Venice and to the protection and purse of Bragadin. The way home took him through Dresden, where he saw his mother for the first time in fifteen years, and Vienna, where he was appalled by the prudery of administration. "Everything in Vienna was splendid," he recalled, "but there was great hardship for those who were votaries of Venus." The devout Empress Maria Theresa considered gallantry a scourge and declared that her people did not "have the devil in their bodies like the Italians." This was inhospitable terrain for the twenty-seven-year-old Casanova, and he was soon headed home. In May 1753, he returned to Venice.

Casanova's homecoming coincided with the celebration of the Feast of the Ascension, the most extravagant of Venice's many public holidays. A cross between Valentine's Day and the Fourth of July, this was a time when young lovers exchanged gifts while the Doge reconsecrated the Serene Republic's commitment to the seas that had made her fortune by marrying the Adriatic at the Lido. For the period of the festivities masking was permitted and the city's inhabitants abandoned themselves to leisure. No sooner had he reclaimed his rooms at the Palazzo Bragadin than his old patron declared his desire to leave the city to the young and retire to the peace of his country home outside Padua. Casanova accompanied him on the journey, dined with him at his estate, and then returned to the city by *barella*, a two-wheeled carriage that traveled down the post road that ran parallel to the Brenta Canal. As he passed through Oriago his *barella* met a speeding cabriolet carrying an officer in uniform and a beautiful young woman. Ten meters or so before the two parties crashed into each other, the driver of the oncoming equipage swerved to avoid a collision and in the process tipped his vehicle river-ward. The lady inside was flung dramatically from her trap and landed perilously close to the edge of the canal. Casanova sprung out of his own carriage to help her, admiring as he did so the "secret wonders" revealed in the disarray of her skirts. The coachmen quarreled, the gentlemen reassured the distressed lady, and then both groups went on their respective ways.

The next day was the scheduled date for the climax of the Ascension Day celebrations. That was when the Doge would make the annual pilgrimage across the lagoon from his palace to the cusp of the Adriatic in his fabulously gold, fabulously top-heavy barge of state, the *Bucentaur*, fling a wedding ring into the sea, and claim it as the city's faithful wife. It was customary for the nobility, foreign diplomats, and other grandees to travel in the *Bucentaur*'s wake in their own craft. Casanova, naturally, was to follow the Doge in Bragadin's gondola. He waited for the appropriate hour on St. Mark's Square, where he enjoyed a cup of coffee and watched the world go by. A masked woman came up to him and rapped him playfully on his shoulder with her fan. She said nothing; Casanova ignored her. Later, on his way to his gondola, he ran into her on a bridge, accompanied by a masked man in an officer's uniform. He asked her why she had struck him with her fan, to which she replied that she was punishing him for his failure to recognize the woman he had so gallantly rescued the day before. He realized his error and invited the duo to ride with him in his gondola. Afterward the group repaired to an inn near the Campo San Moisè, where Casanova declared his love to the mysterious woman. They went from the inn to a box at the opera and thence to another inn. Casanova took them home in his gondola, "in which, under cover of the darkness, the beauty granted me all the favours which propriety permits a woman to grant when there is a third person to be considered." The next day, the officer appeared at Casanova's house and told him that he was Pietro Capretta and the woman was Maria Colonda, without specifying the exact nature of their relations to each other. Casanova was already suspicious of the couple's intentions and suspected that Capretta was Colonda's pimp. The truth was in fact worse. Capretta explained that he had a contract to supply Hungarian beef to the City of Venice but that cash-flow problems were hindering his business. He asked Casanova—on the strength of a chance meeting, and an evening on the town together—to guarantee several bills of exchange on his behalf, taking his future cattle shipments to Trieste as collateral against non-payment. Casanova was left "astonished by such a speech and such a proposition, which seemed to me chimerical and the source of continuous difficulties that I loathed." He refused to be entangled in Capretta's financial machinations and sent him on his way.

This vignette—an upturned carriage on a post road, a serendipitous encounter during a festival, a fumble in a gondola, an artful escape from a financial swindle—is so typical of Casanova's world, yet it triggered a series of events that upended it. That traffic accident on the Brenta Canal was the fateful moment in his existence, one that led to his most beguiling love affair, to his criminal detention in wretched circumstances, and to the triumphant escapade that would become, in the fullness of time, the cornerstone of his legend.

For Casanova broke his promise to himself and did see Pietro Capretta again. The next day he called on the Capretta household as a courtesy. Pietro introduced him to his mother and to his fourteen-year-old sister, Caterina. Casanova was ever exposed to coups de foudre, they were his stock-in-trade, and the ungenerous reader of his life might doubt the sincerity of his many infatuations. In this instance, however, later events would instantiate the feelings he claimed to have felt at once. Caterina fascinated him immediately. "It took her no more than half an hour to enchant me by hear bearing," he recalled. "What chiefly struck me was a lively and unspoiled nature brimming over with candour and ingen-uousness, a gay and innocent vivacity, simple and noble feelings." She had been well-educated by her parents—both learned and pious people, whose library "possessed no novels"—but had lived a cloistered exis-tence. She was excited to meet an envoy from the world outside and peppered him with questions. When it came time to leave, he did so with a heavy heart, convinced he would never see her again and doubly convinced that even if he did he would never be allowed to marry her.

A remedy for his melancholy was quick at hand. The same afternoon he called on a friend from his childhood, Signora Manzoni, who told him that his old flame Teresa Imer was back in Venice. Teresa had spent the previous decade on the road in Europe, building her skill and fame as a singer. She was back in Venice for a short time in between stints in Bayreuth. The two spent the afternoon catching up and then went to the opera together in the evening. The next day he went to breakfast in her rooms, and finding her still in bed joined her therein. The result was a baby girl whom he would not see until she was nearly six years old.

Teresa left for Germany shortly afterward, and no sooner had she gone than Pietro Capretta reappeared, announcing the wonderful news that his sister was obsessed with him. Another trip to the Capretta household confirmed Casanova's affection for her, and hers for him, but it also stirred uncharacteristic misgivings. "I examined the nature of budding passion," Casanova writes, "and I found it cruel. I could proceed with C.C. neither as an honourable man nor as a libertine." He buried his doubts at the card table, losing extravagantly, but he could not shake off Pietro, who seemed intent on making the match between his sister and his would-be benefactor. Casanova knew enough about the world to perceive that Pietro's matchmaking was inspired more by a love of his troubled cattle trade than for his little sister. Likewise, he knew enough about himself to understand that such ancillary schemes would not, ultimately, obstruct the ways of his heart. He allowed himself to be shepherded into a romance with Caterina. The two went to the opera together. They walked arm in arm in the *giardini* in San Biagio. They survived a lurid double date with Pietro and Maria Colonda.[28] Finally, falling ever deeper in love, and swearing solemnly that they should be married or elope, they took a *casino* on the Giudecca and shared a bed for the first time. Casanova was as good as his word. Their affair continued as it had, although he now formally asked Bragadin to help him approach Caterina's father and broker a marriage with his daughter. The plan was delayed by Signor Capretta's absence from the city on business. No sooner was he back than Bragadin arranged a meeting between the two older men. Casanova was sanguine; Caterina did not think her father would let her marry so young. Her pessimism proved correct. Not only did Signor Capretta deny his suit, he declared that his daughter could not marry for another four years, and she would spend those four years in a convent on Murano.

The convents of Venice were one of the city's famed attributes, as much an attraction as its theatres and brothels. By the eighteenth century the lagoon was host to thirty-three nunneries, which housed several thousand nuns.[29] Some of these were respectable educational and charitable institutions, a select few were elite music schools where all-female choirs and bands were trained to the highest standards, for the most part, however, the city's convents enjoyed an insalubrious reputation as hotbeds of dissipation. Passing through the city in 1739, the French visitor Charles de Brosses reported stories of nuns fighting duels with poniards and three convents vying to provide the new Papal Nuncio with a mistress.[30] Carnival was celebrated within the convents as it was in the city more generally, as the exuberant, cacophonous depictions of the convent visiting parlors at such times by painters such as Pietro Longhi, Francesco Guardia, and Giuseppe de Gobbis readily attest. The relative permissiveness of Venetian convents was accepted in recognition that women were placed in them for purely secular reasons: patrician families could not afford multiple marriages and the consequent dilution of their estates. The mazily named French diplomat Abraham Nicolas Amelot de la Houssaye argued in his contemporary account of the city that this accounted for "the irregularity of the *Nuns*" of Venice, who were immured in their droves by parsimonious parents but then, perhaps out of guilt, were allowed "to have some Entertainment in their Cloisters, and at least to be allowed the privilege of seeing their Lovers at a Grate."[31] De la Houssaye's basic insight was correct. The convents were a product of secular needs, and the nuns made a healthy sum from the upper classes' need to shield their daughters from unwanted advances.[32] The money they made from their charges encouraged a more indolent approach to matters of discipline out of kilter with Italian nunnery norms. The particulars of convent architecture revealed the Venetian way. One expatriate Italian, defending the Venetian system to an English audience, remarked that the visiting parlors of Venetian convents were more inviting spaces than was the case elsewhere on the peninsula:

> Both in the morning and afternoon they are allowed some hours
> of parlatory, as they call it. There they receive their visitors, and
> sit chatting with them through the iron-grate. This grate is double
> and very narrow throughout Italy. At Venice only it is not so: nay,
> the partitions there are so very large, that one may conveniently
> shake hands with them. But the largeness of the Venetian grates has
> ruined the reputation of the Venetian nuns.[33]

Questions of convent security were now foremost in Casanova's mind. Lover's bravado had first led him to believe "that I could carry her off even if the convent were guarded with artillery."[34] This was a chimerical aspiration; in the first instance he did not even know which convent Caterina was in. Even once he found out she was in a nunnery on Murano,[35] he could not access her, although a back channel was found by which the lovers could exchange letters. This correspondence revealed a problem far greater than a forced separation—Caterina was pregnant. One July morning, Casanova was woken up to receive a desperate letter from her. She was having a miscarriage and was hemorrhaging badly. The nuns were trying to help her the best they could, but she had not revealed her condition to them and they had not guessed it. She begged him to relay to her via Laura (their intermediary) materials to stanch the bleeding. "I am scarcely dressed," Casanova writes, "before I have another oar put to my gondola, and I go with Laura to the Ghetto, where I buy a Jew's whole stock of sheets and more than two hundred napkins, and after putting them in a bag I go to Murano with her." In Murano, he set himself up in Laura's house while she went back and forth to the convent with illicit supplies of sheets and napkins hidden in her skirt. She went with clean linen; she returned with the news that Caterina was close to death and a stash of bloodied cloth. "When I saw the linen," Casanova recalled, "which she took out from under her skirt I very nearly dropped dead. It was sheer butchery . . . I shuddered when the woman showed me a little shapeless lump in among the blood." Laura's traffic between convent and home continued for two nights. What she carried back in her skirt was a continual reproach to Casanova's careless ways. His moral system quavered, and he began to doubt his whole way of life. "I was really in despair. Seeing myself the murderer of this innocent girl, I did not feel that I could survive her." He shunned female company, not even letting Laura's daughters wait on him. He realized that his uncontrolled passions had turned women into "the instruments of my horrible incontinence, which had made me the executioner of an angel incarnate."

Then Caterina recovered. Casanova returned to Venice and to his usual ways—though he moaned that "without a real and satisfying love affair I could not be happy." He did, however, receive news that he would be able to see Caterina in the convent. This he did, and learned that he could also go to mass at the convent on feast days. Casanova was soon visiting the convent on every possible occasion, and Caterina wrote to him that his repeated attendance at their services had given rise to wild speculation as to his identity and motives.[36] There was no danger of his true purpose being revealed, and in any case, the two earnestly believed themselves to be married in spirit if not in fact—Casanova refers to Caterina as his "dear wife" in this period—and such visits were the very least he could do amid the tragedy of their separation and her brush with death. Nonetheless, he was not a happy man: "I was growing thin, I was wearing myself out; I could not long survive this sort of life. I was born to have a mistress and to live happily with her. Not knowing what to do, I gambled and I won nearly every day, yet for all that I was bored."

November 1, 1753. All Saints' Day. As Casanova left mass and made his way to his gondola, a woman dropped a letter in his path. When she saw he had collected it, she vanished. Once settled in his gondola, Casanova broke the seal and read its contents. It was a long letter in French from someone claiming to be one of Caterina's fellow nuns. It contained a frank proposition and a number of scenarios as to how the two might meet. Casanova surmised from the style and tone of the letter that his anonymous correspondent might be the nun "who was teaching C.C. French and who was beautiful, rich, and a flirt. . . . But I dismissed the suspicion precisely because it pleased me." Casanova decided to hedge, writing back that he would welcome a chance to meet her in the convent visiting rooms, in the company of a woman of her choice. The proposal was accepted, and the necessary arrangements were made. The following Sunday Casanova went to morning mass at the convent as usual. That evening he returned, masked and in the company of the designated woman, at the entrance. His escort "asks to see M.M. The name astonishes me, for the bearer of it was celebrated." With mounting excitement he was led to a private visiting room. M.M. (her real identity has never been uncovered) appeared at the grating, pressed a button that loosened four sections, allowing for the creation of a hole easily large enough for a man to pass through, stepped across the grille, and embraced her friend. Casanova sat in silent rapture as the two the conversed. M.M. was a "rare beauty" in her early twenties,

> tall, so white of complexion as to verge on pallor, with an air of nobility and decision but at the same time of reserve and shyness, large blue eyes; a sweet, smiling face, beautiful lips damp with dew, which allowed a glimpse of two magnificent rows of teeth, her nun's habit did not let me see any hair; but whether she had it or not, its colour must be light chestnut, her eyebrows told me as much.[37]

She completely ignored him, and after an hour or so of conversation she returned through the grating without so much as a nod of recognition. This was more than enough for Casanova, who surrendered himself to the thrill of a nascent affair. He was fascinated by this beautiful, sophisticated woman, who had the ability to pass freely through the convent walls. Discreetly, he interviewed women who knew her, gathering a portrait of an enigmatic woman who had "taken the veil when she is rich, highly intelligent, very cultivated, and . . . a freethinker." She also proved an adept manipulator of male emotions. After the initial excitement of their nocturnal encounter in the visiting parlor, M.M. denied Casanova a meeting. Casanova was thrown off. At night he wrote her bitter letters and then destroyed them in the coolness of the morning. "Such are the terrible moments to which a pursuer of women is exposed," Casanova reflected, "there is nothing more cruel."

> *They degrade, they distress, they kill. In my revulsion and humiliation, my first feeling was contempt for myself, a dark contempt which approached the limits of horror. The second was a disdainful indignation toward the nun, on whom I passed the judgement she appeared to deserve. She was mad, a wretched creature, shameless. My only consolation was to think her such.*

He wrestled with his wounded pride and his rattled emotions which fluctuated between whimsical savagery and profound self-loathing. He knew what reason demanded—"I must pretend indifference"—but he could not impose its sovereignty. After letting him dangle for some days, M.M. came to his rescue, sending a consolatory note that assured him that she had not meant to humiliate him but that a series of honest mistakes had kept them apart. Casanova jumped at the letter, dashing off a florid response ("I cannot live except in the hope of your forgiveness . . . I saw you, you dazzled me."). The two quickly organized another meeting, à deux, at her convent in Murano. There they had an honest exchange despite the inevitable Casanovian histrionics. He admitted that he had a lover in the convent, "but she has been torn from me. For six months I have lived in perfect celibacy." He still loved Caterina, "but I foresee that the seduction of your charms will make me forget her." For her part, she admitted she also had a lover, one of means and rank. He was aware of her flirtation with Casanova and had made his *casino* available for the two to use. They had their first, unconsummated, assignation there shortly afterward. Casanova was charged with organizing their second, and his preparations for it, and the philosophizing that accompanied them, represent one of the great intellectual excavations of the meaning of seduction.

. A belief in the essential benignity of the reasoned pursuit of happiness was at the heart of Enlightenment thinking. The aspiration for all civilized conduct was that rational individuals, endowed with free will and molded by polite society, could make decisions designed to maximize their own pleasure and contentment, without harming others, and, ideally, while benefitting them. Enlightened pleasure was distinguished from animal gratification by the inclusion of reason. Discussing his arrangements for his assignation with M.M., Casanova observes that the three inherent features of life are hunger, the sex drive, and the hatred of competitors. Beasts and brutes can gain satisfaction from the fulfilment of any of these three urges, but "let us not call them pleasures . . . for they do not reason about them."

"Man alone is capable of true pleasures," he continues,

> for, endowed with the faculty of reason, he foresees it, seeks it,
> creates it, and reasons about it after enjoying it. My dear reader,
> I beg you to follow me; if you drop me at this point, you are not
> polite. Let us examine the thing. Man is in the same condition as
> the beasts when he yields to these three instincts without his reason
> entering in. When our mind makes its contribution, these three
> satisfactions become pleasure, pleasure, pleasure.

What has not been planned cannot properly be called pleasurable. Casanova is distrustful of spontaneity for this reason. He knows that the blind gratification of the passions leads to shame, dishonor, and injury. This is not to say that he never succumbs to them, merely that he regards them as inferior to pleasures more rationally won. Some portion of this preference is grounded in a sincere belief that reciprocity is the key to genuine pleasure. The amoral libertine is logical; the ebullient philanderer is impulsive. Both are concerned with smashing through the resistance of their target. Jealous of their own pleasure they pay scant regard to that of the woman at hand. Casanova denies that this can be the highest manifestation of enlightened love. The carefully stage-managed seduction he prepares for M.M. is designed to draw her willingly into the minuet. Delayed gratification is the key. Just as "we bear hunger in order to savour culinary concoctions better," he writes, "we put off the pleasure of love in order to make it more intense."

Casanova's preparations for his second night with M.M. were an earnest testament to his philosophy of seduction. On short notice he found an expensive *casino* near St. Mark's, with a drawing room with a chandelier, mirrors, porcelain-tiled walls, an array of suggestive statuettes, a suite of matching sofas and armchairs. A second room was octagonal and mirrored from floor to ceiling, with counterposed mirrors that allowed the same object to be viewed from multiple perspectives. Adjacent was a hidden alcove that led to a spacious closet and thence to a chamber with a bed and a large bathtub, the paneling here embossed with ormolu and painted over with flowers and a pastiche of foliate Ottoman patterning. The *casino* came with a cook, whom Casanova charged with finding suitable quantities of Burgundy and champagne, food for eight courses plus dessert, clean bedding, and candles for every room. He further ordered that he would have the meal that night that would be served to M.M. the next, to ensure the cooking met his standards. The rooms were designed such that the servants' quarters and kitchens were structurally segregated from the front rooms. Successive courses were passed through a revolving dumbwaiter that allowed for no glimpse of the people on the other side. That evening Casanova solemnly consumed, plate by plate, a feast served on ornate Meissen crockery and then gave his notes to the waiting chef. "Game, sturgeon, truffles, oysters, and perfect wines. I only reproached him with having forgotten to set out hard-boiled eggs, anchovies, and prepared vinegars on a dish. . . . I also said that another time I wanted to have bitter oranges to give flavour to the punch and that I wanted rum, not arrack." The dress rehearsal took two hours, then he went to bed. The next morning he rang for coffee, and before he left he instructed his man to find fresh fruits and ices for their dessert that evening. With nothing to occupy his mind until the appointed hour he went to the Ridotto and gambled until dusk. That evening his careful planning and exacting standards did not go unrewarded. M.M. was as impressed as he had hoped, and when she left in the morning to return to the convent the two were lovers.

Theirs was a quintessentially enlightened affair and represented something of a high-water mark in Casanova's career. There is little in the totality of Casanova's sex life that can be innocently defended. Even allowing for the disparities in norms and mores between his time and ours, it would require the most cynical partisan to make the case that a good deal of Casanova's sexual endeavors were not something more than the meeting of rational, like-minded individuals and strayed somewhere beyond the crooked boundary of the consensually transgressive, past the bogs and marshes of the tolerably deviant, and into the black valleys of sexual crime. His affair with M.M., however, perhaps because it was one that she managed more than he, is free of some of the doubts that trouble his other amours. She insisted that they use the best English-made condoms to ensure that she did not get pregnant. She tutored him in her free thinking ways and made sure he read books from her library.[38] When she informed him that her lover wanted to be a hidden spectator to one of their assignations (concealed in an alcove behind a sofa, where flowers carved in relief in the wainscoting had

unintrusive spy-holes cut out of their carpels), he assented without complaint. M.M. made a mockery of the convent's security, moving freely in
and out to visit Casanova in a *casino*, or to spend the night at the opera
or gambling at the Ridotto. Casanova responded in style. At one point
he learned from Laura that a masked ball was to be held in the convent's
largest visiting parlor. Without first telling either Caterina or M.M. of his
intentions, he attended dressed as the white-frocked clown Pierrot and
danced a dozen *furlane* with a harlequiness in pristine anonymity before
a cheering crowd of nuns and day-visitors. This was nothing compared
to what M.M. did next. One evening, Casanova went to an assignation
with her to find Caterina waiting in her place. The shock of Caterina's
introduction into their affair initially caused a rupture, but M.M. was
able to steer all involved back on to her intended course. Soon she had
inveigled the three into a ménage à trois that quickly expanded into a
ménage à quatre when she brought into the circle her original lover,
who was revealed to be François-Joachim de Pierre de Bernis, the French
ambassador to Venice.

These were the golden days of Casanova's youth, and they could
not last. Geopolitics initiated the unraveling of their coterie. De Bernis
was summoned from Venice, where in truth he was doing very little, to
Vienna to help negotiate an epochal diplomatic settlement between the
House of Bourbon and the House of Habsburg.[39] The departure of her
principle lover cast M.M. into a great depression and also took from her
some of the freedoms and privileges that the mistress of such a powerful
man might expect to enjoy. Meanwhile, Casanova himself was coming
under greater and greater scrutiny from the Venetian Inquisition. In late
1754 he was assigned a spy, one Giovanni Battista Manuzzi, by the
Inquisition. Manuzzi was soon gathering information and producing
reports chronicling Casanova's scandalous behavior. In his telling, Casanova was a parvenu, a con man, and a layabout who consorted with

gamblers and atheists, had contacts with foreign agents;[40] he had been the "ruin of Bragadin, from whom he has extracted much money."[41] While these allegations were swirling around him, Casanova managed to make an enemy of Antonio Condulmer, a patrician who in 1755 became a State Inquisitor. Also around this time, he made the acquaintance of the aforementioned John Murray, the English resident in Venice, and was soon sharing mistresses and making gossip with yet another highly placed foreign diplomat. Other incidents piled up. Manuzzi approached Casanova directly concerning a chimerical diamond deal and, invited into Casanova's room, observed that he had heretical books and manuscripts relating to the cabala littered about his room. Lucia Memmo, from a distinguished patrician family, complained directly to the Inquisition that Casanova was teaching atheism to her son Andrea. Anonymous informants told the inquisitors that he was a magician, a devil worshipper, and a Freemason. Lurid rumors spread that Casanova had sold corrupted love philters to one Countess Bonafede, who had subsequently gone insane and ran naked about the Campo di San Pietro screaming his name.

It soon became common knowledge that Casanova was a marked man. As June turned to July, friends began to urge Casanova to leave town. One morning, after a night spent restlessly walking the streets, he returned to his *casino* to find it had been raided by the guard. At Bragadin's, his old patron had a gondola and purse full of gold waiting for him; he implored his young friend to fly to Florence until it was safe to come back. He refused. Misplaced pride kept him in the city. On the evening of July 25, 1755, he was arrested and taken to the Ducal Palace. He passed briefly before the tribunal; this was formality, as under Venetian law there were no lawyers, no evidence, no witnesses, no real trial to speak of. In the archives his crime is listed as "public outrages against the holy religion," but he was not informed of this. Nor was he told of his sentence: five years in the *piombi*, the prison in the attics above the Ducal Palace.[42]

There were two dungeons in the Ducal Palace. The *pozzi*, or the wells, in the cellars, and the *piombi*, or the Leads, in the rooftops. Both were objects of terror for the Venetian populace, though the dank *pozzi* were lethal, whereas the lofty *piombi*, scorched in the summer and frozen in the winter, were merely very uncomfortable. As a relatively wealthy prisoner, Casanova benefitted from being able to purchase a few luxuries for his cell. These were pitiful recompense for the structural indignities of his detention. The ceiling was too low to accommodate his full height, so he moved in a stoop. The sounds of rats scurrying in the gables were a constant in the background, regularly joined by the booming chimes of the nearby clocktower on St. Mark's. Sitting in his single wretched armchair he was devoured by lice and drenched in sweat. Soon he was in a delirium brought on by the ferocious heat and the equally ferocious boredom of his solitary confinement.[43] When, at last, Lorenzo the jailer brought him two books to read, they were as unappetizing a selection as one might expect: a jesuitical work praising the heart and another religious text, a mystical work by a Spanish nun.[44] Neither provided much stimulus. Denied pen and writing paper or even the company of other prisoners, and running low on money, Casanova was soon an enervated wretch. Summer turned to winter, an event marked by a cataclysm. On November 1, Casanova's cell began to quiver, the beams above bouncing out of position. For a few minutes the whole building threatened to jerk apart. The wardens ran about the corridors of the jail in terror. Inside his cell, Casanova called out for god to collapse the Ducal Palace and release him from captivity. The prayer went unanswered, though two thousand kilometers away the city of Lisbon was near totally destroyed.[45]

The only exercise Casanova was permitted during his imprisonment was an occasional walk in the garret. This was a long dusty room, filled with junk abandoned there by long-dead administrators who had worked in the palace below. In the first weeks of 1756 Casanova made two handy discoveries there. The first was a stick of polished black marble; the second was a long metal bolt.[46] He soon realized he could use the former as a whetstone to sharpen the latter. These were to be the tools of his escape. For the next eight months, Casanova dug through his floor in preparation for a nocturnal escape that would have begun in the Inquisitors' chamber, which was situated directly beneath his cell. Everything was in place when a few days before he was scheduled to make his bid for freedom, he was moved to a larger, airier cell with a view of the city. This was a relief won for him by Bragadin's tireless advocacy on his behalf. The sudden move came at an inopportune time, and he had to start his plotting all over again. Due to various architectural hindrances arising out of his new location in the building, he was obliged to draw in other prisoners into his scheming. With the guards' blessing, he began sharing books with a man in another cell, Marin Balbi, an aristocrat and sometime monk. Communicating via messages secreted in the bindings of the books they exchanged, Casanova conspired to have Balbi start by digging through a ceiling into the crawlspace above the prison, and sent him his precious bolt—hidden in a Bible and carried beneath a tray that carried two heaped plates of macaroni with butter and parmesan—to begin work. Once Balbi had done this, he was able to break into Casanova's cell from above and the two could then begin to work on breaking through the lead-tiled roof. The target date was November 1, when the Inquisitors and many other senior state officials left Venice for three days.

The scheme was almost abandoned completely when, in mid-October, a stool pigeon named Soradaci was added to Casanova's cell. After a few days of panic and despair, Casanova pulled himself together and in a hysterical display of his charismatic powers was able to convince

Soradaci that angels were visiting his cell at night.[47] The angel was, of course, Balbi, who on the evening of October 31 emerged from the ceiling and into Casanova's waiting arms. They spent some time preparing the various items they would need for their escape, as well as attempting to borrow some money from fellow prisoners and having a last-minute shave. Then they ventured out onto the great roof of the building.

After some hair-raising peregrinations around the slippery, fog-bound roof (Casanova nearly died falling off and spent two perilous minutes hanging from the gutter before he could right himself, a moment captured in a contemporary etching), the two found their way into one of the many offices above the Ducal Palace. Exhausted, Casanova then had a three-hour nap. When he awoke he opened a window and recognized that they were directly above the San Marco quarter, where he had passed so many merry nights in *casini*. This was not, however, a suitable place to exit the building. They made their way in the darkness through the building until they came to a large locked door. Using his spike, and heedless of the immense noise it made, Casanova smashed through the paneling until he had created a hole large enough to crawl through. They were now in a passageway that led to the principal entrance to the palace's interior—the Scala d'Oro, which led down to Scala dei Giganti and thence to the Piazzetta di San Marco. When a new Doge was elected he would process in splendor up the Scala dei Giganti and at the summit would be crowned with his cap of state, the golden *corno*. Thereafter, the Scala d'Oro would be the official approach to his offices of state on the second floor of the palace. At the stop of these stairs impassable door which Casanova and Balbi were now stuck behind. Casanova's bolt could do no more for them. The next step was in the hands of fate.

Casanova was by then a total mess: smeared in grime, sweat, and blood, wild-eyed from adrenaline and cortisol, covered in splinters, grazes, cuts, scrapes, and bruises. He laid down and had an hour's rest.

When he awoke the sun was about to rise. He took from his bundle a fine coat, white stockings, a lace-trimmed shirt, and a hat with golden brocade and a white plume. He stashed his ruined clothes behind an armchair and went over to a window. In the courtyard some lackey saw a fine young man in the palace and assumed someone had been locked in overnight. Balbi and Casanova stood at the door and listened to the jangle of keys as the porter made his way up the grand staircase. When it opened it revealed a single man, unassuming and unarmed, now stunned as his brain made the necessary connections as to what he had just done. Casanova brushed past him wordlessly and walked down the Scala d'Oro, turned right and trotted past the two enormous sculptures of Neptune and Mars that bracketed the top of the Scala dei Giganti, went down those stairs and into the porticos of the Ducal Palace and out into the *piazzetta*, where, beneath a Tiepolo dawn, a few Grand Tourists were winding across the flagstones and the coffee shops were opening for a new day's business. Balbi began to beg him to take them to the basilica, where they could claim the medieval right of asylum. Casanova, had he cast a glance in that direction, would have seen the twin ashen columns of the Pillars of Acre, beside them the freckled porphyry dish, *la pietra del bando*, where traitors' heads were displayed for three days and three nights. More likely he veered left without a second thought, passing past the columns of St. Mark and St. Theodore, toward the quay where fishmongers were laying out their stalls beneath the watchful eyes of the cloaked and capped fisherman, fresh from the Adriatic, and a gaggle of *gondolieri* were making small talk. He loudly cried out for a boat to Fusina then halfway across the lagoon he ordered them to take him to Mestre instead. In Mestre all was almost lost when Casanova was recognized by one of the Inquisition's spies while waiting for Balbi to finish flirting with a waitress in a coffeehouse. They took a coach to Treviso—still within the boundaries of the Venetian state—and then left the town on foot, aiming for the independent Bishopric of Trento. Somewhere in the countryside he gave Balbi the remainder of the money, menaced him with his spike, and sent him on his way. Alone, famished, thirsty, and gloriously free, Casanova began his march toward the Alps.

—·— ≡≫◆ —·—

In a characteristically ostentatious display of his classical education, Casanova describes himself as possessing *kerdaleophron*. In Homeric poetry, *kerdaleos* is an adjective used to describe the fox as cunning or tricky. The root of it, *kerda*, literally means "profit" and the heart of the full word as Casanova uses it means something like profit-minded, self-interested, crafty. It is in this sense that Agamemnon hurls it as an insult at Odysseus, the famously sly Greek hero. Casanova's adoption of the word is a fascinating glimpse of how he imagines himself. For following his departure for Venice in 1756 he did become something of an Odysseus in his wayward traveling existence, albeit an Odysseus without an Ithaca, scheming his way around Europe without end or purpose.

Casanova's peregrinations spanned the better part of three decades and defy easy summary. Traveling under the adopted title of the Chevalier de Seingalt he roamed freely around every part of the continent, rarely staying in any one place for more than ten months.[48] Zooming out from the thickets of anecdote to consider the larger story he relates it becomes possible to see Casanova's life as he tells it as something of a greatest-hits tour of Enlightenment Europe. Following his flight from Venice he spent two years in Paris, where, with the aid of his old comrade from the convent, François-Joachim de Pierre de Bernis, he became fabulously wealthy after organizing the nation's first national lottery. In this period he also made the acquaintance of Rousseau, who did not impress him, and the plutocratic dowager Madame d'Urfé, whom he conned with his cabalistic knowledge in order to finance better his extravagant lifestyle.[49] In 1759 de Bernis sent Casanova on a mission to Amsterdam to sell French government bonds to help fund the ongoing Seven Years War. In Amsterdam Casanova ran into an impoverished Teresa Imer accompanied by their daughter, Sophie, and her elder son Giuseppe. Imer persuaded Casanova to take Giuseppe back to Paris, where the poor boy soon became inveigled into a plot by Madame d'Urfé to obtain immortality by transferring her soul into the body of a child. Meanwhile, Casanova went on an extended tour of southern Europe, passing through Geneva, where he was thrilled to spend some hours in conversation with Voltaire, before passing leisurely through Southern France and thence to Rome and Naples.

Returning to Paris in 1763 he received a summons from London. Teresa Imer had metamorphosed into Teresa Cornelys, the impresaria behind the ultra-fashionable Soho pleasure palace Carlisle House. She was at this stage—and admittedly only for a brief period—the wealthiest self-made woman in London, and she wanted her son back. Casanova crossed the Channel in June 1763 and was soon rooming in St. James and making inroads into London society. He was a perfect match for Georgian London and records his visits to Vauxhall and Ranelagh, to the bagnios and coffee shops of Covent Garden, and to the various playhouses, attending the Italian opera—whose performers had once ranked his mother among their number—and the Drury Lane Theatre, where he saw David Garrick perform. At Carlisle House he caroused with the riotous aristocratic elite and attended court, where he met George III and his wife. He discussed etymology with Samuel Johnson, met and refused the charms of the celebrated courtesan Kitty Fisher, and went before the court of the blind judge Sir John Fielding—brother of the novelist Henry Fielding—who interviewed the suspect Venetian in perfect Italian.[50] After London he went to Prussia, where he met, and flirted with, Frederick the Great, and then traveled to Russia, where he had several meetings with Catherine the Great. He met Johann Winckelmann in Rome; he met Benjamin Franklin in Paris. For many of these meetings we have only Casanova's account—Voltaire, for example, barely makes mention of a meeting that takes up many exuberant pages in Casanova's memoir—while others left enthusiastic remembrances of this exotic exile. Not all were impressed. James Boswell met Casanova (whose name he Germanicized as "Neuhaus") at a Berlin tavern in 1764 and recorded the devastating impression of "an Italian, [who] wanted to shine as a great philosopher, and accordingly doubted of his existence and of everything else. I thought him a blockhead."

Along the way there were many dalliances of varying degrees of seriousness and salubrity, though for the reader of Casanova's memoirs the endless sequences of affairs soon cease to beguile and begin instead to bewilder. The governing paradox of Casanova's literary project was that he was the greatest chronicler of a phenomenon that he lacked the self-knowledge to analyze. For even if Casanova failed to articulate it, there was a connection between sex, travel, and Enlightenment and it was forged in the final years of 1760s, as Casanova skittered from capital to court at ever greater velocity, a ball on a perpetually spinning roulette wheel.

In 1767, Captain Samuel Wallis of the Royal Navy discovered the island of Otaheite, now known as Tahiti, in the South Pacific. It soon emerged that sexual mores on Tahiti were very different from those at home. The crew of the *Dolphin* wondered at the beauty of the indigenous peoples and were taken aback by the forwardness of their women. English bashfulness was quickly overcome, and soon a thriving trade was under way with sailors buying favors with local women using iron nails—something the locals coveted above all else—as currency. Soon the *Dolphin*'s crew were pillaging the ship for iron nails, spikes, and rivets with such diligence that the captain feared the craft might disintegrate on open waters—as perfect a metaphor as can be imagined for the capacity of desire to destabilize complex structures. Such behavior might only be expected from sailors, but the official Navy historian sat in judgment of Tahitian mores. "Chastity does not seem to be considered as a virtue among them," he wrote a judgment confirmed later that year, when French captain Louis Antoine de Bougainville arrived on the island.[51] He observed many of the same habits that had shocked the English with a more gracious Gallic eye. "These people breathe only rest and sensual pleasures," he wrote, "Venus is the goddess they worship . . . everything [in Tahiti] inspires sensual pleasure. And so I have named it New Cythera."[52] The association of Tahiti with Venus was confirmed in sentiment and in nomenclature in 1769 when Captain Cook arrived on the island. Cook was charged with conveying botanist and astronomer Joseph Banks of the Royal Society to Tahiti to document the Transit of Venus. Banks and Cook built their observatory on the shore and enclosed it in a palisade they named Fort Venus. When not engaged in astronomical work, Banks explored the island and marveled at its sexual freedoms. "Love is the Chief Occupation, the favorite, nay almost the Sole Luxury of the inhabitants," he recorded in his journal, "both the bodies and souls of the women are modeled into the utmost perfection for that soft science. Idleness, the father of Love, reigns here in almost unmolested ease." Banks described and participated in "Arreoy," gatherings of unmarried Tahitian men and women that involved wrestling, dancing, and sexual orgies.[53]

News of an island in the distant Pacific whose inhabitants knew of no Christian god, seemingly lived in social peace amid a natural cornucopia, and enjoyed "free liberty in love" exploded like fireworks in the imaginations of late-Enlightenment Europeans.[54] Explorations at the

frontiers of the known world had seemingly endorsed the philosophical belief in the naturalness of desires and the healthiness of their free
expression. Satirists, philosophes, and polite conversationalists across
the continent were soon writing and talking about Tahiti and the lessons
it might hold for Europe. The most thorough treatment of the subject
came from Denis Diderot, who in 1772 wrote "Supplément au Voyage
de Bougainville," an imagined dialogue between a Tahitian and a European that he used as a vehicle for a wide-ranging critique of French
society and French colonial practices. One area among many where
Diderot believed Europeans could learn from Tahitians was in matters
of sexual morality. Speaking through his imagined Tahitian (named
Orou), Diderot asserted that "courtship exists in nature" and that the
constraints on sexuality were unnatural contrivances: "There's nothing
natural in modesty; all the rest is convention." "The Tahitian would say
to us," Diderot continues,

> Why do you hide your body? What are you ashamed of? Is it
> wrong to submit to the most noble impulse of nature? Man, show
> yourself openly if you are attractive. Woman, if this man pleases
> you, receive him with candour.

In a final flourish, Diderot declared that "nowhere but in Tahiti will
you find the condition of man a happy one, nor is it elsewhere even tolerable, apart from in a little backwater of Europe." That place, another
island in a smaller sea, was Venice, where "morals are less artificial, and
vices and virtues are less chimerical, than anywhere else."[55]

Casanova's own sexual explorations were less replete with philosophical possibility. A typical encounter was the kind of glancing blow
recorded in Paris. In pursuit of Camille, an actress, he shared a carriage
with her and her occasional lover the Count de la Tour d'Auvergne.

Squeezed in a two-seat trap, Camille sat on the count's lap. In the darkness Casanova made the familiar move:

> *Full of desire, I determine to seize the opportunity, and, wasting no*
> *time, for the coachman was driving fast, I take her hand, squeeze it,*
> *she squeezes mine, I gratefully raise it to my lips, covering it with*
> *silent kisses, and, impatient to convince her of my ardour, I proceed*
> *as my state of bliss demands that I do; but just at the moment of*
> *crisis I hear La Tour d'Auvergne saying:*

> *"I am obliged to you, my dear friend, for a piece of your country's*
> *politeness of which I thought I was no longer worthy; I hope it is*
> *not a mistake."*[56]

Extracting meaning from such episodes is a mystifying endeavor, made harder by the great number of them Casanova includes in his memoirs and the comparative paucity of introspection with which they are recounted. On this point, Byron is once again a useful approach to Casanova. A man who knew as much as Casanova about sex, transport, and the intersection of the two, Byron also had a more fully developed philosophy about the significance of such experiences. Writing from Venice to Lord Kinnaird in London, apropos of *Don Juan*, whose third canto he was then deep into, Byron mounted a brilliant preemptive defense of his work:

> *it may be bawdy—but is it not good English? It may be*
> *profligate—but is it not life, is it not the thing?—Could any man*
> *have written it—who has not lived in the world?—and tooled in a*
> *post-chaise? in a hackney coach? in a gondola? against a wall? in a*
> *court carriage? in a vis-à-vis?—on a table?—and under it?*[57]

Intellectual capabilities aside, the two men shared much in common. The hunger for sensual variety just described by Byron is found on every page of Casanova's memoir as is a corresponding, if implicit, fatigue. Both men were exiles—Casanova from Venice, Byron to Venice—and in exile both adopted a shallow cosmopolitan posture that belied home-sickness and wounded patriotism.[58] Sensualists and travelers, rootless men in rootless relationships, between the two we can scry the essential features of the heroic seducer: a strenuous neophilia, a listless promiscuity, and a naive cosmopolitanism.

On the evening of October 29, 1787, Casanova could be found in a box at the Nostitz Theatre in Prague waiting for an opera to begin. At sixty-two, he was a stiff old man in a short brown wig, dressed in fine if slightly faded clothes, looking on with well-practiced hauteur at the tumult in the auditorium beneath him. For several hours crowds had been gathering before the theatre, eager to secure a ticket and a seat. The crush of carriages had created a mire of churned mud that fashionable ladies and their attendants had been obliged to pick their way through. Inside was chaos: the stalls and the parterre were packed; the gallery was so overwhelmed that spectators clung to the metal rods connecting the rafters, triggering concerns that the crush might collapse the roof. Adrift in the melee were vendors selling beer, sausages, and lemonade. Shortly before seven the conductor entered the pit and received a thunderous reception, the crowd rising to its feet three times to show their appreciation. At last the uproar dissipated, the orchestra struck up, and the curtain lifted on the opening night of *Il Dissoluto punito, ossia il Don Giovanni* by Wolfgang Amadeus Mozart.

The tale of Don Juan was first committed to paper in the early seventeenth century by a Spanish monk named Gabriel Tellez, who under the pen name Tirso de Molina wrote *El Burlador de Sevilla y Convidado de Piedra*. It was an instant hit and had become something of a dramatical and literary standard reworked and reimagined by authors and playwrights across the continent. The plot adhered to a norm: Don Juan Tenorio is a ruthless and cynical womanizer who at the beginning of the play seduces the beautiful Ana and then kills her upstanding father. Much of the action of the play consists of Don Juan escaping justice for his various crimes while seeking to corrupt an assortment of peasant girls and noblewomen. In the final scenes he encounters the shade of the man he killed and insouciantly invites him to dine with him that evening. The vengeful ghost accepts the offer and once dinner has been served insists on returning the invitation by dragging Don Juan down into hell. In its various tellings, the tale of Don Juan was always meant to entertain, but it also contained a strong religious warning. Don Juan's crime is to make a mockery of the sacrament of marriage, a mortal sin for which he must pay with his life.

In the hands of Mozart and his librettist Lorenzo Da Ponte the play took on a very different character. The basic plot structure survived, but the moral message was overthrown. Don Giovanni struts across the stage not as a villain but an embodiment of liberty and libertinism. Donna Elvira is not a seduced maiden but a jilted lover. We laugh at the uxorious Masetto and wonder at the true desires of his fiancée, Zerlina. *Don Giovanni* shuns moralizing in favor of a full-throated celebration of Casanova's world of leisure, travel, and seduction. This was a milieu where sexual adventure was encouraged, and so it is only fitting that the orchestra approaches an ecstatic pitch as Don Giovanni's faithful servant Leporello recounts the conquests of his master:

> *Madamina, il catalogo è questo*
> *delle belle, che amò il padron mio;*

un catalogo egli è, che ho fatt'io.

Osservate, leggete con me.

In Italia seicento e quaranta,

in Almagna duecento e trentuna,

cento in Francia, in Turchia novantuna,

ma in Ispagna son già mille e tre!*

If Casanova was jealous of the don's prodigality he can only have approved of his justification for his liberal loving ways. "I do it because I love them," Don Giovanni explains to Leporello. "Who is faithful to one is cruel to the others. I am a man whose heart is so large that I love all of them."

Since the early nineteenth century there have been those who have claimed that it was no coincidence that Casanova was present at the first performance of an opera that, more than any other work of art, has come to represent one half of how Western culture has thought about

---

* Dear Madame, here's a little list
Of the beauties my master has won.
I've made some notes, just for fun.
Come over here, read it with me.
In Italy, six hundred and forty.
In Germany, two hundred and thirty-one.
In France, a hundred. In Turkey, ninety-one.
But in Spain, it tops a thousand and three.
There are your country girls,
Maidservants and ladies in pearls.
Countesses, baronesses
Princesses, marchionesses.
Women of every rank,
Of any shape, of any age.

This translation is taken from *Seven Mozart Librettos*, trans. J. D. McClatchy, (New York: W. W. Norton & Co., 2011).

seduction. It has been alleged that Casanova was not simply a passive onlooker in the theatre but a librettist admiring his work. The notion that Giacomo Casanova, semi-mythical seducer, had a hand in the composition of Mozart's *Don Giovanni* is so enormously perfect it exerts a kind of gravitational pull on the imagination. The facts are more mundane, though suggestive nonetheless. Mozart's librettist for *Don Giovanni* was Lorenzo Da Ponte, a Venetian who had befriended Casanova during the latter's ill-fated return to Venice in the late 1770s. In his memoirs, Da Ponte speaks very highly of Casanova and specifically praises his writing abilities. In the winter of 1787 Da Ponte was working furiously on three separate librettos: *Don Giovanni* for Mozart, *Axur* for Antonio Salieri, and *Arbore di Diana* for Vicente Martín. He arrived in Prague from Vienna in time for the first rehearsals of *Don Giovanni* in early October but was summoned back to Vienna to help Salieri rehearse for *Axur*, which was to be performed before Emperor Joseph II. Da Ponte's departure threw the preparations for *Don Giovanni* into well-documented chaos culminating in the enraged theatre manager locking Mozart in his room to complete the opera. The theory goes that Da Ponte, who earlier in the year had run into his old friend while strolling around Vienna with Salieri, now summoned Casanova to Prague to help Mozart complete the libretto after he was obliged to return to Vienna to work on *Axur*. The idea that Casanova could be drafted into write a libretto on such short notice is not completely incredible. He was, after all, a published playwright, an accomplished violinist, and a man who through family, friendship, and personal enthusiasm knew a great deal about the stage. Furthermore, the story of Don Juan would not have been new to him. Carlo Goldoni, who had written parts for his mother, had produced his own adaptation of the legend in 1736. More recently, librettist Giovanni Bertati's *Don Giovanni Tenorio, o sia Il Convitato di Pietra* had debuted at the Teatro San Moisè in Venice in February 1787 before moving on to Vienna. Additionally, Casanova knew the impresario at the Nostitz, Pasquale Bondini, as well as some of the troupe. The smoking gun is a few sheets of a draft libretto in Casanova's hand discovered in the 1920s. These seemed to show that Casanova had been tasked with assisting Mozart in completing the libretto in the frantic final days before the October 29 debut. It is now conjectured that Casanova helped write parts of the second act, specifically an aria by Leporello in which he promises to reveal the crimes of his master, Don Giovanni.[59] If true, there is a certain poignancy that Casanova—that son of an actress, that most eager of social climbers—should have written the part of a miserable manservant and not that of the don.[60]

The true extent of Casanova's collaboration on *Don Giovanni* can never be known, nor can we know what thoughts were his when he watched his fictional counterpart descend into hell by way of the trapdoor of the Nostitz stage. Still fifteen years from his death in Castle Dux in 1797, perhaps Casanova saw in Don Giovanni's end an intimation of his own, although his would be attended by neither crowds nor recognition. Maybe he glimpsed in it an allegory for the state of his beloved Europe—aristocratic, cosmopolitan, carefree, somewhat cruel—as it stumbled garrulously toward the French Revolution and the democratizing impulses it unleashed. Venice might have come to mind, his impossible homeland sinking in splendor into the glittering lagoon. Most likely this was but one more night's entertainment and he thought of nothing.

━ ⊰✦⊱ ━

CHAPTER THREE

AN UNSENTIMENTAL EDUCATION

Shortly after Casanova arrived in Paris following his escape from the Leads, a man named Robert-François Damiens tried to kill Louis XV at Versailles. Damiens barely managed to scratch the king but faced the full force of the law nonetheless. The punishment for the attempt on the king's life was a brutal death by torture, held in a public square. On the morning of Damiens's death, Casanova and a mixed party of men and women went by carriage to the Place de Grève to watch the execution from an apartment window overlooking the scaffold. Space at the window was limited, so the three women stood in a row, their elbows on the windowsill, their feet on a little ledge. The men stood behind them, their feet sharing the same ledge, craning their heads over the women's for a glimpse of the bloody spectacle.

Damiens's death was an extensive, baroque affair. Bound to a bier at the scaffold, his body was pierced all over with red-hot pincers and then covered liberally with a boiling mixture of oil, resin, wax, and molten lead. The hand that held the knife that cut the king was burned with sulfur His body was to be torn apart by horses, one animal attached to each limb by a length of rope. This took so long to accomplish that eventually the executioners had to slash his joints and tendons with a blade. This worked, and the horses were finally able to detach his arms and legs from his body. The trunk and head was then thrown onto a fire. According to some eyewitnesses his jaw could still be seen moving amid the flames.[1] Casanova watched some four hours of this butchery. At some point the sight of Damiens's agonies was so appalling that he turned his eyes in revulsion. Dropping his gaze he noticed that the pair of friends to his side were seemingly unaffected by the execution playing out in front of them.

> *Tiretta kept Madame XXX so strangely occupied during the whole execution that it may have been only on his account that she never dared to stir or look around.*
>
> *Being behind her and very close to her, he had raised her dress so as not to step on it, and that was all very well. But later, looking toward them, I saw that he had raised it a little too high; . . . I heard the rustling of the dress for two whole hours, and finding the whole thing most amusing I never swerved from the resolve I had taken. I admired Tiretta's appetite even more than his boldness, for in that respect I had often been as daring as he.*
>
> *When at the end of the execution I saw Madame XXX straighten up, I turned too. I saw my friend as lively, fresh, and calm as if nothing had happened.*[2]

By the time Casanova wrote these words, the Bourbon regime that Louis XV had bequeathed to his son Louis XVI had been swept away by the French Revolution. The sensual world of Europe's courts and palaces were being replaced with an austere modernity with its own code of conduct and morality. The new world sat in harsh judgment of the sexual mores of the old. Casanova's account of fashionable aristocrats fornicating at the public quartering of a failed regicide encapsulated the connection many drew between tyranny and debauchery. In the revolutionary era of the 1790s, sexual questions would become political questions while political rhetoric and iconography would be saturated with sexual imagery and gendered language. The sexual politics of the French Revolution would be parsed best by another writer who stood at another Parisian window in 1793 with a prospect on Louis XVI going to face revolutionary justice. Mary Wollstonecraft's life and work would be a study on both the revolutionary and the reactionary potential for sex and seduction.

Wollstonecraft's long road to that window in Paris had begun in London's Essex hinterland, where she was born in April 1759, the second of seven children of Edward and Elizabeth Wollstonecraft. Her father had started out with a not-insubstantial fortune that he frittered away in pursuit of chimerical agricultural schemes that never returned the expected profits. The background to Wollstonecraft's childhood was her family's gradual descent from lower-upper-middle-class respectability to the most precarious of genteel poverties, a downward social trajectory played out against ever-changing backdrops—London, East Riding, London, South Wales, London—as her father dragged his family across the country on the hunt for his latest doomed scheme. Edward had a furious temper and a taste for alcohol that combined in acts of attempted and realized violence against his wife. Some of Wollstonecraft's earliest memories were of trying to prevent this violence, going so far as to sleep across the boundary of her mother's door when she feared her father might come home drunk that night. These experiences, later reinforced by a Protestant taste for temperance in all things, gave her a lifelong appreciation for the evils of alcohol and a keen eye for the details of male slovenliness.[3] Her father's boorishness was made all the more grotesque by the social sanction he was granted through no earned merit as a man, a husband, and a patriarch. The generational recurrence of this injustice was symbolized by the special privileges ladled out to Wollstonecraft's brothers while the daughters were left largely to fend for themselves. Denied any systematic education, she sought out her own, and from the earliest age showed an appetite for reading, writing, and an exchange of ideas and sentiments. Some of her earliest surviving letters—written when she was just fourteen—are poignant examples of this hunger for intellectual engagement. They also point toward some of her abiding interests, ones that she would carry with her from her adolescence to her adulthood. "I have a heart that scorns disguise," she wrote to her first friend, Jane Arden, "and a countenance which will not dissemble:—I have formed romantic notions—I have been once disappointed:—I think if I am a second time I shall want only some infidelity in a love affair, to qualify me for an old maid."[4] These were prophetic words. Wollstonecraft's life was walked on a tightrope kept taut by the tension between her rational self and her passionate self, between the need for independence and intellectual achievement and her hunger for emotional attachments and her dread of loneliness.

Wollstonecraft was a loyal sister and a constructive meddler in her siblings' lives, but the self-evident failure of the Wollstonecraft family unit made it clear to her that relationships born of mutual affection arrived at by rational decision-making were preferable to those imposed and sustained by gothic customs. Her first great experiment in new modes of social living was conducted in concert with Fanny Blood, whom she met in the mid-1770s while living in the village of Hoxton, just outside London. Hoxton was home to a large dissenting community, observant Protestants who worshipped outside the established Church of England, and who were at the forefront of commercial enterprise, progressive reform, and political activism. The dissenting tradition emphasized personal improvement through formal education and private studies and encouraged the thorough interrogation of established norms across every dimension of human experience. It was through connections made in Hoxton that Wollstonecraft was introduced to Blood and the two were soon inseparable, Wollstonecraft traveling from Hoxton to her friend's home in Newington Butts, south of the Thames, whenever the opportunity afforded. Wollstonecraft, who always wanted more from her relationships, claimed that "to live with this friend is the height of my ambition," but life intervened. Her father moved them briefly to Laugharne in South Wales; less than a year later they were back in London, this time in Walworth, closer to the Bloods, but financial exigencies and a fierce need to flee her dysfunctional family home led Wollstonecraft, then nineteen, to take up a job as the companion to an elderly lady, based first in fashionable Bath and then in Windsor. Wollstonecraft found the work both demeaning and stultifying, but it marked a necessary first foray into the outside world. Whenever she could, she returned to London to spend time with Fanny Blood. Near the end of 1781, Wollstonecraft's mother fell terminally ill, and she quit her work as a companion to tend to her through her long final sickness. Her death in April 1782 liberated her daughter to pursue a daring experiment in economic independence and female collaboration.

In February 1784 Wollstonecraft declared her intention to set up a girls' school. She raised money for the venture from within the dissenting community, recruited her sisters Eliza and Everina and Fanny Blood to staff it, and, after a false start in Hoxton, established their school in Newington Green. The school was on perilous financial footings from the outset and continued to be so throughout its near three-year existence. For Wollstonecraft, whose twin needs were independence and usefulness, it provided a vital function.[5] It also brought her into close contact with the community of dissenters, radicals, and writers who made their home in the area. She began attending the lectures and sermons of Dr. Richard Price, a polymath, a quasi–Unitarian minister, and a prolific writer of tracts calling for reform. She befriended Mrs. Burgh, the widow of progressive politician and activist James Burgh, author of the influential educational text, *Thoughts on Education* (1747). She met and bonded with the Reverend John Hewlett, an aspiring writer whose links to publishers and literary taste-makers in Paternoster Row would later serve Wollstonecraft well. Someone in this milieu took her to have tea with an ailing Samuel Johnson, shortly before his death in the winter of 1784. Wollstonecraft's integration into this world was disrupted by her need to tend to Fanny Blood. In January 1785, Blood, who was suffering from consumption, traveled to Lisbon for treatment with her fiancé, Hugh Skeys. Without Blood, Mary's interest in the school waned; when she learned her friend was both pregnant and still persistently consumptive she decided her place was at her side. In a move she certainly knew would result in the school's closure, she borrowed money from Mrs. Burgh and embarked for Lisbon in November 1785.

These were tense, fretful times. She was abandoning her community, her school, and her sisters. She was borrowing money to attend to a quixotic, sentimental mission. For all this, she was young and starting on an overseas adventure. "When going to Lisbon," she would later write, "the elasticity of my mind was sufficient to ward off weariness, and my imagination still could dip her brush in the rainbow of fancy, and sketch futurity in glowing colours." Not that she saw many signs for future hope upon arrival in Lisbon. She detested the sclerotic Catholic culture, disdaining Portugal as "the most savage part of Europe, where superstition still reigns." Characteristically for her, the retrograde state of the nation was reflected in its convents, places where women were imprisoned, deluded by religion, and denied an education, where the "rust of the mind" would accrue, layer by layer, never to be "rubbed off by sensible conversation, or new-born affections of the heart." Her unfavorable impressions were doubtless enhanced by the presence of personal tragedy. Wollstonecraft arrived in Lisbon as Fanny went into labor. Neither mother or son survived, and after an illicit midnight burial in a Protestant graveyard Mary returned to London.

The year that followed was one of depression and financial misery. The school was shuttered, and Mary was harried by creditors. Out of this barren period, however, was born literary opportunity. Encouraged by Mrs. Burgh and with the generous use of Reverend Hewlett's literary connections, Wollstonecraft won a princely ten-guinea advance from the illustrious liberal publisher Joseph Johnson for a commission to write a short book on education. The result was *Thoughts on the Education of Daughters*, published in early 1787. As an educational book by a woman for women, *Thoughts* was progressive by default. The substance of Wollstonecraft's argument, however, hinted at a germinating radical thesis that linked reason and passion, education and sex, independence and submission. At the heart of the book was a sustained critique of a model of female education that encouraged the development of a passing knowledge of peripheral subjects like music, art, and geography and a dedication to wholly inutile interests such as cards, fashion, and saccharine literature. What was missing from this education was the cultivation of reason. This was a fatal absence, Wollstonecraft wrote, because "reason must often be called in to fill up the vacuums of life; but too many of our sex suffer theirs to lie dormant." In contemporary society, little thought was given to that vacuum, as girls were expected to marry and then busy themselves with children and housekeeping. However, in the gap between her maturity and her marriage, a girl without an education was "in great danger of being seduced," as there were plenty of men ready "to take advantage of the artless tenderness of a woman who loves" but loves without logic. It was not that Wollstonecraft disdained emotion, it was that she feared its power if left unchecked by the countervailing imperatives of reason. A woman who could not divine the difference between a sincere suitor and a cynical libertine faced ruin. The application of reason would filter out the rakes and allow for a more impassioned commitment to a good partner. "We should always try to fix in our minds the rational grounds we have for loving a person," she counseled.

Her book was a moderate success and, combined with her previous educational venture in Newington Green, established her as something of a pedagogue. This reputation, in conjunction with persistent financial need, qualified her for a job as governess to the daughters of Robert King, Viscount Kingsborough, the largest Protestant landowner in Ireland. Lord and Lady Kingsborough were, by the standards of their class, progressive in their attitudes and attentive to the needs of their impoverished Catholic tenants. By the summer of 1787, when Mary accepted a position in their household at Mitchelstown, County Cork, they had produced close to a dozen children together, a fecundity that belied the strength of their marriage.[6] A few years earlier, their household had been roiled by scandal when it was alleged that Lord Kingsborough's agricultural advisor, the famed agronomist (and later accidental chronicler of the French Revolution) Arthur Young, was courting Lady Kingsborough over the chessboard after dinner while the children's governess, Mrs. Crosby, was carrying on an adulterous relationship with the viscount himself.[7] Their new governess was well placed to detect whatever traces of conjugal strife might have lingered when she arrived in the household after a painless crossing in October. For after a period of initial excitement, Wollstonecraft lapsed into a characteristic funk, and by the time she crossed the threshold of the fairy-tale Kingsborough pile at Castle Mitchelstown—set on 1,200 acres of woods, gardens, vineyards, and mountains—her thoughts had taken a melancholy turn. She told her sister Everina, that "there was such a solemn kind of stupidity about this place as froze my very blood—I entered the great gates with the same kind of feeling as I should if I was going into the Bastille.'"[8]

Her misgivings found expression in a contentious relationship with her employer, Lady Kingsborough. In her letters home she disdained her as a frigid mother who cared more for her dogs than her daughters and as a shallow, vain woman, who preferred to pamper herself with expensive dresses and imported Italian cosmetics rather than to tend to her proper duties as a wife and mother. She despaired at the miseducation the King daughters were receiving (they were "literally speaking wild Irish, unformed and not very pleasing") and described the daughters of some other relatives, who also lived in the castle, as "fine girls, just going to market, as their brother says." She saw herself as a savior and a substitute mother to the girls and was drawn particularly strongly toward Margaret King, a spry fourteen-year-old whom she judged to be living in terror of her mother and whom she lovingly nursed back to health when she fell poorly at Christmas. Whatever solaces there were in her role, the uneasy place of the governess in the hierarchy of any grand household was exactly designed to play on her class anxieties. In a ruminative letter to Everina, she described herself sitting alone in her room, the family spending time alone together somewhere in the house while from the cellars came the sounds of the Irish servants dancing to a fiddle. "I am treated like a gentlewoman," she wrote, "but I cannot easily forget my inferior station—and this something betwixt and between is rather aukward [sic]."[9] The solitude forced her into her books, and she was soon teaching herself French by reading Madame de Genlis's wildly popular educational tract, *Adèle et Théodore* (1782), which she found "wonderfully clever." Her subsequent reading led her to one the most important intellectual relationships of her career. By March 1788, the family moved to Dublin, and in her letters she was telling Everina that she had moved on to Rousseau's *Émile, or On Education*. That Wollstonecraft responded positively to this initial encounter with Rousseau is noteworthy as a general contempt for his work permeates much of her later writings. There is scarcely a work of hers that does not contain a snipe at the then revered Frenchman. Wollstonecraft mocked his "fanciful state of nature" and abhorred his views on women's education and his biological determinism as "wild chimeras."[10] However contentious Rousseau's substance, his style was immensely influential on his contemporaries, even those who disagreed with him on everything else. Like Byron after him, Rousseau pioneered a certain personal aesthetic—independent, authentic, unabashedly emotional—that cast a spell on a whole generation of Europeans, including Wollstonecraft. "I love his paradoxes," she wrote to her sister, "he was a strange inconsistent unhappy clever creature—yet he possessed an uncommon portion of sensibility and penetration."[11] Her antipathy toward Lady Kingsborough and her admiration for Rousseau were united by a sense of her own burgeoning sensibility, a treasured aspect of her own personality, and one that she thought went squandered in her loveless existence. In the same letter that she praised *Émile*, she lamented of herself that it was "a sad pity that so sweet a flower should waste its sweetness on the *Desart* air, or that the Grave should receive its *untouched* charms." She signed off "Yours an Old Maid."[12]

During her time with the family, Wollstonecraft remained in contact with Joseph Johnson in London and worked on the manuscript of *Mary, A Fiction*. It was evident to her, however, that her literary ambitions were not going to blossom in the service of the Kingsboroughs, and her conviction that her intellectual and sexual potential was going to waste made her an unhappy presence in the family. Her standing with Lady Kingsborough steadily diminished. When in the summer of 1788, the family and their entourage went to England as part of a leisurely tour to France, Wollstonecraft was let go at Bristol after less than a year in the role. It was a setback and an opportunity. At twenty-eight she now had no excuse not to pursue her vocation as a writer. Throwing herself on Johnson's generosity, she roomed in his home for several weeks until he had found her suitable, if very humble, lodgings on George Street on the south side of Blackfriars Bridge.

Only twenty years before, the patch of South London she now called home had been open countryside, meadows that lay between Lambeth and Southwark. The area had been transformed with the construction of the original Blackfriars Bridge in 1769 and in a relatively short time had become a densely built, densely inhabited working-class neighborhood. Poverty and precarity were visible and audible from George Street. The sounds of an organ grinder make their way into her letters, and the numberless beggars and the crowds of out-of-work mechanics invaded her political writings and her political consciousness. In its short history, the neighborhood had acquired something of a rough-and-ready reputation as the epicenter of the anti-Catholic Gordon Riots in 1780. It was also home to a significant number of philanthropic institutions, including two whose proximity to her new home must have resonated with her. The Asylum for Female Orphans in Lambeth had been established in 1758 by Sir John Fielding and was little better than a workhouse whose treatment of its inmates appalled William Blake, who lived on the same street. A few streets south down Great Surrey Street was the Magdalen House, the rescue house for seduced girls and women that doubled as a site of prurient entertainment for well-off Londoners, who paid to attend the services held there on the weekends to goggle at the fallen women. Their carriages would have rattled past her window each Sunday.[13] For her part, Wollstonecraft was living simply. She had one servant and a very limited wardrobe. She scarcely ate meat and spent nothing on entertainments. A rather condescending account of her physical appearance survives from this period that attests to her asceticism: "Her usual dress being a habit of coarse cloth, such as is now worn by milk-women, black worsted stockings, and a beaver hat, with her hair hanging lank about her shoulders."[14] More generous chroniclers described a hale, passionate young woman, with a thick mass of russet hair, and recognized her careless dressing as part of her radical aesthetic. More precious than any of this was her arrival at a state approximating self-sufficiency. "I must be independent," she wrote to Everina from her desk at George Street,

> I am not without hope—And freedom, even uncertain freedom—
> is dear. . . . You know that I am not born to tread in the beaten
> track—and the peculiar bent of my nature pushes me on.

Johnson published *Mary, A Fiction* to little fanfare in 1788 and was soon keeping her busy with translation work. She also became a prodigious reviewer for the *Analytical Review*, Johnson's monthly periodical with a radical bent. Over the next four years she would contribute hundreds of pieces, mostly short and pungent,[15] on topics as diverse as boxing, bridge design, and French history. She enjoyed the activity and the place it secured her in literary circles, but the possibility of becoming little more than a Grub Street hack loomed large. As her husband would later note, "This sort of miscellaneous literary employment, seems, for the time at least, rather to damp and contract, than to enlarge and invigorate, the genius." The writer whose work only serves the "mere mercantile purpose of the day" risks being touched by "the torpedo of mediocrity."[16] Wollstonecraft needed a larger canvas to work on. In the summer of 1789 a revolution in France provided one.

For much of 1789, the British establishment was cautiously optimistic about political developments across the Channel. The prime minister, Pitt the Younger, initially greeted the revolution as an opportunity for "good order and good government," continuing that "France would stand forward as one of the most brilliant Powers in Europe; she would enjoy just that kind of liberty which I venerate." Many statesman agreed, choosing to draw parallels between events in France and events in England during the Glorious Revolution.[17] This sentiment held through the fall of the Bastille and through a turbulent summer of riots, conspiracies, and rural anarchy. The event that led a good part of the British elite to oppose the French Revolution was an action by a group of Parisian woman that autumn. On October 5, 1789, the fisherwomen of Paris, the famous *poissardes*, heard a rumor that the king's bodyguards were planning some kind of strike against the revolution. A huge crowd of them gathered at the Hôtel de Ville, where they looted weapons and then, dragooning in female bystanders as they went, marched out of the city to Versailles. There they demanded a meeting with the king, skirmished with his bodyguard, and finally "secured" the royal family and brought them back to Paris in triumph the next day.

For some the Women's March on Versailles (as it came to be known) was one of the first great episodes of female agency in the French Revolution. For others, it was a travesty, a subversion of gender roles and political norms. Edmund Burke was very much in the latter group. Burke was a writer and Whig member of Parliament, long admired by artists for his treatise on the sublime and by liberals for his defense of the American revolutionaries. It was well-known that Burke was writing a response to events in France, and his essay was much anticipated by liberals, who believed he would affirm the actions of French revolutionaries in a like manner to his warm support for the American revolutionaries. This was not to be. Burke had been repelled by the anarchy he saw in France, which for him was encapsulated in the chaotic events of the *poissardes'* march on Versailles to claim the king, on October 5 and 6, 1789. Similarly, he was aghast at the gushing reaction to the French Revolution in English liberal and radical circles, whom he regarded as abandoning the finest traditions of the English constitution. Burke's twin criticisms met on the occasion of a speech given by Dr. Richard Price,

Mary Wollstonecraft's friend and mentor from Newington Green, at the Old Jewry Meeting-house in London on November 4, 1789. Addressing the London Revolution Society, a political club that commemorated the political triumphs of the Glorious Revolution, Price reflected on the "imperfect state in which the Revolution left our constitution" before declaring that first the American Revolution and now the French Revolution ("both glorious") had given him new hope for the possibilities of political change in England, in Europe, and all over the world. "I see the ardor for liberty catching and spreading," he concluded, "a general amendment beginning in human affairs; the dominion of kings changed for the dominion of laws, and the dominion of priests giving way to the dominion of reason and conscience."[18] For Burke, Price's utopian reveries were "unfounded, dangerous, illegal, and unconstitutional," an affront to tradition, law, and civility. What angered him even more was the timing of Price's address. Exactly a month after the Women's March, when, for Burke at least, all hope for a positive outcome in France was lost, Price had seen fit to praise "these Theban and Thracian orgies, acted in France and applauded only in the Old Jewry."[19] Burke went on to attack the march of the *poissardes* in gendered terms, conjuring up the image of

> *the royal captives who followed in the train . . . slowly moved*
> *along, amidst the horrid yells, and shrilling screams, and frantic*
> *dances, and infamous contumelies, and all the unutterable*
> *abominations of the furies of hell in the abused shape of the vilest*
> *of women.*

The preposterousness of the revolution in France was symbolized by these women who dared to participate in politics. Sexual subversion and political subversion were now joined in a new rhetoric of reaction, one that saw in the politics of the French Revolution a universe where female "sentiments which beautify and soften private society, are to be dissolved by this new conquering empire of light and reason."

"The age of chivalry is gone," Burke declared, "all homage paid to the sex in general . . . is to be regarded as romance and folly."[20]

Reflections on the Revolution in France was published on November 1, 1790. Besides her anger at what she perceived as his betrayal of his earlier support for the rights and liberties of the American revolutionaries—which was widely shared in her circle—as well his unrestrained assault on the benevolent Dr. Price, the content of what Burke wrote, especially as it touched on questions of gender, could have been little better designed to infuriate Wollstonecraft. In a white heat of wrathful inspiration, she took up her pen and within a month had written and published—by Joseph Johnson, of course—a scathing response to Burke's polemic. In its sheer vitriol, its naked ad hominem style, *A Vindication of the Rights of Men* was like nothing Wollstonecraft had written before or would write after. Her attacks on Burke's person are by turns inventive and hilarious; their gendered nature, though, is a curious choice of rhetorical strategy, given that the first edition of *Vindication* was published anonymously, and one that sits uneasily with her own intellectual project of dismantling sexual stereotypes. There are layers of irony to a radical female writer using the shield of anonymity to treat a conservative male political theorist like a swooning girl, mocking his "infantine sensibility," his "pampered sensibility," and joking that she fears she might "derange your nervous system by the bare mention of a metaphysical enquiry." She was on firmer ground when defending the rights of the *poissardes*, whom she characterized with as much dignity as simplicity as "women who gained a livelihood by selling vegetables or fish, who never had had any advantages of education" in the face of Burke's savage contempt. This stout defense led her argument back to her favored subject—the need to edify women through the illuminating powers of reason—where she welcomed the end of the cult of sensibility that Burke so lachrymosely lamented, declaring that it had turned women into "vain inconsiderate dolls, who ought to be prudent mothers and useful members of society."

Vindication made Wollstonecraft famous and its financial success relieved her of some of her money woes, allowing her to move lodgings to Bedford Square and to buy a new dress. Its publication in December 1790 also marked the moment when Englishwomen manned the barriers of political debate. That month, two responses to Burke's *Reflections* were published, both by radical women—Mary Wollstonecraft and Catherine Macaulay Graham—and Helen Maria Williams published the first volume of her eyewitness account of the French Revolution, *Letters Written in France*, in which she welcomed events in Paris as "the triumph of human kind." The presence of this many women in the political arena drew predictable scorn from conservatives, who mocked them as the "Amazon Allies" of the French Revolutionaries and as "our *poissardes*"—some of the first outings of disdainful gendered language that would soon become widespread, but it announced the arrival of women at the radical table.[21] Quite literally in Wollstonecraft's case. In November 1791 she was invited to attend a dinner at Johnson's in honor of Thomas Paine, author of *Common Sense*, who was then writing another reaction to Burke, *The Rights of Man*. Also present was Wollstonecraft's future husband, the radical philosopher William Godwin. Paine ate his food in silence as Godwin and Wollstonecraft sparred over subjects as various and divisive as "monarchy, Tooke, Johnson, Voltaire, pursuits and religion."[22] Wollstonecraft had found her political voice and would never again be silenced.

For all the attention it brought her, Wollstonecraft had misgivings about the substantiveness of her reply to Burke. She had written it too quickly and had made half-hearted attempts to stop its publication.

Success mollified her, but the desire to offer the world a more complete and more considered declaration of her beliefs remained. Once again it would be events in France that moved her to take up her pen. Throughout the summer of 1791, the French National Assembly had been finalizing the wording of the new constitution that would turn the country into a British-style constitutional monarchy influenced by the American model of the division of powers. This was the end of a two-year process of barter, negotiation, and crisis. In June 1791, the king had tried to escape the country with his family to join the counterrevolutionary forces amassed at France's borders. He had come within a hundred kilometers of freedom before he was captured in Varennes and returned to Paris under armed escort. Shortly after his reinstatement in the capital, the National Assembly formally pardoned the king of the accusation that he had tried to go into exile and instead approved the ludicrous fiction that he had been kidnapped. This obvious falsehood led to a split in the Jacobin Club. The day after the king's exoneration, radical Jacobins staged a protest at the Champs-de-Mars in Paris, calling for the abolition of the monarchy and the creation of a republic. The protest turned violent, and soldiers opened fire on the crowds. Martial law was subsequently declared, and the more radical elements within the simmering Parisian political milieu went underground. It was in this period of relative political moderation that the National Assembly sought to finish the constitutional process.

Frenchwomen had been following the framing of the new constitution closely. From the first days of the revolution women had been political agents, participating in protests, submitting petitions, and writing works of political theory and political journalism. Their demands were consistent. They wanted a resolution to the perennial shortages of basic goods (possibly accompanied by some kind of organized system of welfare), a program of national education that would be open to women as well as to men, and a reform of divorce laws. Women met to discuss these matters in political clubs like the Cercle Social, the Société fraternelle, the Cordeliers Club, and, later, in the Society of Revolutionary Republican Women. The more radical among them identified with the rough-and-ready street activists of the Parisian *sections*, the more genteel were allied with the Girondin faction within the National Assembly. Whatever their allegiance, politically engaged women had a stake in the outcome of the wrangling over the constitution and tried to influence the debates as far as they could. In the summer of 1791, as individuals and as part of clubs and delegations, women let the Assembly know what mattered to them. In one such address, Etta Palm called for marital reform and educational opportunities in language that chimed with many of Wollstonecraft's own thoughts on the matter. "Conjugal authority should be only the consequence of the social pact," Palm said, and that pact ought to be a legal rather than a spiritual one; the law "must give equal protection and maintain a perpetual balance between the two married people." The protection of women's rights, she argued, was inseparable from the larger cause of French liberty:

> *Abuse of liberty is a natural consequence of the oppressive regime*
> *of the indissolubility of marriage and of the dull and enervated*
> *education of the cloisters, haunts of ignorance and fanaticism*
> *which you destroyed in your wisdom. You will complete your work*
> *by giving girls a moral education equal to that of their brothers;*
> *for education is for the soul what watering is for plants; it makes*
> *them fertile, causes it to bloom, fortifies it, and carries the germ*
> *productive of virtue and talents to a perfect maturity.*[23]

The constitution that was passed in September was silent about these concerns. The suffrage provisions assigned women the role of "passive citizens," unable to vote. When Talleyrand submitted a report on education to the Assembly, he couched his argument for the separate treatment of men and women in the educational system in familiar Rousseauian terms. Women "ought not to aspire to exercise rights and political functions," he stated. "One must seek their best interest in the will of nature."[24] There was no move to institute divorce laws. The betrayal of French women's political aspirations produced one of the first great feminist manifestos of the 1790s. Olympe de Gouges was an actress and political activist associated with the Girondins. Shortly after the ratification of the constitution she published her *Declaration of the Rights of Woman*, a blistering document that echoed the emancipatory proclamations of the American revolutionaries. Her pamphlet was "a solemn declaration of the natural, inalienable, and sacred rights of woman" and called for women to have the same rights and responsibilities as men. Like Etta Palm and Mary Wollstonecraft, she saw sex and education as being intimately linked, as the central axis on which the condition of women turned. "Woman, wake up," she wrote, "the tocsin of reason is being heard throughout the whole universe; discover your rights."

> *Under the Old Regime, all was vicious, all was guilty. . . . Reason finds other examples that are even more touching. A young, inexperienced woman, seduced by a man whom she loves, will abandon her parents to follow him; the ingrate will leave her after a few years, and the older she has become with him, the more inhuman is his inconstancy; if she has children, he will likewise abandon them. . . . Marriage is the tomb of trust and love . . . the way can be prepared through national education, the restoration of morals, and conjugal conventions.*[25]

The French context is the key to understanding much of Wollstonecraft's thinking as she began work on her most famous book, *A*

Vindication of the Rights of Woman. Written in the winter of 1791, and published in the new year, her second *Vindication* was framed as a response to events in France just as her first *Vindication* was framed as a response to Edmund Burke. This second, more substantial work was dedicated to Talleyrand, whom she met in London between the publication of the first and second editions of *Vindication* (entertaining him at her flat, she served the famously sybaritic aristocrat wine in teacups), with the intention of dissuading him of the views on education that he had expressed in his *Rapport sur l'instruction publique* to the National Assembly.[26] What began as a debate concerning French education policy became a rich, idiosyncratic, and at a times digressive text that resists easy classification. The core of her book was on the relationship between education and sex, the advancement of women, and the concomitant advancement of humanity. "Contending for the rights of women," she wrote, "my main argument is built on this simple principle, that if she be not prepared by education to become the companion of man, she will stop the progress of knowledge."[27] One of the main intellectual obstacles she had to surmount in pursuit of this argument was the prevalence of physiological beliefs that women by virtue of their biology simply could not be educated to the same level as men. Consequently some of her heaviest rhetorical salvos were reserved for this kind of crude biological chauvinism and the men who expounded it. "I will allow that bodily strength seems to give man a natural superiority over woman," she wrote,

> and this is the only solid basis on which the superiority of the
> sex can be built. But I still insist, that not only the virtue, but the
> KNOWLEDGE of the two sexes should be the same in nature, if
> not in degree, and that women, considered not only as moral, but
> rational creatures, ought to endeavour to acquire human virtues

(or perfections) by the SAME means as men, instead of being
educated like a fanciful kind of HALF being, one of Rousseau's
wild chimeras.[28]

However much she may have wished to, Wollstonecraft did not make the dismantling of essentialist views on sexual difference the cornerstone of her debate. The matter was of vital importance but debating pseudo-science with pseudo-scientists was as sterile a pastime as it was ineffective. Wollstonecraft's watchword was usefulness, and the testimony of her own life experience was that women were best served by attaining an education and, through that, independence. As a result, large parts of *Vindication* deal with the importance of education, pursued under "the sober steady eye of reason," which she contrasts continually with the facile miseducation of women under the influences of "novels, music, poetry, and gallantry," which conspire to "to make women the creatures of sensation." Within the prevailing social norms and structures of her day this "false system of education" could not but have sexual implications. It was a system, she wrote, that was more "anxious to make [women] alluring mistresses than rational wives."[29] This was foolish on two counts. Firstly, ill-educated wives made for unhappy marriages. Female fripperies might be forgiven by a husband in the summer of youth, Wollstonecraft wrote, but "the woman who has only been taught to please, will soon find that her charms are oblique sun-beams . . . when the summer is past and gone." A woman with a well-stocked mind would be better placed to handle "the more important years of life, when reflection takes place of sensation" and intimacy subsides into companionship.[30] More worrying yet were the risks of seduction faced by a population of women raised to be giddy ingénues. "Men of wit and fancy are often rakes," she wrote, "and fancy is the food of love."

Such men will inspire passion. Half the sex, in its present infantine
state, would pine for a Lovelace; a man so witty, so graceful, and
so valiant; and can they DESERVE blame for acting according to
principles so constantly inculcated?[31]

To be sure, Wollstonecraft believed that seducers should be held financially responsible for the women they seduced and abandoned.[32] She was
skeptical, however, of the sentimental trope that women should devote
themselves to reforming men. Instead, she believed women were better
protected from seduction and better served in life by seeking to elevate
themselves through education. "It is time to effect a revolution in female
manners," she declared, "time to restore to them their lost dignity, and
make them, as a part of the human species, labour by reforming themselves to reform the world."[33]

— ◆ —

That reader who comes to Wollstonecraft's writing in search of consistency is bound to be disappointed. Wollstonecraft had a questing mind,
ill-disposed to dogma. She freely (though never casually) changed her
mind as she accrued more experience of the world. There were, besides,
too many conflicting strands to her own biography—her wretched,
roving childhood, her precarious ascent to recognition, the rival influences of her dissenting faith and her freethinking milieu, her intellectual
pride and her material poverty—to permit her to perch too complacently
on any one philosophical position. Permeating all of this was her own
keenly felt psychological volatility. She had felt the tug-of-war between
reason and passion since childhood and tussled with it through to the
end of her life. "I am a mere animal," she wrote to Johnson, at a low
ebb in the autumn of 1792, "emotions too often silence the suggestions

of reason."[34] Yet it was this awareness of the simultaneous attractions of contradictory attitudes that made her such a brilliant analyst of the human heart. She once defined love as "the common passion, in which chance and sensation take place of choice and reason." Love involved a loss of control; that was part of its thrill and its terror. Conversely, in Wollstonecraft's view, reason could always reassert itself, the logical mind stealing back ground from the tumultuous passions. The ideal state was a kind of equilibrium between the parts that produced neither a lusterless partnership nor a firestorm of uncontrolled ardors. These "rational desires," as she termed them, held out the best hope for female love, free from subjugation and indignity. Much of this nuance is lost in *A Vindication of the Rights of Woman*, which stakes out a vision of sexual relations that is far more ascetic and suspicious than Wollstonecraft allowed for in her own private life. Even as she was giving expression to the minatory streak in her sexual politics in *Vindication*, Wollstonecraft was herself immersed in an experiment associated with the theory and practice of Free Love.

In the 1790s notions of Free Love were neither widespread nor fully fleshed-out. There was no key text on the subject, no recognizable groupings, no identifiable movement. The doctrines of Free Love, as far as they were even known, were treated as subversive and degenerate, the domain of cranks and madmen. Wollstonecraft had links to this disparate network of sexual radicals. The 1791 edition of her children's book, *Original Stories from Real Life*, featured engravings by William Blake, another client of Joseph Johnson's. Blake was a radical's radical, and the extensive body of mystical poetry he produced was replete with obscurely phrased paeans to sexual liberation. In *Visions of the Daughters of Albion* (1793) he sang of "Love! Love! Love! happy happy Love! free as the mountain wind!" and unfettered by the bonds of law or custom. His friend George Cumberland wrote *The Captive of the Castle of Sennaar* (1798), which depicted a perfect community living on the fictional island of Sophis in the lake of Zambree somewhere in the middle of Africa. Here a system of free love was practiced with no concept of marriage. When the narrator explains the English system of marital relations the inhabitants recoil and tell him it is a "brutal commerce" and a "legal prostitution." Instead every man and woman should be allowed to "act freely; subject to no restraint while they *violate not the innocent will of another*."[35]

Such imagined sexual utopias were inspired by the apparently real sexual utopias discovered in the South Pacific, especially in present-day Tahiti. The example of Tahiti inspired poets Robert Southey and Samuel Coleridge, who in 1793–94 planned to leave for America and set up a model society, the Pantisocracy, which would incorporate elements of Free Love into its organization.[36] The Pantisocrats were also influenced by Wollstonecraft's future husband, William Godwin, who in 1793 published his seminal work, *Political Justice*. This book's early editions contained Godwin's condemnation of the institution of marriage and his call for reformed sexual relations that was as close as the Free Love coterie came to having a catechism. In its pages Godwin attacked marriage as a despotic and irrational institution that captured in miniature all the failings of society at large. "Marriage is law, and the worst of all laws," he thundered, "marriage is an affair of property, and the worst of all properties." He proposed the abolition of marriage, the abolition of surnames, the free mingling of men and women, and the communal parenting of the children who were subsequently produced. In this condition, he believed, "the intercourse of the sexes will in such a state fall under the same system as any other species of friendship." Each man would "assiduously cultivate the intercourse of that woman whose accomplishments shall strike [him] in the most powerful manner," and each woman would do likewise. If several men formed meaningful affections for the same women, "this will create no difficulty."

We may all enjoy her conversation; and we shall all be wise enough
to consider the sensual intercourse as a very trivial object. This,
like every other affair in which two persons are concerned, must
be regulated in each successive instance by the unforced consent of
either party.[37]

The extent of Wollstonecraft's own participation in these utopian
imaginings varied over the course of her life. Under the influence of Dr.
Price and the Newington Green dissenters, she had been something of a
prude. At the height of the revolutionary fever in 1792 and 1793, she was
an enthusiastic proponent of sexual liberation. Later, jaded by political
and romantic failure, her attitudes mellowed into a qualified commitment to the principle of individual sexual freedom. She was throughout a
consistent critic of existing marital arrangements and a convinced enemy
of the stigmas that surrounded so-called fallen women—the seduced,
the abandoned, the ostracized. She wanted to believe in the possibility
of a liberated sexual order but also struggled with the suspicion that it
would degenerate into mindless sensualism and the further exploitation
of women. It was a model that could only work among people with cultivated sentiments, a thorough education, and moral and psychological
temperance. So many elements had to be present to ensure that Free
Love could work that hers was ultimately an elitist vision of sexual liberation, practicable only by a small minority. "Affection requires a firmer
foundation than sympathy," she wrote, "and few people have a principle of action sufficiently stable to produce rectitude of feeling." This is
less a criticism of her thought than of her age, which bred radicalism out
of what is now considered prosaic. All Wollstonecraft believed was that
consenting men and women should be allowed to enter into voluntary
sexual relations conducted on terms of equality, dignity, and respect, and
untroubled by social censure or legal intervention. If this seems banal

today, then that speaks to the visionary simplicity of her thought. As Virginia Woolf observed, Wollstonecraft's "originality has become our commonplace."

Wollstonecraft's own experiments with Free Love were almost exactly coextensive with the first portion of the French Revolution and provided the emotional backdrop against which she encountered developments in France. Much like the revolution itself, her attempts to live out a new vision of sexual relations was a tale of boundless optimism turned to bitterest despair. It was a shared interest and enthusiasm for events in France that first drew her to Henry Fuseli, the brilliant Anglo-Swiss artist whom Wollstonecraft met at Joseph Johnson's dinner table not long after she arrived in London and whom she began to pursue in earnest in the autumn of 1791—just as she began composing *A Vindication of the Rights of Woman*. Wollstonecraft was thirty-two, famous, and approaching the acme of her radicalism. She had never had a lover. Fuseli was fifty. A short, irascible man with a strong German accent who was wholly convinced of his own genius, his own career had only taken off recently, with a successful exhibition of Shakespeare illustrations in 1788, but he was undoubtedly one of the singular artistic talents of his age. His dramatic gothic compositions shared some of the physical drama of William Blake's (who distrusted Fuseli, describing him as "both Turk and Jew") and much of the otherworldliness of Caspar David Friedrich's. Neither his talents nor his interests were limited to art. Fuseli was fiercely proud of his republican Swiss pedigree and freely advertised his radical credentials around Johnson's table. He had immersed himself in the English literary tradition, and his encyclopedic knowledge of Shakespeare and Milton profoundly influenced his art. He was also a partisan of Rousseau and an obsessive reader of Richardson, who never failed to move this otherwise quite cruel man to tears. For Wollstonecraft, who knew nothing much of art, his political and literary passions provided some common ground with the man, for whom, whatever his failings, and there were many, she was perfectly primed to fall. She was keen to love and drawn to genius. For his part, Fuseli was prideful man who enjoyed his fame and fancied himself something of a womanizer. He took some wicked pleasure in Wollstonecraft's pursuit of him. Well aware of the intensity of her passion, he would not respond to or even open and read her letters to him. Whether she detected it in his art or in his person, Wollstonecraft seemed cognizant of this sadistic streak in Fuseli. A glimpse of this comes in a letter to the Liverpudlian lawyer and radical William Roscoe. Committed, as ever, to being useful, Wollstonecraft was dutifully helping to raise subscriptions for Fuseli's latest project, a series of prints inspired by Milton. In a letter to Roscoe in January 1792, she provided an update on Fuseli's artistic activities that was rich in suggestion:

> *Fuseli is going on with more than usual spirit—like Milton he seems quite at home in hell—his Devil will be the hero of the poetic series; for, entre nous, I rather doubt whether he will produce an Eve to please me in any of the situations, which he has selected, unless it be after the fall.*[38]

The Fuseli imbroglio was made all the more wretched by the fact that he was married to a pretty young actress named Sophia. Consequently, Fuseli could encourage her pursuit when it took his fancy, rise above the fray by playing faithful the husband when it did not, and let Wollstonecraft embarrass herself with her passion for a family man. This was not a healthy cycle to be trapped in. By the spring of 1792, Wollstonecraft's friends were well aware of her debilitating obsession with Fuseli. Johnson occasionally tried to goad her out of London and away from him; he worried about her mental health and her declining literary output. As rumors spread, Wollstonecraft slid deeper into debt and began to nurture ever more unlikely hopes about her future with him. In awe of his intellect, she began to harbor hopes for a purely platonic relationship where she might "unite herself to his mind."[39] This was not a realistic solution. As Godwin later observed, "Mary was not of a temper to live upon terms of so much intimacy with a man of merit and genius, without loving him." Even if she was, one can only imagine what Sophia Fuseli might have thought—had she been consulted—on the proposed inclusion of Wollstonecraft in her household. As the affair began to spiral into scandal, Fuseli (allegedly) tried to reason with her and talk her out of her obsession. "If I thought my passion criminal," she supposedly replied, "I would conquer it, or die in the attempt. For immodesty, in my eyes, is ugliness."[40] The correspondence between the two did not survive, so the truth of Wollstonecraft's attachment to Fuseli is lost, hidden in the penumbra of burnt letters, partisan memoirs, and incomplete archives. What we know glancingly does suggest an all-consuming passion on her part and an equivocal interest in his.

The existence of this unequal and destructive dynamic made their next step even less explicable. On June 20, 1792, Wollstonecraft wrote to her sister Everina that she, Johnson, and the Fuselis had planned a six-week excursion to Paris, where they hoped to meet their revolutionary idols, drink in the atmosphere, and, in her case, bask in the success of the recent French translation of *A Vindication of the Rights of Woman*. France may have also afforded the promise of a new setting for her courtship of Fuseli. The date for their trip was set in early August. On the day, their party set out for Dover by carriage only to learn at the seafront that events in Paris had overtaken them. On August 10, Jacobin radicals and the Parisian sections staged a coup, resulting in a massacre of the royal bodyguard at the Tuileries Palace and the arrest of the royal family.[41] This was not a time to go sightseeing, and the party turned back for London. The disappointment of the French venture seemed to impress on Wollstonecraft the need for a new frankness in her relations with Fuseli. She knew how she felt, and she knew what she wanted. Reason dictated that she make her position clear to him. If the account of his biographer is to be believed, the critical moment came near the end of that summer, when "Mrs. Wollstonecraft appears to have grown desperate,"

> *for she had the temerity to go to Mrs. Fuseli, and to tell her, that she wished to become an intimate in her family; and she added, as I am above deceit, it is right to say that this proposal "arises from the sincere affection which I have for your husband, for I find that I cannot live without the satisfaction of seeing and conversing with him daily." This frank avowal immediately opened the eyes of Mrs. Fuseli, who being alarmed by the declaration, not only refused her solicitation, but she instantly forbade her the house.*[42]

Thoroughly humiliated, Wollstonecraft apologized to Fuseli and swore off further contact. The chaos in Paris was looking more preferable than the chaos in London, and Wollstonecraft became fixated on traveling to France at the earliest possible date. The upheaval there was immense. On August 29 the French citadel at Verdun fell to the Prussians and the road to Paris was momentarily clear. Amid legitimate panic that the city would be put to the sword, the Jacobins orchestrated a bloody purge, murdering several hundred prisoners with knives and clubs on the night of September 2. They also issued orders for the arrest and murder of the Girondin leadership. These went unfulfilled, but the fear of lustration now loomed large over that faction. Madame Roland, one of the leading female politicians of the day, wrote to a colleague that "Robespierre and Marat have a knife to our throats."[43]

Roland's friend and English champion, Helen Maria Williams, whose hotel had a prospect onto the storming of the Tuileries on

August 10, was aghast at the violence and was in no doubt that it had been carefully organized. In a letter to Hester Thrale Piozzi on September 4—to which she was too terrified to even sign her name for fear of interception—she described the orgy of violence in Paris as "a dark stain on the annals of the revolution—you will hear accounts of it as if it were the mob—but it is a well-known fact that the plan was laid & the list of the proscribed marked by those to whom the people have been an instrument."[44] The memory of the September Massacres, as they came to be known, were soon swept up in the torrent of events that followed. On September 20 the Prussian advance was halted by French artillery at the Battle of Valmy. The same day the National Assembly legalized divorce and decreed marriage to be a civil matter. On the twenty-first, the National Assembly abolished the monarchy. On November 6, the French army defeated the Austrians at Jemappes, effectively ending the immediate military threat from outside powers and unleashing patriotic euphoria in Paris. Amid this riot of historical activity Wollstonecraft composed an extraordinary letter to William Roscoe in Liverpool. "I intend no longer to struggle with a rational desire," she wrote, alluding to Fuseli,

> so have determined to set out for Paris in the course of a fortnight or three weeks; and I shall not now halt at Dover, I promise you; for as I go alone neck or nothing is the word.

In her absence, she urged him to stay true to his radical beliefs even as public sentiment turned against the French Revolution with news of the September Massacres. Displaying an astonishing indifference to the brutality of recent events, she joked that "children of any growth will do mischief when they meddle with edged tools" and that he ought not abandon "immutable principles, because some of the mere instrument[s] of the revolution were too sharp." Then, with a nod to the recent divorce law, she returned to romantic matters:

> At Paris, indeed, I might take a husband for the time being, and get divorced when my truant heart longed again to nestle with its old friends.[45]

Desire and politics had merged. Whatever revolution was being forged in Paris would necessarily have sexual implications. She was soon to find out. A month later she disembarked at Calais.

Wollstonecraft arrived in Paris in mid-December with a cold. The days were short, and the city was shrouded in an icy fog. Like all British visitors she was appalled at the filthy streets and was bewildered by the tangle of lanes and alleys, crammed full of teetering timber-frame dwellings that constituted the medieval center. Her own lodgings, on 22 Rue Meslay, between the recently rechristened Place de la Republique and the king's prison cell at the Temple, were far grander than she expected, six floors staffed by a troupe of servants. Her hostess was absent, and so she had the house to herself. Sick, lonely, and ill at ease being waited on in a stranger's house, Wollstonecraft was in no mood to strike out alone into the city. Paris was not, in any event, at its most welcoming. On December 10 the National Assembly brought a formal indictment against the former King Louis XVI, known since the abolition of the monarchy in September as Citizen Louis Capet. When Wollstonecraft arrived, the trial of the king had begun in a paranoid atmosphere of invasion scares and royalist conspiracies. The streets were filled with soldiers recently returned from the front and tetchy National Guardsman. The *septembriseurs*, the

citizen-murderers of the prison massacres of late summer, mingled anonymously with the mob that Wollstonecraft had eyed skeptically as she
entered the city. As chance would have it, Wollstonecraft did not need
to seek out history. The attic window of her tall home on Rue Meslay
afforded a prospect over the road that took the former king from prison
to courthouse. On December 26 she wrote a striking letter to Johnson in
London describing her first encounter with revolutionary justice:

> *About nine o'clock this morning, the king passed by my window,*
> *moving silently along (excepting now and then a few strokes on*
> *the drum, which rendered the stillness more awful) through empty*
> *streets, surrounded by the national guards, who, clustering round*
> *the carriage, seemed to deserve their name. The inhabitants flocked*
> *to their windows, but the casements were shut, not a voice was*
> *heard, nor did I see anything like an insulting gesture. For the first*
> *time since I entered France, I bowed to the majesty of the people.*

The dignity of the former king made a profound impression on her
and his stoicism in the face of his reckoning filled her with foreboding:

> *I can scarcely tell you why, but an association of ideas made the*
> *tears flow insensibly from my eyes, when I saw Louis sitting, with*
> *more dignity than I expected from his character, in a hackney*
> *coach, going to meet* death, *where so many of his race have*
> *triumphed. . . . I cannot dismiss the lively images that have filled my*
> *imagination all the day. . . . twice, lifting my eyes from the paper,*
> *I have seen eyes glare through a glass-door opposite my chair, and*
> *bloody hands shook at me. . . . I wish I had even kept the cat with*
> *me! I want to see something alive; death in so many frightful shapes*
> *has taken hold of my fancy.*[46]

Voting began on Louis's fate in mid-January. The final tally was 361–360 in favor of the death penalty—the deciding vote having been cast by his first cousin and the richest man in France, the Duc d'Orléans. Paris was shuttered the morning of January 21, when Louis was driven in a bottle-green carriage through thick fog to the guillotine at the Place de la Révolution. Wollstonecraft did not see his execution, nor did she see Louis pass through the streets lined with 130,000 soldiers, but sitting in her deserted house she would have heard the solitary, sepulchral drummer that went before his carriage as he traveled to his death. It was the first of many executions during her time in Paris. Already in February she was wondering in a letter to Johnson whether "the turn of the tide has left the dregs of the old system to corrupt the new."[47] Around the same time she wrote this gloomy forecast, she was offered a place in a carriage back to London. She refused it. Whatever her doubts, she was committed to experiencing as much of the revolution as events would allow.

Britain declared war on France on February 1, 1793, effectively stranding Wollstonecraft in Paris for the foreseeable future. She was not alone in her exile. There was a large English contingent in Paris at the time, all enthusiasts of the revolutionary project. Wollstonecraft had connections to some of them through Joseph Johnson, and many of them would have been familiar with her through her writings. The British Club, based at White's, was home to Thomas Paine (who had fled the prospect of treason trial in England in 1791 and was now a deputy to the National Convention despite his nonexistent French) and Joel Barlow, an American writer she had known in London, whose wife, Ruth, Wollstonecraft's friend, would soon join him in Paris. Among this group was a colleague from the *Analytical Review*, Thomas Christie, who, along with his wife, Rebecca, hosted gatherings of expatriates.

Another expatriate hotspot was the salon of Helen Maria Williams, a chronicler of the French Revolution, whom Wollstonecraft met shortly after her arrival in Paris. "Miss Williams has behaved very civilly to me," she wrote to her sister Everina, "and I shall visit her frequently, because I *rather* like her, and I meet french company at her house." Williams was a committed supporter of the imperiled Girondin faction and the French company that gathered at her house included many of its luminaries. There Wollstonecraft mingled with Jacques Pierre Brissot, Madame Roland, Lazare Carnot, and Nicolas Chamfort. Through Williams she likely met Madame de Genlis, the educational writer she had read and admired, who at that time was sporting a remarkable new necklace, a polished stone taken from the Bastille, studded with diamonds that spelt out *Liberté*.[48] Aside from the society she provided, she had much else in common with Williams. They were both writers, they were both committed activists who believed in the contribution women could make to revolutionary politics (Williams once wrote that that "whatever the imperious lords of the creation may fancy" women "act in human affairs like those secret springs in mechanism, by which, though invisible, great movements are regulated"), and both believed that the revolution, in Williams's words, was "an affair of the heart."[49] Williams was engaged in a scandalous, if somewhat obscure, connection with another expatriate Englishman, John Hurford Stone, a merchant, a member of Dr. Price's Hackney congregation, and a divorcé.[50] Eager to forget the Fuseli fiasco in London, Wollstonecraft was keen to immerse herself in a revolutionary fling of her own. She had an inconclusive flirtation with another revolutionary tourist, the Silesian Count Gustav von Schlabrendorf, who left a breathless account of Wollstonecraft at this time. "There was enchantment in her glance, her voice, and her movement," he wrote, she was "the noblest, purest, and most intelligent woman I have ever met."[51] She was fast losing any reservations about the proper place of desire in the brave new world of the revolution. Schlabrendorf overheard her brusquely inform a Frenchwoman that sexual pleasure was *"un défaut de la nature."*[52]

The man who her ardor alighted upon was Gilbert Imlay, a rangy and charming American whom she met at one of the Christies' gatherings upon his arrival in Paris in April 1793. Imlay was a land agent by trade. He had written a widely read book on the opportunities available for settlement and cultivation in the American territories, especially in Kentucky. He had also written a sentimental epistolary novel, *The Emigrants*, that had made progressive noises about the need for divorce reform and the abolition of slavery while discoursing on other modish subjects such as the perfectibility of society, the merits of living close to nature, and the evils of excessive commerce.[53] There was no small irony in his proclaimed suspicion of commerce as his novel as well as his work of topography were props in his sales pitch. Imlay was a land speculator. He was selling the dream of utopia on the American frontier to would-be colonists desperate to escape European tyranny. He was also a man on a political mission. He had secured permission from Brissot to investigate, alongside Joel Barlow, the possibility that the American government might want help in securing Louisiana from British incursion now that the wars of the revolution were spreading into the Atlantic.

Imlay's literary and political pedigree appealed to Wollstonecraft far more than his suspect commercial enterprises. He had besides an energy and an easy humor and had the sexual appetite and experience that she desired so much for herself. For his part, Imlay thought her a glamorous radical celebrity in media res of an erotic awakening in revolutionary Paris.[54] By April 19, Joel Barlow was gossiping to his wife that Wollstonecraft "has got a sweetheart." "A very sensible man," in his estimation.[55] Later events would cast some doubts on this judgment, though Wollstonecraft had no complaints at the outset. After thirty-four years alone, she was finally in the throes of the love affair she had always sought. She was a woman transformed, "playful, full of confidence, kindness and sympathy."

> *Her eyes assumed new lustre, and her cheeks new colour and smoothness. Her voice became cheerful; her temper overflowing with universal kindness; and that smile of bewitching tenderness from day to day illuminated her countenance, which all who knew her will so well recollect, and which won, both heart and soul, the affection of almost every one that beheld it.*[56]

She would need the cheer. The first blossoming of her romance with Imlay coincided with the outbreak of fratricidal infighting between the Girondins and the Jacobins. Those spring days were thick with intrigue. That March the Vendée rose in rebellion against the revolutionary regime in Paris. In response the Convention introduced a slew of authoritarian measures through the month, expanding the number of capital offenses, introducing the Revolutionary Tribunal to expedite trials, and ordering the creation of Surveillance Committees in every municipality. In early April, the Girondin General Charles François Dumouriez defected to the Austrians. Marat and Robespierre, operating through the recently organized Committee of Public Safety, now moved decisively against the Girondins. Many of those whom Wollstonecraft had met at salons and parties were fighting for survival. As the internecine warfare raged through April and May, many of her friends fled Paris either for Switzerland or the provinces. Wollstonecraft herself moved to a cottage in Neuilly-sur-Seine, just north of the Bois de Boulogne. Here she worked on her latest project, a history of the French Revolution, ambled in the woods, and practiced her French on the gardener. In the evenings she would meet Imlay, who had remained in Paris, for assignations at the

Longchamp tollgate at the city limit. The two were planning to emigrate to America, and she was consumed with visions of the blissful future that awaited them there. "You can scarcely imagine," she wrote to him late that August, "with what pleasure I anticipate the day, when we are to begin almost to live together."[57]

As summer turned to autumn, things fell apart, both romantically and politically. By September the first flush of their romance had passed, and a new, sharper edge emerges in her letters to Imlay. "Of late we are always separating.—Crack!—crack!—and away you go." She was still utterly infatuated with him but was growing restive at the amount of time they spent apart and complained that he did not do enough to try to remedy the situation. Her concerns about his commitment increased further in November when she realized that she was pregnant. Sharing in the widely held belief that a mother's emotional state influenced the health of the fetus, Wollstonecraft declared in her letter to Imlay informing him of the pregnancy that she aimed to be "very attentive to calm my mind" to ensure the health of a child "in whom we are to have a mutual interest"[58] This was to prove challenging. Imlay remained aloof in Paris through to December, seemingly immune to Wollstonecraft's pleas and barbs. Shortly before the New Year, he moved to the Channel port of Le Havre. Plans to emigrate to America had been postponed. Imlay had spied a new mercantile opportunity born of the exigencies of war. The Royal Navy was now blockading French ports, leading to shortages throughout the country. Imlay set himself up as a blockade-runner, building connections with traders in neutral Scandinavia who would accept French silver as payment. Wollstonecraft loathed all of this. She missed his presence; she shuddered at his commercial schemings. She wrote him scathing letters, where she called him a tyrant, and then wrote additional letters pleading for forgiveness. The sexual confidence that had animated her less than a year before was dwindling, replaced by increasingly wretched bids for his affection. "I do not want to be loved like a goddess," she wrote to him on New Year's Day, 1794, "but I wish to be necessary to you."[59]

Her relationship with Imlay faltered at the same time as disillusionment with revolutionary politics set in. That October, as she was becoming aware of the first stirrings of her pregnancy, the political center collapsed. At the end of the month, Imlay visited Neuilly with news from Paris. Brissot had been guillotined along with two dozen leading Girondins. A good portion of the glamorous French reformers whom she had moved among in her first hopeful months in Paris had been executed in one go. Their faces rose unbidden in her mind, "but before she was conscious of the effect of the picture, she sunk lifeless on the floor."[60] The Jacobins had finally triumphed over the Girondins; Robespierre was delivering on his promise to make terror "the order of the day."

The coming of the Terror was accompanied by a reconfiguration of the sexual politics of the Revolution. The Girondins had been largely susceptible to the idea that the state could improve the lot of women through better educational opportunities and the extension of social and political liberties to them. The Jacobins held rather different ideas about the place of women in society. The principle influence on the new leaders of France was Rousseau, who had preached the merits of a stark sexual order. In Rousseau's view, the Bourbon state had been corrupted by the influence of women in the halls of power. The stew of mistresses, courtesans, and unfaithful wives at Versailles had turned the politics of the ancien régime into a parlor game manipulated by women. The regeneration of the state and, by extension, of national morality, could be accomplished by simply banishing women from politics and confining them to the home. "If women would only deign to nurse their children," he wrote, "morals would reform of themselves." This insight led naturally to a new equation: sexual virtue equaled political virtue. Mistresses had corrupted the monarchy; mothers would renew the republic.[61] This idea had been on the march since 1789. Any number of political figures had stated in unambiguous terms their opposition to female participation in public life. The 1792 constitution had cemented this principle by denying women the vote. Throughout, the pill of female exclusion was sugared with paeans to their superior virtue. Olympe de Gouges caustically observed that "women are now respected and excluded; under the old regime they were despised and powerful." The ascent of the Jacobins was merely the most extreme manifestation of this outlook. They were intent on purging women from politics, and they relied upon a very crude, gendered political rhetoric to do so.[62]

Ironically, the Jacobins were propelled to hegemony in the high summer of 1793 by just the kind of female political intrusion that they despised. On July 13 a Girondin sympathizer named Charlotte Corday traveled to Paris and murdered the Jacobin propagandist Jean-Paul Marat while he reposed in his bathtub. Marat's assassination and his prompt canonization as a secular martyr to the revolutionary cause further brutalized Parisian politics and further strengthened Jacobin resolve. It also bolstered the conviction that women had to be disbarred from political life. After a dramatic trial Corday was guillotined on July 17. Her body was barely in the ground when women political activists began to notice a sea change in attitudes toward them. Claire Lacombe and Pauline Léon both noted in August that the fear that "they might be designated as new Cordays" was being used to silence politically engaged women.[63] These were prophetic words. What followed were months of murder and misogyny. At the trial of Marie Antoinette in October the former queen's political meddling was constantly linked to her supposed sexual transgressions. The high-water mark of the prosecution's campaign of prurient slander was the allegation that the queen and her lady-in-waiting had taught the dauphin how to masturbate.

These fantastical charges were wholly unnecessary in the pursuit of a guilty verdict—which was readily secured—but central to the rhetorical project of connecting sexual deviance to monarchical, counterrevolutionary sentiment.[64] She was executed on October 16.

In the same period, many prominent women were either arrested or fled the country. Among them were many of Wollstonecraft's friends and acquaintances, including Helen Maria Williams, Madame Roland, and Madame de Genlis. On October 30, the National Convention outlawed clubs and popular societies for women, a move that was justified by recourse to the Rousseauian language of impermeable sexual difference. Deputy André Amar, in explaining the need for the ban, relied on common conventions concerning the proper role of women in society. "We believe," he told the Convention, "that a woman should not leave her family to meddle in affairs of government." If they did involve themselves in revolutionary politics the result would be chaos and corruption:

> If we consider that the political education of men is at its
> beginning . . . that we are still stammering the word liberty, then
> how much more reasonable is it for women, whose moral education
> is almost nil, to be less enlightened concerning principles? Their
> presence in popular societies, therefore, would give an active role
> in government to people more exposed to error and seduction. Let
> us add that women are disposed by their organisation to an over-
> excitation which would be deadly in public affairs and that interests
> of state would soon be sacrificed to everything in which ardour of
> passions can generate in the way of error and disorder.[65]

A few days later, Olympe de Gouges, who in Article X of her *Declaration of the Rights of Woman* had claimed for women "the right to mount the scaffold," went to the guillotine. She was followed soon after by Madame Roland. The bloody enforcement of the new sexual order was accompanied by the introduction of a new iconography. In the new Jacobin France, the temptress of the ancien régime and the street-fighting *poissarde* were comparably subversive. "Liberty is not a nymph from the opera, it is not a *bonnet rouge*, or a dirty shirt," one Jacobin orator proclaimed, "liberty is happiness, reason and equality." Realistic portrayals of women as actors and agents of revolution were replaced by bland allegorical images that purveyed the Jacobin orthodoxy of the serene mother, breast exposed, offering France the milk of liberty.[66]

Wollstonecraft was protected from the bloodletting by a typically astute maneuver on Imlay's part. Early in September he had her registered as his wife at the American embassy in Paris. This had no legal bearing, and they were never married, but it did afford her de facto recognition as an American citizen and kept her safe amid the mayhem of the Terror.[67] Her relative security did not conceal the fear and violence all about her. She visited her imprisoned friends in the overcrowded jails, haunted by the rattle of the tumbril, and she witnessed with her own eyes blood running across the cobblestones after yet another execution. There is a judicious silence on such matters in her letters to Imlay—she was not so secure that she could risk expressing her revulsion in print—but the murderous atmosphere of Paris in those months stayed with her for the rest of her life. It doubtless contributed to her hunger for the stability of domestic life with Imlay and her rage at his departure for the coast.

The issue of geography was resolved in January, when she moved to join him in Le Havre. The following months were ones of relative harmony as the couple established a household on the Rue de Corderie by the harbor and prepared for the arrival of their child. Fanny Imlay was born on May 14, 1794. In a letter to Ruth Barlow, Wollstonecraft reported that their French midwife, who was evidently on-message, had quipped that "I ought to make children for the Republic, since I treat it so lightly." She continued that the "little Girl begins to suck so *manfully* that her father reckons saucily on her writing the second part of the Rights of Woman."[68] This period of family communion around the newborn child was painfully short-lived. Imlay's byzantine commercial dealings were consuming ever more of his time. He spent the summer going back and forth between Paris and Le Havre. Then, in September, he was obliged to travel to London in pursuit of information about a business deal gone awry. Rather than remain alone in the dreary coastal town, Wollstonecraft and Fanny went to Paris, where the Jacobins had been crushed amid a final, apocalyptic round of beheadings at the Place de la Révolution at the end of July. The city was safe now. The rounds of visits and gatherings resumed, albeit with the ranks of the radical depleted and their confidence in their beliefs diminished. The passage of the Terror allowed each a moment of personal reckoning. Wollstonecraft had now been in France for just under two years. Her belief in the merits of rational desires and uncertain freedoms had been tested beyond any limit that she might have imagined as a writer on the make in London. France had given her love, a daughter, and a wealth of experience but at the expense of her idealism. Her experiment in radical love outside the bonds of marriage and the bounds of respectable society had forced her to confront some basic truths about human relationships. They could neither be rationalized or managed. Freedom to love meant freedom to lose. Men could rove, but a woman with a child in her womb or at her breast faced certain constraints. Imlay was now roving an awful lot. Confronted with the compromised state of her sexual beliefs, she nourished herself on elysian memories of the first pangs of her romance. "There is nothing picturesque in your present pursuits," she wrote to Imlay that September.

*My imagination then rather chuses to ramble back to the barrier
with you, or to see you coming to meet me, and my basket of
grapes.—With what pleasure do I recollect your looks and words,
when I have been sitting on the window, regarding the waving
corn!*

. . .

*If you call these observations romantic . . . I shall be apt to retort,
that you are embruted by trade, and the vulgar enjoyments of life—
Bring me then back your barrier-face, or you shall have nothing
to say to my barrier-girl; and I shall fly from you, to cherish the
remembrances that will ever be dear to me.*[69]

This was false bravado. Imlay was flying from her, and she was perceptive enough to detect that in their correspondence. She waited for
him in France until the spring of 1795, subsisting on a starvation diet
of false hope and pat nostalgia. In his letters to her, Imlay breathed
faintly on whatever embers of mutual affection still glimmered, but he
remained stubbornly in London. At the beginning of April Wollstonecraft's patience finally broke and she resolved to return to England after
a two-and-a-half-year hiatus. On April 7, 1795, Wollstonecraft wrote
a curt letter to Imlay informing him to expect her and his daughter in
Brighton within the week.

In London, Wollstonecraft learned that Imlay had taken up with a
young actress and tried to commit suicide. The details of the attempt
are unclear, though she did not succeed and word of her desperate condition reached Imlay, momentarily dragging him back into her affairs.
His response was self-serving. He suggested that Wollstonecraft and

Fanny might travel to Norway on his behalf to uncover the fate of a lost ship of his that had been engaged in running the British blockade. Wollstonecraft agreed, and by early June she was in Hull awaiting passage to Gothenberg. The journey was repeatedly delayed by bad weather, and she peppered Imlay with letters to stave off boredom. In one such letter, she sketched a nascent theory of love that seemed to her to explain why their relationship had failed. Passion was the raw material of love, she wrote, and reason was the necessary cement. The problem was that "the common run of men," which presumably included Imlay, had to "have variety to banish *ennui*." Lasting love, "a unison of affection and desire," could only be achieved through the addition of a third ingredient: the imagination. The exercise of the powers of the imagination allowed the lover access to a higher state of romantic experience "that renders every emotion delicate and rapturous." Not all people could arrive at this state, it was "the distinctive characteristic of genius" to be able to attain this superior kind of love. She was hopeful though that Imlay had the potential to reach it "which would open your heart to me. I would fain rest there."[70]

These musings on the imaginations stayed with her throughout her travels in Scandinavia. She arrived in Gothenburg on June 27 and embarked on a circuitous tour of the peninsula, which took her north up the coast, then across the Skagerrak strait to Risør, a remote coastal outpost in southeast Norway, then northeast to Christiania (now Oslo), before heading south through Gothenburg and thence to Elsinore, Copenhagen, and Hamburg. Her journeys through the wild terrain of rural Scandinavia provided a kind of natural cure for her after months of trauma. She unspooled herself in the landscapes of Sweden and Norway. Communing with nature in the daytime, with only Fanny for company, she jotted down her impressions in the evenings, the polar nights so luminous that she could write without the aid of a candle. These notes in time gathered to become her greatest work, *Letters Written in Sweden, Norway, and Denmark* (1796), a strange and powerful piece of writing, structured as a series of letters to Imlay, who is never named and whose role in her life is never properly explained. Indeed, there is very little biographical exposition provided, so that the casual reader would be only faintly aware of phantoms hovering above the page as she discourses on nature, politics, commerce, and love. There is a tidal quality to the *Letters*; Wollstonecraft allows herself to range out into new waters, testing out ideas, considering images, exploring channels of thought, then the weight of personal tragedy tugs her back in toward familiar shores—the anxieties of motherhood, political disillusionment, heartbreak. A constant in all the letters is the transformative powers of the imagination, which seemed to offer if not an escape route from her troubles then at least a means of momentarily transcending them. The encounter with nature was the catalyst for these episodes of metaphysical release:

> *In the evening they also die away; the aspen leaves tremble into stillness, and reposing nature seems to be warmed by the moon, which here assumes a genial aspect. And if a light shower has chanced to fall with the sun, the juniper, the underwood of the forest, exhales a wild perfume, mixed with a thousand nameless sweets that, soothing the heart, leave images in the memory which the imagination will ever hold dear.*

In the grip of these reveries her imagination was borne off to mystic territory. Wandering across the heath she heard the specter of Fanny Blood calling out to her across the years. Walking among the groves of firs and pines at dusk, she seemed to sense their souls. Cruising down the coast from Helgeroa to Risør she surveyed the barren shore and had a vision of the day when the world would be so overpopulated that even these blighted places would be crowded with humans.

> *Imagination went still farther, and pictured the state of man when the earth could no longer support him. Whither was he to flee from universal famine? Do not smile; I really became distressed for these fellow creatures yet unborn. The images fastened on me, and the world appeared a vast prison.*[71]

In their scope and lyricism, *Letters* represented a bound forward in Wollstonecraft's literary abilities. With her meditations on the role and power of the imagination she was exploring poetic territory that would later be charted more completely by the Romantics—but the discovery was hers.[72]

"If ever there was a book calculated to make a man in love with its author," William Godwin wrote of *Letters*, "this appears to me to be the book." Nothing could make Gilbert Imlay anymore disposed to love Mary Wollstonecraft. As she traveled south to Denmark she tried to persuade him to meet her in Hamburg so that they could travel on to Switzerland as a family. When it became clear this was not going to happen she accepted her lot with prideful resignation. "I am content to be wretched; but I will not be contemptible,"[73] she wrote from Hamburg in late September. She was at Dover by October 4 and in London soon afterward. There she met Imlay and learned that he had a new mistress. All her hopes for the renewal of their love—it was now thirty months since their first meeting—were dashed. The crisis was insuperable. Wollstonecraft had been thinking about suicide for months now. At Hull she had considered the sea as a potential tomb for her worries. At a waterfall at Frederichstadt, she had felt the lure of the thundering water and had "asked myself why I was chained to life and its misery." She had always loved *Hamlet*, identifying with the lugubrious Dane, similarly unlucky in love and family and politics. In the end she played Ophelia, the tormented lover who took too much water in her grief. On the wet night of October 10, she took a boat down the Thames to Putney, where she walked up and down the banks until her dress was heavy with rainwater. Then she mounted the bridge and hurled herself into the dark swift river.

—◦—

In April 1796 Mary Wollstonecraft walked through the lush meadows that covered the way from her new home in Islington to Somers Town, near King's Cross. Seven months after she had been fished out of the Thames and revived by a member of the Humane Society, Wollstonecraft was ready to experiment with love once more. She was heading to the house of William Godwin, the bachelor philosopher, to make a social call, unannounced and unaccompanied, in characteristic defiance of etiquette. At forty, Godwin was a stubby man with a lumpy nose and lumpy chin, as disinterested in social niceties as her, though a little more prone than she to allowing dry philosophical disquisitions to intrude upon regular conversation. He shunned both the rococo clothing fashions of the day and the austere radical chic favored by many in his circle in favor of the fusty, somewhat peculiar sartorial choices of a provincial eccentric—a green coat, a scarlet waistcoat, and pointy red morocco slippers—which in several respects he was. He had neither the natural charm nor the lanky good looks of Imlay. Still, Wollstonecraft and Godwin had much in common both socially and intellectually, as well as a shared past as supper guests of Joseph Johnson—not that these encounters had sparked anything like desire in either of them. In January the two had met at the house of Mary Hays, another female writer who had been courting Wollstonecraft's approval for some time. They had met on a couple of occasions since. Now, striding through the fields on the approach Wollstonecraft was consciously escalating the terms of their acquaintance.

Godwin's diary recorded his daily activity in telegraphic style ("Thursday 21st February 1793: Read the Amorous Cynic. Wedgwood's Concert: sup at Holcroft's.") and as of that January meeting Wollstonecraft had appeared only three times in it. After her April visit, the terse mentions of her presence rapidly increase, charting the rising pulse of their relationship. They struck up a correspondence that soon graduated from the literary to the flirtatious to the amorous. "It was friendship melting into love," Godwin would later write,[74] a process that he nonetheless nearly scuppered by attempting to impose his philosophical precepts on their courtship. This was, nonetheless, the most rational desire either had ever entertained. By the end of August they were lovers. By the New Year she was pregnant. As her condition began to show in the spring of 1797 they decided—with heavy radical hearts—to marry. Godwin thought the need for a ceremony ridiculous and "contrary to the genuine march of sentiment." Wollstonecraft was rather more concerned with the gossip it would give rise to. She had been going by Mrs. Imlay for several years now. Legally marrying Godwin would reveal that she had never been married to Imlay, that she had been nothing more than his mistress. Her fears were borne out. Following their April marriage several of their friends refused to be seen in society with them. There was much wagging of tongues besides about the union of two of Britain's most scandalous philosophers. "You have not, perhaps, heard," Henry Fuseli wrote to a friend, "that the assertrix of female rights has given her hand to the *balancier* of political justice."[75]

Conforming to convention, they now moved in together at Somers Town, but otherwise theirs was a most unusual marriage. They socialized separately or together as the fancy took them. Godwin rented another apartment in Somers Town, where he would work from morning till evening, seeing his wife only at dinner. Godwin was also an affectionate stepfather to Fanny Imlay, refusing, in line with his principles, to indulge in the stigma surrounding bastard children. In his memoir of this period, Godwin was proud of their very rational domestic arrangements. "We were both of us of opinion, that it was possible for two persons to be too uniformly in each other's society," he wrote. By fragmenting the time they spent together while also keeping a traditional household they successfully combined "the novelty and lively sensation of visit, with the more delicious and heart-felt pleasures of domestic life."

It was during this new and welcome period of marital and domestic stability that Wollstonecraft began to write her most radical work, one that foreshadows the concerns of contemporary feminism far more than *A Vindication of the Rights of Woman*. The prescience of *Maria: or, The Wrongs of Woman* is made all the more remarkable given that it was never completed and contains a number of dead ends and fragmentary plot connections that she never had time to correct. For all this, *Maria* is far more compelling a read than her earlier novel *Mary*—yet another sign of her flourishing literary talents. The novel is set in a madhouse, where three characters—a man and two women—tell the tragic tale of their lives. Seduction lies at the center of the life stories of the two women, Jemima and Maria, although the narratives each tell subvert in different ways the tradition of the seduction narrative. Jemima is from a working-class background. Her mother was seduced and abandoned and then died less than two weeks after giving birth to her. Raised in the direst poverty, at sixteen Jemima went into service, where she was raped by her master and, when she became pregnant by him, was evicted from his household. She had a backstreet abortion and became a prostitute. Later she was taken into the house of a gentleman and became his kept woman. "Fate dragged me through the very kennels of society," Jemima says of her life. "I was still a slave, a bastard, a common property." The depiction of Jemima is innovative as it was uncommon to use seduction narratives to focus on the plight of the poor, still less of poor women who were capable of coolly analyzing the circumstances of their oppression. For Jemima is a fierce and astute critic of British society. Whereas most sentimental heroines focus on questions of virtue and appeal to the reform of men through the inculcation of Christian morality, Jemima focuses on the structural problems facing women, especially economic ones:

> "How often have I heard," said Jemima, interrupting her narrative, "in conversation, and read in books, that every person willing to work may find employment? It is the vague assertion, I believe, of insensible indolence, when it relates to men; but, with respect to women, I am sure of its fallacy, unless they will submit to the most menial bodily labour; and even to be employed at hard labour is out of the reach of many, whose reputation misfortune or folly has tainted."[76]

The problems she faced, in other words, ran across more than one vector. The problems of poverty were made different by the fact of her gender. This was intersectionality two hundred years before the fact.

The unremittingly brutal world faced by women that Jemima describes makes Wollstonecraft's depiction of Maria even more remarkable. Unlike Jemima, she is from a respectable, well-off family. Her life arc seems to trace that of the typical sentimental heroine since *Clarissa*. As a young woman in thrall to romantic notions she learned from novels, she is courted by George Venables, an apparently upright young man from a wealthy family. Little does she know, but "in London, George had acquired habits of libertinism, which he carefully concealed from his father and his commercial connections." She finds out his true nature too late. They are wed, only for Maria to discover that George is a boor, a drunk, and a habitué of the meanest sort of brothels. "Marriage had bastilled me for life," Maria tells her friends. Unlike most women, Maria decides to fight back. A woman of sensibility and reason, she decides that her marriage is effectively rendered void by her husband's coarse, unloving behavior. In a brilliant passage she describes what her ideal partner would be like:

> A man of feeling thinks not of seducing, he is himself seduced by all the noblest emotions of his soul. He figures to himself all the sacrifices a woman of sensibility must make, and every situation in which his imagination places her, touches his heart, and fires his passions.[77]

She escapes her unhappy home and heads for London, where she meets and falls in love with Henry Darnford. Maria and Darnford live together for a period, enjoying their outlaw passion, until her husband catches up with them. George sues Darnford for adultery and seduction. Under English law, husbands could sue men who intruded in their marriage, often as a prelude to securing a divorce. Women were considered passive objects in these legal events, alluded to but not given voice.[78] Maria chooses to upend this system by involving herself in Darnford's defense. She instructs his lawyers to plead guilty to the charge of adultery but to deny the charge of seduction. Forbidden by law to give evidence in person, Maria writes a testament that she hopes will be read out in court. In writing this document, "she only felt in earnest to insist on the privilege of her nature" caring nothing for either the letter of unjust laws or for the censure of an hypocritical society. At the core of her argument is an attack on a "false morality" that makes "all the virtue of women

consist in chastity, submission, and the forgiveness of injuries." Maria
insists on challenging the charge of seduction because she exercised her
own powers of reason to love Darnford of her own free will. She agrees
that she was a victim of society in many ways but refuses to go along
with a legal fiction that assumes she could not make her own mind as to
whom to leave and whom to love:

> *I met the man charged with seducing me. We became attached—I*
> *deemed, and ever shall deem, myself free. . . . To this person, thus*
> *encountered, I voluntarily gave myself, never considering myself*
> *as any more bound to transgress the laws of moral purity, because*
> *the will of my husband might be pleaded in my excuse, than to*
> *transgress those laws to which [the policy of artificial society has]*
> *annexed [positive] punishments.*[79]

This carefully modulated defense of Free Love was one of the last
things Mary Wollstonecraft ever wrote. On August 30 she gave birth
to a daughter, Mary Godwin. The birth initially seemed to have gone
well. There were, however, hidden complications. Some sections of the
placenta had become caught in her womb. After several days they began
to rot, eventually leading her to develop septicemia. She took ten agonizing days to die. Godwin tended to her to the best of his abilities. In
moments of lucidity she spoke to him of Fanny and Mary. Otherwise he
busied himself with finding doctors and minding the children while she
lay on the bed, racked with fevers. The end came on the evening of September 10, an event Godwin recorded with fearful brevity in his diary.
"20 minutes before 8," followed by a long ellipsis.

Following his wife's death, Godwin decided to memorialize her in a
biography. He immersed himself in her letters and manuscripts before
setting about writing the story of her life. He worked at a furious pace.

Memoirs of the Author of A Vindication of the Rights of Woman was published in January 1798. It was intended as an homage to a radical life. He did not shy from any fact of her existence. Everything was within its pages: her pursuit of Henry Fuseli, her extramarital affair with Gilbert Imlay, their false wedding in Paris, her illegitimate child by him, their separation and her two suicide attempts, her unusual courtship and premarital sexual affair with Godwin. He was unapologetic about the book's candor. "There are no circumstances of her life, that, in the judgment of honour and reason, could brand her with disgrace," he wrote. "Never did there exist a human being, that needed, with less fear, expose all their actions, and call upon the universe to judge them."[80] Posterity may have arrived at the same conclusion, but in the short term his unbowdlerized account of her life was a public relations disaster of the first order. Even those disposed toward Godwin could not understand why he would publish such things about his recently deceased wife. The poet Robert Southey wrote that Godwin exhibited "a want of all feeling in stripping his dead wife naked."[81] Joseph Johnson had pleaded with him not to publish it in its final form. For conservatives, his revelations about the private life of one of their most implacable foes were read with relish. Wollstonecraft's sex life was used to discredit her political principles.[82] In his poem "The Unsex'd Females" (1798), the Reverend Richard Polwhele put Wollstonecraft at the head of a

> *A female band despising NATURE's law,*
> *As 'proud defiance' flashes from their arms,*
> *And vengeance smothers all their softer charms*
> *I shudder at the new unpictur'd scene,*
> *Where unsex'd woman vaunts the imperious mien;*
> *Where girls, affecting to dismiss the heart,*
> *Invoke the Proteus of petrific art.*

The "unsex'd woman" was politically engaged and sexually liber-
ated—both characteristics were to be feared and condemned in equal
measure. As in France, now in England, sexual virtue was equated with
political virtue. "The moral sentiments and moral conduct of Mrs.
Wollstonecroft [sic]," the *Anti-Jacobin Review* wrote in its review of
Godwin's *Memoirs*, "exemplify and illustrate JACOBIN MORALITY."
Wollstonecraft's travels to France and her early sympathy for the French
Revolution were deemed comparable to her irregular relationships.
Promiscuity and treason made easy bedfellows. In its index, the *Anti-
Jacobin Review* listed her under "Prostitution. See Mary Wollstone-
craft."[83] The cruelest posthumous blow came not from the reactionary
press but from the man who had loved her most. In later life, William
Godwin disavowed much of his youthful radicalism, in particular the
sections of *Political Justice* that dealt with Free Love. His memoirs then
were also edited in order to tone down their sexual content. "Is truth
then so variable?" William Hazlitt wrote in a sketch of Godwin in 1825.
"Is it one thing at twenty, and another at forty? Is it at a burning heat in
1793, and below zero in 1814?"[84] Yet Godwin was not alone in growing
conservative with the years. Many of the radicals of the 1790s made a
similar journey toward the center ground of British politics. Whether
Wollstonecraft would have joined them there is unknowable. Nonetheless, their subsequent defection made her example look all the more
anomalous and all the less encouraging. The prospects for the survival
of her beliefs in the powers of reason, the pleasures of the passions, and
the rights of individuals would reside in the next era. Her shade would
not have to look far. Though she and her daughter Mary had met only
in passing at life's boundary, it was enough to ensure that the line of
succession went unbroken. For whatever piece of the daughter lodged
in the mother, a greater portion of the mother lodged in the daughter,
and the questions that had animated her life were passed along to a new

generation.

—·—≡◆≡—·—

CHAPTER FOUR

CIRCLING MARY SHELLEY

In May 1816, Mary Godwin, the only child of William Godwin and
Mary Wollstonecraft, was staying in the Hotel d'Angleterre in Geneva,
waiting for a visitor from England. At eighteen, Mary was striking if not
conventionally beautiful. Her curly brown hair was gathered in ringlets
around her neck and was pulled up around her temples to expose her
most noticeable feature, her expansive, pear-white forehead that sat like
a great tablet above the rest of her otherwise quite delicate face—an aqui-
line nose; soft, high-dimpled cheeks; an unobtrusive mouth. Even then
there was an intensity apparent to Mary. Later, after tragedy, she would
write that though her outward existence was solitary and monotonous
her inner life was one wonderfully "diversified by internal feeling." This
was characteristic modesty on her part. Mary's intelligence and energy
had always shone through her natural reserve. Her large, hazel eyes at
once hid and conveyed immense thoughts and fathomless analytical
abilities. She was, after all, the daughter of the woman who had gone
toe-to-toe with Edmund Burke, a girl who had been hand-reared by one
of England's greatest living political thinkers, and whose tutor, William
Baxter of Dundee, where Mary lived from 1812 to 1814, was given
simple instructions to raise her "like a philosopher."

It was following the completion of this task and upon her subsequent
return to London that she met and fell in love with the man now by her
side in Switzerland. Percy Bysshe Shelley was short, sickly, and frenetic
with mental and creative energy when she met him in her father's drawing
room in Clerkenwell. He was also married to Harriet Westbrook, whose
charms had diminished for him once she became pregnant with their

second child. Harriet saw the thumbprints of both of Mary's radical parents all over what followed. Her once-faithful husband has turned "profligate and sensual, owing entirely to Godwin's 'Political Justice.'" With her target primed by her father's radical ideas, the daughter had then made her move. "Mary was determined to secure him," Harriet continued,

She is to blame. She heated his imagination by talking of her mother, and going to her grave with him every day till at last she told him she was dying in love for him, accompanied by the most violent gestures and vehement expostulations.

Mary and Shelley did indeed have assignations in St. Pancras Churchyard, where Mary Wollstonecraft was buried, though this was likely for convenience and privacy rather than an attempt on Mary's part to use her mother's sepulchre as a morbid prop for her seduction of Percy Shelley.[1] It also seems to have been here that the first declarations of love were made, though it seems unlikely—as later chroniclers of their romance asserted—that their love was consummated atop the very grave of Britain's foremost feminist. But whatever had passed there between them, Harriet seemed to intuit early on that it could not be undone and that her husband was lost to her forever. "He cares not for me now," she concluded in a despairing letter to *Catherine Nugent*, "the man I once loved is dead. This is a vampire. His character is blasted for ever. Nothing can save him now."[2]

Unpicking the politics from the passion in the youthful affair between Shelley and Mary was a hard task for anyone, let alone his spurned teenage wife. Likewise, judging the merits of any relationship from their beginnings is as myopic as judging them by their endings. But there was enduring significance to the torrid opening phase of Mary and Shelley's remarkable relationship. Mary's whole life would be triangulated between the shifting markers of romantic love, sexual radicalism, and human—predominantly female—suffering. She never forgot what had happened to Harriet. She came to believe it haunted her. The thwarted promise and numerous pitfalls of sexual freedom in a period of systematic and unabashed female subordination would be a recurrent theme in Mary's life, writing, and friendships.

William Godwin was indelibly linked in British minds with the doctrine of Free Love. But the old radical's interest in the subject had diminished considerably since the publication of the first, infamous edition of *Political Justice* in 1793, replaced by a fervid and abiding interest in staying out of debtors' prison. By the time he became acquainted with Percy Shelley, the eldest son of a well-to-do baronet, he was more concerned with securing a large loan from his red-maned young disciple than in passing on the torch to the next generation of radicals. Godwin acquired the loan, with the intense romance between his lender and his daughter thrown into the bargain. At this point all of his philosophical interest in sexual freedom and free association vanished and he expressed his opposition to the couple in unambiguous terms. Undeterred and enthused by the prospect of a romantic adventure, Mary and Percy planned an elopement to Europe. Aiding and abetting their plan was Mary's stepsister Mary Jane Clairmont, the daughter of Godwin's second wife. The date for their escape from London and censure to Europe and liberty was set for July 28. When the carriage appeared at the agreed-upon time and place, the two young lovers darted in and—in a fateful last-minute addition—were joined by Clairmont.

The trip to the war-weary continent was a predictable disaster, and the trio were back in England in less than two months, the principal product of their venture a pregnant Mary Shelley, scared and only sixteen years old. She gave birth in March 1815 to a girl, Clara, who did not live to see the summer. Mary would forever after associate spring not with hope and rebirth but with tragedy, and would date many of her later misfortunes to the original loss of that year. The development of Mary's tragic sensibility coincided with her stepsister's transformation into a self-declared avatar of Free Love. Mary Jane Clairmont rebranded herself Claire Clairmont, daughter of liberty and roaming sexual spirit. She had arrived at this conclusion by a number of avenues: through intense readings of Wollstonecraft, Rousseau, and other radicals; in an attempt to distinguish herself from her brilliant, sober stepsister; from her time spent in the captivating orbit of Percy Shelley. There is strong evidence to suggest that Clairmont and Shelley were romantically involved while Mary was confined during her ill-starred pregnancy. There is good circumstantial evidence that she may have borne, then abandoned, Shelley's illegitimate child near the end of that year. What is clear is that there was some kind of intense rupture in the group in this period, one that, miraculously, seems to have been resolved by the beginning of 1816.

In January, Mary gave birth to a health boy, William, or Wilmouse, and by the spring the three were planning another trip to Europe. In May they set off for Geneva. There Clairmont hoped to pull off a *coup de theatre*. In London, while Percy and Mary had been busy with their newborn, Clairmont had struck up an intimacy with a radical and poet of her own—one even more notorious than her stepsister's. He was something of a reluctant lover, and Clairmont had lured him down to Switzerland using her distinguished traveling companions as bait. They arrived a fortnight before him and settled into the Hotel d'Angleterre. In her letters Mary described the wonders of natural setting—the boats that drifted into their moorings as dusk gathered over Lac Léman, the forbidding Jura mountain range that darkened into pitch as the sun fell behind it, the rolling lightning storms that at night illuminated the sides of the mountain and the surface of the lake—in gorgeous prose. She was less impressed by the English tourists at the hotel. The "haughty English ladies," she recorded, "are greatly disgusted with this consequence of republican institutions, for the Genevese servants complain very much of their *scolding*."[3] The same haughty ladies disapproved of the scandalous poet and his two female companions, scandalous by association. They were shunned by their fellow guests and were greeted with silence in the hotel's dining rooms and public spaces. Each day their visitor from England drew closer.

The person they were waiting for was George Gordon Byron, Sixth Baron Byron, poet, seducer, and now fugitive from English society and the scandals he had conjured therein. Byron's troubles had started in 1812, when he had first begun to consider marriage. That year he had published the first cantos of *Childe Harold's Pilgrimage*, and he and it had become the talk of London overnight. The poem was "on every table" the Duchess of Devonshire wrote to her son in America, and its author "courted, visited, flattered, and praised whenever he appears." One of those who put herself gently in the poet's path was Anne Isabella "Annabella" Milbanke, a pious, intelligent, and very serious young woman who had been sent down from the provincial northeast to find a husband. Her aunt was Lady Melbourne, wife of 1st Viscount Melbourne, one of the most politically engaged and influential women of the era. Under her aunt's auspices, Annabella was soon being courted by several eligible young men, including one of the Devonshires and William Bankes, one of Byron's Cambridge friends, who lent her a copy of *Childe Harold*. The poem seized Annabella's imagination—as it had so many others—and she contrived to meet him. Their first encounter in March 1812 was a taste of things to come. Annabella noted his "natural sarcasm and vehemence," his ill-concealed distaste toward society stalwarts, and his impatience with polite conversation. She also gleaned from gossips stories that "indicated feelings dreadfully perverted" and that he was an atheist. She felt drawn to him nonetheless, sensing, it seemed, the possibility of a great moral adventure, ending with her redemption of the most infamous man in the country. For his part, Byron was impressed by Annabella's intelligence and the breadth of her reading. Like her, he also had his reservations. He was frustrated by her twee Christian moralizing—he would later describe her, rather perfectly, as having been "systematically Clarissa Harlowed"—and her prim, awkward manner in social settings. Still, she was different from most of the respectable young women thrust his way in the London marriage market, and he struck up a correspondence with her that resulted in a rather perfunctory proposal, which she wisely turned down.

Despite later allegations that Annabella's initial rejection inspired Byron to dedicate himself to her ruin, he seems to have taken the snub in reasonably good spirits. In any event, there were other distractions. For much of 1812 and 1813 Byron was consumed by a raging affair with Lady Caroline Lamb, a flighty, scandal-prone society beauty who was both two years his senior and married. Although he would later savage her in verse and disavow their relationship, they were, for a period, genuinely and completely infatuated with each other. "You drew me to you like a magnet," Lamb wrote to him, "& I could not indeed I could not have kept away." Byron felt similarly entranced, later explaining to a friend that "I am easily governed by women, and she gained an ascendency over me that I could not easily shake off." But shake he did, and in the summer of 1812 he began to drift away from her, preferring instead the company of his half-sister Augusta Leigh, the "autumnal charms" of Lady Oxford, and disposable nights with the actresses of Drury Lane. Lamb responded to this attempted disengagement with legendary ferocity. She broke into his house dressed as a page and attempted to stab herself when Byron's friend and accomplice John Hobhouse hustled her out. She ambushed him at a society event, again with a knife, and slashed open her hand in the chaos that ensued. When she could not find her lord in the flesh she contented herself with sending him a locket of her pubic hair in the post accompanied with a note signed off "From Your Wild Antelope." At length she fell silent, and Byron could continue his quixotic quest for marital bliss. But she had not forgotten him.

In late 1813 Byron and Annabella resumed their cagy courtship. Both were torn between a perverse fascination with each other and profound recognition that they were spectacularly ill-suited for life together. "She requires time and all the cardinal virtues," he observed, accurately, to one correspondent, "I am one who demands neither." Annabella was similarly skeptical, but they continued to draw closer. Byron was inspired by a certain fatalism about the necessity of marriage and a particular cynicism about the financial security he (inaccurately) believed that Annabella would bring him; Annabella by Christian concern for the wicked lord's soul and a genuine passion for Byron that overrode her own better judgment. In 1814, Byron proposed again—by letter—and this time Annabella accepted. They were married in the living room of her parents' house in Seaham on January 2, 1815, and then were conducted by coach to Halnaby Hall, in Yorkshire, for their wintry honeymoon.[4]

Whatever doubts Annabella might have had about Byron were soon confirmed in Yorkshire. Her husband was not used to sharing a bed and would use any device to delay having to come up to their room. This meant in practice that he would get wildly drunk—something that Annabella had never been exposed to—and curse the servants. Once in bed his behavior was not much better: he would scream in the night and have violent nightmares that woke him up; once awake he would roam around the galleries armed with a pistol and dagger, muttering to himself. Their stay in Halnaby Hall did, however, succeed in getting Annabella pregnant. The couple moved to London and hoped to settle into a more routine family life. But Byron could not be calmed. The demands of married life grated on him. He was harried by financial woes that he felt he could not discuss with his wife. He remained socially and professionally involved in the literary scene of his bachelorhood—a world that Annabella was excluded from and that was replete with temptations for her husband. Whenever Augusta Leigh was present—and Byron seemed to hunger for her company—he would make astonishingly crude and suggestive remarks.[5] Byron's cruelty and violence of temperament only seemed to intensify as the birth of their first child approached. He remained devoted to his wife in principle, but in practice she was the recipient of his harshest words and most deliberately devastating provocations. Byron was well aware of his volatile nature. "As long as I can remember anything," he later admitted to Lady Blessington,

> I recollect being subject to violent paroxysms of rage, so
> disproportioned to the cause as to surprise me when they were
> over; and this still continues. I cannot coolly view any thing which
> excites my feelings; and, once the lurking devil in me is roused,
> I lose all command of myself. I do not recover a good fit of rage
> for days after. Mind, I do not by this mean that the ill humour
> continues, as, on the contrary, that quickly subsides, exhausted by
> its own violence; but it shakes me terribly, and leaves me low and
> nervous after.[6]

Annabella had an inquisitive, methodical mind. Confronted with the tempestuous Lord Byron and a daily witness to his wild moods and erratic behavior, she set out to diagnose him. As a child she had been trained in the sciences and was a great lover of math (Byron nicknamed her the Princess of Parallelograms), and now she put her formidable mind to work solving the problem of her husband.[7]

On December 15, 1815, their daughter, Ada, was born. About the same time, Annabella's observations on her husband began to cohere into a persuasive hypothesis. She became convinced that Byron was mad, perhaps because of water on the brain. A secret investigation of his letters and personal effects revealed some supporting evidence, to wit a copy of the Marquis de Sade's *Justine* and a bottle of laudanum, which was used, inter alia, to treat the insane.[8] She began to correspond with a doctor in the hopes of achieving a formal diagnosis. In the meantime she revealed her discovery to certain of her confidantes, who were quickly convinced of her reasoning. Quietly, Annabella began to plot a separation from her husband. Byron was in the dark about all this. Wrapped up in his own affairs, he blithely assented to her request to travel to her parents' Leicestershire home with their newborn daughter. On January 15, 1816, Annabella bid farewell to her husband and left their London home with Ada. Byron would never see either of them again.[9]

At Kirkby Mallory, Annabella informed her parents of her findings concerning her husband's mental condition and, presumably, her suspicions about his relations with Augusta. Aghast, they agreed that she should immediately begin separation proceedings. Annabella's mother went to London to meet with lawyers, armed with a testimonial written by her daughter chronicling the story of their marriage. While she was thus engaged, the doctor Annabella had hoped would confirm her home-spun diagnosis of madness contacted her. Lord Byron, he informed her, was not medically insane.

This was a turning point in the affair. Under English law, divorce was incredibly hard to come by. Parliament could issue divorces, but to do so was wildly expensive and very rare.[10] Husband and wife could agree

by mutual consent to sign a deed of separation, but this could be difficult to engineer if the husband (who under the law held almost all the
power) refused to cooperate. Byron was stubborn and could be relied
upon to resist the separation with all his considerable energies. The final
option was to go to court. Up until 1857 the Church of England ruled
on marital matters through the ecclesiastical courts and permitted sepa-
rations only in a few extreme scenarios. One of these was insanity, which
was why Annabella had been so insistent on proving that her husband
was mad. But now a doctor had diagnosed Byron as unstable but sane,
she was forced to find even more radical means of ending their marriage.

In early February, Byron learned of his wife's designs. His response
was a mixture of disbelief, self-pity, and cold rage. He made it known
that he was eager fight the case in the courts. In the meantime, Annabella's parents had redoubled their efforts on their daughter's behalf.
Later that month, they presented their lawyers with evidence that Byron
had had incestuous relations with Augusta Leigh. But here, too, there
was a problem. Wives could not testify against husbands. Consequently,
Annabella's statements on any matter—including incest—would not be
admissible in court. To circumvent this stipulation, Annabella began to
cultivate Augusta as a confidante and tried to obtain written admission
that her and Byron's companionship had been extralegally intimate.

But London gossips operated without any such restraints. By March
scandal threatened to engulf completely all the parties concerned. Rumor
was now rife that Augusta and Byron were lovers and that her daughter
Medora, born in 1814, was their love child.[11] At the time, Augusta was
living with Byron in Piccadilly. In an attempt to temper suspicions she
moved to St. James's Palace, where she had been made a lady-in-waiting
to the queen. But stories continued to circulate. A siege mentality developed in the Byron household. He feared being hissed and mocked if
he went to the theatre. He no longer attended to his lordly duties in

Parliament lest he was insulted or ridiculed by his fellow aristocrats. Crowds sometimes gathered outside his house. Friends tried to fight the allegations on his behalf in public and to lift his spirits in private, but his situation was dire. It was in these circumstances that he responded favorably to a letter from a female admirer, Claire Clairmont. The two had liaisons in his Piccadilly rooms. In the subsequent correspondence Clairmont encouraged him to join her in Switzerland, tempting him with the promise of meeting her distinguished stepsister Mary and Percy Shelley, whose poetry Byron admired. Byron had never needed much excuse to travel, and life in London was fast becoming unbearable. "If what was whispered and muttered and murmured was true," he later observed, "I was unfit for England; if false, England was unfit for me." Nevertheless, at this point he was still well-positioned to fight a divorce suit. That all changed when a vengeful Caroline Lamb reemerged in his affairs. Near the end of March she offered her services to the Milbankes as a witness against her former lover. "I shall tell you that which if you merely menace him with the knowledge shall make him tremble," she promised. Annabella loathed Lamb but was eager to hear what she had to say. On March 27, the two women held a lurid conference in the Milbankes' London, home wherein Lamb revealed that Byron had told her that he had long been "in the practice of an unnatural crime,"[12] a practice he had apparently been schooled in at Harrow and later mastered in Turkey.

Sodomy—"the unnatural crime"—was grounds for divorce. Annabella was triumphant; Byron was now in a hopeless situation. It was not worth destroying his reputation for a court case he would surely lose. He acceded to requests for a legal separation and accelerated his preparations for a flight to Europe. Among these were the acquisition of a doctor to accompany him on his travels. John William Polidori was a young man recently graduated from Edinburgh University who came recommended from Sir Henry Halford, physician to King George. Another was the expenditure of the massive sum of £500 on a custom-made carriage, made to be an exact replica of Napoleon's military carriage captured at Waterloo. This enormous navy and scarlet structure came with bulletproof walls, a gold service set, a foldable bed, a dressing room, a library, and all-weather blinds. On April 21, Byron signed the deed of separation. Two days later, he and Polidori climbed into their Napoleonic carriage and rumbled off toward the Channel. At Dover, as he went into exile in circumstances that would have made a pariah of anyone else, Byron's hold over the minds of Englishwomen persisted. Waiting to embark a local doctor reported that the tavern Byron was staying in was besieged by "many ladies accoutred . . . as chambermaids for the purpose of obtaining under that disguise a nearer inspection" of the most notorious man in the country. It was an outfit those ladies might have avoided if they had known more of Byron's proclivities. After a short voyage, Byron and Polidori arrived at Ostend and checked into a hotel. "As soon as he reached his room," Polidori recorded, "Lord Byron fell like a thunderbolt upon the chambermaid."

Only twenty years old, John Polidori had dark wavy hair, umbrous eyes, and stormy features—more Byronic than Byron himself. Despite his professional background in medicine Polidori had literary ambitions and was thrilled to be in the company of England's most celebrated living poet. His association with Byron had already helped further his progress in this area: John Murray, the poet's longstanding and otherwise loyal publisher, had rather duplicitously contracted Polidori to write a record of his travels with Byron to be published at some later date. He dutifully did so, recording his impressions of Byron and the local scenery as they trundled south through the Lowlands. The surrounding area still bore the marks of war and economic ruin, marks invisible in the landscape—when they visited the site of the Battle of Waterloo less than a year after the fact, Polidori was surprised to discover a few plowed-over fields and some enterprising locals hawking souvenirs for visiting tourists—but evident everywhere in the poverty and exhaustion of the populace. Polidori noted the meanness of the villages, the drawn, unattractive women, the abominable roads, the crowds of beggar boys that ran alongside their carriage.[13,14] Circumstances improved as they drew closer to Switzerland, though as they entered more mountainous terrain they found that their carriage now rolled like a galleon on the high seas as they made their way up hills and down valleys. It broke down repeatedly. On May 19 they finally entered Switzerland and a little less than week later, and exactly a month since they left London, Polidori glimpsed the peak of Mont Blanc and, as was customary for English tourists, he tried his hand at capturing its beauty in writing:

> We saw Mont Blanc in the distance; ethereal in appearance, mingling
> with the clouds; it is more than 60 miles from where we saw it. It is
> a classic ground we go over. Buonaparte, Joseph, Bonnet, Necker,
> Stael, Voltaire, Rousseau, all have their villas (except Rousseau).
> Genthoud, Ferney, Coppet, are close to the road.[15]

This was by some distance the least celebrated account of Mont Blanc that this trip produced. Shortly afterward they arrived at Lac Léman. At the Hotel d'Angleterre an exhausted Lord Byron entered his age in the register as one hundred and went straight to bed. The next day Polidori and Byron went for a swim in the lake. In his diary Polidori gloated over his comity with his noble employer:

> rode *first with Lord Byron upon the field of Waterloo;* walked
> *first to see Churchill's tomb* bathed *and* rowed *first on the Leman*
> *Lake.—It did us much good.*[16]

Claire Clairmont, along with every other English holidaymaker in the vicinity, had received word of Byron's arrival and sent him several letters requesting a meeting. These went unanswered. A few days after they had arrived, the two men sailed across the lake to inspect a villa. On the return journey they spotted three figures walking along the shore where they were to disembark. They rowed over, got out, and met Percy Shelley, Claire Clairmont, and Mary Godwin.

⋯ ▪◆▪ ⋯

The meeting of this variously strange, troubled, and talented group of people on the shores of Lac Léman was consecrated by a bizarre climactic occurrence. In 1815 a volcano had erupted on the island of Sumbawa in modern-day Indonesia. The explosion at Mount Tambora was the largest of its kind in two millennia and put 140 billion tons of tectonic matter into the atmosphere, disrupting global temperatures and resulting in a volcanic winter. The effects were still being felt that June in Europe, producing the famed "Year Without a Summer," which led to famine in some parts and ruined the holiday plans of well-heeled travelers in others. The weather in Geneva was damp, drafty, and overcast—more Midlands than Alpine—obliging this band of young Romantics to spend more time inside than they might have preferred. Indeed, one of their first decisions was to move from the frosty Hotel d'Angleterre to private lodgings across the lake. Byron and his entourage took up residence in the spacious, stucco Villa Diodati; Shelley and his in the more modest Maison Chapuis, a short walk away. Across the lake their fellow English travelers studied the fugitive poets and their female companions through a telescope, and rumors spread that the disgraced Lord Byron was heading up a "league of incest" on Swiss shores.[17]

But otherwise England and its judgments could no longer intrude

upon their lives. After an initial, inevitable period of mutual circum-
spection Shelley and Byron got along like old friends. Shelley won the
older poet's respect on the lake, when their small sailboat was caught
in a storm. Shelley could not swim, and Byron briefly feared for his life
as their boat was pummeled by the waters but was impressed by his
courage and calm under pressure. Theirs was the only relationship to
deepen by waters of Lac Léman. Claire, who had been fantasizing about
her reunion with Byron for weeks and who was now also showing the
first signs of pregnancy as a consequence of their assignations in London
in March, found herself largely ignored by her erstwhile lover. The bored
lord did, occasionally, allow her into his chambers but only for the most
cynical reasons. "If a girl of eighteen comes prancing at you at all hours
of the night," he explained to a friend, "there is but one way."

She was not the only one to feel jilted by Byron. Polidori had jour-
neyed with him from London, believing that this was the beginning of
a great friendship between poets and equals but now found himself
displaced in his lord's affections by Percy Shelley. Sidelined by the two
other men, Polidori became stroppy and ingenuously malicious. On one
occasion, while out boating with the two he challenged Shelley to a duel
after the latter beat him in a sailing race. On another, while rowing
he accidentally struck Byron's knee with the oar. When his employer
remarked that this had caused him some great deal of pain, he seemed
to relish in it. "I am glad of it," Polidori (supposedly) replied. "I am
glad to see you can suffer pain." Byron would later claim that the only
thing had stopped him from tipping his impudent physician into the lake
was the presence of Mary in the boat.[18] Even if true, it is unlikely that
Mary would have much appreciated his gallantry. Byron was now just
one more person preventing her from spending time with Percy. Worse
yet, with the two poets now away together, Polidori turned his scorned
and winsome attentions on Mary. He noted in his diary small details

from daily life that reveal a young man's first hopes for a burgeoning romance ("June 2.—Breakfasted with Shelley. Read Tasso with Mrs. Shelley. Took child for vaccination.") but his ill-conceived infatuation with Mary quickly attracted Byron's expert bullying eye. On June 14 after a rainy spell, Byron and Polidori were sitting on the balcony when they spotted Mary making her way up the wet slope toward the Villa. "Now," Byron said to his lovestruck physician, "you who wish to be gallant ought to jump down this small height, and offer your arm." This he did and duly sprained his ankle on the wet grass. In his diary, Polidori skates over the event, simply noting, "After dinner, jumping a wall my foot slipped and I strained my left ankle." Byron recorded the same in a letter to John Murray, noting that his doctor had injured himself in "tumbling from a wall; he can't jump." He could now only walk with difficulty. His injury magnified his feelings toward Mary, and a few days after the incident he made some kind of declaration to her. Mary, who had a largely philosophical interest in Free Love, soon disavowed him of his notions.[19] The young doctor recorded the moment in his typically elliptical fashion: "June 18.—My leg much worse. Shelley and party here. Mrs. S[helley] called me her brother (younger)."

The days that bore witness to Polidori's tumble and the hapless climax of his longing for Mary were also days of rain, confinement, ghost stories, and literary and philosophical investigations. Trapped together in Diodati because of the appalling weather, the group began to discuss the latest developments in science. Polidori and Shelley talked "about principles,—whether man was to be thought merely an instrument." The doctor might also have told the party of the recent, and scandalous, lectures given by Dr. William Lawrence in London. Lawrence, a surgeon and anatomist with atheistic tendencies who had at one point been Shelley's doctor, had electrified medical London earlier that year with a series of lectures at the Royal College of Surgeons. In these talks, Lawrence had attacked certain "false notions in physiology" that sought to explain the origins of human life by reference to fashionable pseudoscientific theories of vitalism, animal magnetism, and mesmerism. Lawrence had deconstructed the various claims that there existed an "independent living principle, superadded to the structure of animal bodies" concluding, as only a surgeon might, that no such principle could be "discovered amid the blood and filth of the dissecting room." Man was matter—nothing more. But the exact opposite was also discussed at Diodati. Mary recalled that they also talked about the work of Erasmus Darwin,

> *Who preserved a piece of vermicelli in a glass case, till by some extraordinary means it began to move with voluntary motion. Not thus, after all, would life be given. Perhaps a corpse would be reanimated; galvanism had given token of such things: perhaps the component parts of a creature might be manufactured, brought together, and endued with vital warmth.*

Galvanism referred to the work of Luigi Galvani, the Italian scientist who had pioneered the study of electricity. In a series of famous experiments, Galvani had passed electrical currents through the tissue of dead frogs, inducing lifelike motions and begging the inevitable question: Could electricity generate life? His nephew, Giovanni Aldini, had pushed such speculations to the limit in a grisly trial at Newgate Prison in London in 1803. There, Aldini conducted his uncle's experiment on the corpses of recently executed criminals. His attempts to "revive" the heart and circulatory systems of the deceased were largely in vain, but he stunned his audiences nonetheless. The electrified corpses convulsed on the gurney. Eyes jerked and rolled in otherwise lifeless skulls. Arms crashed up and down violently. Chest and back muscles contracted together with such force that they threatened to crush the rib cage.[20] Over a decade later, this attempt to create life electrically had not been forgotten by England's poets. "This is the age of oddities let loose," Byron joked, as darkly as ever, in Canto I of *Don Juan*, where "galvanism has set some corpses grinning."[21]

Talk of science intermingled with literary creation. On the stormy night of the eighteenth, around about midnight, the group "began to talk ghostly." Byron read from a volume of German supernatural stories and then recited parts of Coleridge's "Christabel," passages so haunting that Shelley fled from the room in hysterics and had to be treated with ether by Polidori—one of the very few occasions on which the young doctor applied his medical training to someone other than himself. Bored with simply reading ghost stories, Byron then suggested that each of them compose one of their own. They all spent a few days writing—except poor Clairmont, excluded once again—and regrouped a few days later to judge the fruits of their labors. It was not an impressive harvest. Shelley had "commenced one story of his earlier life" but had become bored and abandoned the attempt. Byron had sketched the plot of a story involving two wealthy young friends on an ill-fated Grand Tour; then he, too, got bored, and left the story unfinished. Polidori's tale was slightly more complete but was, in Mary's telling, not much to behold, based as it was around "some terrible idea about a skull-headed lady, who was so punished for peeping through a keyhole—to see what I forget." The exception to this collection of botched and mediocre productions was, of course, Mary's own, which became *Frankenstein*.

Mary's first novel would be published two years later after a number of agonizing rewrites and months of fretful editing. Nonetheless, it was recognizably the same tale that she began that June. Subsequently, there has always been the temptation to assume that the basic premise of the book—a monster constructed from body parts by a maniacal medical student and then given life by an electric spark—was a product of the pseudo-scientific conversations that Mary had participated in during those June days. Frankenstein's monster, in this telling, was built of those highflown speculations and animated by the lightning that crackled over Lac Léman. There are a number of problems with this rather clean-edged narrative. Erasmus Darwin had never claimed that electricity could create life, and Mary was well aware of it. Similarly, it is hard to see how Dr. Lawrence's intense materialism could readily inspire the heady theoretical speculations that undergird *Frankenstein*'s plot. Of course, Mary's genius was to take this mélange of ideas and then "to innovate upon their combinations." The result was an astounding work of science fiction *avant la lettre*, a parable about the moral pitfalls of scientific creation that looked two hundred years ahead to the ethical dilemmas posed by cloning, robotics, and artificial intelligence.

Such, at least, is the conventional telling of how *Frankenstein* came to be. But while the scientific explanation of its genesis is alluring, it also seems to miss an earthier, more proximate version of the book's backstory. *Frankenstein* is a book about the perils of reckless creation. However, Dr. Frankenstein's generative powers are not unique to him; are common to all humans. Every man and every woman possesses the potential to create life. In an age before widespread contraception this potential was not easily controlled. Sexual liaisons, consensual or otherwise, produced children. Seduction, which was defined as occurring either outside of marriage or in violation of existing marital bonds, produced illegitimate children—bastards.

No reader of *Frankenstein* can forget the moment of the monster's creation—the dreary November night when the young doctor animates his creature surrounded by the muck and filth of his makeshift surgery—but what he does immediately afterward is equally important: Dr. Frankenstein runs away. He creates life and then absconds. He dodges responsibility for what he has made. Later, when the monster finally confronts his maker on one of the Alpine summits around Geneva he speaks to him as an abandoned child to a father. "I am thy creature," the monster tells Dr. Frankenstein, "I ought to be thy Adam." When Dr. Frankenstein cruelly disowns him, the monster's response cuts to the heart of matter:

You, my creator, detest and spurn me, thy creature, to whom thou
art bound by ties only dissoluble by the annihilation of one of us.
You purpose to kill me. How dare you sport thus with life?

The double tragedy for a bastard was both their rejection by their parent, usually their father, and their subsequent rejection by a society that held illegitimacy to be taboo. The illegitimate child became, like the monster, "the scorn and horror of mankind." This was a condition that Mary understood all too well. Her stepsister Claire Clairmont was the illegitimate child of an absentee father who now bore a child who, absent an outlandish act of chivalry on Byron's part, was destined to be illegitimate, too. Her lonesome half-sister Fanny Imlay, the bastard child of the rakish Gilbert Imlay, who had charmed their mother in Revolutionary Paris all those years before, would kill herself in October 1816, while Mary was working hard at the novel. Sleeping in his crib while she wrote the first pages of the book by Lac Léman was her treasured son, Wilmouse, born out of wedlock. The desperate position of bastard children in English society was one of the reasons that Shelley had attacked the exclusionary institution of marriage in the notes to *Queen Mab* (1813). "Society avenges herself," he wrote there, "on the criminals of her own creation."[22]

At the end of 1816 another tragedy born of the paranoia concerning the legitimacy of newborns paradoxically gave Mary her route to respectability. At some point early that summer, Harriet Shelley, Percy Shelley's lawful and unloved wife, took a lover. His identity is not clear, though he is thought to have been an officer in the British army. He, whoever he was, soon moved on and Harriet soon found herself alone, shunned by her family, abandoned by her husband, and living a solitary existence in London with little money. On November 9 she wrote a final letter to her family and then vanished into the night.[23] A month later her body was fished out of the Serpentine, and an autopsy confirmed what was readily apparent: she was in an advanced state of pregnancy.

With Harriet dead, Percy was now free to marry Mary. They were wed in London on December 30, 1816, and nine months later their daughter Clara Shelley—their first legitimate child together—was born. Clara's future seemed secure. But as 1817 drew to a close the question of what to do with Claire Clairmont and Lord Byron's love child was becoming ever more pressing. Clara Allegra Byron, whom her mother lovingly called Alba, was born a few weeks after Mary became Mrs. Shelley. For the sake of appearances, Mary had mingled Alba in with the rest of the brood and raised her publicly as if she were her own, though Claire continued (to her frustration) to live with them. Mary had also considered incorporating Alba into the large and welcoming family of their friend and literary booster Leigh Hunt. This, ultimately, came to nothing. Then in 1818, with his health declining, Percy Shelley went to see his doctor, William Lawrence, who suggested that a move to warmer climes would be beneficial. The Shelleys (and Clairmont) began to prepare to relocate to Italy, where Byron was now based. Mary and Percy hatched a plot to deliver Alba to her father, who, they believed, would be able to provide for her future in a way that Claire never could. Byron had not shown the least interest in his daughter by Claire—he had refused, even, to come and visit the Shelleys when they settled in Lake Como that spring—but then in April some caprice inspired in him some paternal feeling and he ordered Claire to send their daughter to him in Venice, minus mother. Near the end of the month, one of Byron's servants arrived to collect the fifteen-month-old girl. Claire was herself only twenty but was now in a heartbreaking position. By law Byron had no automatic right to custody over his illegitimate child. But he was an aristocrat with an income, she, in her own words, "a miserable and neglected dependent." She loved and cared for their daughter, and she had every reason to suspect that he did not. It was a choice between some hope for her baby's future social and financial security and the certainty of a warm and loving childhood. With Byron's footman waiting to deliver the child to his master, she wrote a final, anguished note to go along with Alba:

> If I have been faulty I have suffered enough to redeem my error,
> my child was born in sorrow and after much suffering—then I love
> her with a passion that almost destroys my being she goes from me.
> My dear Lord Byron I most truly love my child. She never checked
> me—she loves me most she stretches out her arms to me & cooes
> for joy when I take her. . . . I have wept so much to night that now
> my eyes seem to drop hot & burning blood.

The child left for Venice, and soon after their reduced party moved to Tuscany. Then in August two alarming letters arrived from Venice. Alba's nurse Elise had accompanied her charge to Venice and she now wrote to them that life in Lord Byron's Venetian household was intolerable and that Claire needed to come at once to rescue her daughter. Stricken with worry, Claire immediately set out to reclaim her daughter, taking Shelley with her and leaving Mary, Wilmouse, and a sickly Clara behind. Mary struggled to keep the house together by herself and was concerned with her daughter's fever, which she was powerless to treat in the ferocious heat of the Italian summer. In the midst of her worries another letter arrived from her husband, instructing her to come to Venice at once. She was needed to take receipt of Alba, whom Byron refused to surrender to Claire under any circumstances. On August 31, Mary, despite all her forebodings, left for the arduous trip to Venice accompanied by her son and her fading daughter. The four-day journey to Este, a day's travel from Venice, took them through the malarial swamps that then encircled the city and broke the health of Clara. They rushed her to the city to consult with Byron's doctor, but it was too late. She died in Venice and was buried in an unmarked grave on the Lido. Shelley, meanwhile, had been conducting his own investigations into Alba's circumstances and found nothing unduly amiss. Elise, it seemed, was more concerned with her own well-being and, possibly, was seeking a way back into the Shelley household, as she had developed an attachment to their servant Paolo, with whom she did, indeed, later elope.

After a few days with her mother, Alba was returned to her father's care. Byron promptly entrusted her to Richard Hoppner, the British consul in Venice. Alba, or Allegra as Byron now renamed her, proved to be a handful, and the arrangement with the Hoppners did not last long. After passing through several homes, Byron finally decided to send her to receive a convent education in Bagnacavallo, near Ravenna. Claire protested vociferously, but her complaints went ignored.[24] At Mary's urging Shelley tried to intervene, offering to take Allegra into his own household in the circumstances of Byron's choosing. The proposal was met with threats that if the Claire and the Shelleys did not cease meddling, Byron would move Allegra to a secret convent where they would have no access to her at all. "No one can more entirely agree with you than I in thinking that as soon as possible Allegra ought to be taken out of the hands of one as remorseless as he is unprincipled," Mary wrote to Claire, but in the meantime nothing could be done.[25] Nor would it. As Claire had predicted, the climate at Bagnacavallo did not agree with

Allegra. She would die there of typhus in April 1822. She was five years old.

A year after Allegra's death Marguerite Gardiner, Countess Blessington, was traveling through Genoa and struck up a friendship with Byron, who was then living there. The two engaged in long, rambling conversations, which Blessington recorded and later had published in London. At one point Byron mused on how a death had a way of magnifying, postmortem, his affections for those who he had found so tiresome to deal with in life.

> How did I feel this when Allegra, my daughter, died! While she
> lived, her existence never seemed necessary to my happiness; but no
> sooner did I lose her, than it appeared to me as if I could not live
> without her.

The words of the monster on the mountaintop resound: *How dare you sport thus with life?*

· ⚊ ▰ ⚊ ·

The question of culpability—of who is the real monster—lurks behind every line of *Frankenstein*. Another book that also arose out of that summer by Lac Léman would make the question explicit and answer it in an incendiary fashion. In 1819, Byron, still idling in Venice, received a concerning piece of news from London. A scandalous novella had been published under his name, first in a literary journal and then as a bound volume. It was called *The Vampyre*, and it told the story of the friendship between a wealthy orphan named Aubrey and the mysterious Lord Ruthven. Ruthven was an obvious stand-in for Byron. His name was an allusion to the antagonist of Caroline Lamb's roman à clef *Glenarvon* (the thinly fictionalized account of her affair with the poet that was also published in that turbulent summer of 1816) and his cold good looks and icy social manner were recognizably Byronic, literally and literarily. Furthermore, the description of Ruthven dwells on his "irresistible powers of seduction" and discusses at some length how the dark lord shuns adventuresses, adulteresses, and society flirts in favor of virtuous women and the most innocent young girls whom he can then corrupt. This is abhorrent in itself, but what is even more appalling is the aftermath of Ruthven's seduction of previously chaste women:

All those females whom he had sought, apparently on account of their virtue, had, since his departure, thrown even the mask aside, and had not scrupled to expose the whole deformity of their vices to the public gaze.

Ruthven leaves a trail of destruction in his wake wherever he goes. Aubrey learns this the hard way after he foolishly agrees to go on the Grand Tour with his new friend. After a period he becomes disgusted with Ruthven's appalling behavior and the two part ways. Continuing on alone, Aubrey soon arrives in Greece, where he falls in love with a local girl named Ianthe. She inducts him into the local lore concerning the "vampyre," and in her description of the supernatural being the lovestruck Aubrey dimly discerns "a pretty accurate description of Lord Ruthven." Ianthe is struck down by this monster a few days later. Plunged into grief Aubrey enters a delirium. Ruthven visits his sickbed, and the two resume their travels only for the lord to be killed by bandits during an ambush on their party. But when Aubrey returns to England he finds Ruthven alive, shape-shifted into Earl Marsden, and now courting his sister, who has fallen prey to his "serpent's art." Unable to prevent their marriage, Aubrey enters into a kind of fugue state and then goes mad and dies. The story ends with his sister found dead, her husband vanished, and a gothic flourish: "Aubrey's sister had glutted the thirst of a VAMPYRE!"

Byron was appalled—both by the fact that his name had been attached to this rather prosaic piece of prose but also by the inclusion of an anonymous preface that claimed that this was the story he had told the night that Mary Shelley had read the first tentative pages of *Frankenstein*. As a defensive measure he instructed his publisher to include what he actually composed in the forthcoming edition of his new poem, "Mazeppa."[26] Meanwhile, the genuine author of *The Vampyre* had been given no warning of its imminent publication and received virtually nothing by way of royalties despite the book's massive success in England and especially on the Continent.[27] A letter-writing campaign to correct even the most basic authorial facts of the book's origins met with limited success. *The Vampyre* was still being billed as the work of Byron's hand as late as the 1880s, an irony that might have amused the slighted author had he been anyone other than John William Polidori.

Polidori had originally written *The Vampyre* in 1816, shortly after he was released from Byron's service. The relationship between doctor and patient had been in decline ever since they had arrived in Geneva. Aside from bashing his patron with an oar and threatening Shelley with a duel, there had been numerous more mundane lapses in judgment on Polidori's part, many of which involved the day-to-day running of Byron's household. There were problems with servants, horses, and, in one instance, a questionable batch of magnesium procured from a local apothecary. These small failings were doubtless exacerbated by the larger incompatibility of the two men's personalities. Byron was soon seeking to avoid Polidori's company as much as he was Clairmont's. There is a telling anecdote from Shelley and Byron's trip together around the lake at the end of June. The two men had gone off alone on a mini-pilgrimage around sites associated with Jean-Jacques Rousseau. On the trail of his great novel *Julie* they wandered together in stunned silence through the vineyards of Nerni, in awe of the beauty all about them. "Thank God," Byron suddenly exclaimed, "Polidori is not here." When, at the end of August, the Shelleys left and John Hobhouse arrived, Polidori's days as Byron's companion were clearly numbered. He was let go at the beginning of the September, and Polidori began work on *The Vampyre* shortly after. Polidori's only famous work was in a sense a high-Gothic retelling of his angst-ridden relationship with England's most notorious poet, and a very modern parable about the dangers of meeting one's idols.

But *The Vampyre* is more than simply a fictionalized account of a friendship gone askew. It is also principally and, given the circumstances of its inspiration and composition, perhaps ineluctably a story about seducers and their "serpent's art." Hanging over the Villa Diodati was both the detritus from Mount Tambora and the wreckage that Byron had left behind in England. Both cast their shadow. Inside, the pathetic, pregnant figure of Clairmont and the mute and nameless Alba she bore were a palpable reminder that actions have consequences. Mary also posed a problem. Why had she wrecked the home and life of another woman, simply to traipse after an unstable and dissolute baronet's son, their own illegitimate child in tow? Added to the complexity was the fact that Polidori's own attempts at courting Mary had met with rejection and ridicule. His failure in this arena might have led him to speculate on why reckless and sporadically wicked men like Byron and, to a lesser degree, Shelley were able to attract women while he could not. *The Vampyre* was also an attempt to solve the mystery of attraction. Hidden within it was a solution to that mystery, and it was an answer born of the same speculative science that infused *Frankenstein*.

In the final passages of *The Vampyre* Aubrey goes mad as he watches Ruthven charm his beautiful, chaste younger sister. As his mental condition declines, strange things occur. He hears Ruthven's voice in his ear and feels his presence about him at all times. Ruthven consumes his thoughts and exerts invisible but decisive control over his actions. Aubrey seems to hover somewhere between life and death. He is physically present in the world but is practically powerless to intervene in it. He is living in a kind of suspended animation, having lost his free will but having retained his normal bodily functions. Polidori conveys Aubrey's odd condition convincingly, for it resembles a state that he had studied extensively as a medical student: somnambulism.

In his final year at Edinburgh University, Polidori had submitted a thesis in Latin entitled *De Oneirodynia,* "On Sleepwalking."[28] The study of sleepwalking, or somnambulism, as it was referred to, was an interesting and unusual choice for the young medic. Unusual because somnambulism was inextricably connected to mesmerism, which was among the most contested subjects of the day. Mesmerism, also known as vitalism and animal magnetism, was an attempt to understand the origins of life. Its students, like the English radical John Thelwall, were concerned with "how life and death may be accurately discriminated." They sought, like Dr. Frankenstein, to "penetrate into the recesses of nature, and show how she works in her hiding-places." Mesmerism flourished in the spaces opened up by new discoveries in physiology. Breakthroughs in the study of circulation, of the brain, and of muscle tissue meant that scientists and natural philosophers increasingly understood the mechanics of life— but they still had no explanation for what caused it. Mesmerists did: they believed variously in the existence of a vital principle, a universal fluid, or some kind of invisible force field that accounted for why some categories of matter were inert and others were alive. Mesmerists were fascinated by somnambulism because it appeared to be an intermediate state between life and death. The somnambulist was physiologically alive but neurologically incapacitated in some way. The condition of the somnambulist seemed to demonstrate that the body and the will could be temporarily separated, that man could become an automaton. Pseudo-scientists and quacks were not alone in this fascination. Somnambulism attracted the attention of serious scholars. Among this group the consensus was that somnambulism was, like most sleep disorders, a kind of insanity or mania. Sleeping and dreaming had long been associated with madness. When the body rested so, too, did man's faculties. This was "when monarch Reason sleeps," wrote one nineteenth-century doctor, quoting Dryden.[29] This association with madness explained why somnambulists seemed to do such strange things: attempting to climb walls and trees, shouting incoherent and nonsensical phrases, brandishing weapons. But what was truly unique to the condition was the curious pliability of somnambulists. They were totally docile, content to obey commands without question, and were thus ripe for manipulation. In Richerand's *Elements of Physiology* (1815) the French doctor observed that in somnambulism

> *Sometimes one organ of sense remains open to impression, and then you can direct, at pleasure, the intellectual action. Thus, you will make him that talks in his sleep, speak on what subject you choose, and steal from him the confession of his most secret thoughts.*[30]

The mesmerists had noticed exactly the same phenomenon. But where the staid men of science believed that this strange state arose out of some kind of neurological disorder that could neither be controlled nor predicted, the mesmerists believed that they could induce this same condition. Starting with the pioneering work of Amand-Marie-Jacques de Chastenet, Marquis de Puységur, mesmerists began to experiment with "artificial somnambulism," a precursor to hypnotism, whereby patients were put into a somnambulistic state through the (supposed) manipulation of their natural magnetic fields by a skilled mesmerist. In the years before the French Revolution thousands of such experiments were performed, often before large audiences. Joseph Deleuze, a contemporary scholar of the phenomenon, claimed that in the half century following Puységur's initial experiments in the 1760s as many as fifty thousand Frenchmen witnessed successful attempts at artificial somnambulism. He also stressed that "there are prodigious differences between magnetisers, as to the power which they are capable of exerting," and that while "some have frequently produced the state of somnambulism . . . others have made numerous efforts for that purpose, without obtaining such a result." Those who possessed that special ability became powerful indeed, for their patients were "subjected to the will of his magnetizer."[31] But with power came responsibility. Puységur had stated from the outset that his fellow magnetisers should "fear the effects of animal magnetism in the hands of dishonest men" and was particularly concerned about artificial somnambulism being used to sexually exploit women.[32] His worries were soon borne out. In the 1790s the credibility of animal magnetism as a field of study had been fatally discredited because of its connection with certain unscrupulous men. Among them was Alessandro Cagliostro, an Italian con man, rival of Giacomo Casanova, and sometime resident of the Bastille for defrauding Marie Antoinette during the "Affair of the Diamond Necklace." Cagliostro was also an occultist and "healer" who dabbled in mesmerism. His abilities in this field had attracted a devout following in certain Parisian social circles and the unscrupulous Cagliostro then

Inflamed them with the desire of beholding extraordinary things;
abused their credulity and seduced the imagination of females,
whom he rendered instrumental to various deceitful purposes,
without their even suspecting it.[33]

Things were not much better in England. There a certain Dr. John Bell gave accounts of his many experiments in artificial somnambulism in his 1792 treatise *The General and Particular Principles of Animal Electricity and Magnetism*. The work reveals Dr. Bell to be not a first-rate fabulist but a scientist and ethicist of indeterminate rank. His reports are full of his deft exploitation of women in the name of science, including making them drink wine, remove their garters, break wind, and, on one extraordinary occasion, be groped by a lunatic.[34] It was unsurprising, then, that mesmerism became connected in the public mind with underhand attempts to sexually control women. This distrust seeped into popular perceptions of more reputable fields of research. When Humphry Davy conducted his famous experiments with laughing gas— another, more scientific attempt to put the human body into an intermediate state between life and death—he was ridiculed by London satirists who accused him only half-jokingly of putting women "in a state of gas" for purposes less pure than the plain advancement of human knowledge. The anonymous author of "The Skeptic" (1800) claimed that a network of doctors pimped their patients to Davy, who treated them with gas and then

> *In this insidious manner gained admittance to their lovely persons;*
> *he warms their snowy bosoms; blows up the latent spark of*
> *soft desire; explores each hidden source of human bliss, and*
> *unsuspected, riots in their charms!*[35]

"More than one fair patient," the author scurrilously concluded, "has become a mother in consequence" of Davy's experiments.

These new sciences were treated with all the more suspicion because of their French origins. Horror, first at the revolution, and then at Bonapartism, inspired general revulsion at all things novel and French, and at that time one tended to be synonymous with the other. In a lavishly scatological cartoon from 1800, James Gillray depicted the Channel awash with excrement emanating from a huge dunghill in France. Napoleon floats foremost among them in his iconic bicorne, labeled "First Horse Turd." Lesser effluvia—Robespierre, Marat, Talleyrand—bob about him, while in the dunghill itself sit the names of other French agitators mixed in with their English confederates: Thomas Paine, William Godwin, and Joseph Priestley—a radical, a scientist, and the man who first synthesized laughing gas.[36] Among English reactionaries it was taken for granted that radical science and radical politics were dangerously intertwined. John Thelwall had lectured on vitalism in 1793 and had then spent 1794 in the Tower of London on charges of treason. In 1806 the *Anti-Jacobin Review* commented on a recent French work on universal fluid, in which animal magnetism was decried as a 'scandalous delusion' funded by Bonaparte. Artificial somnambulism was the target of the *Review*'s especial contempt, and its editors aligned themselves with "the enemies of *somnambulism*" who "exclaim, that all these pretended wonders are but impostures, the sport of delirious imaginations, the intrigues of silly mean women, the frauds of intriguers."[37]

This, then, was the medical field that the precocious student John Polidori chose to specialize in while at Edinburgh. The study of somnambulism was sexually and politically subversive, indelibly linked to the French enemy, and treated with the greatest skepticism by reputable scientists. Polidori could not have been ignorant of these facts. Indeed, as the son of Catholic immigrants he must have been doubly aware of these negative associations. But such considerations do not seem to have restrained his enthusiasm. Polidori remained fascinated by somnambulism even after he had graduated. In his journal from the summer of 1816 he records that he visited a certain Dr. Odier in Geneva, "who talked with me about somnambulism. . . . Odier gave me yesterday many

articles of *Bibliothèque*—translated and *rédigés* by himself, and to-day
a manuscript on somnambulism."[38] This meeting with Odier took place
only a few days before the night that gave birth to *Frankenstein*, and it
may well be Odier's manuscript that was the basis for Polidori's conversation with Shelley on June 8 that, in his estimation, left Mary and
Claire's "brains whizzed with giddiness."[39] Somnambulism was at the
forefront of Polidori's mind that summer, where it mingled with his frustrations, his fantasies, and his literary ambitions. It was there when he
sat down to compose *The Vampyre*, in which he used it as a device to
explain Lord Ruthven's/Lord Byron's "irresistible powers of seduction."

Despite the botched circumstance of its publication, the success of
The Vampyre made Polidori's name as a writer. But it did not cure his
melancholy. A troubled, turbulent young man, he died in obscure circumstances in his rooms in Golden Square, Soho, in August 1821. He
was buried in a Catholic graveyard, but all London knew that he had
taken his own life, most probably poisoning himself with prussic acid.
Polidori's death was but one of a wave that swept the male members of
the party that had gathered by Lac Léman in 1816. A year later Percy
Shelley would drown in the Gulf of Spezia, when his boat, *The Don
Juan*, sank in a storm. Mary was left numb with grief, and it fell to
Byron, Leigh Hunt, and a newcomer to the party—the leonine, fero-
ciously Byronic Edward Trelawny—to burn the dead poet's body on the
shores of the Tyrrhenian Sea, near Viareggio. Pouring out her misery in
a letter to Maria Gisborne, Mary remarked parenthetically that "Lord
Byron has been very kind—but [his mistress] restrains him perhaps—she
being an Italian is capable of being jealous of a living corpse such as I."
If in tragedy she finally saw something to commend in Byron's character
she did not have much time to enjoy his company. Nine months later,
Byron was dead in Missolonghi, struck down by disease as he fought
for Greek independence. In a letter to Trelawny, Mary, clear-eyed as

ever, noted that while Byron "could hardly be called a friend" she had admired his poetry and had bonded with him at an intellectual and emotional level. She felt a pang when she saw his cortège pass beneath her window in Kentish Town on its way up Highgate Hill to his final resting place in Nottinghamshire. Not even little Wilmouse survived the massacre. He had succumbed to a fever in Rome in 1819 only a few months after the death of his younger sister, Clara.

Within a few years of *Frankenstein*'s publication all the men who had been present at its birth were dead. But the women they had known and loved and loathed, lived on—as did the problem of Free Love. Mary believed in Free Love philosophically even as she doubted it practically. In contrast to her stepsister, she had always been wary of the consequences for women for the free pursuit of their desires. Nothing she had experienced in the first twenty-five years of her life could have disabused her of this precaution. The problem was not one of principles but of underlying structures. The terms of engagement in courtship were wildly skewed in favor of men. Men risked relatively little in seduction; women risked their reputation, their health, and the lives of their unborn children. This inequality was sustained by a series of interlocking systems of control and censure, some formal, others less so. Mary's parents had believed that these might be overthrown in a single motion, but by the 1820s the likelihood of a revolution in Britain was small. What was needed was tactical legal reform that would pave the way to lasting equality. What was also needed was a reformer with the will to make it happen. A decade after her husband's death Mary met her.

Caroline Norton and Mary Shelley had much in common. Caroline was also the heir to a great literary and political tradition. Her grandfather was the great Anglo-Irish playwright and founder of Drury Lane Theatre, Richard Brinsley Sheridan, who was also a leading Whig parliamentarian. Like Mary's, this distinguished pedigree did little to materially improve the quality of her upbringing, and she grew up in genteel poverty, the family surviving on a mixture of aristocratic patronage and royal charity. Consequently, though she never knew the kind of social ostracism that was the water Mary swam in, she could not depend, like most of the women of her class, on marrying or inheriting herself into financial security. Her mother strove to win good matches for her daughters, but all she could secure for the flirtatious, playful, endlessly talented Caroline was the hand of George Norton, a dullard and a vulgarian with little money, a titled older brother, and a marked aversion to practicing his chosen profession of lawyer. As a result of Norton's reluctance to work, his bride was obliged to turn her childhood passion for writing into paid work. She published her first poetry collection, *The Sorrows of Rosalie*, to a warm reception in 1829 when she was twenty-one—almost exactly the same age as Mary had been when she published *Frankenstein* a decade earlier. Over the next forty years Caroline would publish over a dozen novels, plays, and volumes of poetry, as well as a number of profoundly influential political pamphlets, and through her salons and dinner parties, as well as the journals she edited and contributed to, she helped shape literary and political life in London for a generation. This is a body of work and an enterprise that has now been almost totally forgotten, which is regrettable since it was Caroline—just as much as it was Mary—who helped create the modern conception of the independent female intellectual.

It is not exactly clear when the two women met. There is good evidence to suggest that Mary wrote an 1831 profile of Caroline in the *New Monthly Magazine*. The sketch reveals a writerly appreciation of form and a preference for Norton's refined phrasing to the "gaudy glittering sentences" of her rivals. It also shows a pronounced interest in her literary pedigree, "in that long chain of hereditary talent . . . the rich cluster of genius and talent which is wreathed round her name she inherits." This lineage fostered a childhood of scribbling, a "*furor scribendi*," that blossomed into adolescent precocity, and, by the time of this piece's writing, several works of poetry, some plays, and half a novel.[40] The accompanying portrait shows a beautiful young woman, with rich brown hair, thick eyebrows, and a Grecian aspect that recalled the Mediterranean temptresses of Byron's verse. In her own lifetime, Caroline was frequently compared to Byron—she was the "Byron of poetesses"—but he was at least as Nortonian as she was Byronic.[41] The two shared an energy, an indefinable attraction, and a mastery of the written and spoken word that persists even at the distance of two centuries. Above all, they shared an unrivaled capacity for mischief-making. As a younger woman she had been known simply as one of the "strange girls" of the Sheridan clan, "who swear and say all sorts of odd things to make men laugh." But she soon came into her own as especially volatile company. In 1828 the whig grandee Henry Edward Fox recorded in his diary her teasingly declaring her love to one John Talbot in front of her "astonished husband before a roomful of people at Chesterfield House."

The whole of it was a fiction; but such allusions are both dangerous and indecent for so young a woman. Her oddity makes her at present the fashion; and people admire her prodigiously.[42]

By 1832 she was putting her considerable charms to nobler use, throwing herself into the effort to pass the Great Reform Bill. That year also marked the definite beginning of her relationship with Mary—the journal Caroline edited, *The Court Magazine and Belle Assemblée*, published a short story called "The Pole," written by the "author of

'Frankenstein.'"[43] By 1833, Caroline had borne her unloving and unlovely husband three sons (Fletcher [1829], Brinsley [1831], and William [1833]) and remained a source of fascination in society. A remarkable account of her effect on men survives in the diary of the society painter Benjamin Haydon, who was a regular at Caroline's salon in Storey's Gate that year. Haydon appears to have been a particularly easy mark, but his breathless account of her performance at a dinner party in July gives a flavor of the otherworldly effect she had on the men in her circle:

> Mrs Norton . . . lightened up at midnight, and gave us specimens of her exquisite humour. Her fine black eyes shone like Arsinoe's! Her Aegyptian mouth, her sublime head, looked quite inspired! It was a sight, & never to be forgotten!

A few weeks later he entrusted to his journal more of the same florid prose:

> A more unaffected creature on thorough acquaintance does not exist. There she sat, looking like a Divinity, calm, self possessed. I could hardly trust myself to look at her! Grand Creature! . . . She told me she was fierce in her temper! Let her be. . . . She has beauty, Genius, & is not blue! which I abhor.[44]

Haydon, unsurprisingly, proved to be too insistent in his affections of Caroline and eventually had to be eased out of her circle.[45] But there were many more admirers waiting in the wings. In 1835, Edward Trelawny, Byron and Shelley's former accomplice and Mary's onetime suitor,[46] returned from a tour of America and reentered London society. He soon encountered and was immediately bewitched by Caroline Norton. Known as "Corsair Trelawny" in London social circles, the tall, lean Trelawny, his jaw visibly scarred from a gunshot wound to the face sustained during a failed assassination attempt in Greece, cut a piratical figure in London drawing rooms. But he was no match for Caroline. He was lavish in his pursuit of her, too much so, and within two years she was bored of this "mysteriously awful, & vaguely sublime, but very fierce" man who, though fifteen years her senior, played the part of the lovestruck younger beau, made scenes in public, and ended the relationship with a rude, incoherent, and faintly threatening letter.

While Trelawny had been making a fool of himself, Mary and Caroline became close friends. Mary participated in the London season of 1835 and had joined Trelawny on the social circuit. She followed Trelawny's courtship of Caroline with some amusement and no little encouragement—though whether this support was well-intentioned or otherwise is not wholly clear. In a letter sent to Trelawny that October, Mary dwelled at length on Caroline's charms, declaring that

> *I never saw a woman I thought so fascinating. Had I been a man I should certainly have fallen in love with her; as a woman, ten years ago, I should have been spellbound, and had she taken the trouble, she might have wound me round her little finger.*

She then went on to praise in fulsome manner her wit, her beauty, her centrality to London social life. Perhaps she meant all of this—she certainly repeated similar sentiments, in less rococo phrasing, on other occasions—but perhaps she was tempting Trelawny in this vain endeavor, dangling before his hungry rake's eyes the prospect of an immortal conquest. The very next day she sent a letter to her friend Maria Gisborne. "Trelawn[e]y is in England," she wrote, "he is enchained by Mrs. Norton—I do not wonder at the latter—she is a wonderful creation possessing wit, beauty and sweetness at their highest grade—They say a stony heart withal—so I hope she will make him pay for his numerous coqueteries [sic] with our sex."

In any event, Caroline and Mary's friendship proved genuine. By April 1836, Mary was writing to Caroline for help with a delicate matter. That month, her father had died at-age-eighty. To prevent her stepmother from lapsing into abject poverty she sought to have Godwin's modest pension transferred over to his widow. From the outset Caroline was willing and happy to help, though she was clear that Mary's chances would be significantly improved if she appealed to the prime minister, Lord Melbourne, directly. In the letters that followed, Caroline demonstrated her familiarity with the British patronage system while also revealing her wit, her powers of social observation, and her vivid, antic prose:

As to petitioning, no one dislikes begging more than I do, especially when one begs for what seems mere justice; but I have long observed that though people will resist claims (however just) they like to do favours. Therefore, when I beg I am a crawling lizard, a humble toad, a brown snake in cold weather, or any other simile most feebly "rampante," the reverse of "rampant," which would be the natural attitude for petitioning, but which must never be assumed except in the poodle style, standing with one's paws bent to catch the bits of bread on one's nose.

Forgive my jesting. Upon my honour, I feel sincerely anxious for your anxiety, and sad enough on my own affairs; but Irish blood will dance. My meaning is, that if one asks at all, one should rather think of the person written to than one's own feelings. He is an indolent man—talk of your literary labours; a kind man—talk of her age and infirmities; a patron of all genius—talk of your father's and your own; a prudent man—speak of your likelihood of the pension being a short grant (as you have done); lastly, he is a great man—take it all as a personal favour.

Those last, intimate lines could not have been written at a more germane moment. A few months later, in the summer of 1836, the extent of Caroline Norton's relationship with Lord Melbourne would become the subject of a legal battle as well as a national fixation. It would also begin a heroic, decades-long struggle on the part of Caroline that would result in the transformation of the rights of Englishwomen.

Under English law there were four civil actions available in the instance of seduction. Only one of these actions was open to women. This was the "Breach of Promise to Marry" tort, which allowed seduced women to seek damages in court if a man proposed marriage and then reneged on the offer. The tort for "Seduction" allowed for fathers to sue the seducers of their daughters under a largely defunct but socially useful legal fiction of *per quod servitium amisit* ("whereby he lost services") that held that a seduced daughter meant a loss of services for the father—anything as small as the making of his cup of tea at breakfast—for which he was allowed to seek compensation.[47]

The final two actions were open only to husbands. The first was "Alienation of Affection," which was open to any husband whose wife deserted him because of the interference or meddling of another man. Alienation of affection was distinct from the second, more serious charge of "Criminal Conversation" in that it did not require sexual relations to have occurred between the defendant and the wife. Criminal conversation (abbreviated as "Crim. Con.") provided for damages in the instance of adultery, with the court requiring reasonable evidence that a "criminal intercourse" had existed between alleged adulterer and alleged adulteress. The legal complication in such cases came in meeting the burden of proof. Neither husband nor wife could testify in court against the other. Consequently, servants were called upon to stand in judgment of their master's and mistress's actions in public. The ensuing drama was always a source of public fascination. There were whole magazines, such as *The Crim. Con. Gazette*, that existed to feed the appetite for information about the sexual lives of England's rich and titled. But for all the shame involved in the public disclosure and society scandal that Crim. Con. entailed, it remained a perennial temptation. The court awards could be enormous—the highest was £20,000—and so the suit became a magnet for blackmailers, troublemakers, and those out to destroy the fortunes as well as the reputations of their rivals.

William Lamb, Second Viscount Melbourne, and twice prime minister of the United Kingdom (in 1834 and 1835–1841) knew all about Crim. Con. cases. Had he cared to, he could have easily brought such a case against Byron when the latter cuckolded him quite spectacularly with his wife, Caroline Lamb. But to do so would not have been in Melbourne's character. A raffish, charming, liberal gentleman, he had been raised in a permissive aristocratic atmosphere that regarded discreet affairs as the norm. Following Caroline's death in 1828, Melbourne had sought companionship in the arms of married women and had thought nothing of it. Husbands had thought otherwise. In 1828 a Crim. Con. case was brought against him by Lord Branden, the spouse of his mistress, Lady Branden, which Melbourne dodged only by means of a generous out-of-court settlement. In June 1836 he found himself accused again, this time by George Norton.

By the time that court case began in the stifling heat of Court of Common Pleas in Westminster, George Norton had known Lord Melbourne for over six years. The relationship was cordial and, for Norton, financially beneficial. In 1830 Melbourne (at Caroline's request) had secured Norton a lucrative job as a magistrate in Aldgate, East London, where he presided over the legal conflicts of London's working classes. What divided them was politics—Melbourne was a Whig, Norton the most reactionary kind of backcountry Tory—and Caroline Norton. Caroline and Melbourne had become friendly during the great flurry of political activity that preceded the passage of the Great Reform Act of 1832. For much of the 1830s he was a regular at her salon and in her larger social circle. Melbourne was everything that Caroline sought in a man: powerful, intelligent, a great performer passionately involved in the issues of the day. Soon Melbourne was stopping by her home with great regularity on the way home from work and was keeping up a daily correspondence with her. While Caroline's relationship with Melbourne was intensifying, her marriage was falling apart. Norton was stupid, priggish, and vindictive. He periodically beat her. In 1835 she moved to separate from him, but when he denied her access to her sons she submitted to a reconciliation with him. In the spring of 1836 there was another contretemps. Again she moved out of his house and again, when her sons were taken from her, she moved to mend fences. But this time Norton refused her. Spite and wounded pride almost certainly played their part, but it also seems that the prospect of trashing the reputation of the sitting Whig prime minister was too much of a temptation for him and his Tory handlers. A Crim. Con. suit was brought again the PM and *Norton v. Viscount Melbourne*, dubbed the "Trial of the Century," was scheduled for June 22, 1832.

For all the hype, the trial lasted a day and a night and resulted in a victory for the prime minister. Norton failed to win any of the £10,000 he had sued for and went home in the identical condition in which he had begun. Neither of the named parties in the suit had been present in the courtroom, though both had been represented by veteran barristers. The trial's real victim was Caroline Norton, who had neither been present nor advocated for. Crim. Con. cases were strictly clashes between men. The women they squabbled over were treated as collateral damage—and for Norton there was a great deal of damage done. An array of servants—many of whom had been clearly well-trained by the prosecution's team of lawyers—had testified that they had observed many "familiarities and such things as would make you wonder" at Storey's Gate when Melbourne had come to visit Caroline. The star witness, the dipsomaniac, tragicomic figure of former servant John Fluke, who readily admitted to having a few drinks before taking the stand and then went on to claim to have caught the couple *in flagrante*, with Caroline spread on a rug, thigh exposed, "like a Spartan virgin."[48] Caroline's letters to and from Melbourne, many of them achingly banal in content, were scoured for proof of lustful intention. Even though the jury (a diverse crowd of ten merchants, a banker, and a retired Admiral) found for Melbourne, Caroline's reputation in polite society could not survive such exposure.[49] She was forever afterward associated with scandal, a point made clear when upon her accession to the throne a year following the trial Queen Victoria refused to allow Caroline to appear at court—a rite of passage for all well-born men and women.[50] "A woman," Caroline wrote to Mary, a few days after the end of the trial, "is made a helpless wretch by these laws of men."[51]

For Caroline the most harmful legacy of the trial was her separation from her three young sons. After a period of initial uncertainty as to whether her estranged husband would allow her access to them, it became clear that he would not and that his refusal to do so was perfectly within the limits of the law. Confronted by unjust laws she took up her pen and determined to change them. As she began her campaign in latter half of 1836 the woman she turned to for support was Mary Shelley.

In between her humiliation in 1836 and her triumph in 1839 with the passage of the Custody of Infants Act, Caroline published no fewer than three pamphlets arguing for immediate reform of the law. Mary only worked closely with her on the first of these—*Observations on the Natural Claim of the Mother to the Custody of Her Infant Children* (1837)—but all three shared a common refrain, and Caroline's objectives and reasoning were all laid out in a long letter to Mary in January 1837. The aim was simple: "that children under the age of seven should belong, at all events, to the mother; and after that access dependent, not on the father, but on the Court of Chancery." This, she noted, and what Mary must likely already have known, was simply extending to married mothers the rights afforded to the mothers of illegitimate children. Her reasoning was twofold. The first was a straightforward Enlightenment argument in favor natural rights. The court-sanctioned separation of a mother from her children was a clear "perversion of natural rights" that had to be corrected. The second argument attacked the organizing principle of English common law: the sovereignty of property rights. "In this commercial country," she wrote to Mary, "the rights of property are the only rights really and efficiently protected; and the consideration of property the only one which weighs with the decision made in a court of justice."

> The great obstacle, in all the cases I have looked through, to the woman obtaining her child, or even obtaining that it should be in the hands of a third party as a proper guardian, has been the want of property to justify the interference of the law.

The radicalness of Caroline's reasoning can be easy to miss. Courts were unwilling to help mothers in her position and vulnerable women in general because "the interference of the law" was usually premised on a violation of property rights. By making a legal case premised on the violation of *natural* rights, Caroline was essentially arguing the courts should concern themselves with questions of morality, not just property. This was revolutionary. Early-nineteenth-century Britain was a modernizing society with a medieval legal system. The focus on property rights organized relations vertically. The fundamental question in the overwhelming majority legal actions was: Who owned what? By injecting morality into the system Caroline was calling for an equalization of legal identities. Relationships would now be organized horizontally on the basis of rights, not upward and downward on the basis of ownership, tithes, and obligations.

Working through her able and courageous parliamentary proxy Sir Thomas Talfourd, Caroline secured the passage of the Custody of Infants Act in 1839. The bill was the first feminist piece of legislation in English history. It identified rights unique to women and guarded them from abuse by men. In so doing it created a precedent that would reverberate throughout the English legal system.

But Caroline's victory was not without its ironies. In a letter from February 1837, Caroline informed Mary of Talfourd's first attempt to introduce the bill to Parliament. "I thought you would be glad to know this," she wrote, "both for the sake of the sex (whom you have not the clever woman's affectation of thinking inferior to men) and for me." Here we see Caroline invoke a sense of sisterly camaraderie in pursuit of legal reform: they are two feminists working side by side for social change. The letter is revealing because everywhere else Caroline tended to distance herself from feminists and in an 1838 letter to John Murray explicitly complained of scabrous political writers who "erect an imaginary Mrs. Norton, something between a barn-actress and a Mary Wollstonecraft, and . . . hunt her down with unceasing perseverance."[52] Elsewhere she refuted "the wild and ridiculous doctrine of [gender] equality." It is hard to know what Mary made of this dualism in her close friend. She had spent her whole life in the company of radicals who had achieved little, so must have admired the practical Norton who said what was necessary to do the transformative. Nonetheless, given how much she treasured the memory of her father, her husband, and, above all, her mother, she surely must have resented this disavowal of her family's radical legacy.

The most poignant irony was the fact that the new law did nothing for Caroline. Following its passage, Norton moved the sons to Scotland and into the separate Scottish legal system, where the act had no power. In the end, only tragedy reunited Caroline with her sons. In 1842 her son William fell from a horse, contracted complications from his injuries, and died of septicemia soon afterward. The loss softened her husband's attitude, and for the rest of her life she enjoyed more or less unrestrained access to her sons. The rapprochement had other welcome consequences. In 1848 she signed a legal deed of separation with her husband that guaranteed her an income.

The 1840s were a period of peace for both Mary and Caroline. The two women spent their time writing, traveling, and worrying about their sons. Their correspondence continued, and they shared with each other the travails peculiar to women in their then uncommon position: single, self-supporting, intellectual. In an amusing letter from the time, chiding Mary for her lack of financial nous, Caroline joked about how she and Mary "run about alone like . . . young bachelor[s]." Their lives were unconventional for their age, but their letters reveal very modern concerns. They fret over their sons' education, securing payment from publishers, and finding suitable housing in London for a single woman.

In the wider world, political reform was gradually coming to English society. Ever since the Great Reform Act women's rights had been a staple for parliamentary debate. The Custody of Infants Act had been a high-water mark, but there was hope in other areas as well. Married women's property rights and divorce were two subjects of perennial discussion, as were seduction and prostitution—two issues that were regularly conflated. The rights of seduced women had been discussed during the debates surrounding the 1834 Poor Law and were to come to parliamentary attention twice more in the 1840s. Throughout the decade, petitions flooded in to Parliament, calling for the greater policing of seduction and prostitution. The two phenomena were seen as fundamentally intertwined as a seduced woman was not far from becoming a fallen woman. Seduction was a gateway to prostitution—the Great Social Evil, as it was known. In 1844, Henry Phillpotts, Bishop of Exeter, took up the issue. "There were none so thoroughly Satanical as the seducer," he told the House of Lords, "and if it were possible for human laws to reach him, there was no punishment that ought to be forborne."[53] The bishop's concerns came to nought that year, but in 1847 the question came before the Commons. There the Birmingham MP Richard Spooner introduced the Seduction and Prostitution Suppression Bill. Under the bill's provisions men found guilty of seduction would have faced imprisonment "with or without hard labour, in the common gaol or house of correction for any term not exceeding two years." The bill was supported both by Tory moralists and by radical members, such as the flammulously named Henry Galgacus Redhead Yorke, who growled from the floor "that in his opinion it was the province of the House to put down every abomination that came under its cognizance, and, therefore, he came with the intention of supporting the measure of the hon. Gentleman opposite."[54] Despite these encouraging displays of bipartisanship, and the great support for the bill in the country at large, its opponents in the Commons were more numerous and no less convinced of their cause.[55] Members argued against the bill along legal lines that the offense was ill-defined, that the accused had insufficient avenues for appeal, and that the burden of proof would always be insufficient in such cases, and along moral lines that publicizing lewdness in the courts would only aid its spread in the public at large. More worrying yet, men would be exposed to all kinds of new perils from scheming, cynical women. John Arthur Roebuck summarized the threat to British men:

> *Under this Bill any man could be made the victim of the vilest conspiracy. . . . Under the provisions of this Act no one would be safe, from the Archbishop of Canterbury downwards—nay, not even the hon. Member for Birmingham himself.*

The bill was withdrawn. But once again the new fault line in British politics had been re-demarcated. Did the law exist to protect men or women, to guard morality or property, to buttress the existing order or to bring about reform?

These were big questions that touched every area of English life. But when the focus was narrowed down to issues of love, sex, and courtship—and the potential of all those to impinge upon the law—then what was really at stake was the institution of marriage. Marriage was at the heart of English society. It was an event that everyone strove toward in the course of their own lives. It reaffirmed the bonds of law and religion that organized the nation and those of status and property that organized society. Marriage also entrenched sexual inequality. At the altar the woman ceased to exist. Her legal identity was subsumed into her husband, and the two became indivisible in the eyes of law. This was the terrible significance of Miss Caroline Sheridan's transformation into Mrs. George Norton. This was the principle of coverture, so-called, as Blackstone noted, because while married the wife's existence was "incorporated and consolidated into that of the husband: under whose wing, protection and *cover*, she performs everything.[56] What made coverture so terrifying was the inflexibility of wedlock. Because a marriage could be dissolved only with great difficulty and at great expense, it acted as a one-way filter: one could enter but could not leave. This immovable reality defined the sexual lives of all women. To follow their desires outside of marriage was risky precisely because it threatened to preclude the possibility of security inside marriage. The pursuit of sexual freedom brought with it social ostracism, economic insecurity, illegitimate children; submission to marriage meant individual extinction and a life spent at the mercy of one's husband who could beat, rape, and otherwise abuse his wife without "the interference of the law." Men, by contrast, faced none of these dilemmas and could be libertines within or without wedlock. For women, Free Love, or even enjoyment of the most prosaic of sexual freedoms, was chimerical while marriage remained monolithic. Nothing would liberate women more—legally, socially, sexually—than the liberalization of marriage, and in the 1850s Caroline Norton did just that.

The near decade-long truce between George and Caroline Norton ended in 1851 with the death of Caroline's mother. In her will she left a bequest to her daughter and, knowing all too well of her son-in-law's covetous ways, she did all she could to ensure the money would go to Caroline and not to him. When Norton learned of this he simply ceased to pay Caroline the money owed to her as per their 1848 legal separation. The money she inherited from her mother was less than the amount now withheld by her husband. Newly impoverished and once more enraged, Caroline turned the logic of the law upon itself. Because of her husband's vindictiveness she could no longer afford to pay various tradesmen for services already rendered, nor pay off her other creditors. However, under coverture her and he were indistinguishable. She did not exist and all the debts she accrued were in his name and were liable to the legal entity known as Mr. George Norton. Caroline simply ceased to pay and told the various bailiffs and debt collectors sent her way to seek payment from her husband. This was an early and exquisite example of the tactic of "heightening the contradictions." In August 1853 it resulted in a lawsuit, when one of these unpaid tradesmen, the carriage-builder Thrupps of Oxford Street, took George Norton to court for failing to meet his—meaning his wife's—contractual agreements. Caroline was called in as a witness and before a crowd of two to three hundred spectators the litigious couple sparred for several hours. Caroline was a child of the theatre, and if she did not exactly revel in the performative aspect of court proceedings she well knew how to manage them to her own advantage. Before a rapt crowd who periodically burst into supportive applause she chronicled how her husband had slandered her, taken the copyrights to her books, refused to pay his debts, private and public, and had kept her from her children. She concluded with a final, blistering assault on Norton's character:

> I know Mr. Norton can cheat me, and I have no doubt that my
> friends will assist me more than ever when they learn that the man
> who calls himself a magistrate, a barrister, and a gentleman, and
> who can also cheat poor tradesman, because I am called his agent,
> and it is not binding upon me. I do not ask for my rights. I have no
> rights—I have only wrongs.[57]

This final flourish was rhetorically devastating but not wholly true. It was Caroline's particular genius that she combined the ability to play the part of the wronged woman with that of the hardheaded political reformer. In the weeks after the trial she restated her complaints against the legal system in general and her husband in particular in a furious

Above: William Hogarth's *The Harlot's Progress* (1732). The two men lurking in the background are Colonel Francis Charteris and his henchman, John Gourley. CREDIT: Harris Brisbane Dick fund, 1932 *Below:* An image of the Magdalen Hospital in St. George's Fields, Southwark, circa 1798. CREDIT: Wellcome Collection

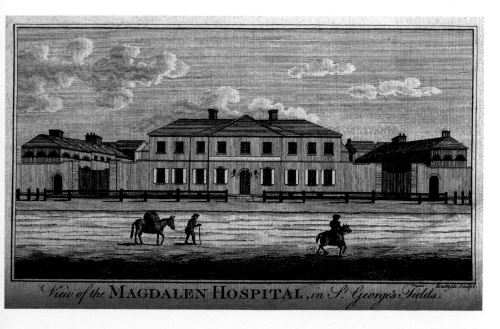

The chapel of the Magdalen Hospital in Southwark, London. Society men and women would pay generously to attend the Sunday services and experience the vicarious thrill of sharing a space with the seduced and abandoned. The magdalens themselves are in the gallery, behind a screen. CREDIT: The Elisha Whittelsey Collection, The Elisha Whittelsey Fund, 1959

Below: The Covent Garden Piazza—the meeting place of London's literary and leisure classes. CREDIT: Yale Center for British Art, Paul Mellon Collection

Two images from the Venetian master Pietro Longhi that capture the social and sexual freedoms that women enjoyed in the Venetian Republic. In *The Visit*, a woman is attended to by several men, one of whom (in yellow) may well be her *cicisbeo*, or male concubine. In *The Meeting*, several women (each wearing a different kind of mask) flirt with men during Carnival. CREDIT (above): Pietro Longhi (Pietro Falca) (Italian, Venice 1701–1785 Venice), Gift of Samuel H. Kress, 1936; CREDIT (below): Frederick c. Hewitt Fund, 1912

Above: The stairs exiting the Ducal Palace that Casanova ran down on the final stretch towards freedom and exile. CREDIT: courtesy of the author

Right: Casanova dangling from the roof of the Ducal Palace during his escape from prison in Venice in 1757. An engraving from his widely circulated memoir *Story of My Flight* (1787).
CREDIT: Wikimedia Commons

Below: The Brenta Canal, which connected Venice and Padua, was the scene and source of much adventure throughout Casanova's life.
CREDIT: Gift of Samuel H. Kress, 1936

A scene from *Pamela* (1740), a French engraving after Joseph Highmore. In this scene, Mr. B— has inveigled his way into Pamela's bedroom with the assistance of his corrupt servant, Mrs. Jervis. CREDIT: Wellcome Collection

A depiction of the Harlowe family with Clarissa standing on the left. Richardson declared his message in *Clarissa* to be twofold: to "explode . . . that pernicious Notion, that a Reformed Rake . . . makes the best Husband" and to "to admonish Parents against forcing their Children's Inclinations, in an Article so essential to their Happiness, as Marriage." This scene, which shows Clarissa's family chastising her for her independence and her self-proclaimed "right to a heart," is crucial in explaining how she ends up ensnared by Lovelace's designs. CREDIT: Yale Center for British Art, Paul Mellon Collection

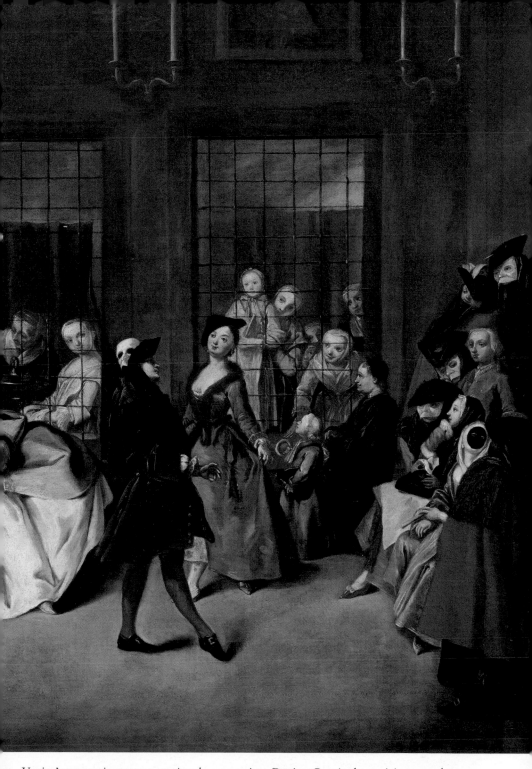

Venice's nunneries were notoriously easy-going. During Carnival, musicians, revelers, and clowns came to their visiting parlours to entertain the nuns, who were usually the daughters of moneyed Venetians. Note the size of the bars on the windows. "The largeness of the Venetian grates has ruined the reputation of the Venetian nuns," lamented one contemporary. CREDIT: Wikimedia Commons

Above: A satirical cartoon depicting Caroline Norton's adulterous affair with Prime Minister Lord Melbourne (christened William Lamb—hence clothed in sheepskin) while her husband, the cretinous George Norton, looks on, sporting his cuckold's horns. The 1836 legal dispute that resulted from the affair led indirectly to the reform of women's marital rights—a campaign spearheaded by Caroline Norton. CREDIT: Wellcome Collection *Below*: A pair of overindulged rakes and their companions. CREDIT: The Elisha Whittelsey Collection, The Elisha Whittelsey Fund, 1959

James Gillray's portrayal of the aftermath of the Women's March on Versailles in 1789, which led to a militia ransacking the palace and menacing the royal family. On the far right, Marie Antoinette can be seen fleeing down a corridor. On the far left, Reverend Richard Price—Mary Wollstonecraft's mentor—watches with pleasure in the company of a demon. The incident led Burke to famously complain that "The Age of Chivalry is gone. That of sophisters, economists, and calculators has succeeded; and the glory of Europe is extinguished for ever." CREDIT: Yale Center for British Art, Paul Mellon Collection

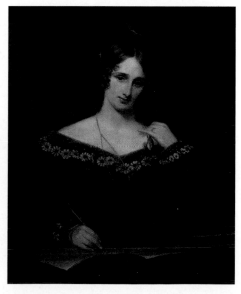

Mother and daughter: Mary Wollstonecraft and Mary Shelley.
CREDIT: Wikimedia Commons

A portrait of William Godwin, philosopher, novelist, apostle of free love, and husband to Mary Wollstonecraft. The most notorious radical of his day, his posthumous biography of Wollstonecraft had the unintended effect of discrediting her ideas for generations to come. CREDIT: Wikimedia Commons

The moment in *Frankenstein* when the monster wakes up and his creator flees. Mary Shelley's novel was many things, including a critique of male sexual irresponsibility. Note the rakishness of Dr. Frankenstein's attire. CREDIT: Wikimedia Commons

A depiction of the Women's March on Versailles in 1789 when the *poissardes*, the fisherwomen of Paris, seized control of history. This was the inciting incident for Edmund Burke's *Reflections on the Revolution in France*. Mary Wollstonecraft and other female radicals in Britain would be referred to disdainfully as "our *poissardes*."
CREDIT: Wikimedia Commons

The Nightmare by Henri Fuseli (1781) was one of the most disturbing and widely reproduced depictions of Romantic sexuality. CREDIT: Wikimedia Commons

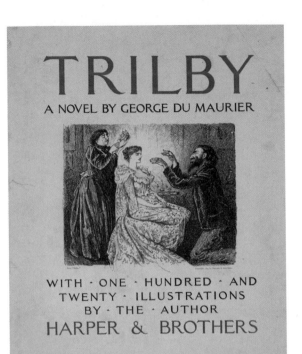

A poster for the transatlantic bestseller, *Trilby*, featuring the most nakedly anti-Semitic illustration from the book, where Svengali hypnotises the helpless Trilby O'Farrell. CREDIT: Wikimedia Commons

An anti-Semitic cartoon from 1930s Germany.
CREDIT: Reproduced with the kind permission of Randall Bytwerk

THE FIRST STEP
Ice cream parlors of the city and fruit stores combined, largely run by foreigners, are the places where scores of girls have taken their first step downward. Does her mother know the character of the place and the man she is with?

Two images from the voluminous literature on the "white slave traffic." It was a standard technique of white slave trade activists to recast normal heterosocial behaviour as the gateway to sexual bondage. CREDIT: Wikimedia Commons

Right: A cartoon from a sensationalist book on the white slave trade. Seduction was depicted as the fatal first step toward sexual bondage. Here, the young man spins a yarn about their future together, helpfully portrayed at the top of the image, where they gad about in expensive cars. CREDIT: From *Fighting the Traffic in Young Girls* © 1911, L. H. Walter

Below: An eighteenth-century depiction of animal magnetism. Note the woman swooning in the bottom left-hand corner. Patients in Paris receiving Mesmer's animal magnetism therapy. Colored etching after C-L. Desrais. CREDIT: Wellcome Collection

LE MAGNÉTISME ANIMAL

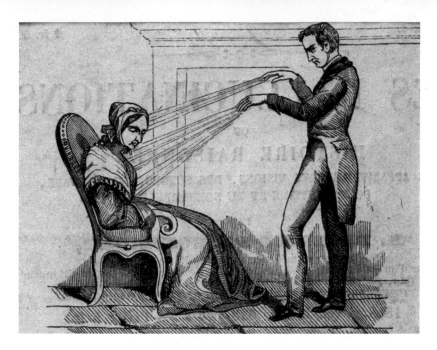

Above: *A Practitioner of Animal Magnetism*, a late eighteenth-century engraving.
CREDIT: Wellcome Collection

Below: A nineteenth-century depiction of Jean-Martin Charcot's world-famous experiments in hypnotism at the Salpêtrière hospital in Paris. By the turn of the century, hypnotism and seduction were intimately linked in the popular consciousness. CREDIT: Wikimedia Commons

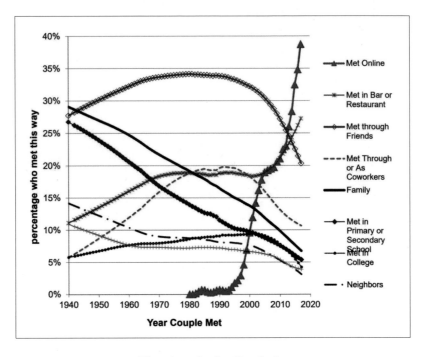

The triumph of online dating.

CREDIT: Reproduced with the kind permission of Michael J. Rosenfeld

correspondence with George Norton in the letters pages of *The Times*. Then she took up her pen and wrote two powerful pamphlets—*English Laws for Women in the Nineteenth Century* (1854) and *A Letter to the Queen on Lord Chancellor Cranworth's Marriage & Divorce Bill* (1855). As the title of the latter suggests, Caroline was writing amid a revival of interest in the legal status of married women. While she was only one voice among several arguing for reform, she was easily the most virtuosic. Her lines of attack were almost identical to those elucidated to Mary in 1837. Coverture, she argued, was a self-evident absurdity. It held that a married woman was "non-existent in law" and no more deserving of legal protection than a slave laboring in the cotton fields of the American South. This was a clear violation of natural rights—not to mention common sense and common decency. She simultaneously brought morality into play, condemning "England's merchant spirit" where "property, not morality, [was] the thing held sacred." Caroline pointed out how morally injurious existing marital law was. Adultery was grounds for divorce for husbands but not for wives. Married women were held to the highest standard of individual morality, and rightly so, she argued, but married men could act the libertine without fear of legal rebuke. Caroline mocked the logic that the moral significance of a wife's adultery was magnified by the prospect of giving "the husband a spurious son to inherit."

> *Truly: and the husband's adultery may give his friend,—into whose house he has crept like a thief, to steal faith and honor,—a spurious son to inherit. Or it may give some wretched victim of his seduction, a spurious son to drown or strangle. Or it may give him a spurious son, by some wanton, on whom he lavishes the patrimony of his legitimate sons. No matter! The wrong done by him cannot be measured by equal weight with the wrong done to*

him: for he is a man, and claims his right of exemption, by natural superiority.[58]

Unchecked male immorality within marriage resulted in damage to society at large. Creating avenues of legal redress for wives would benefit the institution of marriage and also protect public morality. Left unsaid was how new marital laws would change the choice architecture for unmarried men. Perhaps all men would start to rethink their behavior toward women once they saw that not even husbands were invulnerable to legal challenge. Perhaps such reforms presaged an end to a legally sanctioned double standard and would hold men and women to the same ethical norm—what the next generation of women's rights activists would call the "Single Moral Standard."

Between 1853 and 1857 Parliament debated the topic of married women's rights in fits, their work impeded by the waging of the Crimean War. But in 1857 Lord Palmerston determined to have the proposed Matrimonial Causes Act passed that summer, and the bill began its final passage through the Lords and Commons. Caroline was absent from the chamber, but her voice was heard everywhere. Her closest proxy, Lord Lyndhurst, essentially quoted directly from her pamphlets, and even her erstwhile opponent Lord Brougham declared her *Letter to the Queen* to have been "as clever a thing as ever was written" and decisive in shaping the terms of the debate. In the heat and stench of the London summer, "when men would almost give up Magna Charta itself to avoid another sitting" (according to *The Examiner*), the new law was passed.[59] Four of the bill's clauses would not have been included were it not for Caroline's agitation and her vivid use of her own autobiography to illustrate the wrongs of the existing system.[60] Many of those clauses fatally undermined coverture and ensured its dismantling over the next generation. Both men and women could now sue for divorce on grounds of adultery, and the process of divorce was simplified and handed over to a single, civil court. There had been 193 divorces in England from 1800 to 1857. By the end of the century there would be close to a thousand each year. Most pairings were still for life, but the institution was now a great deal more porous. With marriage less restrictive, love could be more free.[61]

Neither Mary nor Caroline gained much benefit by the new law. Mary, whose health was marred in the late 1840s by crippling headaches, had died in 1851 from a brain tumor. By the time the Matrimonial Causes Act came into effect in 1858, Caroline's own marriage was so marred by legal complexity and procedural convolution that its benefits did not extend to her. She was only liberated by the death of the Right Honourable George Norton in 1875. In 1877 Caroline married again, this time to a far better match—Sir William Maxwell-Stirling, a Scottish baronet, Hispanist, and writer—though their marriage was a short one, for Caroline died, age sixty-nine, only a few months after the two took their vows.

By the end of the 1870s only one member of the original party that had gathered by Lac Léman in the gloomy summer of 1816 was still alive. Unwanted, neglected, and systematically wronged, Claire Clairmont proved to be the great survivor, living to eighty, a life lived half a century longer than those of her great male antagonists, Lord George Byron and Percy Bysshe Shelley. For all her other theatrics, Clairmont had always made clear that she was not a writer. Although a lover of literature, she had never sought literary plaudits for herself. When the rest of the party sat around the Villa Diodati composing their ghost stories she had sequestered herself and occupied herself with more worldly matters. It was the final twist in the serpentine tale of the Shelley-Byron circle (that oddly named group, whose principals died so soon) that it was

Clairmont who would have the final word on the men she had known in her youth and whose poetry and radical doctrines she had admired. In the 2000s a fragment of a memoir Clairmont had written in her old age was discovered in the archives of the New York Public Library. "I have to relate my recollection of two great Poets," it began, "on their account I hope this recital will awaken many profound reflections."

I will commit this sad tale to paper and finally to the public, it is with the intention of demonstrating from actual facts, what evil passion free love assured, what tenderness it dissolves; how it abused affections that should be the solace and balm of life, into a destroying scourge what . . . bitter tears [it] caused to flow, and what victims it immolated [the reader] will behold how the worshippers of free love not only preyed upon one another, but preyed equally upon their own individual selves turning their existence into a perfect hell.

Such will be the picture my recollections of two great poets S[helley] & B[yron]—will present; they were the fondest and most obstinate advocates and partisans and followers of free love . . . it appears to me that in the eternal interest of religion and morality of truth and right require a plain straightforward description of their opinions and conduct.

Under the influence of the doctrine and belief of free love I saw the two first poets of England . . . become monsters of lying, meanness, cruelty and treachery—under the influence of free love Lord B[yron] became a human tyger slaking his thirst for inflicting pain upon defenceless women who under the influence of free love . . . loved him.

The age of Free Love was over.

CHAPTER FIVE

——— ⚊✦⚊ ———

OF MANN AND MEN

In 1902 a burly young man in worker's overalls ducked into a storefront in Los Angeles. He was there to see a fortune-teller. The outfit he wore was a disguise. Jack Johnson was far from the zenith of fame that he would achieve within the decade, but he was still a recognizable figure. Wary of being identified by the fortune-teller and drip fed flattering forecasts he had assumed the outward appearance of an average workingman to ensure his fortune was read fairly. "But I did not fool her. She at once told me that I was a boxer, and recounted some of my past life with such accuracy that I was astounded."

> *She proceeded to tell me many things concerning my future, some*
> *of them so fantastic and so improbable, viewed from the place I*
> *then occupied in life, that I departed from her presence feeling that*
> *she had drawn a highly imaginative picture of my life. She predicted*
> *that I would be the heavy-weight boxing champion; she told me*
> *of my forth-coming marriages and of various affairs that I was*
> *destined to have with women; she told me, almost in detail, of the*
> *adventures and travels that were to mark my later life [and] of my*
> *conflicts with the law.*

Johnson did not give much credence to the woman at the time, but over the years all her prophecies came true. He did become the heavyweight champion. He did have many affairs with many women. Those affairs did bring him in conflict with the law. "The Los Angeles fortune teller still looms conspicuously in my memory," Johnson later wrote, "and there are few developments in my life that do not in some way echo that incidental visit, many years ago, when I stood on the threshold of a life that was to be one of the most picturesque in American history."[1]

Jack Johnson was prone to grandiosity, though his verdict on his own life is hard to dispute. For Jack Johnson was no ordinary celebrity. He was black, and his race would be the single factor that would tip his remarkable career from the atypical to the extraordinary. His insistence on his right to pursue love affairs with white women and his singular success in this field brought him into direct conflict with prevailing racial mores. It also put him on a collision course with one of the great (and largely forgotten) American social experiments: the attempt to regulate seduction through the criminal justice system.

John Arthur Johnson was born in Galveston, Texas, on March 31, 1878, fifteen years after the presidential decree that had freed his parents from slavery and one year after the Corrupt Bargain of 1877 that threatened to return to them, him, and all other black Americans to a kind of bondage. The first thirty years of Johnson's life were shaped by the failed attempt, known as Reconstruction, to heal the wounds of civil war and slavery. This Northern-led attempt to reconstruct the South was bitterly resisted and came to an end following the contested election of 1876. Thereafter, Southern white supremacists tilted the trajectory of their section toward what they called "Redemption." This aimed to put black Americans squarely back in their place and to ensure that white rule would remain unchallenged in the South for generations to come. These were the years of lynching, the institution of the Jim Crow caste system, the de facto disenfranchisement of a de jure enfranchised people.

In his childhood, Johnson was partially protected from these bleak historical conditions. Reconstruction had created space for a small, besieged but tenacious business- and property-owning black middle class who had their own newspapers, their own schools and universities, and, most visibly, their own elected officials at the state and local level. The Galveston of Johnson's youth exposed him to these kinds of black success stories. Furthermore, his hometown was one of the great Gulf ports, like Mobile and New Orleans, and tolerated a far greater degree of cultural and racial diversity than was typical in the vast Southern hinterland. Johnson grew up knowing of black politicians, playing with white street kids, and exposed to the great carnival of human folly that always accompanies the presence of large numbers of thirsty sailors on shore leave. His parents, Henry and Tiny Johnson, had a profound respect for education and ensured their children had access to as much schooling as their straitened circumstances allowed. Johnson loved learning and would remain an omnivorous autodidact, but he hated school and by the age of thirteen was working on the docks in Galveston. However positive his own memories and experiences of Galveston, he was still a black man living in a former Confederate state. The threat of violence always hovered about the edges of his experience. When Johnson was fourteen, a brutal incident in Texas was a stark reminder of the omnipresence of racial discipline in the Old South.

Near the end of January 1893, four-year-old Myrtle Vance was found murdered in the woods near Paris, Texas, a small city in the northeast of the state not far from the Oklahoma state line. The community was shocked by her death, and this shock was soon compounded by the spread of rumors that she had been raped during the assault. The sexual aspect to her murder gave it at once a racial dimension. Bishop Haygood, in an apology for what was to follow, described a community inflamed by the gruesome details of the attack on a white child. Vance, Haygood stated, had been "first outraged with demoniacal cruelty and then taken by her heels and torn asunder in the mad wantonness of gorilla ferocity." Later investigations would prove that she had not been so outraged, but the damage was done and the hunt was on for the necessarily black "gorilla" who had raped and killed little Myrtle Vance. Myrtle's father was a former policeman with a reputation for the rough treatment of those in his custody. Locals began to suspect that some former prisoner of his was avenging the father's sins upon the child. Their interest alighted upon Henry Smith, a mentally impaired black teenager who did chores and odd jobs for whites in Paris. For a few tense days the sinister attentions of the town's white citizens began to concentrate on poor Smith. The twin facts of Smith's innocence and his disability prevented him from readily understanding the horrifying position he was now in. When, at length, he realized what was alleged, he fled to Hope, Arkansas. A posse was formed and sent to fetch him, which they did. Upon learning of his capture, Ida Wells reported,

> News flashed across the country that the white Christian people
> of Paris, Texas and the communities thereabout had deliberately
> determined to lay aside all forms of law and inaugurate an entirely
> new form of punishment for the murder. They absolutely refused to
> make any inquiry as to the sanity or insanity of their prisoner, but
> set the day and hour [of his lynching].

The nation was given fair warning about what the citizens of Paris intended to do to Henry Smith, but the savagery with which they did it appalled even those long-accustomed to intense racist violence. Back in Paris, Smith was met at the train station by a crowd of an estimated ten thousand people and was then paraded down "Main Street to the square, around the square down Clarksville street to Church Street, thence to the open prairies about 300 yards from the Texas & Pacific depot." There in a dismal field, a drab wooden scaffold with "Justice" daubed in white paint on a plank on its front awaited Smith. According to witnesses, Smith did not seem to understand what was to happen to him and had seemed cheerfully overwhelmed as he was led through the crowded, queerly jubilant town. It was only as he was being lashed to the stake on the scaffold in that field that the reality of what he was to endure finally dawned on him. The town had now emptied into the field before him. The mayor had order schools and whisky shops closed. Additional police had been called in to manage the crowds, but not to interfere with their purpose. Men, women, and children, on foot, horseback, and wagon, some with picnics, others with snacks and alcohol, watched as the men of the Vance family systematically tortured Smith with hot irons for close to an hour. They had come "from every part of this section," one newspaper reported, they "came from Dallas, Fort Worth, Sherman, Denison, Bonham, Texarkana, Fort Smith, Ark., and a party of fifteen came from Hempstead county, Arkansas, where he was captured. Every train that came in was loaded to its utmost capacity, and there were demands at many points for special trains to bring the people here to see the unparalleled punishment for an unparalleled crime." Some turned away, but most looked placidly on as the Vance men went about their butchery:

> *Every groan from the fiend, every contortion of his body was cheered by the thickly packed crowd of 10,000 persons. The mass of beings 600 yards in diameter, the scaffold being the center. After burning the feet and legs, the hot irons—plenty of fresh ones being at hand—were rolled up and down Smith's stomach, back, and arms. Then the eyes were burned out and irons were thrust down his throat.*

According to some accounts Smith was still alive "when kerosene was poured upon him, cottonseed hulls placed beneath him," and he was set on fire.

In the crowd was one Reverend King of New York state. He had known Smith and privately doubted that he was responsible for Myrtle's death. He attended Smith's murder with the intention of silently praying for the condemned man. But once witness to the full horror of the spectacle King could no longer contain himself. He begged the crowd to stop the torture or at the very least to remove the children from the crowd of spectators. King had gravely misjudged his audience. He was knocked to the ground with a rifle butt, beaten, dragged to his home, allowed to pack a travel bag, and then placed on the first train North with a one-way ticket. Back home in the Empire State a journalist for the *New York Sun* asked the reverend if he would ever return to Paris. "I shall never go south again," he replied, "the impressions of that awful day will stay with me forever."[2]

All racial politics are sexual politics because all racists fetishize racial purity, and purity can only be sustained through the enforcement of a strict sexual apartheid. In the American South, lynching was the most infamous form of this socio-sexual policing and is rightly remembered and memorialized as such. For all its variety and brilliance, Jack Johnson's own life would be played out in the shadow of the scaffold. Nonetheless, it was another form of sexual discipline that would ultimately ensnare him. For alongside the extrajudicial phenomenon of lynching existed a de jure system for the punishment of sexual transgressions.

The Americans had inherited from the English the four civil law actions—Criminal Conversation, Alienation of Affections, Breach of Promise to Marriage, and Seduction—that policed marriage, sex, and courtship. In the United States they were referred to by the wonderfully

saccharine name of the "heart balm acts," a group of legal instruments
that sought to salve wounded hearts with cash compensation. In the
mid–nineteenth century these English legal devices were used as the basis
for a peculiarly American exercise. Between 1848 and 1935 the United
States embarked on one of the most ambitious, most expansive, and
most intrusive judicial experiments in all its history: the attempt to regulate seduction by legal fiat. Initially this involved the reform of the civil
suit of Seduction such that women could bring suits against men on
their own initiative.[3] The movement began in Michigan in 1846 and
soon spread around the country. By 1913, eighteen states had enacted
reforms liberalizing the use of the seduction tort.[4] These reforms led to
the development of a new language to describe sexual behavior. Courts
combined legal and moral principles to articulate what seduction was,
who a seducer was, and who the law would identify as a victim of seduction. In the 1856 Iowa case of *Gover v. Dill* the court held that evidence of active and organized misrepresentation was key to determining
whether seduction had occurred. The victim had to have been moved
"by some promise or artifice, . . . by his flattery or deception." Likewise
consent, or failure to resist, or evidence that "she had previously prostituted herself to the embraces of other men" could be a defense for the
man. All men could be seducers; only certain types of women could be
seduced. Using a variation of a phrase that would recur throughout the
great American legal experiment in seduction, the Iowa court ruled that
"the person seduced must have been previously of chaste character—
that she has yet preserved that priceless jewel that is the peculiar badge
of the virtuous unmarried female." This was a shift from an economic
understanding of a woman's worth to a moral one. From an interest in a
loss of services to a loss of moral standing. But it also created a new kind
of moral economy—who possessed that priceless jewel? For if a court
decided that a woman did indeed possess it, then the plaintiff could be in

for a major windfall. Damages could run into the thousands of dollars. The high watermark came with the 1915 decision in *Eller v. Lord*, where a South Dakota court awarded $25,000 to the plaintiff—$650,000 in 2019 terms.[5]

But this tinkering with civil suits was fairly minor when compared with the revolutionary decision to criminalize Seduction. Starting with New York in 1848, states began to threaten men with fines and imprisonment for what was deemed consensual but exploitative sexual behavior. The text of the New York law was typical of what was to come. Seduction was a "crime against society" and those found guilty of it could face a maximum of five years in prison and a fine of up to $1,000. Crucially, a seduced woman had to be "an unmarried female of previous chaste character."[6] These laws were adopted throughout the country. By 1885, twenty-seven of thirty-eight states had such statutes. By 1921, thirty-seven of forty-eight states had them on the books. These laws had common features. They all required that plaintiffs meet certain subjective moral standards. Lewd women, bawds, and adventuresses were not welcome in courts, nor were prostitutes or immoral characters. Most, but not all, states required that the women involved had to be unmarried and some held that they had to be below a certain age. When it came to defining seduction, most states understood seduction in relation to marriage with twenty-two of thirty-seven state laws requiring that the "prosecution must show either a promise of marriage or a feigned or pretended marriage." More generally, seduction was understood as the

> Use of arts, persuasions, or wiles to overcome the resistance of the female who is not disposed, of her volition, to step aside from the path of virtue. . . . Any seductive arts or promises, where the female involuntarily and reluctantly yields thereto, are sufficient.

In all but three states with these laws the offense of Seduction was classified as a felony, and conviction could lead to a sentence of between one and twenty years in prison as well as a fine. Some states allowed for men to avoid the jailhouse by marrying their victims, but women were by no means obliged to accept such legally induced proposals.[7]

The proponents of this legislation were largely married, middle-class women. They claimed to be acting in the interest of vulnerable unmarried girls, but the stories of those whom they looked to protect were far from flattering. The landmark New York statute of 1848 was the result of over a decade of sustained activism on the part of the New York Female Moral Reform Society (NYFMRS), a female-run association that by the 1840s had fifty thousand members and hundreds of affiliate organizations. The women of the NYFMRS were deeply concerned about the moral dangers faced by young women coming from the countryside to seek work in the city. In their literature they dwell repeatedly on the threat posed to innocent provincials by the theatre, the dancehall, and other urban arenas where men and women met and mingled without parental oversight. The seduction of young women in such places would result in a fall from chastity to sin, followed by a life of spinsterhood or, worse, prostitution. These fears were premised on a belief that women were by nature ingenuous and could be easily tricked into engaging in harmful behaviors. The female mind was so impressionable, these activists believed, that it had to be protected from all kinds of malign influences. They were particularly preoccupied with the threat posed to the young consciences by literature. All NYFMRS members had to pledge upon joining to "discountenance all lewd books, poems, and pictures." The organization's journal, *The Advocate*, warned against "the wondrous powers of fiction," which worked upon the female mind just as alcohol worked upon the male body. The works of Byron and Edward Bulwer-Lytton were singled out

as being singularly pernicious. The characteristics of fiction— its artifice, its mastery of rhetoric and storytelling, its capacity to beguile the
mind and suspend reason—were the same of the "wily arts by which
the young and unsuspecting are seduced and ruined." Men who used
flowery language or rhetorical trickery in conversation were to be
avoided. The use of double entendre and wordplay by a man were a
sure sign that he had ruinous intentions.[8]

The tropes of the successful New York campaign would be repeated
across the country over the next seventy years. The forces of the law had
to be mobilized to protect women who lacked the faculties to navigate
the modern sexual market themselves. However, not all women were
deemed worthy of protection. Courts and juries now got to choose who
was worthy of legal protection by deciding whether a woman was of
"previous chaste character." This meant that men now sat in judgment of
women's characters even though those women came to court as plaintiffs,
not defendants. Middle-class men tended to be much more magnanimous
in their rulings when middle-class women were involved. Questions of
moral standing inevitably collided with questions of social standing, and
courts were haunted by the bourgeois presumption of working-class dissolution. Poor and working-class women who brought suits against their
social betters were regularly smeared as whores and hussies. Race also
came into play. There was not infrequently a correlation between the
severity of a state's racial laws and the severity of its seduction laws.

The state of Alabama had some of the harshest laws in both spaces.
The wording of the seduction statute was so open to interpretation that
virtually all consensual sexual activity fell within its purview. Running
parallel to the state's stringent seduction laws were its even more stringent laws on what was then known as "miscegenation," or interracial
sexual relations. Under Alabama law, "any white person and any negro,
or the descendant of any negro to the third generation" were not allowed

to "intermarry or live in adultery or fornication with each other" and risked jail time or "hard labor" if they were found guilty of so doing.

The laws regulating seduction and the laws regulating interracial love formally overlapped, as well. Seduction laws did not tend to mention race, but their companion laws governing racial love affairs had direct bearing upon who could and could not file a seduction suit. A black woman who wanted to bring a seduction suit against a white man in the state of Alabama faced two barriers. First, as interracial marriage was illegal, she could not realistically claim to have been tricked into sex by the promise of marriage. Furthermore, as interracial sex, or fornication, was illegal, she would essentially be pleading guilty to a charge of misce-genation and would consequently be vulnerable to judicial persecution. On the other side of the equation, black men were at constant risk of accusations of sexual impropriety made by white women. In a culture that granted white women a great deal of judicial freedom to bring suits against men on the grounds of sexual misconduct, allegations made by white women—inside or outside the courts—against a black man were almost never fact-checked and were almost always enthusiastically pun-ished, though in those instances it was more often lynch law that pre-dominated rather than any statute on the law books. The Texas of Jack Johnson's youth had strict seduction statutes on the books and a grim record of extrajudicial lynchings.[9]

Although it would later upend his life, the development of an elaborate legal structure to police seduction was far from Johnson's life on the Gal-veston docks. The world of the Galveston stevedores was a harsh one, and his experiences there would set him on the path to the heavyweight championship. His colleagues on the docks were "some of the toughest

and hardest-boiled men imaginable," he recalled. "To them, fighting was
one of the important functions of existence. They fought upon every occasion and on any pretext. They shot craps and indulged in other forms of
gambling with almost as much ardor as they fought." Johnson's young
age did not spare him from participation in these scraps and confronted
with their inevitability he sought out boxing lessons to survive his workplace. Athletic, fast, and powerful, Johnson quickly gained a reputation
on the docks as a strong fighter and was soon taking on all comers.[10]

Even outside the rough-and-tumble world of the Galveston dock-
workers, boxing in the 1890s was a very different sport from what it is
now. Bare-knuckle boxing persisted into the 1880s, and the first formal
heavyweight title fight did not take place until John L. Sullivan fought
Gentleman Jim Corbett in New Orleans in 1892. Even as it was being
gradually formalized, boxing—or prizefighting, as it was commonly
known—remained an astonishingly violent enterprise. Fighters wore no
mouth guards, and the gloves were so small (customarily around five
ounces) that they were no more than leather sheaths affording little protection. The average fight was scheduled for twenty rounds, forty rounds
was the norm for title fights, and matches as along as sixty rounds were
not unheard of. Inside the ring there was no limit on the number of
knockdowns a fighter could sustain and no neutral corner that a boxer
had to retreat to in the event of one. There was no ringside doctor;
fixed fights were so frequent as to be unremarked upon; it was not
uncommon for referees, cornermen, and audience members to be armed
with revolvers. Not a few fighters died in the ring.

As a consequence of all this, boxing was illegal in several states,
including Johnson's native Texas. Johnson's first formal fight, in 1895,
against a dockworker named John "Must Have It" Lee in Josie's Beer
Garden in Galveston, ended up being fought on the beach after the
police raided the original site. Johnson won the bout and the $1.50 in

prize money that came with it. Johnson spied a path to easy money and sought to make boxing his profession, despite the plethora of legal, medical, and social risks that accompanied the pursuit.

The gamble seemed to pay off. Johnson's abilities rapidly outgrew the opportunities on offer in the Galveston area, and at nineteen he decided to "cast myself wholly into the lap of fate" and start riding the rails in search of fighting opportunities. Johnson's account of these early years are tinged with his customary good humor and love of sly understatement. A powerfully built young black boxer hoboing about the South in the last years of the nineteenth century could not expect a warm welcome in many towns. Life on the rails and on the road was lonely, financially insecure, and unsafe. Johnson recalled the kind of reception he became accustomed to receiving in provincial America:

> [In] some of the smaller towns where a stranger was quickly
> discovered, police officers and constables manifested deep concern
> in me. In fact, they were generally so deeply interested that they
> often insisted that I remain as a guest of their town. On these
> occasions, I was introduced to the town Judge, who pried into my
> personal affairs and asked me embarrassing questions. Usually,
> after my meetings with the Judge, I was instructed to hasten out
> of town, which was exactly what I wished to do, and what I was
> trying to do when the police interfered. Sometimes I was detained,
> quarters being assigned me in the town jail.[11]

But he loved the freedom of a life on the move, and success and adventure came easily to the voluble young man. At a battle royal in Springfield, Illinois, his masterful performance caught the eye of a promoter named Johnnie Connors, who brought him to Chicago for the first time. There, in 1899, he fought the fearsome black boxer Klondike Haynes and lost, and then lost what money he had earned from the fight at a nearby racetrack. It was a rocky introduction to a city that would become his base of operations for close to two decades. Heading east, he went to New York City, where he fell in with the legendary welterweight Joe Walcott, the Barbados Demon, who took him up to Boston to work in his training camp as a sparring partner. When that gig ran its course he returned south, fighting Klondike twice more in Memphis and Galveston, and meeting with more success on those occasions. Back home, local promoters began to tire both of Johnson's winning streak and his brash self-confidence. They sought out a white fighter whom they believed would beat the upstart black boxer. They chose Joe Choynski, a Jewish boxer based out of California. In February 1901, Choynski duly arrived in Galveston, stepped inside a ring in Harmony Hall, and in the third round knocked out Jack Johnson for the first time in his professional career. At this point, with Johnson flat on the canvas and Choynski celebrating a quick fight and a fast buck, five Texas Rangers entered the ring brandishing pistols and arrested both men for violating the state's ban on prizefighting.

Johnson's arrest and subsequent detention in the Galveston lockup was arguably the most propitious event in his long and celebrated career. The terms of their confinement were not as uncomfortable as they might have been. Sheriff Henry Thomas allowed both men to sleep at home, but they had to spend the daytime in the prison compound. There, for the entertainment of law enforcement and curious locals, the two interned boxers sparred for several hours each day. This was to be a formative experience for Johnson. At a time when most boxers, and most boxing fans, considered the essence of the sport to be the brute application of power along linear lines of attack, Choynski treated pugilism as an art form. He had studied its nuances, earned an appreciation for its delicacies, and in the process formed his own unique, evasive style that privileged an intelligent defensive method over a hard-charging offensive manner. Over the course of twenty-three days together, he imparted the secrets of the sweet science to Johnson. He taught him how to feint, dodge, slip. He taught him how to catch punches, how to counterpunch, how to manage his opponent around the ring. He taught him the dark arts of the clinch, where an opponent could be tied up and savaged with invisible but deadly body shots. Choynski gave Johnson the tools that would turn him from a good fighter into a great boxer. Johnson would scarcely lose a fight over the next fifteen years.[12]

Johnson's newfound style was the perfect match for his ostentatious appearance and teasing personality. A photo of him from the year of the Choynski fight shows a powerful, trim young man with shoulders like cannonballs and enormous, veined forearms. But what stands out is his head. Johnson shaved his head (he would later go bald, joking that this was from too much "makin' babies"), and this, coupled with his large ingenuous eyes and soft features, lent him an appearance that was not so much youthful as baby-faced. Johnson's great size and strength was made all the more eerie by these gleefully neotenous features and by his famously exuberant smile, made all the more eye-catching by the gold-capped front teeth he had fitted once his finances allowed for the luxury. The final component of Johnson's style was his permanent good humor toward the press and public and the unaffected condescension with which he treated his opponents inside the ring. Johnson loved conversation and the back-and-forth of barroom banter and saw no reason why it should stop inside the ring. The Johnson who marches spasmodically around the ring in the surviving fight films from the period is constantly talking. Looming above his opponents he laughs at their missed hits, applauds when they somehow land a blow, and just smiles and shakes his head when they charge forward at him. In the clinch he would maneuver his opponent around the canvas, pausing to flirt with his girlfriends at ringside, or to taunt the opposing cornermen, or to dispense thoughts to the assembled ring reporters. The effect was maddening; the jibes made unbearable to white boxers by the blackness of his skin.[13]

In 1898 Johnson had married a black woman from Galveston named Mary Austen. Not much is known about her, except that the she left him in 1902. Johnson was fond of Austen and mourned her departure, but freed from the constraints marriage he was now able to immerse himself in the sporting world. To be a sport or a sporting man (or sporting women) meant something quite significant in the first decades of the twentieth century. A sport could be an actual athlete like Johnson. It could also refer to someone who associated with sporting activities, like a racehorse trainer or boxing promoter. Furthermore, it could be applied to someone who simply enjoyed going to the races, or to a fight, or who liked to gamble on the outcome of either. A sport might be someone who simply sought the company of other sportsmen. Most cardsharps, bookies, dandies, and hustlers could be classified as sports. A sporting woman was often, but not always, a prostitute. A sporting house was a brothel. The capacious world of the sports was something halfway between the violent world of the frontier and the sanitized world of celebrity. It had one foot in the underworld and the other in the headlines. At a time when sex, liquor, and organized sports themselves were subject to a high degree of control, the sporting scene was one of relaxed social and sexual standards. Importantly, it was also a world where blacks and whites mingled much more readily than they did in the rest of society. As Johnson's boxing career took off he became the uncrowned king of the sports and one of the great witnesses to one of the most decadent and unrestrained social scenes in all American history.[14]

In 1903 Johnson fell in with a new woman. Her name was Clara Kerr, and she was most definitely a sport. Kerr and Johnson spent, by his account, two years of bliss on the road together, her dutifully accompanying him across the country in pursuit of fights. Money was tight at times—Johnson was still not earning purses as large as he would have liked but was nevertheless spending prodigiously—but Johnson believed the relationship to be stable and loving. Then in Los Angeles, in October 1905, a rival sport appeared in Johnson's household. His name was William Bryant. He was a horse trainer whom Johnson had known back east, and Johnson considered him an "old and intimate friend"—intimate enough that he invited Bryant to share their home. But there was no honor among sports. While Johnson was not looking, a relationship developed between Bryant and Kerr and one day Johnson returned home to find the two had vanished along with his money, his jewelry, and a good deal of his wardrobe. He informed the police and soon the two fugitive lovers were tracked to Tucson, Arizona. Kerr and Johnson made sweet, somehow, and then relocated to Chicago. But the move to the Midwest did little to mend their relationship or reform Clara Kerr. In September 1906, with Johnson low on money again, she absconded taking what little he had with her. Once more Johnson came home to find his home ransacked and his lover gone. Once more he searched for her. But this time she had gone for good.

This second loss and doubled humiliation was too much for the prideful boxer. "The world became a void for me," Johnson recalled, a void he tried to fill with alcohol and hard living. Within weeks he was penniless, psychologically scarred, and physically wrecked. Concerned friends lent him money, and at length he decided to travel New York City to seek out more fights. He was so poor that before boarding the train a friend had to forcibly lend him a dollar to sustain him on the journey. Johnson might have had a single dollar to his name, but he was still a sport, and he spent the money in fine style:

> Of this dollar I gave the train porter 50 cents; I bought two cigars
> with another quarter and the remaining quarter I tossed to a
> newsboy at the station when I arrived in New York.[15]

If Johnson is to be believed, this second betrayal by Clara Kerr also resulted in a radical and fateful sexual decision. "The heartaches which Mary Austin and Clara Kerr had caused me," he wrote, "led me to forswear colored women and to determine that my lot henceforth would be cast only with white women."[16] From 1906 onward he would never again be seen in public with a black woman by his side. There would be three legally recognized Mrs. Johnsons, and a couple of other Mrs. Johnsons introduced with a wink and a smile. All of them would be white. This at a time when black Americans were regularly lynched for much less. Johnson knew the risks he was taking, but he did not seem to care. Besides, his decision owed more to egotism than to provocation. "I will never believe that he married his white woman just to spite white people," one friend later wrote. "I just think he did what he wanted to do because he wanted to do it."[17]

Johnson's fateful decision to cross one color line came just as he was figuring out his passage over another. By 1906, Johnson was confronted by a problem familiar to talented contenders. He was twenty-eight; he had won fifty-three of fifty-six fights (as well as scores of undocumented bouts); he was in possession of a difficult, dangerous fighting style. It was both demeaning and unprofitable to seek matches with fighters of a lower caliber; his pugilistic peers—and they were few—did not want to meet him in the ring. What Johnson wanted, needed, and believed was already his was the title of heavyweight champion. But he could not have it. Ever since John L. Sullivan had been recognized as the first heavyweight champion in 1885, white boxers had drawn the color line. Though most had fought black boxers on the way up, they considered it their duty once champion to keep the title in white hands. Jim Jeffries, the glowering ex-boilermaker who had watched from the sidelines as Johnson dismantled his younger brother, Jack, in 1902, was typical in this respect. Jeffries held the championship for six years from 1899, and while he did he would not defend it against a black man. "I will never fight a negro," he stated, "back to the boiler works first."[18] But in 1905 Jeffries retired. There was nobody to fight, or at least nobody white to fight, he claimed, and so he would relinquish the championship and retreat to his California farm undefeated. The title then passed briefly into Marvin Hart's hands. He had beaten Johnson only months before, in a controversial decision acceding to the title, but once champion he too drew the color line. Then, in February 1906, Hart lost the title to Tommy Burns in Los Angeles and Johnson had his chance.

Burns had stated that he would fight anyone of any race, creed, or nationality to prove that he was the world heavyweight champion. This did not mean, however, that Burns was willing to fight Johnson straightaway. A childhood of despairing poverty had impressed on Burns a thoroughly realistic attitude toward personal enrichment. He understood that the heavyweight title was license to print money—but only while it was in your possession. A title lost was worth nothing. If Johnson wanted a title fight against Burns, he was going to have to find a way of making it worth the champion's while.

What followed was a very public and very global attempt by the contender to shame the champion into fighting him while enlisting the press—who were as skeptical of the stubby, unprepossessing Tommy Burns as they were of the brash, showboating Jack Johnson—into his campaign to get a title fight. Burns toured North America, Europe, and Australasia, taking easy fights, participating in vaudeville and variety shows, and generally cashing in on the title wherever he went. Johnson was hot on his heels. He fought all over the United States, in Kansas, Maryland, Pennsylvania, and Oregon; he fought in Australia, twice, and once in Britain. He followed Burns to his fights and heckled him from ringside. He spoke to the press constantly, mocking the regnant champion and outlining ad nauseam why he had earned the right to face

Burns inside the ring. Still Burns would not fight him. "I virtually had to
mow my way to Burns . . . even King Edward of England was disgusted
by Burns" tactics and called him a "Yankee Bluffer" The true thoughts
of Edward VII on the matter of the Burns-Johnson matchup are likely
unknowable, but on the other side of the British Empire Johnson's noisy
campaign for the title had convinced one man to put up the money necessary to get Burns into the ring with the black contender.

Hugh D. McIntosh was an Australian businessman and impresario
with a singular vision of how to profit from the confluence of sports,
race, and naval power in Sydney Harbour in 1908. That year, President Theodore Roosevelt's newly constructed armada was scheduled
to stop in Australia as part of its two-year demonstration of American
sea power. The flotilla was known as the Great White Fleet. Its mission
served no formal military purpose. Its two-year circumnavigation of
the globe was presented as a gesture of fraternal goodwill to its fellow
Anglo-Saxon powers. It was also a carelessly concealed challenge to
two of them: Great Britain and Germany. Finally, it was a clear bid
for mastery in the Pacific, where a Japanese naval empire was consol-
idating following the destruction of the tsar's fleet at Tsushima during
the Russo-Japanese war of 1905. The imperialist logic of the day held
that geopolitical struggles were also racial struggles. The clash of great
powers on land and at sea was simply the Darwinian struggle for existence writ large. It took a man with McIntosh's peculiar, cynical entrepreneurial genius to see that in this perfervid atmosphere an interracial
heavyweight title fight was simply the same struggle for existence writ
small. The gate would be made by rowdy American sailors, Australians bloated with racial comity, and the promise of international film
sales. McIntosh met Burns's demand for $30,000 and offered Johnson
$5,000. Both men accepted. The fight was set for Sydney on Boxing
Day, 1908.

"In Australia I was warmly received," Johnson recalled, "not with-standing the fact that Burns was the favorite in the betting, which was to be expected because of the racial element involved."[19] As ever, he was downplaying the extent of the animus displayed toward him. McIntosh's whole marketing plan was premised on racializing the bout, and the global anglophone press was rooting for Tommy Burns on purely racial grounds. Not for the last time, both the press and the bookies allowed racial longing to obscure pugilistic judgment. The match was a mismatch. Johnson toyed with the smaller Burns for thirteen rounds before putting him out in the fourteenth. The police intervened to stop the filming seconds before the final blow landed. As such, the moment when Jack Johnson became the first black heavyweight champion was never recorded on film. Sitting at ringside was Jack London, then the most highly paid novelist in America, covering the fight for the *New York Herald*. "There was no fight," he told the *Herald*'s readers. "No Armenian massacre could compare with the hopeless slaughter that took place today. The fight, if fight it could be called, was like that between a pygmy and a colossus . . . But one thing now remains. . . . The White Man must be rescued."

The urgent need for white rescue would become apparent to all when Johnson returned to North America in the spring of 1909. After spending a few months enjoying himself in Australia, Johnson steamed home, arriving in Vancouver on March 9, 1909. The press corps was waiting for him. When he appeared on the gangway, looking resplendent in a trilby and full-length double-breasted overcoat, the newsmen got their glimpse of the first black champion. They also made the acquaintance of a small, toothy women, wrapped in furs, and sporting a huge white plume in her hat. She was introduced as Mrs. Jack Johnson, formerly Ms. Nellie O'Brien of Philadelphia. She was white.

Nellie O'Brien was in fact Hattie McClay of Mississippi, and she was not Johnson's wife. She was a sport and an all-round good-time girl who had fallen in with Johnson in New York in the summer of 1907. She liked to drink, dance, and play music—the couple had entertained the press in Sydney by playing the fiddle together—and was endlessly tolerant of Johnson's caddish ways. McClay could not by any means be described as a great beauty, and it seems that Johnson enjoyed her company more than anything else. "Hattie was a splendid gal," Johnson sighs in his memoir, a description more cousinly than amorous.[20] Not that these nuances mattered to the upholders of America's stark racial order. The apparent marriage of a white woman to the slayer of white manhood caused grave consternation. Galveston's planned homecoming celebrations were quickly canceled, the authorities stating that Johnson would be arrested for violation of Texas's anti-miscegenation statutes if he entered the state with McClay. But Johnson had long outgrown his hometown. He headed first to New York, and then to Chicago, a city that he now knew well and that would become his home for the next four years.[21] With his winnings Johnson set himself and his mother up in a house in the heart of the South Side's Black Belt, a community populated by tens of thousands of African-Americans, and only a few blocks away from pleasure houses of the Levee, Chicago's vice district, where racial divisions were relaxed in service to the higher cause of making merry. Sometime that spring, he met Belle Schreiber, a twenty-year-old from Milwaukee then working in the Everleigh Club, the most exclusive bordello in the Levee. Johnson quickly wooed her, at which point the proprietors of the Everleigh Club fired her for breaching their own strict rules on interracial relations. Belle started touring the country with Johnson (and, at times, McClay). That October she was in the crowd when he devastated Stanley Ketchel, the middleweight phenomenon and arch-rake, in San Francisco. Less than two weeks after the Ketchel fight, Johnson was in New York where he met a third woman at a Long Island racecourse. Her name was Etta Duryea. A cultivated woman from a privileged home, Duryea was a sometime actress and former loving wife to a wealthy property developer named Clarence Duryea. By the time she met Johnson, she and Clarence were living apart and Etta was dipping her toes in the sporting scene. Johnson's courtship was swift. By the end of the year she was immersed in his world, spending Christmas with him and Tiny Johnson at their Chicago home on South Wabash Avenue. Also present were Belle Schreiber and Hattie McClay. It was not, by any account, a peaceful holiday period.[22]

What white America made of the spectacle of a black champion cavorting around the country with several white women can be readily imagined. The white press endlessly editorialized against Johnson's very public flouting of the color line. The black press pleaded for modesty, lest Johnson's antics endanger the lives of his kinsmen. Death threats flowed in from all over the country. Johnson lived in full knowledge of white society's lethal disapproval of his interracial relations. While touring in the Midwest in 1909, a taxi carrying him and Etta broke down in Minneapolis–St. Paul. A mob quickly gathered, and the couple were only saved from harm by police intervention.

What many whites craved was to see Johnson cut down to size. Some wanted him lynched and were happy to say so. But many more would settle for his lawful humiliation in the ring. They had just the man for the job: the undefeated Jim Jeffries. Ever since Burns had hit the canvas in Sydney, the cry had gone up for Jeffries to return to the ring to defeat Johnson and redeem the championship. Jeffries resisted for some time. He was in his mid-thirties and grown fat from sitting on his farm and watching the alfalfa grow. He was also a legendary drinker, and years of whiskey consumption had dulled his reflexes. But he hated Johnson sincerely. He hated his "yellow" fighting style. He hated his white girlfriends. He hated his black skin.[23] For months the press did little else but tout Jeffries's Olympian strength and belittle Johnson's abilities. Journalists, ex- and active fighters, and concerned citizens had visited Jeffries on his farm to beg him to take up the mantle. Then, in November 1909, boxing promoter Tex Rickard stepped up with an offer of a $101,000 purse. Avarice and misplaced racial pride won out over realism and a quiet retirement. That month Jeffries and Johnson met with Rickard in New Jersey to finalize the details. In December the contracts were signed in a public ceremony in Manhattan. The Fight of the Century was on.

The bout was set for July 4, 1910. The symbolism of the date was crude but compelling. This was to be the day that the white championship was liberated from black hands—a second Independence Day. Jeffries needed the time. He had been out of the fight game for five years. He had to regain his touch and shrink from an unwieldy 340 pounds to his old fighting weight of 220 pounds. The task ahead of him was daunting; the pressure put upon him by an increasingly hysterical public intense. Johnson, meanwhile, had to straighten out his own affairs. McClay and Schreiber were being edged out by Duryea, and the two sporting women were increasingly living apart from the champion. This suited Duryea, but she found it hard to adjust to Johnson's peripatetic lifestyle and serial infidelities. She never would.

Whatever pain he caused her and whatever her misgivings about their relationship, she was dutifully in the crowd as Mrs. Jack Johnson when he met Jim Jeffries in the ring in Reno that July. Jeffries had done what many thought was impossible and shed over one hundred pounds during training. He had sparred with Johnson's old foe Joe Choynski and his training had been supervised by revered former champions John L. Sullivan and Gentleman Jim Corbett. The press feasted on every trace of Jeffries's return to form, and going into the fight the betting odds began to widen in favor of the grizzled ex-champion. As the day drew near white Americans succumbed to a kind of collective delusion concerning Jeffries's invincibility. The outcome of the fight was already known:

Jeffries would whip Johnson, and whip him bad. The only problem was that Johnson was not behaving like a man about to be obliterated by a vengeful white fighter. "The man is a puzzle," the *Chicago Tribune* wrote of Johnson,

Physically, the greatest athlete the coloured race had produced and mentally as keen as a razor in a sort of undeveloped way, he fiddles away on his bull fiddle, swaps jokes with ready wit, shoots craps, plays baseball, listens dreamily to classical love songs on the phonograph and is going to fight Jim Jeffries for the world's championship one week from tomorrow.[24]

This was not the countenance of a condemned man. The *San Francisco Examiner*, channeling, perhaps, submerged memories of Henry Smith's unwitting progress to the scaffold in Paris, Texas, suggested that Johnson's carefree demeanor was evidence of "the same cheerful indifference to coming events [that has] marked others of the same race even while standing in the very shadow of the gallows."[25]

Once again the press and the bookmakers had it badly wrong. The fight was scheduled for a grueling forty-five rounds. Jeffries made it through fourteen, lurching forward repeatedly to get his man, only to get tangled in Johnson's longer arms and then savaged in the clinch by vicious uppercuts. In the fifteenth Jeffries went down, then he went down a second time; he was pulled to his feet by several cornermen only to be knocked to his knees for a third, final time.

The victory in Reno made Johnson a rich man and the undisputed heavyweight champion. It also made him a hero to black Americans, many of whom took to the streets to show their appreciation. But nationwide celebrations at Johnson's victory morphed into nationwide race riots as whites lashed out against jubilant blacks. Racial violence roared through the nation, afflicting provincial towns and major cities alike. In Roanoke, Virginia, "a small race war" broke out, according to the local newspaper, because of "the word of a fresh Negro" on the subject of Johnson's victory. In Norfolk, Virginia, white sailors staged pitched battles against celebrating blacks. In Washington, D.C., marine units hunted down black soldiers, seeking vicarious revenge for Jeffries. In towns as large as Atlanta and as small Covington, Kentucky, the whole police force and reserves were called out to keep the peace. In New York, mobs of thousands of white men gathered in central Manhattan and attacked any and all black faces they saw. When the police waded into rescue one victim they found him (alive) with a rope around his neck.[26] In his autobiography, Louis Armstrong recalled the day of Jack Johnson's victory as one of the most terrifying of his life. Armstrong was eight years old and working as a newsboy in New Orleans:

> That day I was going to get my supply of papers from Charlie, who employed a good many colored boys like myself. On Canal Street I saw a crowd of colored boys running like mad toward me. I asked one of them what had happened. "You better get started, black boy," he said breathlessly as he started to pull me along. "Jack Johnson has just knocked out Jim Jeffries. The white boys are sore about it and they're going to take it out on us." He did not have to do any urging. I lit out and passed the other boys in a flash.[27]

Such scenes were repeated in Cincinnati, Kansas City, St. Louis, Omaha, Houston, and Los Angeles. In Congress, politicians from both parties started to peddle the tendentious narrative that the race riots had been stoked by nationwide access to the film footage of the fight. A move was made to ban the interstate transportation of fight films—the same use of the Commerce Clause to control public morality that later underwrote the legal logic of the Mann Act—which ultimately led to the passage of the Sims Act in 1912.[28] The debates that initiated this piece of legislation introduced the nation to the florid racist rhetoric of Congressman Seaborn Roddenbery of Georgia. Speaking in support of the proposed ban, Roddenberry reached new heights of magniloquence:

> *I call attention of the house to the fact that the recent prizefight*
> *which was had in New Mexico presented, perhaps, the grossest*
> *instance of base fraud and bogus effort at a fair fight between a*
> *Caucasian brute and an African biped beast that has ever taken*
> *place. It was repulsive. This bill is designed to prevent the display*
> *to morbid-minded adults and susceptible youths all over the*
> *country the representations of such a disgusting exhibition.*[29]

It would not be the last time that Roddenbery invoked Jack Johnson in the House of Representatives.

For now, Congressional bloviating could not harm Johnson. Ensconced in Chicago's South Side, he was for the most part safe. But white America was now fixated on him. Unable to beat him in the ring, they now sought to destroy him in the courts. The instrument of his destruction would be a law that passed with little fanfare two weeks before his meeting with Jim Jeffries in Reno: the Mann Act.

Technically known as the White-Slave Traffic Act, the Mann Act was the closest America came to having a federal seduction statute. It arose out of a campaign led by the Woman's Christian Temperance Union (WCTU) and its formidable leader, Frances Willard, to bring about the end of the white slave trade. The "White Slave Trade" was the melodramatic name that Progressive campaigners gave to the alleged existence of a global traffic in young white women to feed the insatiable demand for prostitutes in the vice districts of all the major American cities. While it was conceptualized as an international phenomenon, akin to the actual global traffic in black slaves that evangelicals had crusaded against in the eighteenth and nineteenth centuries, the white slave trade was understood at a granular level as the mass seduction of white girls by unscrupulous men. White slave narratives bore striking resemblances to the narratives employed during the earlier campaigns to illegalize seduction. "Procurers and procuresses" had fanned out across the country to "pursue their vile business of enticing young women and girls from the country, from railroad trains, from steamboats, and from their homes by false promises unmolested," one WCTU activist told a New York audience in 1901.[30] One of the most popular collections of white slave trade tracts was *Fighting the Traffic in Young Girls: The War on the White Slave Trade*, which contained an actual taxonomy of the methods of "Snakes Charm Canaries." Some of these were typical employment ruses, but many were simply grotesque misinterpretations of contemporary courtship rituals or even simply the willful miscomprehension of the rudimentary components of normal social existence in turn-of-the-century America. In the hands of white slavery campaigners almost every aspect of modernity became a way of entrapping women in sexual slavery. "Women are also used to beguile other women for the trade," one campaigner noted,

> *These infamous creatures sometimes go as agents for books, gramophones, or machines. A woman now in the penitentiary said she canvassed communities to sell toilet articles, for the purpose of finding girls. Victims are looked for in railroad depots, and trains are watched for young women traveling alone. General*

deliveries in post offices are watched where young women call for
letters. Recruiting stations are found in dance halls, in the cities
and amusements parks with drinking places as attachments. Ice
cream parlors and fruit stores sometimes serve as spiders' webs for
entanglement.[31]

The war on the white slave trade was really a war on some of the
disconcerting aspects of American modernity. What campaigners were
truly concerned about was the uncontrollable dynamism and mobility
of modern society. Trains, cars, and transport depots loom large in
white slave narratives because these were the means by which young
women could move beyond parental control. They were also the means
by which hundreds of thousands of non-white and non-Protestant
men were moving into white American society. The rise of white slave
activism coincided with the first wave of African-American migration
north by trains and the arrival of hundreds of thousands of European
immigrants by steamboat across the Atlantic. White slavers were almost
always described as lying outside the traditional white, Anglo-Saxon,
Protestant norm. French, Italians, Poles, Austrians, and Russians were
involved. "All Europe, North America, Panama, South America, Egypt
and other parts of Africa, India, China and Japan are the fields of operation of these atrocious men and serpentine women." Jewish communities were the alleged ringleaders and were singled out as "the backbone
of the loathsome traffic in New York and Chicago."

Activist concerns converged on Chicago, a city at the heart of the
national railroad network and teeming with newly arrived blacks
from the South, and Italians, Poles, Jews, and others from Europe.
Chicago was also home to one of the nation's most notorious vice districts, the Levee—where Jack Johnson had made his home. In the first
decade of the twentieth century Chicago became synonymous with

the white slave trade. The *Chicago Daily Tribune* filled its pages with lurid stories from the slave markets in the city, warning its readers that beneath their very noses America's second city was "becoming the 'white slave' center of the world" and that city's commerce in female virtue had become one of its "great industries" alongside meatpacking, garment-making, and construction. The apparent crisis in Chicago attracted the attentions of some of the most talented and determined campaigners in the country.

In 1908, United States Attorney Edwin W. Sims, fresh off a landmark anti-trust suit against Standard Oil, turned his considerable powers to solving the problem of white slavery in Chicago. He was horrified at what he found. "In view of what I have learned in the course of the recent investigation and prosecution of the 'white slave' traffic," he reported, "I can say, in all sincerity, that if I lived in the country and had a young daughter I would go to any length of hardship and privation myself rather than allow her to go into the city to work or to study." Sims teamed up with District Attorney Clifford G. Roe, a prominent white slave activist and future author of the seminal text *Horrors of the White Slave Trade: The Mighty Crusade to Protect the Purity of Our Homes*. The two men believed that problem warranted federal intervention and drafted a model law that made the transport of prostitutes across state lines a federal crime. This was a creative use of the Commerce Clause—the clause in the United States Constitution that arrogated to Congress the right "to regulate Commerce with foreign Nations, and among the several States"—to regulate an essentially moral concern. Sims and Roe took the proposed law to Illinois congressman James Robert Mann, a politician with impeccable Progressive credentials who agreed to champion the law in the House. The law was introduced to the nation as the White-Slave Traffic Act, and in case there was any doubt as to who it aimed to protect Mann defined the white slave trade as "the business of securing white women and girls and selling them out-right, or of exploiting them for immoral purpose." The bill won the support of President Taft and became law in June 1910. Henceforth, it would be illegal to

> *Knowingly transport or cause to be transported, or aid or assist*
> *in obtaining transportation for, or in transporting, in interstate*
> *or foreign commerce, or in any Territory or in the District of*
> *Columbia, any woman or girl for the purpose of prostitution or*
> *debauchery, or for any other immoral purpose, or with the intent*
> *and purpose to induce, entice, or compel such woman or girl to*
> *become a prostitute or to give herself up to debauchery, or to*
> *engage in any other immoral practice.*

Those found guilty of violating the law, which became universally known as the Mann Act, faced up to five years in a federal prison and a fine of up to five thousand dollars. The law was described as a measure to combat prostitution and sex trafficking, but its focus on suasion, its expansive wording, and its missing definition of "immoral purpose" meant it functioned as a federal seduction statute. Those charged with executing the law were the zealous young agents of the Bureau of Investigation, the forerunner of the FBI. It soon became apparent that the young men of the Bureau were more interested in policing public morality than monitoring the movements of professional sex workers. In no time at all the new law was catching out sexually adventurous young men throughout the country. In 1913 it ensnared the most sexually adventurous of them all: Jack Johnson, the first black heavyweight boxing champion of the world.

The Mann Act was the means; Chicago was to be the place. What was needed was a trigger. That came in the form of personal tragedy that hit Johnson in September 1912. In the months after the Jeffries fight, McClay and Schreiber had drifted further from the champion's interests and his relationship with Duryea intensified. In January 1911 they were quietly married in Pittsburgh, and that summer they sailed to Europe. Marriage had done little to dampen Johnson's appetite for the sporting life, however. In America, he maintained contact with courtesans and fast women—Schreiber included. In London and Paris he was besieged by female admirers, to Duryea's horror and disgust. Back in America, Johnson struggled to find suitable fights and so busied himself with a new enterprise: the construction of a cabaret in the Levee, where he would be owner, principal attraction, and revel master. Johnson poured his efforts into the Café de Champion. He intended it as an embassy for the Johnson that he wished to project rather than the Johnson who was harangued and reviled in the press. Johnson spared no expense on decorating his club and freely displayed in it many works of art that he had collected over the course his career.[32] Pride of place were several large portraits of Etta and himself. These portraits were intended as a monument to their marriage but were also a statement of intent for the club itself. Just like its owner, the Café de Champion was from the outset an interracial affair.

The club opened in bacchanalian style in July 1912. Pretty soon, the Johnsons were living there full time: Jack entertaining special guests for hours in a private dining room upstairs; Etta confined to a top-floor suite with only a couple of maids for companions. As sports flocked to the café, the champion's infidelities increased commensurately. Johnson struck up affairs with Ada Banks, one of the in-house singers, and with eighteen-year-old Lucille Cameron, a white girl from Minneapolis, among countless others. Etta's mental health, which had always been fragile, now disintegrated.

Late in the morning of September 11, 1912, Johnson returned to the Café de Champion from the train station, where he had been organizing tickets for a planned trip out West. Pulling up outside 41 West thirty-first Street, Johnson saw the sidewalk was crowded with police vehicles. Worried, he entered his beloved cabaret. Inside,

> *Friends told me to hurry upstairs that something had happened to Etta. Those ominous words gave me the worst fright I had ever had and I sped up the stairs not knowing but dreading what I was to find. She lay on the floor, her beautiful long hair hiding her face. Near her was a revolver. On one exposed bare arm was a red spot, I took courage and tried to convince myself that the shot had not been fatal. I gathered her up in my arms, and as I did so her hair fell back, revealing an ugly wound in her head. She died a few hours later.*[33]

Earlier that morning, Duryea had asked her maids to pray with her and then sent them out the room, locking the door behind them. On the first floor Ada "Bricktop" Smith was singing in the private dining room. On the ground floor the orchestra was in full swing. The noise was such that the band did not hear the single gunshot. Smith and others did, however, and ran upstairs and broke down the bedroom door. Etta had shot herself through the head. She was thirty-one.

Johnson was distraught and plunged into a deep depression. His friends rallied to his side, and plans were made for a funeral at St. Marks AME in the South Side followed by a fine burial in Graceland Cemetery. The national press were less sensitive to Johnson's plight.

MRS. JOHNSON TRIES SUICIDE.; Pugilist's Wife, Tired of Being a Social Outcast, Shoots Herself.

Such was the *New York Times*'s reaction to Duryea's passing.[34] Tabloid coverage was even more lurid, with many papers dwelling at length on the alleged psychic consequences of interracial relations. Duryea, they declared, had clearly gone insane on account of shame, more evidence, not that any was needed at that time, that interracial love was unnatural and morally damaging. Others explored Duryea's ostracism from her family and her Long Island hometown. The *New York World* recorded with some delight how her entanglement with Johnson had resulted in her parents, siblings, and extended family severing all links with her. Not even some of the wayward members of the Duryea clan would associate themselves with Etta, "not even her cousin," the *World* reported. "Florette Whaley—who had eloped with the Rev. Jerry Cooke, the Long Island clergyman who deserted his wife in running away with the young choir girl—had sent her a word of condolence." Duryea's mother, meanwhile, told the press that she hoped that her prodigal daughter's death might warn off other girls who were considering love across the color line.

If the press were content to cover the tragic death of a depressed young woman in tones morbid and flippant, they were still willing and able to scold Johnson for his romantic decisions. Johnson soon gave them an opening. Within a fortnight of his wife's entombment in Graceland, Johnson had promoted Lucille Cameron from concubine to main squeeze. In October he introduced her to the press as the new Mrs. Johnson. The resulting spasm of media outrage led Lucille's mother, Mrs. F. Cameron-Falconet, to come to Chicago to try to rescue her recalcitrant daughter from the heavyweight champion of the world. This short, fearsome woman was more than a match for Jack Johnson. Within a day of her arrival she had confronted Johnson and demanded to see her daughter. When he complied she then ordered Lucille to come away with her. When her daughter stated that she loved Johnson and wanted to stay with him, Cameron-Falconet hired a lawyer and requested the police arrest Johnson for abduction. She also began to mobilize public opinion against Johnson. In a series of sensational interviews she begged the authorities to intervene and save her daughter—only nineteen—from the black boxer. She told the *Chicago Daily News* that "Jack Johnson has hypnotic powers and he has exercised them on my little girl." She then gave a vivid and macabre account of her confrontation with Johnson at his South Side home. There, in her version of events, she pleaded with him to release Lucille from his hold. Johnson refused and then (allegedly) boasted of his immense powers of seduction:

> *I told him I could not understand how she could be attracted by such as he, and he said he could "get" any woman he wanted. "I could even get you, too, if I wanted you."*[35]

Those words, that fictitious declaration, stirred something deep within the white psyche. The ensuing furor had been primed by many things: decades of sexualized racial rhetoric and racialized sexual legislation; the popularization of white slave narratives peopled by desperate white mothers, fallen white daughters, and shameless, swarthy seducers; the raw wound of Jim Jeffries's defeat at Reno; the bittersweet memory of the racial violence that swept the nation after that fight; the limpic belief that only, if only Johnson could be destroyed then the White Man would be rescued. But that single phrase, *I could even get you*, represented the totality of white fears. The mask had slipped and fallen. Johnson was bent on destroying the foundations of the American order. He had to be destroyed in turn.

What followed had the dimensions of a national crisis and the details of a farce. Despite massive public pressure and intense institutional willingness, the police were unable to arrest Johnson for abduction for the simple fact that in every interview she gave Lucille stressed that her relationship with Johnson was consensual. Confounded by legal facts, Captain Max

Nootbaar of the Chicago police—a German migrant, a former caval-
ryman, and the legendary scourge of the Levee's bordellos—had Lucille
arrested for disorderly conduct. "I am doing this for humanity's sake," he
told the press. "Legally, I have no right to hold the girl . . . but I believe the
case warrants my action." Johnson personally drove Lucille to the police
station, where he was confronted by Nootbaar and Mrs. Cameron-Falconet. Again they begged Lucille to hand over Johnson; again she refused.
"I would rather see you spend all your life in jail," Lucille's mother said,
moments before her daughter was led to the cells, "than one day in the
company of that nigger." Johnson hurried to the Café de Champion to get
bail money. There he was greeted by a spurned and furious Ada Banks,
who tried and failed to shoot Johnson. Rumor soon spread that she had
mortally wounded the boxer, leading to a cartel of wealthy Southern racists
to wire north an offer to fund her legal costs to the tune of $50,000.[36]

In the meantime, Cameron-Falconet and her lawyer succeeded in
having a judge order Johnson's arrest for abduction. Johnson was briefly
held and then released while he arranged the terms of his bond. Angry
crowds now greeted him wherever he went—at the bank, at the courthouse, anywhere outside the Levee and the Black Belt—and when he
tried to hire private security, neither the Burns nor the Pinkerton Detective Agencies would accept his custom.[37]

The black community's support for Johnson also started to slip. Some
of the criticism from that quarter was more mordant than urgent, as
with *The Philadelphia Port News*'s wry headline:

> *Jack Johnson, Dangerously Ill, Victim of White Fever*

But much of it was damning. On October 20, Booker T. Washington,
who had long been wary of Johnson's ostentatious style, now denounced
him publicly, telling an audience at the Detroit YMCA that "undoubtedly

Johnson's actions are repudiated by the great majority of right-thinking people of the Negro race." Washington dwelled on the fact that Johnson's actions endangered the lives of his fellow black Americans. "This man is harming himself the least," he said, "I wish to say emphatically that his actions do not meet with the approval of the colored race." Washington's speech was met with acclaim in many of the bastions of black opinion, newspapers like the *Baltimore Afro-American Ledger* and the *Indianapolis Freeman*, which now also editorialized against the black champion.[38]

But whatever Washington might have believed, the threat of lynching was at this point directed principally at Jack Johnson. In Chicago, a large crowd gathered at Montrose and Clark—only a block away from where Etta Duryea Johnson laid freshly buried—and hung an effigy of Johnson from a tree. On its chest someone had pinned a note reading: "This is the last of Jack Johnson."[39] Against this hysterical backdrop Johnson went to the Appomattox Club in the South Side to defend himself before an assembly of black businessmen and community leaders. Before a largely silent audience, Johnson began with a refutation of Cameron-Falconet's account of their meeting and then proceeded to give a defense of his right to live and love in freedom worthy of any of the great Enlightenment champions of liberty.

I want to say that I never made a statement attributed to me to the effect that I could get any white woman I wanted. I can lay my hand upon the Bible and swear that I never made such a statement. My father was a Christian and my mother is Christian, and I know what it means to swear by the Bible. I want to say that I never said anything of the sort about any woman of any color.

I have been quoted falsely. The newspapers and the public have taken advantage of me because of my color. If I were a white man not a line of this would have reached the newspaper.

But I do want to say that I am not a slave and that I have the
right to choose who my mate shall be without the dictation of any
man. I have eyes and I have a heart and when they fail to tell me
who I shall have as mine I want to be put away in a lunatic asylum.
So long as I do not interfere with any other man's wife, I shall claim
the right to select the woman of my own choice. Nobody else can
do that for me. That is where the trouble lies.[40]

A few days after this speech, the Chicago authorities, which thus far had been unable to legally detain Johnson, ordered that entertainment cease at the Café de Champion and two days later effectively shuttered the business by revoking its liquor license. This vindictive piece of bureaucratic warfare did substantial damage to the champion's financial position, but he remained stubbornly free.

In the course of their search for any legal pretext to arrest and hold Jack Johnson, Chicago authorities called upon the Justice Department. Knowing Johnson's long and convivial history with prostitutes and prostitution and his nomadic lifestyle, they wanted to explore whether it could be proved that his relationship with Lucille Cameron was a violation of the Mann Act. The effort came to nothing. Such cases relied upon hard evidence of interstate traffic, and there was none in the case of Johnson and Lucille. Nonetheless, once this avenue of investigation was opened, the Bureau of Investigation became convinced that witnesses could be found from among the sporting world who would testify that Johnson had engaged in such behavior since the law came into effect in the summer of 1910. What followed was a kind of phony war, as the Bureau combed through the various vice districts of the United States looking for people to turn state's witness on Johnson while the boxer engaged in his own search to find and silence potential turncoats with cash and a ticket out of town. Then in early November, as the prospect of using Lucille

Cameron to ensnare Johnson was rapidly diminishing, the Chicago office got an anonymous tip about a sporting woman who it could be proved that Johnson had shipped across state lines for "immoral purposes." She went by many names—Belle Gifford, Belle Baker, Belle Allen, Mrs. Jacques Allen—but there was indisputable evidence that she was "FOR-MERLY INMATE EVERLEIGH CLUB, CHICAGO, SAID TO HAVE BEEN ILLEGALLY TRANSPORTED BY JACK JOHNSON." She was, of course, Belle Schreiber, Johnson's former lover, who had fallen out with him after he married Etta Duryea and who was now eking out a precarious existence as a prostitute in Washington, D.C.

The Bureau's agents quickly tracked her down. She was a dream witness: eager to revenge herself on Johnson and in possession of a vast collection of letters, receipts, and other such material that would furnish the infrastructure of a successful prosecution under the Mann Act. On November 7, she was quietly taken to Chicago, where she gave evidence before a grand jury. Within a matter of hours of her testimony the grand jury had issued seven indictments against the black champion for violation of the Mann Act's prohibition on interstate traffic in "White Slaves." Johnson was arrested that evening and briefly put in cuffs before being allowed to spend the night at home. The next day he went before a judge who refused to accept Johnson's request for bail. Johnson was sent to the Cook County Jail. They finally had him where they wanted him.

The case against Johnson was based on an incident that had happened in October 1910. At that time, Johnson had only just made Duryea's acquaintance and was still intimate with Schreiber. She had fallen on hard times and had contacted Johnson—who was flush after the fight in Reno a few months before—from Indiana, asking for some money to set herself up as a prostitute. Johnson wired her $75 and told her to meet him in Chicago. When they met there a few weeks later, Johnson, a firm believer in independent living, suggested that she might

establish and run her own brothel rather than simply tying her fortunes
to another madam. Schreiber agreed and chose an apartment near the
Levee. Johnson paid the first month's rent, helped her pick out furniture,
and also organized a beer supplier. The furnishings alone cost close to
$1,200. The champion had been generous to Belle Schreiber, and she
could prove it because she had kept the receipts.

The occurrences of that October had all the makings of an open-and-
shut Mann Act prosecution. In any event, Johnson would not have his
day in court until the spring of 1913. In the meantime he was out of jail
and free to try to enjoy what he could of his shattered public and private
lives. One diversion was his relationship with Lucille Cameron. Despite
the most incredible pressure, she had remained by his side, and she now
asked that he marry her.[41] After some hesitation, Johnson agreed. On
December 3 Lucille formally became Mrs. Jack Johnson following a ceremony in Johnson's South Side house. Her despairing mother gave up
and went home. "MRS. CAMERON FALCONET HAS WASHED HER
HANDS CLEAN OF THE WHOLE WHITE AND BLACK MESS," *The
Chicago Defender* told its readers, "AND HAS RETURNED TO HER
HOME IN MINNEAPOLIS, MINN. IN UTTER DISGUST."

Mrs. Cameron-Falconet was not the only one to begrudge Johnson his
hopes for marital bliss. News of his marriage to Lucille became public
just as the National Governors Conference was getting under way in
Virginia. From the podium, Governor Cole Blease of South Carolina
called for Johnson's lynching, asking, "If we cannot protect our white
women from black fiends, where is our boasted civilisation?" He continued:

*In the South we love our women, we hold them higher than all
things else, and whenever anything steps between a Southern
man and the defense and virtue of the women of his nation and*

his states, he will tear it down and walk over it in her defense,
regardless of what maybe the consequences.[42]

A vocal and enthusiastic proponent of lynch law, Blease told the assembled governors that his position was that if the constitution forbade mob justice in defense of white female virtue then "to hell with the Constitution."[43] Not to be outdone by his fellow Southerner, Seaborn Roddenberry once again brought his idiosyncratic oratorical style to the floor of the House of Representatives, this time calling for a constitutional amendment to ban interracial marriage:

No brutality, no infamy, no degradation in all the years of
southern slavery, possessed such a villainous character and such
atrocious qualities as the provision of the laws of Illinois, New
York, Massachusetts, and other states which allow the marriage
of the negro, Jack Johnson, to a woman of the Caucasian strain.
[applause] . . . Intermarriage between whites and blacks is
repulsive and averse to every sentiment of pure American spirit. It
is abhorrent and repugnant. It is subversive to social peace. It is
destructive of moral supremacy, and ultimately this slavery of white
women to black beasts will bring this nation to a conflict as fatal
and as bloody as ever reddened the soil of Virginia or crimsoned
the mountain paths for Pennsylvania. . . . Let us uproot and
exterminate now this debasing, ultrademoralizing, un-American
and inhuman leprosy.[44]

Such statements are obscene, but they reveal the unifying rhetorical power of the white slave narrative. The campaign to end white slavery crossed party and sectional lines. Progressives understood it as a policy project. Moralists viewed it as a quest for national purification. Racists grasped its versatility as a tool of racial control. In a country that within living memory had torn itself apart over the very real evil of black slavery, the crusade against a fictitious white slavery offered an opportunity to experience an alternative history where Northern white women were slaves, Southern white men, like Blease and Roddenberry, were abolitionists,[45] and non-whites, like Jack Johnson, were slave masters. In the context of the rolling back of Reconstruction and the reassertion of a de facto bondage in the South, the myth of white slavery in the North was also an excellent way of diverting attention from the failure of the North to change circumstances for former slaves and their children and grandchildren. Turning inward was an escape. Horror at the apparent spectacle of white slaves being traded in the streets of Northern cities became a way of redirecting the moral energies that should have gone into a proper reckoning with the condition of the postwar South. Perhaps Jack Johnson's greatest sin was to embody both the fiction of white slavery and the fact of Southern injustice in one very public person.

United States v. John Arthur Johnson began on May 5, 1913, in Chicago's monumental Federal Building. Federal prosecutors had originally tried to expand the number of charges to include the colorful and suggestive crimes of unlawful sexual intercourse and committing the crime against nature. There was no evidence for these charges, but they were a tactical ploy to further defame the black champion in the eyes of the jury. At the request of Johnson's lawyers, the judge threw out these supplementary indictments. The case was to be purely judged on the merits of whether Johnson had or had not violated the Mann Act.

In his memoirs, Johnson would decry the trial as "a rank frame-up"— an act of judicial persecution against a black man who refused to conform to the racial order of the day. Historians have tended to take the same view. The Johnson case was so clearly politically inspired, so obviously motivated by racial prejudice and moral panic, that its outcome was never in doubt. This was a judicial lynching, not an impartial execution of the law. This is evidently true. There was not a jury in Illinois that would have found Johnson innocent under these circumstances. The atmosphere in the courtroom was as poisonous as that in the press. Johnson was never going to get a fair trial; very few black men did in such cases.

Nonetheless, it is important to confront the case as Johnson, the jurors, and the lawyers involved had to. They were dealing with the law as they found it, not as they might have wished it to be. To demonstrate his innocence, Johnson would have to prove that he had not transported Belle Schreiber across state lines for the purposes of prostitution. Johnson's defense was based on a stout denial of all the events described by the prosecution. In reality she was a prostitute and he had always known that. Johnson might have seen nothing out of the ordinary with consorting with such women—it was all part of the sporting lifestyle— but to the average juror it would have been impossible to interpret their relationship as anything other than that of a prostitute and a client, or, if they were so inclined, white slave and a white slaver. As a consequence, any evidence that Johnson and Schreiber had ever traveled together across state lines or that Johnson had facilitated Schreiber's passage across state lines after July 1910 was evidence that the Mann Act had been violated. Then there was the question of the apartment in the Levee. There were receipts for the purchases made in connection with it, and the vendor testified at the trial that Johnson had paid for them. If this looked like Johnson establishing a brothel, that is because it is what he had, in essence, done. It was what sports were wont to do.

Johnson was ultimately a victim of the Mann Act's capacious wording. The law potentially criminalized all interstate travel involving sexually active adults. It was less a question of whether someone was guilty and more a point of whether there was the motivation to pursue a prosecution. Johnson had clearly violated the loose letter of the law and had certainly offended its puritanical spirit. That did not make the timbre of the trial any less distasteful or diminish the fact that every aspect of Johnson's treatment was shot through with racism. Johnson was both guilty in law and guilty in color. His infraction was legal; his crime was racial. As Sol C. Johnson of the *Savannah Tribune* observed, "While it is true that he has done wrong, it is also true that he has been persecuted. The Negro-hating firebrands have had their inning. The prison wall yearns for Johnson."[46] When the trial ended on May 14 the jury quickly found Johnson guilty on all counts.

Johnson's conviction was met with the predictable headlines. Most were simply unadulterated expressions of schadenfreude. Some went further and foresaw that the case would be a spur to new and more invasive laws against interracial marriage. "Jack Johnson Guilty Means Race Reforms," the *Cleveland Daily News* bellowed. "Laws Prohibiting Intermarriage of Blacks and Whites Sure to Come. Black Pugilist Will Be Made An Example." Black newspapers, whatever their view of Johnson as an individual, recognized that the case was a terrifying confirmation of the place of black Americans in white society. "Every branch of the government is permeated with race prejudice," the *Richmond Planet* said of Johnson's sentencing, though

> There has been no colored man in the history of the country who had done more to injure himself in particular and the colored race in general than Mr. Johnson. He agitated the debilitating race question, this intermarriage of the races.
>
> There are sad hearts in the country today among the colored people. Their idol is shattered. It is painful to contemplate. There is mourning in the Southland.
>
> Farewell, Jack Johnson![47]

In the ring, Jack Johnson was known for his elusive style and his mastery of feints and bluffs. But all his guile seemed to have abandoned him in the confines of the Federal Building. On June 4 the court handed down the sentence: a $1,000 fine and one year and one day in a federal prison. Johnson had two weeks to file an appeal. Confronted with the prospect of prison time and utterly disenchanted with the justice system, Johnson rediscovered his old nimbleness. On June 24, Johnson slipped his police surveillance and drove to Englewood train station. There, as had been planned, he ran across the tracks and bundled aboard a train "carrying a bag of bats and other baseball equipment" in his arms.[48] On board were dozens of other athletic black men with baseball gear—the members of an all-black baseball team called Foster's Giants who were traveling to Canada for a series of matches. Johnson and an associate jumped off in Hamilton, Ontario, and made their way to Montreal, where Lucille was waiting with tickets for a steamer to Le Havre. As an alien in transit with paid tickets to a third country the Canadian authorities were unable to detain or extradite the fugitive boxer. On Sunday, June 29, the couple were aboard the liner *Corinthian* as it left harbor for France. Jack Johnson was free.[49]

The American public might have approved of the particular prosecution of Jack Johnson under the Mann Act, but doubts about the wider application of the law were rife. The law did not deliver on its promise of imprisoning packs of sexually voracious men. Instead, many women were sent to prison for their involvement in the sexual economy. The very first arrest under the law had been that of Nettie Jenkins, a madam arrested while escorting five women from Chicago to Houghton, Michigan. Furthermore, many of the women being protected from apparent exploitation were willing participants in the sex trade. This was so with the five women in the case of Nettie Jenkins. It was also the case of Belle Schreiber and many other sporting women. Bureau agents soon realized that many of the women they were seeking to rescue did not actually want or need their help. Moreover, the agents themselves had often signed up to guard white virtue, not intervene in the existences of women who, in their eyes, were irredeemably lost to a life of vice. Such prejudices were only compounded when the women involved had a history of interracial relations. A certain Agent Lamarioux investigating the case of Violet Hall in October 1911 informed his superiors that Hall "had one or more Jap lovers . . . [and so] can hardly be classed as a white slave."[50] The same was certainly true of Schreiber, who had been freely enjoying the champion's company for some years before turning against him in court.[51] Doubts about who deserved protection under the Mann Act and who should forfeit it hinged on that single ambiguous phrase: "immoral purposes." For agents and activists who were eager to use the law to police sexuality expansively, it was self-evident that immoral purposes encompassed a whole range of behaviors, from adultery to fornication and elopement. More conservative officials assumed that the purpose of the law was narrowly focused on the commercial dimension of the interaction. Inevitably, the two sides clashed, with one side alleging that the other was not enforcing the letter of the law and the other ridiculing attempts to micromanage the private lives of United States citizens. What was needed was clarification from a higher court, and in March 1913, as Johnson was preparing for his court date, the seeds of just that were sown in Reno when local police arrested two men for violation of the Mann Act.

The men concerned were Drew Caminetti and Maury Diggs of Sacramento, California. They were friends and scions of wealthy and politically connected Sacramento families. Caminetti was the wayward son of

California state senator Anthony Caminetti, who in 1913 was nominated by Woodrow Wilson to be the United States Commissioner for Immigration; Diggs was from a family of property developers and was himself a promising young architect. At twenty-seven and twenty-six, respectively, both were married, and both were having affairs. Maury was in love with Marsha Warrington, and Caminetti was involved with Lola Norris. The affairs were no secret: the men flaunted their younger girlfriends around town and even invited them to dinners where their wives were present. By March 1913, their behavior was causing such a scandal that they began receiving threats from the outraged male relatives of all the four women involved. The local press started to take an interest, and Marsha narrowly succeeded in quashing an article on the foursome that was due to run in the *Sacramento Bee*. When the social scrutiny became unbearable the men and their mistresses decided to flee to Los Angeles. They arranged to meet at a restaurant near the train station and travel to the city as a group. That afternoon, however, Caminetti got drunk and lost his wallet and so was late to the meet-up. By the time he arrived they had missed the train to Los Angeles and decided to take the next train out of town. This was going to Reno, Nevada, fourteen miles outside the California state line. In Reno the four found hotel rooms; Caminetti and Diggs then busied themselves with plotting divorces from their wives. But local police soon got wind of their presence in the city and arrested them under the Mann Act.

The men were shipped back to California and tried in a federal court. The affair soon became national news, with Democrats alleging that the case was cooked up by Republicans looking to smear Anthony Caminetti and by association President Woodrow Wilson. Nonetheless, the trial went ahead, with proceedings beginning the day after *United States v. John Arthur Johnson* got under way, and the two men were duly found guilty. The *Sacramento Bee* welcomed the verdict on behalf of "all good men and all decent women."[52] South Carolina senator Ben Tillman called for Diggs's and Caminetti's lynching. Diggs vowed to appeal, telling the press that "If I am a white slaver, 90% of men living are as guilty as I am." A substantial number of people agreed with him. It was one thing to use an expansive interpretation of the law to punish an upstart black boxer, but it was quite another to use it to imprison two respectable, wealthy, white young men. Neither Caminetti nor Diggs stood to gain financially from taking Marsha and Lola across state lines, making nonsense of the legal logic of the Mann Act as arising out of the constitutionally sanctioned right of the federal government to monitor interstate commerce. In other jurisdictions, judges had denied that the law applied to private romantic adventures. The same year that the two friends were convicted a federal judge in Wichita, Kansas, ruled that "it was not the aim of Congress to prevent the personal escapades of any man."[53]

As confusion spread as to the scope of the law, press skepticism grew. As the Caminetti and Diggs appeals drifted from court to higher court, the newspapers began to uncover ever more cases of blackmail and extortion arising out of the Mann Act. Furthermore, the law seemed to victimize men—especially wealthy ones—but never women. In 1916 the *New York Times*, under the headline "Uncle Sam, Blackmailer," noted caustically that

> If two immoral persons pass a state line in the course of their immoral proceedings the man is guilty of a crime but the woman is not. The result has been that this law has acted as a direct inducement to blackmail. . . . The law is in itself an absurdity, but that is less serious than its direct inducement to crime. It breaks up no "white slave" traffic, but it does make the Federal Government the accomplice and instrument of blackmailers and facilitates their operations.[54]

The *Times*'s editorial hinted at a sea change in public attitudes toward women, sex, and the law. Implicit in its criticism of the Mann Act was that the law's exploitation by devious women was evidence that the moral premise of the law—namely, that women were meek and morally superior and needed special protection—was erroneous. That same year the Supreme Court accepted the appeal of Caminetti and Diggs and announced that a ruling would be handed down in 1917. The court's ruling would provide legal clarity concerning the parameters of the law, but it would also serve as a unique opportunity to either halt or sanction the concept creep that had transformed a law designed to prevent the commercial trade in prostitutes into something more expansive and intrusive. The court's ruling in *Caminetti v. United States* was to be referendum on the state of American sexual politics, an inflection point that would decide whether American courts had to double down on Victorian morality or could accept a more complex, more jaundiced, and more modern vision of human sexuality.

In the event, the court's ruling in January 1917 confirmed the broadest possible interpretation of the "immoral causes" clause. The court did so by essentially denying that there was any doubt as to the meaning of the clause at all. "There is no ambiguity in the terms of this act," the court stated,

> *Statutory words are uniformly presumed, unless the contrary appears, to be used in their ordinary and usual sense, and with the meaning commonly attributed to them. To cause a woman or girl to be transported for the purposes of debauchery, and for an immoral purpose, to-wit, becoming a concubine or mistress, for which Caminetti and Diggs were convicted . . . would seem by the very statement of facts to embrace the transportation for purposes denounced by the act, and therefore fairly within its meaning.*

The justices continued that although the crime would be all the baser "if accompanied with the expectation of pecuniary gain," the absence of such a motive did not diminish the moral offense of transporting a woman across state lines for sexual purposes and certainly did not place it outside the scope the Mann Act. "To say the contrary," the court concluded, "would shock the common understanding of what constitutes an immoral purpose when those terms are applied, as here, to sexual relations."[55] The court upheld the original conviction, and that April Diggs and Caminetti were imprisoned on McNeil Island, a federal penitentiary on an islet in the Puget Sound.[56,57,58]

Just as the unhappy defendants of *Caminetti v. United States* were preparing to head to prison, the exiled principal of *United States v. John Arthur Johnson* was beginning to accept that a stint in an American jailhouse might be inescapable. Johnson's life had not been quiet since the *Corinthian* had steamed out of Montreal in June 1913. Johnson was never one to languish in silence and misery, and, if anything, his exile transformed him from a mere celebrity into something mythic. No longer confined to the leisure districts of urban America, Johnson was now free by threat of imprisonment to live a peripatetic existence, full of adventure, disaster, pageantry, and narrow escapes.

Johnson and Lucille arrived in Paris in July 1913 and spent much of the rest of the year bouncing around Europe. Paris and London were no longer as welcoming as they had been—the stigma of criminal conviction carried across the Atlantic—and the Johnsons found themselves drifting further afield to Vienna and Budapest. At the start of 1914 they circled back to Paris, where Johnson hoped to earn some easy money in the ring. As ever the chief problem was finding boxers of a suitable caliber

to fight and promoters who could stump up the money that would moti-
vate the Epicurean champion into the gym. A proposed fight in London
with Sam Langford, a fellow black boxer from Boston, was rejected. The
purse was only a couple of thousand pounds, and Langford was a dangerous opponent. In a high-handed letter to the British sporting authorities Johnson declared that he would not fight for less than $30,000.
Frenchman Georges Carpentier was another option, but the closest
Johnson came to him was when Carpentier refereed an uninspiring
encounter between Johnson and the bruising but artless Irish-American
fighter Frank Moran in Paris on June 27, 1914. The bout went the full
twenty rounds. Johnson won on points but won no money: the earnings
from the fight went straight into the pocket of a promoter Johnson had
jilted earlier that year. The next day Archduke Franz Ferdinand was shot
and killed in Sarajevo.

As Europe's armies stirred to war, Johnson and Lucille were on a train
to St. Petersburg at the invitation of another extraordinary African-
American: George Thomas, who had risen from poverty in Georgia to
become a successful restaurateur and society favorite in tsarist Russia.
Their progress east was repeatedly interrupted by special trains carrying troops. In Germany they observed from their windows reservists
marshaling in stations and drilling in fields. "The whole of Europe,"
Johnson mused in his memoirs, "would be under powder smoke before
long." In the meantime the preparations for war simply interfered with
Johnson's latest moneymaking schemes. Thomas had been organizing
several lucrative theatre appearances in Moscow and St. Petersburg
for Johnson, scheduled for that July, but these now came to nothing.
Exactly a month after their arrival, Germany declared war on Russia,
and the Johnsons now fled to London via Warsaw, Berlin, Belgium, and
Paris, cutting an unlikely path through the chaos of mobilization. Amid
desperate scenes on the Channel coast, they secured passage aboard a

boat to England and were soon in London and, for the moment, safe. Johnson was relieved to be back "among English speaking people" and was laconically appreciative of the relative tranquility that prevailed in London. But the organized violence of a general war obviated the need for organized violence in the ring. The era of liberal borders and nomadic sportsmen was now over.[59] Many patriotic fighters, such as Georges Carpentier and Bombardier Wells, were now serving in the ranks.

Johnson was adrift, until one day he bumped into promoter Jack Curley while walking his dog in Paddington. Curley had come across the Atlantic with a proposal: $30,000 plus training expenses to fight Jess Willard, the latest and the largest of the Great White Hopes, in Mexico. Johnson agreed, and at the end of 1914 he and Lucille sailed to Argentina and then onward to Barbados, finally arriving in Cuba in mid-February. It soon became clear that the fight was not going to happen in Mexico. The country was in a civil war, and the pro-American faction, led by Venustiano Carranza, made it clear that they would hand over Johnson to federal agents if he stepped foot in the parts of the country under their control. Peaceful, placidly corrupt, and close to Florida, Havana was fast emerging as the better location for the title fight. Near the end of February Curley announced the location change. The fight was to happen on April 5; it was scheduled for forty-five rounds.

Johnson was an admirer of Napoleon and saw in Bonaparte's rise from Corsican obscurity to European mastery a historical parallel to his own startling ascent. Napoleon's story had ended in a mire of defeat, betrayal, and imprisonment, and Johnson had at times pondered whether his life would meet a similar end. But his confidence was at its usual high as he settled into his training routine in March 1915. He was not aware that the fight with Jess Willard, an overgrown farmhand from Pottawatomie, Kansas, would be his Waterloo. Johnson was now thirty-seven, and he had fought only four times in the last five years. The championship had bred complacency; age brought arrogance just as it quietly sapped him of his strength, stamina, and reflexes. Willard was younger, hungrier, and perfectly conditioned. After the fact, Johnson would claim that he had thrown the fight. One of the few moments in his memoirs where he forsakes his usual strident tone for a folksy, down-home manner is when he claims that he had planned to lose to Willard as part of a plea bargain that would allow him to go back to Chicago unmolested to "again be with my folks" and "settle down quietly and live in peace with my fellow man." But on April 4, Johnson certainly did not fight like a man who intended to lose. For the first fifteen rounds he gave the challenger a beating and at times came close to putting the lumbering, straight-punching Willard down for good. But Willard stayed upright, and the fierce heat began to sap the champion's strength. As the fight entered the twenty-fifth round it became clear that Johnson had no answer for the fitter, stronger Willard. He was pummeled repeatedly that round, one left hook among them knocked out Johnson's two gold-capped front teeth. Rather than spit them out and let Willard and the crowd see that he had been hurt Johnson elected to swallow them. On his stool at the end of the round he told his cornermen to get Lucille out of the audience. He did not want his wife to witness his downfall. But the end came seconds later and Lucille was still in the crowd to see it. After a final devastating flurry Johnson was on the canvas, counted out under the fierce Cuban sun, before an ecstatic white crowd. He had reigned for six years, four years less than his French idol.[60]

The fact that he was no longer the champion did nothing to change his legal status in the United States. Johnson was still a wanted man. In May he returned to London, via Spain and France, where he signed on with a theatre in Elephant and Castle. One night the performance was interrupted by a zeppelin raid. When the threat had apparently passed, Johnson fetched his white Benz and began to drive through the debris back home to Haverstock Hill. "But the trip was not to be made undisturbed,"

> *for suddenly there came roaring out the black sky more bombs. The*
> *raiders had returned. Between blasts of bombs which were falling*
> *all around us, we could hear the whir and swish of the Zeppelin*
> *overhead. I speeded the car up in an effort to get outside of its*
> *bombing radius, but was surprised to learn that no matter how*
> *fast I traveled or in what direction I turned, the bombs were close*
> *upon us. It was then that I learned with considerable alarm that the*
> *Zeppelin was following us.*[61]

At length Johnson got home, bombed all the way, and then scrambled into his shelter. In his fanciful account the airships continued to bombard his house through the night, leveling the whole neighborhood. He emerged the next morning to a scene of total destruction, his home ringed by smoking ruins. It is a glorious account, worthy of some of the more apocalyptic episodes found in Waugh or Fitzgerald—and equally fictitious. But the choice of the fiction reveals something of the man: his egoism (naturally, the bombing of London had to be all about him) but also his weariness at his persecution. Real or not, his pursuit by that zeppelin was the perfect metaphor for his condition.

The Johnsons soon tired of the deprivations of wartime London, and in the spring of 1916 they moved to Spain. In Barcelona, Johnson's existence, which had always tiptoed on the edge of unreality, became surreal, both figuratively—he became involved in an advertising agency and did a few turns in La Monumental as a matador—and literally: in April 1916, he fought, and handily beat, Arthur Cravan, the nephew of Oscar Wilde and a Dadaist poet in his own right. He was still in Spain when the United States entered the war in 1917 and ever the patriot offered his services to the American embassy in Madrid as a spy. Incredibly, they took him on, and for a period Johnson was a paid member of the United States' Spanish intelligence-gathering operation until, characteristically, Johnson had a falling-out with his superiors over his expenses. By now Johnson's situation was parlous. Where he had once simply dabbled in the demimonde he now risked becoming a permanent member of it. He could not get fights, he could not earn money in any other field, and he remained an outlaw in the only country where he had any prospects for long-term financial stability. To add to his misery, his beloved mother, Tiny Johnson, died in 1918 and was buried in Chicago without her son at the graveside. In 1919 Johnson sailed for Mexico, going first to Mexico City and then moving to Tijuana, less than twenty miles from San Diego.[62] Johnson was now very close to America, and with the passage of the Volstead Act, better known as Prohibition, in January 1920, Americans were soon very close to him, as thousands of his fellow citizens descended on Tijuana to drink and make merry free from legal interference.

Johnson had been in sporadic contact with government officials for years and over the course of 1920 an arrangement was made. Johnson would surrender to federal agents on the border and would then be escorted back to Chicago and thence to a federal prison to serve his original sentence. There would be no handcuffs, and he was assured that he would be treated with all civility. On July 20, 1920, he was driven to the border. He began to walk toward America. Waiting for him on the other side were U.S. marshals and some members of the press corps. Although it meant imprisonment and a loss of his treasured freedom, he felt only relief as he stepped over the dividing line and into the United States. "I was back on American soil again and the realization thrilled me quite as much as though I were entering the realms of a strange and unexplored land."[63]

If America seemed strange and unrecognizable to Johnson after a seven-year absence, it seemed increasingly foreign to those who had never left. It is perhaps only human vanity to believe that something as arbitrary and cosmically insignificant as the start of a new decade necessarily inaugurates a new stage in society's development. But in the twenties America was transformed, and the contours of that transformation were described in a triptych of short stories published in May 1920 by a young F. Scott Fitzgerald. Physically, Fitzgerald was then in his lunar phase—he stares out of the photos from the period pallid, even, and complacent, his face having yet to acquire the ruined grandeur of his bibulous majority—but his literary career was stellar. That March he had published *This Side of Paradise* to a rapturous reception, earning him a fair amount of money and guaranteeing higher prices for future works. Professional accomplishment translated into amorous success. In the spring, after a volatile year, Zelda Sayre of Montgomery, Alabama, finally accepted his proposal.[64] Zelda was Fitzgerald's great love and also the archetype for his female protagonists. She was the ur-flapper, a species America was becoming fast acquainted with that year and which Fitzgerald helpfully taxonomized in three stories published sequentially in *The Saturday Evening Post* in May: "Bernice Bobs Her Hair," "The Ice Palace," and "The Offshore Pirate."

The aesthetic profile of the flapper is well-known. The bob, the revealing, androgynous clothes, the chain-smoking, the drinking, the slang, the moody pose—best exhibited in the back of a speeding car. But in these stories Fitzgerald offered a more substantial philosophical perspective of what she represented. The fundamental principle of flapperdom was a total rejection of the moral, and specifically sexual, values of their parents' generation. Flappers were bored stiff by the ladies of the WCTU and repulsed by their image of soft, Christian femininity. An episode in "Bernice Bobs Her Hair," a brilliant account of one provincial girl's transformation into a liberated modern woman, captures the attitude perfectly. Bernice is the country cousin, confounded by the smarter, more desired Marjorie. Confusion and jealousy breeds conflict and produces the following immortal exchange:

"Don't you think common kindness——"

"Oh, please don't quote 'Little Women'!" cried Marjorie impatiently. "That's out of style."

"You think so?"

"Heavens, yes! What modern girl could live like those inane females?"

"They were the models for our mothers."

Marjorie laughed.

"Yes, they were—not! Besides, our mothers were all very well in their way, but they know very little about their daughters' problems."

The problems of 1920s daughters, or at least daughters of privilege, were principally those associated with sex, seduction, and courtship. The hallowed features of the Jazz Age—the music, the dancing, the cocktails, the fast cars—were really just aspects of a revolution in sexual manners. Jazz was the soundtrack; seduction was the action, a fact illustrated in "The Offshore Pirate," in which Curtis Cayle seduces Ardita Farnham on a beach while

Over across the silver lake the figures of the negroes writhed and squirmed in the moonlight like acrobats who, having been too long inactive, must go through their tacks from sheer surplus energy.

In single file they marched, weaving in concentric circles, now
with their heads thrown back, now bent over their instruments
like piping fauns. And from trombone and saxophone ceaselessly
whined a blended melody, sometimes riotous and jubilant,
sometimes haunting and plaintive as a death-dance from the
Congo's heart.

It is a fitting image of how young, white Americans preferred to engage with black people and black culture: at a safe distance, preferably divided by a body of water. The flappers and their male accomplices were not yet ready to overturn their parents' racial assumptions, which was ironic given that their parents regarded the new youthful fashions as worrying evidence of the negrification of white society. In fiction, Ardita's uncle calls her behavior a reflection "of the demi-monde"; in fact, the *Ladies' Home Journal* called for a legal prohibition on jazz dancing.[65] In truth, the new youth culture was an appropriation of the sporting culture of the prewar era. (Ardita even takes her dates to see boxing matches.) But where the sports were rough, ready, and defiantly interracial, the flappers and philosophers of the Jazz Age were safe, spoiled, and exclusively white.

Jack Johnson had firsthand experience of this bleached and sanitized new vision of his former lifestyle. After getting out of jail in July 1921, Johnson bounced around Chicago and New York looking for fights, working the remnants of the vaudeville circuit, and taking jobs as a sparring partner for the new generation of heavyweight contenders. In 1923 he briefly became involved with a new cabaret called the Café de Luxe in Harlem. The venture was so successful that it was soon taken over by bootleggers and Johnson was cut loose.[66] Not that the former champion seemed to mind much. He had never liked jazz, preferring classical music instead. The club itself was an all-white affair and was gaudily decorated with the style and motifs of a Southern plantation manor. The black musicians onstage were instructed by management to play crude "Jungle" jazz, to cater to the tastes and prejudices of the white clientele. It was a pastiche and an affront to the venerated memory of the Café de Champion. Later, rebranded as the Cotton Club, it would become one of the cultural cornerstones of the Jazz Age and the concomitant Harlem Renaissance. Duke Ellington would make his name there, so too would Louis Armstrong, whom Johnson had indirectly terrorized as a child. Fitzgerald also drank there, and likely found in the decor a pleasing physical echo to the equally artificial vision of the Old South that he returned to repeatedly in his shorter fiction, a place that he describes in the "The Ice Palace" as a "languid paradise of dreamy skies and firefly evenings and noisy niggery street fairs—and especially of gracious, soft-voiced girls, who were brought up on memories instead of money." A place that never existed.[67]

For all its limitations, the Sexual Revolution of the twenties was real and lasting, and did ultimately have progressive consequences. Furthermore it was felt throughout the country rather than experienced in a few elite enclaves. The causes were many and familiar (urbanization, secularization, increased female participation in the workforce, increased mobility due to widespread automobile ownership, better information and access to healthcare, including birth control) and the symptoms were everywhere. Like all reformations in manners it proceeded gradually, unevenly, invisibly, and largely unquantifiably—although some have tried to quantify its progress. Among them were the authors of a monumental 1930s report commissioned by the Roosevelt administration entitled *Recent Social Trends in the United States*. A dour, statistical affair, its contributors studied magazines and journals from the preceding decade in an attempt to chart the rise of the new sexual morality. "Attitudes toward extra-marital sexual intercourse have undergone rather violent fluctuations since 1900," the presidential report concluded, "and particularly during the past 15 years. Correlated with attitudes on adultery, seduction and the like, have been those relating to sex 'thrill,' promiscuous petting and the exposure of the human body."

> *The height of sentiment against traditional sex morals occurs*
> *between 1922 and 1929 . . . Particularly from 1923 to 1927 it was*
> *more frequently asserted than denied in these magazines that love,*
> *not marriage, was the only justification of sex relations, that sexual*
> *intercourse was a private matter in which society had no concern*
> *as long as children were avoided, that celibacy was abnormal and*
> *deleterious and the like.*[68]

Changing attitudes were matched by changing behavior. Another survey from the 1930s revealed that of women born after 1910 only 32 percent were virgins at marriage compared to 74 percent of those born in the period 1890–1900. Kinsey report data showed much the same trend. Put simply, beginning in the 1920s Americans started having a lot more extramarital sex and were comfortable to admit as much to pollsters and social scientists.[69]

The paradox is that this Sexual Revolution coincided with the zenith of authoritarian moral, sexual, and racial legislative activity. Virginia led the nation. In 1922 agitation by the WCTU and other women's groups resulted in the passage of an act that forbade the screening of any film containing "obscene, indecent, immoral, inhuman" material or that might "tend to corrupt morals or incite to crime." In 1924 lobbying by the newly formed Anglo-Saxon Clubs of America (ASCOA) led to Virginia's law to Preserve Racial Integrity that criminalized intermarriage between whites and any "colored" person, including blacks, Asians, American Indians, Malays, or members of other "non-Caucasian strains." The act also tightened the definition of whiteness, introducing the notorious "one-drop rule," where previously anyone with 1/16 or less non-white blood could claim legal status as white. Now "no trace whatsoever of any blood other than Caucasian" was required. It was a quest for purity and segregation so radical that even the Nazis thought it too extreme. In the same session the nation's first state sterilization act was passed, allowing for state intervention in the bodies of those "defective persons" who, if allowed to breed, would constitute a "menace to society." Interestingly, one of the supposed symptoms of such defectiveness was sexual promiscuity.

In 1926 the legislature passed the Public Assemblages Act, which forbade interracial gatherings of any kind in a public space, including theatres, cinemas, schools, and university lecture halls. Walter Plecker, the director of Virginia's Bureau of Vital Statistics, later described total social separation as a means to an end of total sexual separation. "If near-white children are allowed to attend white schools," he stated, "sympathy is aroused, attachments are formed, public sentiment is weakened, and ultimately marriage either in their home counties or elsewhere naturally follows." At the heart of segregation was an effort to prevent the possibility of any situation where interracial courtship or seduction might occur. To the racist men of Virginia the stakes could not have been higher. "Fifty-thousand near-white mixed breeds are pressing down on the color line," John Powell, the founder of ASCOA, declared, "and if we let down the bars, our civilization is doomed."[70]

Versions of all these laws soon spread to other states. At a federal level, sexual behavior was monitored by the Federal Bureau of Investigation. In the aftermath of the *Caminetti* ruling, agents were now free to police virtually all forms of interstate courtship, dating, adultery, and extramarital sexual activity of any kind. Between 1921 and 1936 the FBI investigated 47,500 Mann Act violations, resulting in 6,335 convictions.

Most of the cases were brought by private citizens, often parents seeking to reassert control over their increasingly rebellious children. As sexual freedom diffused throughout the country, decentralized forms of social control ceased to function and parents had to look to the central government to discipline their children. The intense policing of courtship revealed a collapse of parental authority and an underlying shift in attitudes. The vigor of the effort expended had the perverse effect of demonstrating the normality of the behaviors being policed.[71]

The product was a generation of young people whose two chief interests—drinking and sex—came with a potential jail term. Naturally, this made both more exciting, but it also led to serious social distortions. Just as Prohibition led to the massive manufacture of bootleg alcohol, the Mann Act and the state-level seduction laws led to scores of unjust cases. Abuses were rife; the opportunities for blackmail and extortion were obvious. Gangs of criminals systematically blackmailed men by luring them with a single woman into committing acts that broke the letter of the law. The *New York Times* reported on the case of Robert A. Torbillon (AKA "Dapper Don" Collins), a professional criminal who used the Mann Act as a vehicle for blackmail. It was claimed that he earned $200,000 through extortion rackets involving the Mann Act. Similar frauds were conducted—by gangs and by opportunistic individuals—that used Alienation of Affection and Breach of Promise suits. Numerous high-profile men were entangled in these schemes: opera singer Enrico Caruso; the son of 1928 presidential candidate Alfred E. Smith; the heir to the Gimbel department store fortune, Frederick Gimbel; plutocrat and playboy Cornelius Vanderbilt; the boxers Gene Tunney and Jack Dempsey.[72]

The press was quick to point out that a new double standard had emerged: the law treated women as unimpeachably pure and chaste when they were, in fact, lascivious, scheming, and exploitative of the law's trust in their being otherwise. Lawyers declared the heart balm actions as "instrument[s] of oppression, blackmail, and fraud," not tools "for the righting of the wrongs of injured innocence." It is no coincidence that the twenties gave the world the word "gold digger," a term that captured the new cynicism associated with modern women and that was personified in Lorelei Lee, the protagonist of Anita Loos's best-selling 1925 novel *Gentlemen Prefer Blondes*. Largely unread today, Loos's book was one of the outstanding literary hits of its day, so popular, its author liked to boast, that James Joyce read it, despite his reading being strictly rationed because of his incipient blindness. The plot follows Lorelei's fantastically successful attempt to marry in to money by any means, fair or foul. Lorelei is glib, philistine, shallow, and practically illiterate. She has her hair in a bob and wears slight, figure-hugging dresses. She drinks, dines, and travels and does it all on someone else's dollar. Yet for all her superficiality, Lorelei demonstrates a remarkable knowledge of the law. At one point in the novel Lorelei is at a loss as to whether she should marry the plutocratic moral campaigner Henry Spoffard, who has confessed his love to her. She worries that Henry might be too attentive a husband, constantly busying himself with her private affairs. Nonetheless, Lorelei has him write her a letter containing his proposal and his declaration of love:

> So it is quite a problem and I seem to be in quite a quandary, because it might be better if Henry should happen to decide that he should not get married, and he should change his mind, and desert a girl, and then it would be only right if a girl should sue him for a breach of promise.

Elsewhere in the book, she refers in passing to the "Man Act." Lorelei might be vulgar and poorly read—but she knows her legal rights.[73]

Lucille Cameron knew hers, too. In 1924 she filed for divorce because of her husband's serial infidelity. Despite its fractious ending, her marriage to Jack Johnson had been remarkable for its longevity. The couple had been thrown together in what was practically a shotgun wedding in the chaotic aftermath of Etta Duryea's death. They had spent twelve long, eventful years together, touring the world, witnessing war and revolution, experiencing the vagaries of celebrity. Johnson was married within a year of Lucille's departure to Irene Marie Pineau, whom he met—like he had Etta—at a racecourse. She, too, was white. In August 1925 she became the third Mrs. Jack Johnson.

It was at around this period that Johnson starts to diminish in stature. Winnowed out of history he starts to shrink from view. He made a few attempts to get back into boxing after his release from prison. He made a show of going after Jack Dempsey, the new and genuinely terrifying heavyweight champion. To his enduring shame Dempsey drew the color line and declared he would not fight a black boxer for the heavyweight title. As an older man, Dempsey would claim that he had used the color line as an excuse to dodge the still-dangerous Jack Johnson. This seems like a gracious old man seeking pardon for the sins of youth. It was probably best that Johnson never met Dempsey in the ring. Johnson had taken twenty-six rounds to lose to Willard. Dempsey had taken three to destroy him, and did so with a ferocity scarcely seen again in a heavyweight title fight. In any event, the fight never happened. The closest Johnson came to Dempsey was when he served as one of Luis Firpo's sparring partners in the run-up to his shot at the title in 1923. Johnson fought a few more bouts in the mid-twenties and lost most of them. He was now over forty, and his time had passed. There was a new era of fighters and new era of fight fans. Jack Johnson, once the most notorious man in the country, had been largely forgotten. At the height of the Depression he was to be found in variety shows, available to be gawped at for a couple of cents, an exoticism with a golden smile from a vanished age.

By the mid-thirties Jack Johnson was not the only aspect of the prewar world that was beginning to look dated. In 1934 Roberta West Nicholson was elected to the Indiana state legislature. Born in 1903 into a prosperous, Republican Cincinnati family, Nicholson had married at age twenty-one into a wealthy, Democratic family from Indianapolis. Her in-laws were fiercely progressive at a time when Indiana was controlled by the Republicans, and the Indiana Republican Party—everyone from the governor down—was controlled by the Ku Klux Klan. The Klan burned crosses on Nicholson's father-in-law's lawn and sent her own father a handwritten note on his daughter's wedding day describing her as a "nigger loving Jew." Firsthand experience of Klan hegemony turned her into a Democrat; a native Midwestern sense of independence and civic concern led her into progressive activism. Nicholson, though conservative in her actions, had the liberal mind typical of her times. She had driven her first car at age twelve. She did not drink—though she had attended many country club parties where bootleg gin was served behind the bar and vomited up in the ladies' room—but she smoked, something unthinkable for a woman to do a generation before. She and her sister had been raised to be autonomous, adventurous, and the equal of their male peers. Her brother was part of what she called "the restless generation." He had been shot through the throat at the Battle of Argonne then gone West to be a stockbroker in California. Her life, milieu, and outlook matched up exactly with those described in so many Fitzgerald plots, except that she was no ditzy flapper. In Indiana she threw herself into public life, first as an activist for the Women's Organization for

National Prohibition Repeal and later as the founder of the first branch Planned Parenthood in Indianapolis—the first in the state. In 1934 following a scandal in the state Republican party she spied a route to office and in the midterms rode Franklin Roosevelt's long electoral coattails into the Indiana state capitol. There she legislated like a typical New Deal technocrat: she proposed a new insurance code; she helped pass an expansive new welfare bill (what one of her saltier colleagues called "terrible communist social security"); she lent her vote to a (successful) measure to allow for the sterilization of the criminally insane.

Then, in early 1935, she chanced upon an issue and made it her signature reform: the campaign to abolish the seduction statutes and their companion heart balm suits. Nicholson's campaign to pass what became known as anti–heart balm legislation was born of a deep sense of the laws' injustice. "My feeling about the law," Nicholson later told an interviewer,

> is that it just seemed perfectly silly to me, that from time immemorial, a female being engaged to be married could change her mind and say, "Sorry Joe, it's all off." But if a man did, and if he had any money, he could be sued. I thought it was absolutely absurd. I had no understanding whatsoever that I was bucking up against the basic tenet of English common law. . . . I thought it was undignified and disgusting that women sued men for the same changing their mind about getting married.

Nicholson began running a high-profile public campaign for the laws' repeal. It triggered first a statewide debate and then a national debate about the place of seduction legislation in American society. Nicholson proved adept at courting publicity, her charge that female plaintiffs in seduction suits exhibited "itching palms in the guise of aching hearts" drew laughter and applause throughout the nation. Suddenly, legislators who had long been silent on the issue found their voice. State Senator Wade called such legislation a boon to "unscrupulous jackleg lawyers" and a disaster for everybody else; his colleague Senator McNabe challenged the very notion that lost virtue had a court-determined cash value. The press hailed Nicholson as the gold digger's bane and portrayed her in cartoons as a shield to the depredations of vamps, temptresses, and blackmailers adept at exploiting the law. When debates on the proposed bill began in the state assembly some expressed disbelief that women would want to lose these legal protections. "Do you mean to tell me," Republican Senator William P. Dennigan asked the floor, that "you will help women by taking away their civil rights against philanderers and men who prey upon them?" Nicholson was unmoved by such criticism. "We have an opportunity to pass a piece of progressive legislation, in keeping with the times. . . . Women do not demand rights, gentlemen, they earn them, and they ask no such privileges as these which are abolished in this bill."[74]

Nicholson won the day. In the spring of 1935 Indiana passed the nation's first piece of anti–heart balm legislation. The law, known as the "Gold-Diggers bill," abolished the heart balm actions of Breach of Promise to Marriage, Criminal Conversation, and Alienation of Affection, and limited seduction cases in criminal courts to instances in which the plaintiff was under twenty-one years of age. The legislation soon spread to other states. Another six states would pass legislation that year; another four would do so over the next decade.[75][76] In many states, as in Indiana, reform would be led by women, often from among the first generation of female legislators and often ardent feminists. Repealing seduction laws had become a feminist issue.[77]

In retrospect Nicholson's victory was ambiguous and only half-realized. She understood her cause as a straightforward pursuit of equality before the law and an end to the implied condescension to women that she identified at the heart of seduction legislation. But many men clearly viewed the anti–heart balm campaign as a way of avenging themselves on the new women born of the 1920s. The language and imagery of the campaigning in the press—where it was predominantly men, not women, shaping the message—largely evoked modern, negative ideas of womanhood. Women were flappers, gold diggers, blackmailers. At a deeper level, the repeal of protection for women in one arena represented a kind of revenge for their accrual of gains in others, most notably in the workplace and in the voting booth. Furthermore, even if it were true that anti–heart balm legislation was passed for good, progressive reasons then it only met with partial success. Of the twenty-three attempts to pass anti–heart balm laws in 1935, fifteen failed. Clearly a majority of states still believed in the old ideals of feminine meekness, chastity, and vulnerability before the seducer's wiles. This speaks to the incomplete nature of the social and sexual revolution of the 1920s. Snubbed out by the 1929 Crash and the Great Depression that followed, it failed to transform mores and only served as a prelude to the thoroughgoing revolution of the sixties and seventies.[78]

What Jack Johnson thought of all this is unknown. By the mid-thirties very few people asked his views on anything. He featured in the press, if at all, largely as a lone critical voice on the skills and prospects of Joe Louis, the black heavyweight boxing sensation. Johnson had briefly attempted to bring Louis under his wing, and when the younger man sensibly rebuffed him he went into opposition, critiquing Louis's abilities and loudly supporting his great rival, the German Max Schmeling. For his part, Louis, like many black contenders, was wary of Johnson. Since his Havana bout with Jess Willard, no black fighter had been allowed to challenge for the heavyweight title. Louis's management correctly surmised that the only way to get their man the shot he deserved was to market him as the Anti-Johnson. Louis was never seen drinking or gambling. He was never seen outside a church or out of a sober suit. He was never seen with a white woman, at all. Joe Louis had to play dumb—in both senses—to get the title that Johnson had won with a big mouth and a golden smile.

Nonetheless, it is highly unlikely that Johnson would have cared about the anti-heart balm laws. After all, heart balm acts and seduction statutes had never bothered him much when they were on the books and nothing had changed for him with their repeal. By comparison, both the federal Mann Act and the state miscegenation laws were both still on the books, and were both still energetically policed, for the remainder of his life. There was no small irony that the United States went to war in 1941 with a Nazi racial state that considered American state racial laws too harsh for Hitler's Germany. There was perhaps no greater sign of Johnson's fundamental equanimity and graciousness that he would nonetheless appear at boxing exhibitions during the war to help raise money to fund a war for a government that once waged war on him. His three marriages were still considered criminal in over half the states of the union on the night of June 9, 1946 when his speeding car flipped on a bend outside Franklinton, North Carolina, while traveling home from Texas to New York. Johnson died as he lived, racing across state lines for no purpose other than his own. He would be laid to rest in Graceland next to Etta Duryea. Their marriage and their love would not receive universal legal recognition in America for another two decades. *Loving v. Virginia*—the Supreme Court ruling that both annulled all anti-miscegenation laws and served as one of the few occasions where legal shorthand rose to the level of cosmic poetry—was not handed down until June 1967, during the Summer of Love.

CHAPTER SIX

BLOOD OUT

The American mania for policing seduction was never fully embraced in Europe. Though this was not due to a lack of interest in the subject. In Britain and continental Europe the same sexual fears that loomed large in the American psyche were nourished by many of the same anxieties. If in the historical imagination late-Victorian Europe slumbered in self-satisfied complacency, to its inhabitants it seethed with danger and novelty. The outward forms of industrial capitalism—filthy metropolises, mass migration, proletarian mobs, choking air and stinking rivers—were given a terrifying new significance by Darwinian theories that popularized the language of struggle, degeneration, and extinction. As natural selection begat racial theorizing, so did social transformation beget gender trouble. Like their American counterparts, European cities were home to a flourishing public sex trade. They were also incubators for a new generation of feminist activists intent on upending the dominant sexual order. For conservatives, the rebellion of the "New Women" of the 1880s and 1890s was directly connected to the new, racialized discourse that saw sexual permissiveness as the gateway to racial collapse. As in America, the panic over seduction was grounded in antagonistic and contradictory male attitudes toward race and gender. In Europe these fears found expression less in the law than in a complex of cultural tropes that dredged up tales of the supernatural to give form to the anxieties of modernity. "Witch-tales in this enlightened age!" marveled the London-based occult guru Madame Blavatsky in the 1880s. "You will have such witch-tales as the Middle Ages never dreamt of. Whole nations will drift insensibly into black magic." Nowhere was this drift

more in evidence than in the mind and milieu of one Londoner, operating out of a theatre in the city's West End.[1]

The first thing people noticed about Bram Stoker was his height. At
a time when the army had by force of necessity to reduce the minimum
height for prospective recruits from five foot six to five foot, Stoker
was an easy six foot two and muscularly built. Everything about him,
from his tidy russet beard, his ruddy cheeks, and his legendary, booming
voice spoke of good health and vitality. Stoker's energy, good cheer, and
unthinking courage impressed everyone he met. On at least one occasion
it also made the national press when, at age thirty-five, he dived into
the Thames from a steamboat after witnessing the attempted suicide
of a fellow passenger. Without a second thought, the papers reported,
"Mr. Stoker threw off his own coat, and pluckily jumped in after the
drowning man, grappled with him, and succeeded in bringing him up
from to the steamer, where he was laid on the deck in an unconscious
condition." When he could not revive the man himself he took him back
to his home in Chelsea so his brother Thomas, a doctor, could have
a go. The man died; Stoker seems to have survived his plunge in the
rancid river unscathed. His wife, according to lore, was appalled when
she came home to find a cadaver laid out on their dining room table.

Abraham Stoker was born in Clontarf, Ireland, in 1847, but spent
almost his whole life to the age of the thirty in Dublin where his father,
also Abraham, was a civil servant. His mother Charlotte was a respectable housewife who bore her husband seven children and involved
herself in the charitable causes fashionable among middle-class women,
which in her case meant an abiding interest in women's education and
the rescue of poor, vulnerable girls from the streets and workhouses of
Victorian Ireland. The Stokers were Protestant, like much of the Irish
elite, but their bourgeois status was hard-won. Abraham Senior was the
son of an artisan and had raised his family's place in society by grinding

his way up through the ranks of the colonial bureaucracy. The result was that his sons got the best education that could be hoped for, which in Ireland meant attending Trinity College, Dublin. Bram, their third child and second son, had been a sickly boy and a mediocre student but was transformed from the moment he arrived at Trinity in 1864, at age sixteen.

Trinity was an intensely competitive social and intellectual environment which consciously selected and shaped the future Irish leadership. Stoker's contemporaries were the sons of the elite and the fathers of Ireland's revolutionary generation. In ambitious company, Stoker stood out as being a high-achiever with a hunger, easily worn, for success and recognition. There seemed no limit on the range of his interests and offices. He was President of the Philosophical Society and Auditor of the Historical Society (founded by Edmund Burke) where he composed, read, and discussed papers on everything from Shelley, Faust, Byron, and supernaturalism in literature, to science, politics, and racial theory. For his efforts in these fields he was awarded medals and certificates in history, oratory, and composition which sat alongside the dozen or so trophies he won for his athletic achievements in sports as varied as rugby, swimming, distance running, gymnastics, high jump, long jump, vaulting, slingshot, and rowing. Years later his classmates would remember their friend's great strength, his flexibility, and his daring stunts on the rings and the trapeze. He was also a presence on the Trinity stage—performing in productions of Richard Sheridan's *School for Scandal* and *The Rivals*—and a participant in student literary life as an avid if average short story writer. Alongside this packed schedule, Stoker also worked in the Dublin Civil Service for the final four years of his six-year stint at Trinity, a job he would apply himself to with mixed interest until 1878. Stoker formally left university in 1870 but remained intimately bound up in Trinity life which was only to be expected given

the university's dominant position in Dublin society. In 1871, already
established as a local character and universally admired as an avatar of
the Victorian values of thrift, industry, and muscular Christianity, Stoker
joined the *Dublin Evening Mail* as a theatre critic. There he reported to
the *Mail*'s proprietors Dr. Henry Maunsell and Joseph Sheridan Le Fanu,
a descendent of the playwright and the author of the sapphic vampire
thriller *Carmilla* (1872). He was soon ubiquitous in Dublin thespian
circles where he mingled with actors, playwrights, critics, and managers,
became a stalwart presence in the audience at the Theatre Royal, and
grew easily into the role of assiduous networker—he started a correspondence (uninvited but happily received) with Walt Whitman, struck
up intimate friendships with stage beauties like Genevieve Ward, and
won the respect and attention of the dramatists who periodically came
through town on tour.

One of the men who was drawn to Stoker would change his life.
Henry Irving was one of the great Victorian freaks. Born in obscurity in
the West Country, Irving had received little education—George Bernard
Shaw liked to gossip that he was a virtual illiterate—but had acquired
at a young age an obsession with the theatre. He began his dramatical career in the provinces, in Sunderland, and spent the better part of
two decades perfecting his art and striving his way into London acting
circles. A tall, stooping man, with habitually hunched shoulders, Irving
had thick hair, an expansive, bald brow, and a very large, very curious
head, the great bulk of which began beyond the jawline as though it
always sought to tip him downward and that it took conscious effort on
his part to keep himself upright. On the stage Irving was known for his
harsh, stentorian voice, his hypnotic eyes, and his bizarre incorporation
of an affected limp that left one foot dragging after the other whatever
character he played. Irving was an enigmatic man, more comfortable in
playing a fictional persona than inhabiting a real one, but he was acutely

aware of his capacity to enchant his audience. Bram Stoker learned of this up close during his first meeting with Irving in Dublin in 1876 after an evening at Trinity. By this stage in his career, Irving was one of the most respected British actors and commanded audiences wherever he went. Wanting, perhaps, to bring this promising young man under his influence, he treated Stoker to a private recital of "The Dream of Eugene Aram," a melodramatic narrative poem by Thomas Hood concerned with murder, guilt, and gothicism. The poem was a well-known part of Irving's repertoire and one that Stoker knew. Nonetheless, when the famed actor launched into a rendition of these familiar lines after dinner at the Shelbourne Hotel in Dublin, something changed in Stoker forever. "There are great moments even to the great," Stoker later wrote, but

> *That night Irving was inspired. Many times since then I saw and heard him—for such an effort eyes as well as ears are required— recite that poem and hold audiences, big or little, spellbound till the moment came for the thunderous outlet of their pent-up feelings; but that particular vein I never met again. Art can do much; but in all things even in art there is a summit somewhere. That night for a brief time, in which the rest of the world seemed to sit still, Irving's genius floated in blazing triumph above the summit of art. There is something in the soul which lifts it above all that has its base in material things. If once only in a lifetime the soul of a man can take wings and sweep for an instant into mortal gaze, then that "once" for Irving was on that, to me, ever memorable night.*

At the end of the performance Stoker collapsed to the floor in unmanly hysterics. It was the beginning of a great friendship.[2]

"Every Irishman who felt that his business in life was on the higher planes of the cultural professions," George Bernard Shaw observed, "felt that he must have a metropolitan domicile and an International culture: that is, he felt that his first business was to get out of Ireland. I had the same feeling. . . . [the] English language was my weapon, there was nothing for it but London." Bram Stoker felt much the same way. He and Irving stayed in close contact after the night of Eugene Aram and in 1877 Irving began to involve him in his plans to acquire a major London theatre, the Lyceum. When in November of that year Irving's designs for Stoker swam into focus, the younger man recorded three triumphant words in his diary: "London in View!" It would take another year to get there but by December 1878 Stoker had resigned from the Dublin civil service, handed over his last review for the *Mail*, and was ready to sign on with Irving. The two met at Birmingham, where Irving was finishing a tour. Stoker visited Irving at his hotel in Edgbaston and later recalled that his new employer "was mightily surprised when he found that I had a wife with me."

Oscar Wilde once described Florence Balcombe as an "exquisitely pretty girl . . . with the most perfectly beautiful face I have ever seen" and he was well-positioned to know, as were it not for Bram Stoker's mysterious appearance in her life he would have likely married her. Almost nothing is known about how Stoker and Balcombe met, how he won her, and how they lived together for the four decades of outwardly calm married life that followed. Very little is known about Mrs. Stoker at all, except that she was exceptionally physically attractive, easily meeting the exacting standards of ethereal feminine beauty that the Victorians so coveted. Socially, she was a cipher. Biographers of her husband have had to survive on rumors and throwaway remarks to paint a picture of Florence Stoker as a frigid, vain, ambiguously cruel woman. In reality little is known of her except that she was sought after by painters and sculptors wanting to capture her likeness and that she won the sympathy of London society after surviving a major maritime disaster in 1882, when the steamer *Victoria* she and her son were aboard hit rocks near Dieppe in the Channel, resulting in the death of 20 of 120 passengers and crew and a public shaming of the traveling Italian men who jumped into lifeboats reserved for women and children.

One interesting absence in the sketchy surviving portrait of Florence Stoker is that total lack of love for her evinced by her only child, Irving Noel Thornley Stoker, born on New Year's Eve 1879. Noel's memories of childhood feature his enormous, bear of a father who existed as if visiting from a fairytale on the periphery of his life, always dressed up and about to leave for Theaterland, but there is nothing about his mother. There is, however, an unnerving public window into the Stoker household from an image of Bram, Florence, and Noel drawn by George Du Maurier that appeared in *Punch* magazine in September 1886. It is a scene of late-Victorian bliss: a garden party in the grounds of fine country house; in the foreground the hulk of a dark-hatted, heavily bearded Stoker leaning forward in his wicker chair, a tennis racket at his feet; sitting a good meter and a half apart from him is his wife, beautiful, glamorous, and distant, looking down, either lost in her knitting or ignoring both the attentions of her husband sitting morosely across from her and her only child standing in boater and knickerbockers behind her, seemingly bemused by her refusal to play with him. The caption beneath reads:

> FILIAL REPROOF: *Mamma to Noel, who is inclined to be talkative, 'Hush, Noel! Haven't I told you that little Boys should be Seen and not Heard?' Noel's reply "Yes, Mamma! But you don't Look at ME!*

It is an odd piece of Victorian sadism, inexplicable in its casual confusion of public and private.[3]

Within less than a year of their marriage in Dublin, the newly married couple found themselves plunged into the maelstrom of London life. Eventually the Stokers would make their home in and around Cheyne Walk, near the sleepy western end of the Thames Embankment, but in those first hectic years they lived only a few streets away from Stoker's new place of employment at the Lyceum Theatre, at almost the exact center of London life. The Lyceum was and remains a large faux-Palladian structure situated at one of London's great meeting places. Perched on Wellington Street, just off the eastern tip of the Strand, the theatre's entrance was visible to the stream of Londoners and London traffic that traveled south to north across Waterloo Bridge each day and who could not have avoided the two huge illuminated signs that hung invitingly on the theatre's facade. The theatre also connected the Eastern and Western hemispheres of the city. Aldwych, which the Lyceum looked over, was the meeting place of the Strand and Fleet Street. The former was the great London thoroughfare that led to Westminster and thence to the wealthy districts surrounding Piccadilly and Hyde Park before petering out in the bohemian villages of Kensington and Chelsea; the latter was the mainline to the old City of London whose course began as a tour of the great institutions of Victorian Britain—the Royal Courts of Justice, the Bank of England, St. Paul's Cathedral—only to end in the scene of one the nation's great shames: the teeming slums and rookeries of Whitechapel, Shadwell, and Stepney.

The larger paradoxes of Victorian London were played out in the Lyceum's immediate environs. On the Strand, well-heeled shoppers rubbed shoulders with prostitutes, beggars, and pickpockets. Clerks and dukes alike came to Covent Garden for the playhouses—as they had done since the eighteenth century—but also for the seedier pleasures of neighboring Soho, a zone of gin shops, brothels, and flophouses wedged uneasily between the more desirable districts of Mayfair, St. James's, and Bloomsbury. The contradictions that the Lyceum bore witness to were captured by Arthur Conan Doyle in *The Sign of the Four* (1890). When Holmes and Watson meet outside Irving's theatre on a mysterious errand for a client they experience the strangeness of the West End where the thick crowds "of shirt-fronted men and beshawled, bediamonded women" spilling out of private carriages before the entrance to the Lyceum existed alongside a mass of undifferentiated humanity that "flitted from the gloom into the light, and so back into the gloom once more."

The gloom, smoke, and smog that typified late-Victorian London—and which was at its worst close to the river, where vapor from the Thames met with air-borne effluent that gathered naturally in the water basin—was something that the Stokers would have noticed as soon as they arrived from Dublin. The period they lived in the city coincided roughly with the heyday of the Pea-Soupers, the London Particular, the London Ivy—the infamous London fog that defined the visual and olfactory experience of London living in this era. The yellow-brown fog, that, depending on the light, atmospheric conditions, and the peculiar composition of local sources of air pollution, could also shade into purple, vermillion, pale green, and bog black, influenced and obstructed all life in this capital of global finance, industry, and science. In December and January it regularly killed several thousand Londoners a month from respiratory disease. The fogs also provided cover for crime and public disorder. The cast-iron London gaslights—those great symbols of rational civic planning—could not contend with the choking fumes and in the shallow half-light that the city consisted moody crowds and groups of petty thieves could and did run riot with scant fear of the police. In 1886 there was a spate of such disturbances in Trafalgar Square and Pall Mall, on the Lyceum's doorstep. More generally the fog made mockery of Victorian pretensions to the conquest of nature and superstition by reason and investigation. A famous 1888 *Punch* cartoon depicted a hadean "King Fog" accompanied by his imps sweeping over the British capital while the figure of Science lies defeated in the ground. The "shores of Styx were bland matched with Fleet Street or the Strand," *Punch* declared, where "a foul and foetid pall fell over each and all; its ingredients were mist, and much, and smoke." The "ruthless reign of King Fog" had turned the citizens of London into ghosts—an image that artists, journalists, and writers would return to repeatedly in those decades. Indeed, the whole city became a specter existing as the hostage of an unreal, unfathomable, wholly capricious haze that had neither source nor purpose. Oscar Wilde, who had moved to London at the same time as the Stokers and lived nearby, on the Thames side of the Strand, recalled watching the yellow fog roll up the river each winter morning until it consumed the whole city leaving nothing in view apart from the dull white dome of St. Paul's hanging like a chandelier above the mustard cloudline. Victorian London was a nightmare waiting to be populated.

The Lyceum's role was to keep the nightmares out. Irving positioned it as a safe, conservative space that catered to the London elite and the aspirational middle classes. The selection of plays reflected this ethos. Irving rejected suspect new trends in theatre and playwriting in favor of lavish sets, high-end special effects, and a focus on the classics. Over a quarter of the plays performed in the Lyceum under Irving were Shakespeare; the rest were for the most part historical pageants or tried-and-true audience favorites. Irving steered clear of the Ibsen revolution, an insistence which won him the disdain of the avant-garde, especially Bernard Shaw who, though a regular presence in the stalls, considered the Lyceum little better than a high-end music hall.[4] Irving did not care for such matters. A conservative by nature and by politics he was interested in form and craft, and had little time for Bernard Shaw's socialist aesthetics which were, in any case, philistine in the extreme. Irving also needed to turn a profit. Before the curtain even lifted on the first performance under his management, he and Stoker had already spent some £12,000 renovating the building. This included a complete structural and decorative make-over of the two thousand capacity theatre; a retouching of the existing ornaments; the refurbishment of the grungy auditorium in more fetching shades of green and blue; and the commissioning of an entirely new act drop. The faithful green stage curtain was kept, and Irving's son would later recall how when the lights went down

> *and only the lower part of it was softly illumined by footlights,*
> *this green curtain seemed to fade into infinity—veiling, as Charles*
> *Lamb, once said, a heaven of the imagination. It was the veil*
> *between the world of reality and of make-believe; when it rose the*
> *world before and behind the proscenium were blended; the illusory*
> *gained substance from the prosaic which in turn reflected something*
> *of the glittering image of the illusion.*

Stoker's specific role in the running of the Lyceum was that of acting manager. Irving and his stage manager, Harry Loveday, had complete control of the artistic direction of the theatres, of the conduct of the rehearsals, and of what was performed and who performed in it. Stoker had the arguably more complex role of mediating between the world of the stage, the world behind the stage, and the world outside the stage. Most actors only had to play a handful of roles each year; Stoker had to shape-shift between countless each day. Outside the Lyceum he repre-sented Irving's interests in court, in theatrical associations and cultural charities, on a few occasions in Parliament, and defended and promoted him and his work in the press. Stoker also had to handle the police and encourage them to combat the petty crime that always threatened to make the West End unappealing to middle-class theatregoers and to crack down on ticket forgeries—a problem that repeatedly took him to Bow Court to testify on the matter. In the front of house, Stoker was in charge of meeting the crowds who came to see Irving's plays and ensuring that grandees, reviewers, and Irving's mother were seen to their seats with all due care and courtesy. This was his most public function and the sight of this rugged, smiling Irishman deftly marshaling the audience into position before each performance became a familiar and welcome fixture in London life. Behind the scenes he managed all the money that passed through the theatres—over two million pounds over the course of his career—dealt with the salaries, gripes, and idiosyncrasies of the several hundred actors, engineers, and tradesmen in their employ, and otherwise ensured that the enormous operation that was the Lyceum Theatre ran smoothly and profitably.

From the outset Irving's venture was a magnificent success. The opening night of his first Lyceum production—*Hamlet*, with Irving in the lead role—on December 30, 1878 was a major society event with an audience that numbered among them the Prince of Wales, former Prime Ministers and great rivals Gladstone and Disraeli, poets Swinburne, Tennyson, and Wilde, the musical duo Gilbert and Sullivan, and painters—and later Chelsea neighbours of Stoker—Whistler and Millais.[5] Irving went on to secure the enduring patronage of the Prince of Wales and through him the favor of the British and Continental aristocracy. The Royal family would book boxes for the premiers of Irving's plays; Horace Wyndham would later write that in the last decades of the Victorian era an opening night at the Lyceum drew "an audience that was representative of the best of the period in the realms of art, literature, and society. Admittance was a very jealously guarded privilege."

As master of the box office, Stoker was the gatekeeper to each first night at the Lyceum and Wyndham wryly described how the proud

Dubliner "looked upon the stalls, dress circle, and boxes as if they were annexes to the Royal Enclosure at Ascot, and one almost had to be proposed and seconded before the coveted ticket would be issued."[6] Success in London gave Irving a license to print money in the provinces. Starting in 1881, the Lyceum troupe began to tour regularly in Northern England, Scotland, Canada, and the United States. To Stoker's mammoth workload was now added the logistical horror of having to organize the travel arrangements of several hundred thespians and workmen along with their costumes, scenery, and lighting equipment. For the Lyceum's first tour a separate train had to be booked just to transport the stage-sets and lighting paraphernalia. But the profits were enormous. That tour netted £24,000; the nine tours of North America that Stoker organized between 1883 and 1904 brought in lesser but still considerable amounts. It was on the road where Stoker earned his reputation for omnipotence and ubiquity. On an 1893 tour of America he managed to negotiate a stage electrician out of jail after his arrest for violating immigration laws. On tour the actors of the Irving troupe learned to fear and obey their acting manager. Stoker disciplined any dramatist who developed ideas out of sync with Irving's aesthetic vision and personal preferences. An actor who tried to go on stage without wearing his makeup because he believed the foundation would run in the heat of the night was told "to forget his theories and to go and get made properly up like everyone else." Stoker's powers were almost uncanny. "That devil Bram Stoker," actor William Terriss told a colleague, "he can see through a brick wall—God help you." This was only a little short of the truth. Ever in a hurry, Stoker did travel through a plate glass divider while moving at speed through the lobby of the Chestnut Street Opera House in Philadelphia, though, invincible as ever, he emerged on the other side without a mark on him.

After their 1884–1885 tour of the United States, Irving and Stoker went home to the Lyceum. They returned to London that summer of 1885 to find the city in a tumult. Moral outrage led to disturbances in the street. Newspapers editorialized, ministers sermonized, and social reformers agitated for change with new vigor. Committees of bishops and elder statesmen were formed, as were new alliances among previously fractious groups of nonconformist ministers, trade unions, and bourgeois campaigners. Massive meetings in Hyde Park were discussed, organized, and attended. Rumors of conspiracy, cover-up, even revolution bounded around. Questions were asked in Parliament; dormant bills were revived and propelled through the two houses. By autumn English law and English democracy had been transformed. The subject of the outcry was the sexual rights of English women. The source of the intense public furor on the issue was a series of revelations in the London afternoon daily, *The Pall Mall Gazette*. At the center of it all was the *Gazette*'s editor, a professional acquaintance of Bram Stoker's, William Thomas Stead.

With his dark, three-piece suits and pocket chain, his full brown beard, and piercing zealot's eyes, W.T. Stead was emblematic of a new force ascendant in late-Victorian politics. Born in Northumberland in 1849 and raised in a Congregationalist household, Stead's three declared passions were "Christianity, Cricket and Democracy" and his calling was as a campaigning journalist and editor. He had begun his career at the *Northern Echo*, England's first morning halfpenny paper and the champion of its restless working class. Initially a Gladstonian liberal, Stead had been converted to a jingoistic socialism by the late 1870s and believed in "the duty of England as a civilising power among the weaker and more degraded nations of the earth" and was frank in his acknowledgment that the "Anglo-Saxon idea has gained possession of my brain." At home in the provinces where he corresponded with the great and the good in splendid isolation from London, Stead professed no desire to move to the corrupt and dissolute British capital. He claimed that he had been to London once and had no desire to go again. "If the Lord wishes me to go," he declared, "He will have to drive me thither with whips." The Lord did wish for Stead to go to London. In 1880 he was offered a job with John Morley, editor of *Pall Mall Gazette*, an afternoon daily based out of offices on Strand, which he accepted. In 1883 Morley retired and he became editor himself. Under Stead's authority the *Gazette* became an influential force in British life. Despite having a circulation of less than 40,000, the newspaper weighed in on the great issues of the day and not infrequently changed the course of events. Stead's advocacy helped send General Gordon to his martyrdom in Khartoum; his patriotic affront at the retrograde state of the Navy resulted in a massive increase in the Admiralty's budget; a campaign against slum conditions moved the ultra-conservative Tory administration of Lord Salisbury to action on the matter. Then, late in the spring of 1885, Stead had a conversation which would change his life.

In 1880, Benjamin Scott, a committed social reformer and the Lord Chamberlain of London, had been appalled by a new book. That year, Alfred Dyer published *The European Slave Trade in English Girls* in which he declared the existence of an underground economy selling English girls into sexual bondage in the brothels of France and Belgium. In a bid to combat this threat, the London Committee for Suppressing the Traffic in British Girls was established, with Scott as its Chairman. Its committee included many reformist luminaries such as Josephine Butler, the pioneering Victorian feminist and head of the Ladies National Association—a group that lobbied for improved sexual protections for women. Scott's lobbying led to an investigation into white slavery by a House of Lord's Select Committee which reported in 1881 that British laws were not sufficient to protect the bodies and morals of British women and girls. The trade in British girls was symptomatic of a larger failing. British law sought to regulate vice rather than promote virtue. British women were vulnerable to sexual exploitation and social ruin, all too often ending up on the streets as the sexual playthings of debauched aristocrats.[7] "In other countries female chastity is more or less protected by law up to the age of 21," the Lords observed. "No such protection is given in England to girls under the age of 13." They recommended an increase of the age of consent from 13 to 16; the introduction of penalties for indecent assault; criminalizing the solicitation of women for employment in an overseas brothel, as well as tough new measures for those who aided and abetted the procurement and prostitution of minors. These formed the basis for a new Criminal Law Amendment Act which lingered in Parliament for several years without ever becoming law. After another setback in 1884, an infuriated Scott decided that only a major scandal would secure the bill's passage and so he went to W.T. Stead of the *Pall Mall Gazette* with a horrific story.

Scott told Stead that English virgins were being bought and sold on the streets of London in enormous quantities. Outraged, Stead sought the opinion of a retired senior Scotland Yard detective who confirmed the story in no uncertain terms. A now thoroughly scandalized Stead concluded that a conspiracy of silence—whose confederates were the press, senior politicians, and the capitalist and landlord class—was keeping the ghastly truth from the electorate. He was now determined to expose the truth of the matter and in June he embarked on a journey into London's underworld.

"I have been a night prowler for weeks," Stead would later write of this voyage into the pit,

> *I have gone in different guises to most of the favourite rendezvous*
> *of harlots. I have strolled along Ratcliff-highway, and sauntered*
> *round and round the Quadrant at midnight. I have haunted St,*
> *James's Park, and twice enjoyed the strange sweetness of summer*
> *night by the sides of the Serpentine. I have been at all hours in*
> *Leicester-square and the Strand, and have spent the midnight in*
> *Mile-end-road and the vicinity of the Tower. Sometimes I was*
> *alone; sometimes accompanied by a friend; and the deep and*
> *strong impression which I have brought back is one of respect*
> *and admiration for the extraordinarily good behaviour of the*
> *English girls who pursue this dreadful calling. In the whole of my*
> *wanderings I have not been accosted half-a-dozen times, and then I*
> *was more to blame than the woman. I was turned out of Hyde Park*
> *at midnight in company with a drunken prostitute, but she did not*
> *begin the conversation.*

Stead's elegy to the working girls of London spoke to his basic compassion toward women trapped in a life of prostitution. They were not to blame for their condition. On his travels through "the maze of London brotheldom" Stead met the real culprits: the madams who groomed the nurses and shop-girls promenading in Hyde Park on the weekend; the professional seducers who corrupted girls and delivered them to brothels; the drunken mothers who sold their daughters for gin money; the trafficker who spoke in brisk, commercial terms of the slave routes that took London girls to continental brothels via Dover and Ostend; the employment agencies and servants registries and bars and theatres whose business facade concealed a pernicious effort to corrupt and exploit working class women. At the heart of the labyrinth he met the men whose lust kept the market in existence, men taken almost exclusively from "the very wealthy and the immoral idlers of the 'upper ten.'" These were aristocrats and capitalists, the sons and guardians of privilege. Somewhere along the way Stead also found the final proof of Scott's initial claim. A thirteen-year-old girl from West London, her virginity proven by a medical examination, had been sold by her sodden mother for £5, chloroformed, and the delivered up to a wealthy gentleman in a Regent Street brothel.

Overwhelmed by moral revulsion, Stead struggled to find words to explain to the readers of the *Pall Mall Gazette* what he had witnessed in the capital of the British empire. He raided Dante, Homer, even the Koranic accounts of hell to find parallels. In the end he settled on myth of the Cretan Minotaur who took as tribute the flower of the Athenian youth. London was the new Crete, its wretched and exploited women the sacrificial offering. Stead's series of exposes, including his ghastly account of the purchasing of a virgin, duly appeared in the *Pall Mall Gazette* over the course of the first ten days of July under the heading of the "Maiden Tribute of Modern Babylon."

In the first instalment of his exposé, Stead had emphatically denied that he was seeking a revolution in British sexual manners. "However strongly I may feel as to the imperative importance of morality and chastity," he wrote, "I do not ask for any police interference with the liberty of vice. I ask only for the repression of crime." Only three weeks later his tone had sharpened. In the intervening weeks his revelations had sent the country into a frenzy over women's sexual rights and this public outpouring in turn inspired Stead to raise the stakes. Parliament had hastily scheduled a third reading of the Criminal Law Amendment Act on July 30. On July 28 the *Pall Mall Gazette* noted that the MPs were now faced with a "national uprising against the loathsome abnormities

[sic] of sexual vice." Parliamentary intervention was needed to forestall insurrection. "If ever there is a social revolution in this country," the *Gazette* warned, "it will be over this very question."[8]

What Stead and his allies knew was that Parliament could not discuss the issue of prostitution and the alleged "white slave trade" without also addressing the question of seduction: the two issues were inextricably linked in reformers' minds. The condition of England's prostitutes was understood as the dark reflection of the glistening ideal of the "Angel of the House." Women either met a male standard of meek femininity and unquestioning submission to patriarchal authority or they were expendable outlets for unbridled male desire. It was no coincidence that one of Stead's greatest supporters in the struggle to pass the Criminal Law Amendment Act was Josephine Butler, Victorian England's lonely champion of women's sexual rights. Butler and the Ladies National Association (LNA) had spent the previous fifteen years campaigning against the hated Contagious Diseases Act of 1867 that empowered police to detain any woman they suspected to be a prostitute and have them subjected to a forced inspection by a doctor to ensure that they were not carriers of venereal disease. Those who campaigned against the act loathed its partiality, its brutality, and its ineffectiveness, but above all they recognized that alleged prostitutes' powerlessness before the combined specters of "medical despotism" and "police despotism" was a dramatization of every woman's impotence before an all-encompassing male despotism.[9]

For championing the cause of one of Britain's more despised and unsympathetic groups Butler attracted little praise and a great deal of mockery. One of her critics once attacked her as "an indecent maenad, a shrieking sister, frenzied, unsexed, and utterly without shame." "Unsexed" was the key word. It was the same that had been used to describe Mary Wollstonecraft and it referred to a specific idea of womanhood. Butler was "unsexed" because she contravened the norms of her sex—understood quite literally as referring to her genitals. In Victorian medical literature women were portrayed as "the Sex," hostage to their wombs (hence prone to hysteria), sent temporarily mad during menstruation, and finally ruined by menopause. Their biology determined the roles they could play in life: either as "an instrument to the convenience and lust of men" (through a life of prostitution) or as the mute, submissive bearer of children within marriage.[10]

Victorian feminists and their allies knew that the only way they could make progress on major issues—women's education, employment, and voting rights, among others—was to escape a framework that viewed them purely as sex objects. But paradoxically they had to do that by talking about sex. Women had to sexualize politics in order to desexualize themselves. Butler perfected this sinuous rhetorical strategy. One of her most powerful devices was an attack on the double standard of sexual morality. Why was it, she famously asked, that while society mindlessly indulged male libertinism "we never hear it carelessly or complacently asserted of a young woman that 'she is only sowing her wild oats'"? Men and women should be held to the same standard. This was an ostensibly banal assertion that contained a radical germ. Implicit in the argument was the assumption that women were *already* abiding by this superior standard and that only men had to change in order to meet it. Female purity was constantly juxtaposed with male dissolution. Butler and her fellow activists encouraged a view of women as essentially innocent and men as essentially rapacious. Male allies like Stead came to share in this opinion wholeheartedly. "Girls, and I say this emphatically, are not seducers," he later wrote. "They have innate delicacy and refinement. I say honestly that I do not believe that one woman in 10,000 would cast herself at the feet of lust except under duress or under the force of circumstances." Female perfection required radical male change to meet the same standard. Another one of Stead's allies, Edward White

Benson, Archbishop of Canterbury, founded the Church of England Purity Society that later merged with Ellice Hopkins's British White Cross Army (established in 1885) to form the White Cross League, an organization which encouraged single men to take public vows of chastity until marriage and to wear a white ribbon on their lapel to identify themselves as embodiments of the new morality. But individual change was not enough—the law had to protect the special needs of women in this area. Prostitutes had to be protected, but so too did girls, mothers, and wives—all women.[11]

The staid members of the British Parliament were wholly unprepared for the complexities of the reformers' arguments and methods. Gathered together at the height of summer, many were perplexed by the fact that a law that was apparently meant to deal with the problem of underage prostitution actually aimed at the total reformation of sexual norms. Members were not unduly troubled by the request to raise the age of consent from thirteen to sixteen—albeit the few that grumbled about the risks of blackmail for teenage boys—though that measure did not meet the hopes of some feminists who had argued for an age of twenty-one. Similarly, proposed new measures to combat sexual assault and to tackle those who enabled juvenile prostitution were not seriously challenged in the chamber. What did cause consternation was the language used to describe procuring. The law defined procuration as

> *Any person who Procures or attempts to procure any girl or woman under twenty-one years of age, not being a common prostitute, or of known immoral character, to have unlawful carnal connexion, either within or without the Queen's dominions.*

Those found guilty with of procuration faced a two-year prison sentence. The problem was that this looked a lot like a seduction law. The description of "not being . . . of known immoral character" seemed to mimic American seduction statutes that spoke of "previously chaste character." An "unlawful carnal connexion" was defined as "sexual intercourse is unlawful where no valid marriage exists" which seemed to be revive the old crime of fornication. Finally, the additional crimes of procuration "by false pretences or false representations" echoed the language of suasion commonly associated with seduction and courtship, not sexual enslavement. Confusion reigned as to whether the bill actually criminalized seduction or not. The attorney general, Sir Richard Webster, stated it did; Lord Bramwell—one of the most senior jurists in the land—declared that it did not. In between lay every shade of opinion. Many members observed the injustice that the new protections applied only to women and girls and put men and boys of the same age at legal disadvantage. Others stated that the door was now open to blackmail and extortion. Edward Lyulph Stanley, Liberal member for Oldham, called for a clarification of what "false pretences, false representations, or other fraudulent means" looked like in practice. He suggested that, like in American seduction statutes, a promise of marriage ought to be the benchmark for a false pretense that resulted in sex. In any event,

> *There ought to be some illustration given to show what kind of false pretences would be punishable. It would be too much for a woman to induce a man knowingly and willingly to go with her, and then to turn round and give him two years' imprisonment on the charge that she had been influenced by the false representations made to her. . . . That would be carrying the Criminal Law to a dangerous length.*

But no clarification was forthcoming in the final bill. Many parliamentarians clearly believed that the bill acted as a de facto seduction

statute and that it was open abuse and exploitation by cynical women
and "vicious girls." Outside of Parliament there were those who agreed
with them. "This Act of Parliament," complained a columnist in the
radical publication *The Anarchist*, "places the power of irreparably
injuring the character and prospects of innocent men, into the hands
. . . of rash and meddling philanthropists." "The bill," the anonymous
writer continued, "opens a wide door for . . . fraud and intimidation."[12]

But such concerns could not now prevent the passage of the Act.
Public pressure and media scrutiny was too intense. The bill passed the
Commons on August 7 and the Lords on August 10. As promised, Stead
hosted an enormous public protest in support of the new measures in
London at the end of August, shortly before the bill was signed into law
by the Queen.[13]

Shortly after this triumph, Stead suffered what most would consider
a painful personal setback. It transpired that the man whom he had
described in his reporting as having paid £5 for a virgin was none other
than Stead himself. Working through a network of former prostitutes
and madams Stead had arranged for Eliza Armstrong's delivery to that
hotel in London's West End. Keen to play the part of the pederast rake
convincingly, Stead, who was a teetotaller, drank a bottle of champagne
before making his way to the hotel where he paid his £5 and then burst
into the room where the drugged and thoroughly terrified Armstrong
lay in a stupor. Then, in order to prove the transnational trade in girls
was a going concern, he had her transported to France where she was
taken into the care of the Salvation Army. When the facts of Stead's
behavior emerged he was promptly put on trial and sentenced to serve
three months in jail. A farcical end to a farcical enterprise, but in fact
from Stead's perspective it was a triumph. Not only had he succeeded in
changing the law but his martyrdom was providential proof that he was
fighting the good fight.[14] Stead had also ruptured the complacent calm

of high-Victorian England. His dispatches from Babylon had revealed another London—a filthy, fogbound world bubbling over with perversion and sexual danger. A world of monsters.

Stoker knew W.T. Stead. One of his duties was the management of the Lyceum's relations with the press, and the *Pall Mall Gazette* regularly reviewed their productions. Stoker also knew the many politicians, journalists, and Establishment worthies who gathered after hours in the Lyceum's Beefsteak Room to discuss the issues of the day with Henry Irving. That summer talk must have turned from time to time to the antics of W.T. Stead and those whom Irving's circle knew dismissively as "the psalm-singing mob."[15] More prosaically, the wild scenes outside the *Gazette*'s Strand offices that July—the huge crowds, the ranks of policemen—would have obstructed Stoker's morning commute to work and would have naturally drawn comment from the Lyceum's employees. For the women of the Lyceum, Stead's reports would have had a special resonance. In the public mind, actresses had long been interchangeable with prostitutes, an association that Stead reinforced again and again in his journalism that summer.[16] All actresses had to live with this stigma. Ellen Terry, the Lyceum's leading lady, was all too familiar with it. The daughter of strolling players, as a teenager Terry had been an artist's model for George Watts, a painter associated with the Pre-Raphaelites.[17] Despite a forty-year age difference, Watts and Terry had married in 1865. In their subsequent divorce papers, Watts had claimed that he had wed Terry "to remove an impulsive young girl from the dangers and temptations of the stage."[18] By 1885, Terry was twice divorced, had two children out of wedlock, and was among the highest salaried women in the country, earning a massive £200 per week as an actress. Although she largely toed Irving's ideological line at the Lyceum, in her intellectual, creative, and financial independence Terry was something of a harbinger of the New Woman, and would later become a patroness of the suffragist movement. Even the staid confines of Irving's theatre were not completely removed from the torrid sexual politics of late-Victorian London.

— ◄◆► —

In the summer of 1888, when he and his company departed London for an extended tour of the provinces, Irving leased out the Lyceum to an American actor-manager named Richard Mansfield. It was to prove one of Irving's few missteps and one that let the violence and despair of London's dark places onto his hallowed stage, puncturing the veil of reality and make-believe once and for all. Mansfield's production was a stage adaptation of Robert Louis Stevenson's *Dr. Jekyll and Mr. Hyde.* Published in 1886, Stevenson's novel had been rapturously received and quickly became a bestseller. In a long, effusive review, *The Times* declared the story a *tour d'espirit*, Stevenson Edgar Allan Poe's better and George Eliot's equal, and the book a "a finished study in the art of fantastic literature."[19] But *The Times* did not regard *Dr. Jekyll*, as simply a work of fantasy. The reviewer understood its plot—the gradual uncovering of the schizoid split between the avuncular, Anglo-Saxon Dr. Jekyll and the malevolent, simian Mr. Hyde—as taking place on "strictly scientific grounds." Stevenson's work was of a piece with the latest biological and psychological research, specifically those unleashed in the wake of Charles Darwin's two masterpieces: *On the Origin of Species* (1859) and *The Descent of Man* (1871).

Darwin's theory of evolution by natural selection initially took an optimistic view of biological development. "As natural selection works solely by and for the good of each being," he wrote in the famous closing passages of *On the Origin of Species*, "all corporeal and mental endowments will tend to progress towards perfection." But in the 1880s this whiggish view of evolution was called into question. Ray Lankester's *Degeneration, A Chapter in Darwinism* (1880) had argued that if the conditions of life softened then organisms would cease to elaborate in response to threat and instead undergo "a gradual change of the structure in which the organism becomes adapted to less varied and less complex conditions of life. Degeneration was the "stippression [sic] of form, corresponding to the cessation of work." Parasites were the classic example. Once a parasite found a way of living off the life essence of another organism their genetic development eschewed all evolutionary "work" irrelevant to the improvement of their parasitic existence.[20] Lankester's two great scientific influences were the German biologists Anton Dohrn and Ernst Haeckel. Dohrn and Haeckel were both pioneers in the field of embryology. Haeckel had become known for his embryological theory of recapitulation, whereby a fetus in the womb passed through its species antecedent stages as it developed from a scattering of simple cells to, in the case of humans, a fully developed baby. Along the way, Haeckel postulated, the future organism climbed its own family tree. En route to personhood a future human was a group of cells, then a fish, then a primate, and then finally a human. "Ontogeny," Haeckel and his acolytes endlessly explained, "Recapitulates Phylogeny." As the embryonic organism underwent this process they developed and then shed the features of their species' previous incarnations. Human fetuses at one point have a monkey-like tail but they have lost it by the time they are born. But, Haeckel argued, it was possible that these traits would not be lost—that vestigial traits, or atavisms, could persist in otherwise fully developed individuals. However it found expression—physiological, psychological, anatomical—an atavism was the equivalent of a human infant being born with a prehensile tail.

Cesare Lombroso observed atavistic humans everywhere or, to be more precise, everywhere he looked, which was in prisons and penal colonies. Lombroso was an Italian criminologist and an acolyte of the Darwinian theories expounded by Haeckel and others. In the 1860s, while examining the skull of the deceased Italian brigand Vilella, Lombroso had what he described as a revelation. Criminals were not like the rest of the population. The criminal was in fact, "an atavistic being who reproduces in his person the ferocious instincts of primitive humanity and the inferior animals."

> *Thus were explained anatomically the enormous jaws, high cheek-bones, prominent superciliary arches, solitary lines in the palms, extreme size of the orbits, handle-shaped or sessile ears found in criminals, savages, and apes, insensibility to pain, extremely acute sight, tattooing, excessive idleness, love of orgies, and the irresistible craving for evil for its own sake, the desire not only to extinguish life from his victim, but to mutilate the corpse, tear its flesh, and drink its blood.*

As this (partial) list of traits and features demonstrates, for Lombroso physical and behavioral traits were comorbid in the biological criminal. Behavior and biology were intimately linked. In the process, causation became hopelessly confused. Lombroso readily embraced both hard theories of heredity and softer environmental explanations. "The aetiology of crime," he wrote, "mingles with that of all kinds of degeneration: rickets, deafness, monstrosity, hairiness, and cretinism, of which crime is only a variation." This was, of course, music to the ears of social conservatives and connoisseurs of decline throughout the West. Although his works were only translated into English in the very last years of the nineteenth century, his ideas soon gained currency outside of his native Italy. His breakthrough work, *L'uomo Delinquente* (*Criminal Man*), was published in 1876. By 1881 the *Pall Mall Gazette*—which published Stoker's short fiction and reviewed the Lyceum's plays—was discussing the Italian's writings in its columns, concluding gravely from it that "savagery is always very close to our civilization, and that the criminal and indolent easily glide back into the manners of Australians and Red Indians."[21] A few years later, in 1887, the *Gazette* uncritically told its readers that "Lombroso asserts that no less than 40 per cent. of prisoners are born, or habitual, criminals, whom no house of detention, no penal servitude will change, and to whose existence the public had better accustomed themselves, adjusting their minds to the existence of this latest natural phenomenon."[22] In England, the novel notion that there existed a criminal genus mingled easily with a preexisting belief in the existence of sociologically defined "criminal class," not to mention a general phobia of the poor and concomitant and lurid fascination with their moral, social, and domestic condition—as Mansfield's adaption of Stevenson's novel, and the appalling historical backdrop to its run at the Lyceum, would soon demonstrate.

Like Lombroso's biological criminal, Mr. Hyde is both physically and behaviorally different from the upstanding Dr. Jekyll. Jekyll is tall and hale; Hyde is decrepit. Both Hyde's appearance and actions are described in relation to monkeys—animals lower down the evolutionary scale. Jekyll, as a physician, a gentleman, and a man of culture, represents the apex of civilization. Hyde mocks his learning by scrawling obscene marginalia in Jekyll's books. Stevenson used London's geography to symbolize the distance between the two men. Jekyll lives in a large, clean, spacious home with a garden, previously owned by a well-known surgeon. When Utterson, the narrator, tracks Hyde through the "great chocolate-coloured pall" of the London fog, his pursuit leads him to Soho, "a district of some city in a nightmare":

> As the cab drew up before the address indicated, the fog lifted a
> little and showed him a dingy street, a gin palace, a low French

eating house, a shop for the retail of penny numbers and twopenny
salads, many ragged children huddled in the doorways, and many
women of many different nationalities passing out, key in hand, to
have a morning glass; and the next moment the fog settled down
again upon that part, as brown as umber, and cut him off from his
blackguardly surroundings.

Jekyll is home, hearth, and a well-stocked library; Hyde is gin, foreigners, and fog.

Mansfield's great stunt was to play both Jekyll and Hyde at once. In
the famous promotional photo advertising the play he is depicted both
guises simultaneously, the wretched figure of Hyde double exposed over
the dapper Jekyll, an image which visually recalled Darwin's famous
illustration in the *Descent of Man* of the monkey loping upward into
homo sapiens. All these theatrics and all the knowing nods to contemporary science could not help Mansfield. The play opened on August 4,
1888. From the outset it underperformed both critically and commer-
cially. The failure of an intensely psychological novel to translate onto
to the stage might be no great surprise. But circumstance dictated that
Mansfield's misfortune be of a different order all together. *Dr. Jekyll and
Mr. Hyde*, as *The Times* had insisted, was meant to be an entertaining
fantasy but the city determined to turn it into something horrifically real.

In the early hours of August 31, Mary Ann Nichols was found dead in
Buck's Row, in Whitechapel. A week later the body of Annie Chapman
was discovered in Hanbury Street in Spitalfields. Then there was a
hiatus of three weeks before two women, Elizabeth Stride and Catherine
Eddowes, were murdered in the same hour on the night of September 30,
one in White Chapel the other on the eastern edge of the City of London.
There was then another, longer break in the violence until November 9
when the appallingly mutilated body of Mary Kelly was found in her

flat in Spitalfields. All the victims were allegedly prostitutes; all lived in London's East End; all had been subjected to varying degrees of savagery and dismemberment by an unknown killer.

The Jack the Ripper killings, or the Whitechapel Mystery as it was known in the press at the time, gripped the nation at the exact same time as Richard Mansfield was staging *Dr. Jekyll and Mr. Hyde* at the Lyceum. The media descended on Whitechapel and its environs and their coverage of the crimes and their setting was inflected by the same social anxieties and Darwinian theorizing that ran through Stevenson's novel. In a famous series of *Punch* cartoons on the murders, the denizens of London's East End were portrayed as little more than animals— hunched, bestial, idiotic—living in an environment as degraded as its inhabitants. Echoing W.T. Stead, *Punch* compared the lattice of streets, alleys, and courtyards in the East End to the Minotaur's lair; echoing Lankester, Lombroso, and the rest of the Darwinian declinists it asked: "Held Dante's Circles such a dwelling-place? Did primal sludge e'er harbour such a race?" Whitechapel was the monster lurking within an otherwise civilized London; the Hyde to the capital's Jekyll.

The connection between what was going on in the streets of the East End and what was being played out nightly on the Lyceum's stage (only two miles from the sites of the murders) was not lost on the press, the public, or Richard Mansfield. On October 2, the *Pall Mall Gazette* offered its readers a summary of the various theories concerning the identity of the murderer, among them was "The Jekyll and Hyde Theory.—that the murderer lives two lives, and inhabits two houses or two sets of rooms." On October 5, the City of London police received an anonymous letter alleging that Mansfield was himself the Ripper. The author had apparently seen the Lyceum production and though he had a "great likeing for acters" upon seeing Mansfield in the role "I felt at once that he was <u>the Man Wanted</u> & I have not been able to get this Feeling out of my Head."[23] This was not, presumably, the kind of audience response Mansfield had been hoping for. Touring in Scotland, Stoker and Irving looked on with some concern as negative publicity accrued to their theatre and ticket sales plummeted. Pressure mounted on Mansfield to cease performing his play and to switch to less controversial fare. Mansfield decided to do just that. In mid-October the *Daily Telegraph* approvingly reported that the production was being abandoned. "There is quite sufficient to make us shudder out of doors," the paper noted, "few will regret Mr. Mansfield's determination to show us, before he leaves England, a pleasant side of human nature in contrast to the monsters he has conjured up." Hoping to win back public favor, and perhaps allay questions as to his personal culpability, Mansfield announced that he would give the receipts from an evening's performance of the comedy *Prince Karl* to the Refuge Fund for the Poor of the East-end of London.[24] Nothing, however, could save Mansfield now. The abject failure of *Dr. Jekyll and Mr. Hyde* left him in a disastrous financial position: the rent on the Lyceum went unpaid and he had to borrow money from Irving to get back to the United States. The fiasco served to confirm "Irving's distaste and suspicion of contemporary authors." The next Lyceum production would be a dramatical stalwart: *Macbeth*. Stoker, as the man in charge of the theatre's finances would have been intimately familiar with the fiscal problems arising out of Mansfield's woes.[25] But Jekyll, Hyde, and Jack the Ripper also resonated with him artistically. The killings and the mysterious powers of their mysterious perpetrator would linger in his mind and reemerge in the novel he was just starting to plot.

While *Punch* was content to portray the Ripper killings as the work of an atavistic brute, other, more perceptive, observers noted that the reverse was likely the case, namely, that the culprit was charming, socially intelligent, and capable of winning over scared and suspicious women. *The Spectator* argued that judging by his "success in pacifying the women" the murderer must be "respectable, and even gentle in appearance" and manner.[26] The notion that the killer was physically and socially attractive seems, judging by the weight of contemporary evidence and modern research, substantially true. In this way, the Whitechapel Mystery reaffirmed the Victorian narrative that connected seduction, prostitution, and male rapacity. It also added, or rather emphasized, a new dimension to the sexual dangers English women faced: Jewishness.

British anti-Semitism had always been an odd thing, defined by the absence of its object, not its presence. In 1290 Edward I had banished all English Jews from the country and it was not until the seventeenth century that they were permitted to return. By the middle of the nineteenth century there were only around 30,000 living in the country. For the vast majority, Jews were an exoticism—spoken of but never seen. Many Englishmen only saw a Jew in the flesh when they went overseas. In this period, Jewishness in the English imagination was normally associated with the Sephardic Jews that lived on the Mediterranean littoral, who tended to be part of a prospering mercantile caste rather than a segregated ethnocultural one. Henry Irving's encounter was typical. He spent the summer of 1879 yachting around the Mediterranean with some wealthy friends. Boating from port to port he found his attention at every harbor drawn to the local Jewish population, many of whom conducted business at the quayside. These majestic rather romantic figures confounded the native stereotypes he had grown up with. The crystallizing moment came, according to his son, in a port on the Maghreb:

He had seen a Jew in Tunis, beside himself over some transaction, tear his hair and his clothes, fling himself upon the sand writhing in

rage, and a few minutes later become self-possessed, fawning and
full of genuine gratitude for a trifling gift of money. Picturesque in
his fury, having regained his composure, the Jew had stalked away
with kingly dignity behind his mule team.[27]

Irving now had his way into one of the most controversial and, to his
mind, misunderstood figures in dramatical history: Shylock. Upon his
return he revealed his plans for a radical reinterpretation of *The Merchant of Venice* to Loveday and Stoker and on November 1, 1879 the
play opened at the Lyceum. Irving's performance as the title character
won him widespread acclaim and was considered a watershed moment
in Anglophone depictions of "the Jew."

Irving could not have known it, but his portrayal of Shylock came
at a pivotal moment in the history of English Jewry. Between 1881 and
1905 approximately 100,000 Jews came to Britain, driven overseas by
persecution in the Russian empire. Jewishness ceased to be a distant phenomenon and became a component of urban life in many of England's
great cities. Thousands went to Liverpool and Manchester, but the overwhelming majority gathered in relatively small parts of East London.
40,000 lived in Stepney, where they constituted a quarter of the population. Whitechapel and Spitalfields played host to much of the rest, but
communities sprung up all over the East End, in Goodman's Fields, Mile
End, Shadwell, Cable Street, Dock Street, and elsewhere. The shock of
mass Jewish immigration into these neighborhoods was compounded by
their hitherto relative demographic stability—the populations of many
East End neighborhoods were over seventy percent London born—and
the inescapable fact of the newcomers' difference. The complexion of
English Jewry had previously been defined by the cosmopolitan, busi-
ness-minded Sephardim but the Russian and Polish Jews were Ashke-
nazim. Their world was defined by shtetls, pogroms, yiddish, and, for

the radical element among the émigrés, conflict with the Tsarist state. Their self-consciousness as a defined community and their concentration in specific neighborhoods created immediate tension. Jews were accused of undercutting wages, driving up rents, and generally adding to the squalor and misery of the East End. As anti-Semitic feeling began to take root the established English Jewish community took defensive actions. The Chief Rabbi criticized Jewish slum landlords in the press, adding for good measure "Thank God I live under a Christian landlord." The *Jewish Chronicle* begged the newcomers to cease drawing attention "to their peculiarities of dress, of language and of manner" less all English Jews suffer from a recrudescence of "vulgar prejudices." The Jewish Board of Governors went so far as to repatriate about 26,000 of their coreligionists and paid for the onward passage of another 13,000 to America and the Commonwealth.

By the end of the 1880s there was a sense of gathering crisis in the East End. The Ripper murders were the outlet for many of the anxieties that had been conjured up by the experience of mass immigration. From the outset, Jews were held guilty for the killings. The police detained and released several Jewish immigrants in relation to the killing and interviewed many more as witnesses. Leather Apron, the local boogieman believed to be behind the deaths, was universally believed to be "a Jew or of Jewish parentage, his face being marked of a Hebrew type."[28] The murderer's skill with a knife and anatomical knowledge was connected to the preponderance of traditional Jewish butchers in the area. A Viennese correspondent to *The Times* suggested that the killings fitted into a pattern of ritual murder known to be sanctioned by the Talmud. *The Pall Mall Gazette* reprinted the allegation, writing that "among certain fanatical Jews there exists a superstition to the effect that if a Jew became intimate with a Christian woman he would atone for his offence by slaying and mutilating the object of his passion." In the same article the *Gazette* also suggested that the killings might be revenge for the execution of Israel Lipski, a Jewish migrant hung for the murder of his Jewish landlady the year before.

The belief in Jewish culpability was bolstered by the profile of the Ripper's victims. Prostitution was inextricably linked with Jewishness. One of the unifying features of white slave trade narratives from Moscow to San Francisco was that the Jews were somehow behind it all. This was of a piece with the generalized prejudice that viewed Jews as a corrupting force. Jews corrupted politics with socialism, economics with usury, and morality with prostitution.[29] Lombroso had claimed that though Jews committed a lower percentage of crimes compared to other groups, their criminal activities were concentrated in "fraud, forgery, libel, and chief of all, traffic in prostitution."[30] Among rabid anti-Semites it was taken as writ that Jewish wickedness found gleeful expression in the immiseration of gentile girls. For many more it was simply a lazy conclusion drawn from the geographic coincidence of poverty, prostitution, and Jewish arrivals. Moral campaigners had often associated the rise of prostitution with the demise of traditional morality and the incursion of alien faiths. During his early forays into the field, W.T. Stead had characterized the haunts of sex workers as "colonies of heathens and savages."[31] Established English Jews responded vigorously to these allegations. In 1886 Jewish Ladies' Association for Preventative and Rescue Work issued its first report into the matter and the association sent representatives down to the docks to help prevent newly arrived women from falling into the hands of "Men-sharks, and female harpies of all descriptions" set on entrapping them into sexual bondage. In 1888 the *Jewish Chronicle* described East End prostitution as "a blot upon our community at large" and the Chief Rabbi Hermann Adler voiced concern about alleged Jewish involvement in white slavery.[32]

The association would prove hard to shed, for the simple reason that it blurred so easily into the belief that Jews possessed the special ability to influence and seduce the gentile mind. "Intellectual superiority, Oriental subtlety, and the training of sorrow," English anti-Semite Arnold White wrote in *The Modern Jew* (1899), "accredit the Jews with a complex and mysterious power denied to any other living race." This had been a trope of English anti-Semitism since the Romantics and one that had gained widespread credence with the rise to power and preeminence of the uniquely suave and winning Benjamin Disraeli.[33] The idea that Jews had ill-defined magical abilities was, of course, centuries-old but it fused perfectly with the late-Victorian mania for the occult.[34] Hypnotism, mesmerism, and telepathy remained stock subjects for scientific debate and fictional embellishment. The notion that hypnotism could be used to seduce women persisted, albeit as a hotly contested subject among true believers in the practice.[35] Its connection to the Jewish community was merely an extension of old prejudice to new circumstance which long survived the immediate crisis surrounding the Whitechapel Mystery.[3637]

In the 1890s the trinity of Jewishness, hypnotism, and seduction was consolidated in one of the first great modern literary phenomenon. For much of his life, George Du Maurier had been a draughtsman and cartoonist working for London magazines. Since the 1860s he had found regular employment at *Punch*—in 1886 he had contributed the strange Stoker family scene mentioned above—and other popular publications. But in the 1890s his sight started to fail him and he switched from drawing to writing. His first novel made little impression. Then, in 1894, he published *Trilby*.

Set in certain bohemian neighborhoods of 1850s Paris, *Trilby* tells the story of Trilby O'Ferrall, a beautiful if uncouth Irish laundress and artist's model who falls under the influence of a musician and impresario known only as Svengali. Svengali is a Jew and is repeatedly described in the crudest terms. Svengali is a "filthy black Hebrew sweep," "a big hungry spider," with "bold, brilliant black eyes, with long, heavy lids, a thin, sallow face, and a beard of burnt-up black which grew almost from his under eyelids." He bullies, cringes, borrows, hides, spits, performs, insults, and manipulates the whole novel long. Attracted by Trilby's beauty he brings her under his sway through mesmerism, takes her as his mistress, and uses his hypnotic powers to turn her into the most sought after singer in Europe, making himself fantastically wealthy in the process. When he suddenly dies mid-performance, her musical abilities disappear and Trilby withers and dies, used, consumed, and discarded by her Jewish controller for whom she had been "a flexible flageolet of flesh and blood—a voice, and nothing more."[38]

Trilby was a phenomenon on both sides of the Atlantic. Du Maurier's novel sold two million copies in the first two years. Trilby-mania resulted in innumerable commercial spin-outs (of which only the eponymous Trilby hat survives in common parlance). Stage adaptions proliferated. At one point twenty-four separate productions of *Trilby* were touring the United States, among them a burlesque of the novel performed at the Garrick Theatre, New York, by Richard Mansfield.[39] When it was announced that Paul Potter's acclaimed production was coming to England there were high hopes that it would be staged at the Lyceum. "It would be a pity if the Lyceum company did not secure the English rights," one commentator opined, "for Mr. Irving would make an inimitable Svengali, and Ellen Terry would be Trilby without trying."[40] Irving and Stoker had good reason to be optimistic—after all, Trilby was directly compared to Ellen Terry in the text of the novel—but it was not to be.[41] Potter's *Trilby* went to the Haymarket Theatre in Piccadilly, ran by actor-manager Herbert Beerbohm Tree. *Trilby*'s run at the Haymarket lasted three years and 260 performances making Tree so much money that he could afford to buy and rebuild a whole new venue,

Her Majesty's Theatre, across the road. The Lyceum management team's chagrin can be readily guessed at.

By the mid-nineties Bram Stoker had arrived at a crossroads in his career. He had been at the Lyceum for the better part of two decades. He was a known and respected member of London society. In partnership with Irving he had traveled the world meeting statesmen, artists, and magnates along the way. Still, Stoker wanted more from life. Many of his friends and associates had already achieved recognition. Hall Caine was a millionaire novelist, as were George Du Maurier and Arthur Conan Doyle. Bernard Shaw's career was rapidly picking up steam. Henry Irving's long reign at the top of London's theatrical world was crowned in 1895 when he was knighted at Windsor Castle by Queen Victoria, the first actor ever to attain the distinction. Some of his contemporaries had risen so far, so fast they had already experienced collapse and ruin. The same day that Irving's knighthood was announced, Oscar Wilde was sentenced to two years hard labor for gross indecency. The law he had violated was the Criminal Law Amendment Act of 1885, section 11, that had criminalized homosexual sex.

Stoker's restlessness had led him down a number of avenues. In 1886 he stunned his colleagues by announcing his interest in training to become a barrister, an endeavor which seemed scarcely possible given his enormous responsibilities at the Lyceum. Nonetheless, he quietly did the work and was duly called to the Bar at Inner Temple in 1890. In 1891 he invested alongside Arthur Waugh, Hall Caine, and others in an ambitious European publishing scheme. This went awry and a great deal of money was lost. He had continued to write, publishing several novels between 1890 and 1895. None of these made much of an impact in a crowded literary marketplace. Yet he persisted. In 1896 he borrowed some money from Hall Caine, took some time off from the Lyceum, and went to Cruden Bay to put some serious work into writing the novel that had bubbled away in his mind for five years. The commitment paid off. On Friday May 28, 1897, *The Times* announced in its Publications To-Day column, amid a list that included such timeless works as *His Dead Past* by C.J. Wills, *An Exile From London* by Colonel R. H. Savage, and *A Frisky Matron* by Percy Lysle, the release of "DRACULA. By Bram Stoker."[42]

There was no single reason why Bram Stoker chose to write a vampire novel. He had some personal connections to the genre—his former employer Sheridan Le Fanu had written *Carmilla*, one of the major books in the vampiric canon, and his friend Hall Caine was very close to Dante Gabriel Rossetti, John Polidori's nephew—but by the 1890s it was familiar territory for writers and dramatists.[43] Stoker was writing for honest reasons: he needed the money. It seems probable that he identified the vampire narrative as a suitable vehicle for the kind of middle-brow mystery-thrillers so popular at the time. It was also a literary genre that leant itself to engagement with many of the themes and interests of the day. Reading *Dracula* in light of the larger trends and concerns of late-Victorian England, it is striking how many he involved in the plot. Mesmerism, immigration, urbanization, racial theory, imperialism, Jewishness, feminism—all are present in his book. But *Dracula* is more than just a *gemischt* of topical issues. It is clear from Stoker's very earliest extant notes for the book that he intended it to be a book about sexual danger.

In its essentials *Dracula* is a seduction narrative. The Count is the seducer; he pursues friends Lucy Westenra and Mina Harker, seduces them by means of his hypnotic powers, uses and corrupts their bodies, and then abandons them. Lucy and Mina's contrasting sexual personas mimic those of the conventional morality of the day which, as of 1885, had been embedded in law. Mina is the model woman: Christian, domesticated, almost pathologically disposed to supporting her husband. It takes all the count's wiles to ensnare her and their encounter amounts to rape.[44] Lucy is a pampered aristocrat, who speaks suggestively of her appetites, and is desirous of male attention. She craves her assignations with the count, sleepwalking from her bed each night in Whitby and making her way up to meet him at the abbey on the cliff. There she swoons on a bench overlooking the sea while Dracula feasts on her throat. When Mina notices Lucy's somnambulism she locks her doors and windows only to observe her trying to escape through them at night to meet with her vampiric lover. Lucy's corruption by the count results in her becoming a sexually predatory vampire herself though it is implied that this is not so much a perversion of her true self but a vindication of the old belief that "blood will out." Lucy was primed for immorality and was lewd and vicious before the count he arrived—he simply revealed her. Mina, even after her assault, remains a redemptive figure and eventually helps bring about his destruction and her own rescue.

Nothing here departs from the basic literary model handed down from the eighteenth century. The modern spin Stoker puts on it—and *Dracula* is a very modern book—is that of race. The men arrayed against Dracula—Mina's husband Jonathan Harker, Arthur Holmwood, the English peer and Lucy's fiancé, the American adventurer Quincey Morris, the English doctor James Seward, and the Dutch vampire slayer Abraham Van Helsing—are all Anglo-Saxon. The count is from Transylvania, a place that loomed large in the Victorian imagination as a disconcerting goulash of tribes, creeds, and ethnicities.[45] "Its population," the *Spectator* declared in 1888, "is a singular mixture of nondescripts Wallachs, Aryan Teutons, Turanian Huns, Semitic stragglers, and Hindoo nomads, who have existed side by side for ten centuries without the least approach to fusion."[46] Whether Count Dracula is one of those Semitic stragglers is not wholly clear, though much in the text points toward that conclusion. Much emphasis is placed on the shape and size of his nose; in general the descriptions of his physiognomy align with those of workaday Jewish caricatures. He bears a striking resemblance to Svengali, still fresh in the public's mind, and like him he mesmerizes his victims.[47] Like Leather Apron, the count stalks London's streets, scouring the capital for prey. Dracula's portrayal contains other anti-Semitic tropes, not least his avariciousness. The count eats off a solid gold service and Harker finds piles of bullion and paper currency stacked in his bedroom.[48] Later, in London, Harker slashes at Dracula with his kukri:

> *The blow was a powerful one; only the diabolical quickness of the Count's leap back saved him. A second less and the trenchant blade had shorne through his heart. As it was, the point just cut the cloth of his coat, making a wide gap whence a bundle of bank-notes and a stream of gold fell out.*[49]

It is surely not insignificant that the count cringes before the cross— both the symbol of Christianity and a reminder of the Jewish deicide. In the latter part of the book his flight from London back to Transylvania is enabled by one Immanuel Hildesheim "a Hebrew of rather the Adelphi Theatre type, with a nose like a sheep, and a fez."[50]

Jewish or no, Dracula is explicitly linked to the racial theories of the day. "The Count is a criminal and of criminal type." Van Helsing tells his posse of vampire hunters. "Nordau and Lombroso would so classify him, and *qua* criminal he is of imperfectly formed mind."[51] Van Helsing dwells at some length on the count's "child-brain."[52] It is important to the ideological architecture of the book that the count is definitively the intellectual inferior of his Anglo-Saxon pursuers. The Count's "child-brain" is one feature of his atavistic nature that manifests itself—as Lombroso had always claimed—both physiognomically and behaviorally. Dracula is associated with the primordial past, the Hobbesian world of the virgin forest, and his behavior is unimproved by contact with civilization. Holmwood, Harker, and the rest embody the virtues of that civilization and use its strengths to destroy the count. Rational planning, moral force, and, above all, the judicious use of cutting-edge technology, are their weapons. They represent the apex of Victorian civilization. The count's powers, by contrast, are of a cruder order. As a bloodsucker, Dracula is literally a parasite. Like any parasite he has highly developed feeding faculties but his others functions have atrophied. Given that he feasts on women and uses mesmerism to access their bodies, his seductive powers are paradoxically a feature of his biological degeneration. The racialized seducer is not simply a parasite or even an ethnocultural other, but a destabilizing force that threatens progress—evolutionary, social, and moral—itself and does so by corrupting the Anglo-Saxon woman.

That the count uses hypnosis to seduce his targets is significant. The history of seduction is the history of the post-Enlightenment tension between reason and passion. To the racist mind it was impossible to accept that Anglo-Saxon women might actually rationally choose to partner with their racial inferior. Sexual panic and racial panic met in a discourse that imagined the racial "stock" of the West being overwhelmed or "swamped" by lesser races. Of course, such a discourse only made sense if Anglo-Saxon women were breeding with these racial outsiders and if they were—and were doing so consensually—then the very cornerstone of Victorian gender ideology, namely that women were meek, submissive, and faithful, was called into question. Hypnosis helped explain away this quandary. The mesmerized subject has their

reasoning faculties suspended; some hypnotists argued that the mesmerized individual was in a state of hysteria, they were lost to their emotions. Either way, they could no longer be held responsible for their
actions. The cultural trope that connected seduction, hypnotism, and
race thus worked to salvage the myth of Victorian womanhood while
reinforcing the belief that "undesirable aliens" were subversive inferiors
possessed of atavistic sexual powers.[53]

The dark heart of *Dracula* is the unspoken fear that those precious
women may actually desire the outsider, the alien, the count. This
anxiety is connected in the novel to a trend at large in late-Victorian
society—the specter of the New Woman. Between the passage of the
Criminal Law Amendment Act and the publication of *Dracula*, the
place of women in Victorian society had been transformed. A series of
new laws had granted married women new rights. The movement for
women's suffrage was gaining momentum. Women's access to and enrol-
ment in higher education had boomed. A quarter of British women now
participated in the workforce, and a number were beginning to make
incursions into the hitherto exclusively male professions. These developments met with suspicion, and those suspicions found expression in the
figure of the New Woman.[54]

In so far as she actually existed, the New Woman was a bridge between
the fusty world of high-Victorian sexual role-playing and the more
relaxed gender order of the 1920s and 1930s. She was looking ahead
to a post-suffrage world and beginning to experiment with how women
would be after basic civil rights had been won. The New Woman was
engaged, passionate, and independent. To her detractors she was little less
than a harbinger of social collapse.[55] The reformulation of gender roles,
male critics warned, would lead to chaos. These fears were explored on
the stage. The 1880s and 1890s saw a deluge of New Woman theatre.
In Sydney Grundy's *The New Woman* (1894) the Colonel complains

"Why can't a woman be content to be a woman? What does she want to make a beastly man of herself for?" and suggests that the New Woman is "a sex of their own . . . They have invented a new gender." The drive toward greater independence, often defined against the institution of marriage, was associated with a perversion of biological norms. "No, to be a woman trying not to be a woman," the protagonist of Arthur Wing Pinero's *The Notorious Mrs Ebbsmith* (1895) declares, "that is to be mad."[56] These New Woman plays tended to share a common, and comforting, narrative arc. An allegedly emancipated woman toys with gender-bending behavior (smoking, flirting, intellectual activity, employment) then falls in love with a masculine man, realizes the errors of her ways, and is won back to the feminine "norm."

Stoker would write a novel, *The Man* (1905), which conformed exactly to this model, and had as its protagonist the New Woman archetype Stephen Norman, a woman with a man's name. Stoker's domestic life reflected his gender politics. When Walter Osborne's rococo portrait of Florence Stoker was exhibited as the Royal Academy in 1895, the press noted how pleasingly she conformed to classical femininity. "Mr Osborne has evidently taken pains to give a correct idea of the intellectual features of the lady," *The Era* intoned,

> *we might say, with Hood, that everything about Mrs Bram Stoker is "pure womanly" according to the old-fashioned notions respecting the sex. One has no impression of the "new woman" in the fine intelligence, the lady-like dress, and refined manner, the artist has depicted. Mrs Bram Stoker appears in white, the folds of the gown being arranged with simplicity and artistic taste.*[57]

If his home was safe from the New Woman, then by the 1890s Stoker's workplace was not. In 1890, Ellen Terry's daughter Edy Craig joined

the Lyceum's troupe of actors and actresses. She was the very embodiment of the New Woman, who had turned down Girton College, Cambridge to pursue a career on the London stage. If the Lyceum resisted
dramatical modernism in all its forms, Edy Craig immersed herself in
the new modes of theatre and acted in productions—then considered
radical—of dramatic works by Ibsen and Bernard Shaw. A passionate
feminist, she would later establish theatre troupes devoted to publicizing
the suffragist cause.[58] Edy worked alongside Stoker in London for seven
years including a tour to America in 1895. Exactly what he made of her
is not known, though if *Dracula* is anything to go by his views on the
New Woman were dim indeed.

Central to the attempt to pathologize female independence was a
boorish caricature of the emancipated woman as slatternly and sexually
aggressive. Male on female courtship was the respectable norm; female
on male seduction was an abomination.[59] George Bernard Shaw explored
this theme in his play *Man and Superman* (1903). In the preface, Shaw
explained that the idea for the project arose out of a suggestion from a
friend that he produce a play based on the legend of Don Juan. Shaw
complied, after a fashion, but made it clear in the preface that "my Don
Juan is the quarry instead of the huntsman." The inversion of roles
reflects what Shaw saw around him. Women, he wrote, were now

> *Aggressive, powerful: when women are wronged they do not group*
> *themselves pathetically . . . they grasp formidable legal and social*
> *weapons, and retaliate.*

They asserted this new power in all areas of life, including sex. "As
a result," Shaw concluded, "Man is no longer, like Don Juan, victor
in the duel of sex." Independent women were sexually voracious and
their lust could dominate men. The vampire was increasingly an image

applied to women, not men, as a metaphor for the sinister new appetites women were supposedly exhibiting.[60] The same year *Dracula* was
published there was a major public contretemps over the exhibition of
Edward Burne-Jones's *The Vampire* at the Royal Academy. Burne-Jones
was a friend of Stoker's who had done design work for the Lyceum and
had also sketched Florence Stoker. His painting is an inversion of Henry
Fuseli's *The Nightmare*, and depicts a voluptuous, bare-armed women
astride a slumbering, bare-chested man. In *Dracula* almost the exact
same scene is portrayed in print. From the very beginning of the novel
Lucy Westenra is linked to the New Woman.[61] In a letter to Mina she
boasts that three men (Holmwood, Morris, and Seward) had proposed
to her on the same day. "Why can't they let a girl marry three men, or
as many as want her, and save all this trouble?" she complains. This
outrageous wish is realized later in the book. With her blood drained by
the count, Holmwood, Morris, and Seward all volunteer their veins to
provide urgent transfusions into Lucy's own. "Then this so sweet maid
is a polyandrist," Van Helsing thinks aloud. In death, Lucy becomes a
vampire and stalks Hampstead Heath. When the men trace her to her
den in Highgate Cemetery, she attempts to seduce her former fiancé:

> *She still advanced, however, and with a languorous, voluptuous*
> *grace, said:—*
> *"Come to me, Arthur. Leave these others and come to me. My*
> *arms are hungry for you. Come, and we can rest together. Come,*
> *my husband, come!"*

Van Helsing intervenes in time and Lucy is driven back to her grave.
There her sexual transgressions are punished in horrific fashion. Holmwood plunges a stake into her heart; Seward and Van Helsing saw
off her head and stuff her mouth with garlic; her butchered corpse is

then sealed in a lead coffin, like some kind of radioactive material. The savagery with which Lucy's cadaver is treated might leave us to wonder who or what is being punished: a fictional vampire or a very real, independent, and sexually awakened young woman.[62]

The New Woman's sexual aggression was chimerical, a useful fiction invented by her male critics.[63] In reality, many fin de siècle feminists were themselves skeptical of sexual liberation. Sexual freedom was often countenanced in theory and recoiled from in practice. "We none of us know what exactly is the sexual code we believe in," Beatrice Webb observed, "approving of many things on paper which we violently object to when they are practised by those we care about."[64] While there were feminists who staked-out a radical position premised on the merits of free love and sexual experimentation, they were always a minority and were frequently regarded as a harmful distraction from the serious work of securing reform.[65] Most women simply wanted to experience freedom, to see "with our own eyes, and not, as the women of the past have done, with the eyes of men" as one pamphleteer eloquently put it.[66] They wanted at least the prospect of a life lived without reference to men, even if only for a period before marriage. Many centrist feminists did not seek to destroy the institution of marriage or to live outside it in perpetual libertinage, they simply desired its reformation. Marriage ought to be made more accommodating of female independence. Part of this could be achieved by legal reform; part of this had to be brought about by voluntary changes in male behavior. In riposte to the patronizing image of the New Woman, they proposed instead a New Man, who would welcome and support female autonomy in education, the workplace, and the home. This partnership between New Man and New Woman would usher in a new sexual order that would "exemplify reciprocity and cooperation."[67] The more battle-hardened among them were, however, doubtful of the prospects for the New Man.

They argued that sex was a trap laid by men and inherently degrading to women. It was better, they declared, to refuse to play the game. To live independently of men, sexlessly if necessary, was better than to flirt with subjugation. This vestal vision of committed feminism was encapsulated in Margaret McMillan's motto "Marriage is bad and Free Love is worse."[68] Christabel Pankhurst went further, calling for a total rejection of heterosexual sex until feminist victory had been declared on all fronts. Her rallying cry was immortal: "Votes for Women and Chastity for Men."[69]

These nuances are lost in *Dracula*, which should be no surprise as the Stoker's novel is essentially one of male anxiety, not a condition tolerant of complexity. Stoker embodied Victorian values and *Dracula* manifests Victorian fears. The notion that Jews were hypnotizing gentile women was as absurd as the notion that marginally less oppressed women were now sexually harassing men. Nonetheless, change was afoot in English society. Immigration was changing the complexion of the country and, in the racial terms of the day, the make-up of the national stock. New gender norms were ascendant and a growing number of women were living increasingly independent lives. Feminism seemed to be subverting the gender order just as immigration was threatening the racial order. In the minds of the male establishment the two phenomena were closely connected: rebellious women shirked their reproductive duties leaving the nation open to "swamping" by racial inferiors.[70] Foreign men, meanwhile, stood by to capitalize on their host's weakness and the availability of English women. The quandary was that the impulse to protect women—measures like the 1885 Criminal Law Amendment Act—only seemed to embolden the women's movement further. The apparently hopeless position of English men is captured in the dynamic at work in *Dracula*. Van Helsing and his team spend the first part of the novel keeping Lucy alive by elaborate means and the second part hunting her down and elaborately butchering her body—as good a metaphor as any for Victorian attitudes toward women.

— ✴✦✴ —

Bram Stoker died in April 1912—the same week that his friend W. T. Stead perished aboard the *Titanic*—but his most famous creation lived on. Following his death Florence Stoker became his literary executor and the guardian of his royalties and copyrights. By the 1920s all her late husband's works ceased to generate an income, with the exception of *Dracula*. In straitened circumstances following his passing, Florence was understandably proprietorial about Bram's vampire tale and she was enraged when she learned in April 1922 that an unlicensed adaptation of *Dracula* had premiered at the Berlin Zoo the month before. Through lawyers in London and Germany Florence established that Prana-Film had commissioned director F.W. Murnau, who had recently produced a German language version of *Dr. Jekyll and Mr. Hyde—Januskopf* (1920)—to make a free adaptation of Stoker's *Dracula*. Murnau's film had a number of differences. Count Dracula became Count Orlok; the action was moved from London to Bremen; the dramatis personae was dramatically reduced. But these changes were not enough to save the Germans from Florence's wrath. The plot of the film was clearly her husband's and no permission had been obtained from his estate to use it. From her flat in Knightsbridge, Florence orchestrated a multiyear legal campaign to receive compensation from Prana-Film. When the film company went bankrupt she demanded in lieu of payment the destruction of all copies of the film. Her wish was finally achieved in July 1925 and *Nosferatu*, considered the apogee of German expressionist film-making, was consigned to oblivion.[71]

Murnau's Count Orlok was not the only vampire to haunt the imagination of the Weimar Republic. German screens and German novels were filled with tales of the supernatural. Films like *The Cabinet of Dr. Caligari* (1920), and *Dr. Mabuse the Gambler* (1922) and books like Hanns Heinz Ewers's *The Vampire* (1921) and Arthur Dinter's *The Sin Against the Blood.* [72] All blended racial and sexual panic and featured Jewish or quasi-Jewish villains in prominent roles.[73] The presence of esoteric themes in Weimar culture was a continuation of a pre-war fascination with the occult; their proliferation, however, was the consequence of the tectonic shocks that German society had experienced in 1918 and 1919.[74] For thousands of *völkisch* mystics, far-right demagogues, and disillusioned veterans, defeat was not simply a national trauma but an eschatological event, a fissure in reality that had unleashed monsters on Germany.[75] "Yesterday we experienced the collapse of everything which was familiar, dear and valuable to us." Rudolf von Sebottendorf, founder of the mystic right-wing Thule Society told his followers on November 8, 1918. "In the place of our princes of Germanic blood rules our deadly enemy: Judah."[76] In 1919 members of the Thule Society formed the *Deutsche Arbeiterpartei* (DAP) which, upon the rise to prominence of one of its more compelling speakers, Adolf Hitler, became the *National Sozialistische Deutsche Arbeiterpartei* (NSDAP) in 1920.

For the hard-right, the vampire was the perfect metaphor for the Jewish threat they saw all about them. In his monstrous person met the competing fears of sex, race (specifically, blood) and biological degeneracy. It was no surprise then, that when Hitler sat down in his cell in Landsberg Prison in 1924 to pen his personal and political testament, *Mein Kampf*, that the language and imagery of vampirism mixed readily in his prolix diatribes against the Jews. Hitler returned repeatedly to the vampire metaphor, referring to Jews as the "eternal blood-sucker," as "parasites"[77] always on the hunt "for a new feeding soil for his race," lamenting the "blood-sucking tyranny" of "Jewish" financial interests and darkly predicting that the Jewish "vampire" will die soon after "the

death of his victim." Such epithets mixed freely with the familiar associations made between the perils of seduction and the menace of the
racial other. Recalling the Vienna of his youth, Hitler writes that "in
no other city of western Europe could the relationship between Jewry
and prostitution, and even now the white slave traffic, be studied better."[78] The Jews were the "seducers of our people," who had degraded
modern ideas of health and beauty—through, of all things, their alleged
control of the fashion industry—to allow "for the seduction of hundreds
of thousands of girls by bow-legged, disgusting Jewish bastards." Such
language was common among Nazi demagogues. Julius Streicher's *Der
Stürmer* endlessly mixed demonic and vampiric imagery with frenzied
allegations of Jewish sexual predation. In a 1926 edition of the paper, he
claimed that Aryan girls subjected to street harassment by Jewish men
could ward off their by pursuers by the prominent display of nationalist
icons, like the Iron Cross, on their persons—just like a vampire could
be scared off with garlic and crucifixes.[79] In *The Riddle Of The Jews'
Success* (1927) Theodor Fritsch declared that the "Hebrew displays
the features of the parasite" and did not "derive his means of existence
directly from Nature . . . but only by means of an intermediary system
of living, the essential members of which he sucks dry."[80] Fritsch married
his disgust with the Jews physical condition with a perverse admiration
for their seductive powers. "One is also inclined to assume the presence of some hypnotic power," he noted, "when one observes how even
old and ugly Jews render young females docile and submissive to their
desires."[81]

Upon their ascent to power in 1933, Nazi lawyers quickly went
about laying the groundwork for a new set of racially inspired laws that
would protect Germany from this imagined Jewish threat. In September
1933 a group of Nazi lawyers, including the future head of the People's
Court, Roland Freisler, issued a legal manifesto known as the Prussian

Memorandum. The Memorandum laid out a vision of Nazi race law that would supplant the liberal laws of the Weimar republic. Just like the Americans of the Progressive era, Nazi racial thinkers in the 1930s were obsessed with racial mixing—what Hitler had called "race-poisoning"—and wanted to use the law as an instrument to protect the purity of the German race. To this end the authors of the Memorandum proposed the creation of a new crime: race treason. "Every form of sexual mixing between a German and a member of a foreign race," they wrote:

> *Is to be punished as* race treason, *and indeed both parties are to be subject to punishment. . . . Particularly deserving of punishment is the case in which sexual intercourse or marriage is induced through malicious deception.*

Their judicial model as to how to implement this new law was the United States, the home of inventive and expansive laws on race, sex, and seduction. "It is well known," the Memorandum continued, "that the Southern states of North America maintain the most stringent separation between the white population and coloreds in both public and personal interactions." Here was a system that the Nazis could emulate.

In 1934 Nazi lawyers, Freisler again among them, met once more, this time at the Commission on Criminal Law Reform, to discuss how to legislate into existence the Nazi racial utopia. At the forefront of their minds was sex, specifically how to introduce an "effective quarantine separating the racially foreign elements in Germany from the people of German descent." First to speak was Fritz Grau, a member of the Academy of German Law, a future SS Colonel, and future Nuremberg Trial defendant. The American example, Grau said, was laudable but the Commission had to consider the difference in condition between the black American in the Jim Crow South and the Jew in Nazi Germany.

It was all well and good to go down the "path of social segregation and separation" but the sexual threat posed by Jews could not be mitigated so long as the latter held economic power within the German state. "As long as they have the most beautiful automobiles," Grau told his colleagues, "the most beautiful motorboats, as long as they play a prominent role in all pleasure spots and resorts" they would exist as a temptation to German women.[82] The answer was in the first instance "positive statutory measures that forbid absolutely all sexual mixing of a Jew with a German, and impose severe criminal punishment" but also, Grau suggested, economic dispossession.[83][84]

A year after this meeting the Nuremberg Laws were instituted. Echoing the exacting racial and sexual laws in place throughout the United States, the Nuremberg Laws forbade marital and extramarital relations between Jews and those "of German or related blood." Furthermore, Jews were forbidden to employ as domestic helpers "female subjects of the state of German or related blood who are under 45 years old"—a preventative step against the mythical white slave trade, which German anti-Semites had long believed the Jews controlled.

Nor was Nuremberg the end of the Nazi campaign against the Jewish-Vampire-Seducer. As the 1930s wore on anti-semitic legislation intensified, with a whole host of exclusionary laws, injunctions, and regulations put in place to further deny German Jews a place in the society of their birth.[85] In 1938, Fritz Grau's dream of destroying the economic power of German Jews was realized when new statutes were introduced that forbade Jews from operating business and engaging in the trade of good and services of any kind and had to provide the state with details of their bank accounts and declare all wealth in excess of 5000 reichsmarks.[86] No longer would Jewish-owned cars and speedboats tempt the racial honor of German women. A year later, as the Third Reich prepared for war, Nazi theorist and Himmler protégé Gregor

Schwartz-Bostunitsch published *Jew and Woman: The Theory and Practice of Jewish Vampirism*. The book reinforced the connection between Jewishness, vampirism and racial pollution through sex just as the Nazis were about to become sovereign over the largest concentration of Jews in the world. The successes of the 1939 campaign against Poland and Operation Barbarossa against the Soviet Union would ultimately bring some 10 million Jews under Nazi control. This inevitably posed a distinct problem to the Nazi mind. If, after all, the Jews were a supernatural force, an "eternal blood-sucker," a vampire forever thirsting for German blood, then the most radical solutions to the "Jewish Question" had to be entertained. At the Wannsee Conference in Berlin in 1942, fifteen men gathered round a table and planned the Final Solution. Among them was Roland Freisler, the lawyer who had spearheaded anti-Jewish racial and sexual legislation throughout the 1930s. That same week, also in Berlin, a Nazi screenwriter penned a memo about Weimar-era cinema for the Party Education Office entitled "Superstition in Film." There was much decadence in the German cinema of the pre-Nazi period, Hans Fischer-Gerhold declared, but there were also some films from that time that contained political and racial messages that the Nazis could make use of. One such film was *Nosferatu*, F. W. Murnau's unauthorized retelling of *Dracula*. Fischer-Gerhold praised *Nosferatu* as the story of a "vampire of Slavic origin" who preys on innocent Aryan blood. The message of the film was clear. Only one race could survive the confrontation: "either the German or the Jew."[87]

CHAPTER SEVEN

SEDUCTION REMAINS

A mong the first wave of refugees following Hitler's rise to power was a German-Jewish philosopher with a compelling explanation as to how Europe had succumbed to fascism. Herbert Marcuse had been born to a prosperous Berlin family in 1898. A bookish young man, he had been conscripted in 1916 but was spared frontline service due to his poor eyesight. He was in Berlin in 1918 when the Hohenzollern regime and the German war effort collapsed amid mutiny, revolution, and incipient civil war. Already a committed Marxist, Marcuse manned the barricades as fighting broke out between right-wing paramilitary groups and communist insurgents. The nascent revolution was crushed, right-wing factions either co-opted or indulged by the new government, and a disillusioned Marcuse moved to Freiburg and studied Hegel.

As the 1920s wore on the National Socialists grew in political influence and Marcuse began to search for academic positions outside the Nazifying German university system. In the early 1930s this led him to an association with the Institute for Social Research, a coterie of heterodox Marxist thinkers gathered around philosophers Theodor Adorno and Max Horkheimer. Marcuse joined the Institute in Geneva in 1933 and then followed it to America in 1934, where it found shelter within Columbia University in New York City. A passionate opponent of the Nazi regime, Marcuse did not hesitate in offering his assistance to the Americans during the Second World War. He was given a position in the Office of Strategic Services (OSS), a forerunner to the CIA, as an analyst focused on parsing the dynamics of German society. At the war's end he returned to academia, taking up a succession of posts at Columbia, Harvard, and Brandeis.

Marcuse's entire adult life had been shaped by the Nazi catastrophe. In the immediate aftermath of the war, he now sought to turn his formidable intellectual powers into explaining how it had come about. To do so he would depend on theories of human sexuality grounded in Marxism and Freudianism. From the Marxist tradition, Marcuse drew upon a long-established set of beliefs about the relationship between capitalism and sexuality. In *The Communist Manifesto*, Marx and Engels had argued that capitalism led to the commodification of all social ties. In all aspects of intimate life—in the family, in courtship rituals, and in the bedroom—they observed the influence of exploitative sexual relations that mirrored exploitative economic relations. The revolution they envisioned would necessarily transform sex as much as it would economics. They looked forward to the abolition of the family, the demise of prostitution, and the extinction of seduction itself. All these phenomena were relics of a corrupt bourgeois sexual culture ripe for destruction.[1] Subsequent Marxist intellectuals took up this sexual theme. In *Women and Socialism* (1879) August Bebel imagined the "woman of the future" as being "socially and economically independent,"

She is no longer subjected to even a vestige of domination or exploitation, she is free and on a par with man and mistress of her destiny. In choosing the object of her love, woman, like man, is free and unhampered. She woos or is wooed, and enters into a union from no considerations other than her own inclinations. . . . Under the proviso that the satisfaction of his instincts inflicts no injury and disadvantage on others, the individual shall see to his own needs. . . . No one is accountable for it to others and no unsolicited judge has the right to interfere. What I shall eat, how I shall drink, sleep and

dress, is my own affair, as is also my intercourse with a person of
the opposite sex.[2]

Socialism would liberate women and in so doing liberate sexuality. One corollary of the emancipation of women would be the obsolescence of seduction. Men and women would now meet on terms of parity. Sexual partners would be chosen frictionlessly on the basis of mutual attraction. This was a recurring theme in socialist literature, popularized in best-selling books such as Edward Bellamy's *Looking Backward* (1888) and William Morris's *News From Nowhere* (1890).[3] Following the implementation of Marxist precepts in Russia after 1917, Bolshevik politician and feminist theorist Alexandra Kollontai foresaw the emergence of a "communist morality" that demanded an end to "the buying and selling of caresses."[4] The end of seduction, along with the abandonment of other manipulative and exploitative sexual practices, would be but one of many happy side-effects of the new socialist order.

What interested Marcuse was why capitalism depended upon this repressive sexual order. It was here that the writings of Sigmund Freud became relevant. In *Civilization and Its Discontents* (1929), Freud had argued that repression was central to the entire enterprise of human civilization. Each individual was a seething cauldron of appetites and desires which, left to their own devices, would preclude the possibility of collaboration in pursuit of a larger, more harmonious social order. The solution was to prevent the individual, by coercion where necessary, from realizing their own selfish, chaotic impulses and instead divert their energies into productive and peaceable activities. Marcuse sought to challenge Freud's pessimistic prognosis by reference to Marxist theory. It was surely the case, he reasoned, that modern industrial economies were capable of producing enough goods and services for their populations, yet humans were obliged to work harder than ever. Marcuse suggested that Freudian repression was indeed going on in these economies, but that this repression was in excess of what was needed to meet the material needs of the workforce. Echoing the classical Marxist theory of "surplus-labour," he referred to this phenomenon as "surplus-repression." Marcuse believed that surplus-repression was a feature of the capitalist economic order and that it was having disastrous effects on the collective psychology of those trapped within it. "Suppressed sexuality," he wrote, leads to "hideous forms [of release] so well known in the history of civilization; in the sadistic and masochistic orgies of desperate masses, of 'society elites,' of starved bands of mercenaries, of prison and concentration-camp guards."[5] By marrying Freud and Marx, Marcuse believed he had identified the sexual origins of fascism that lurked within all capitalist societies. The delusion of the capitalist system was that there was no alternative to this system of repression—that human progress and civic order depended upon it. Marcuse argued that this was not the case and that "the possibility of a non-represssive civilization is predicated not upon the arrest, but upon the liberation, of progress."[6] He imagined a new kind of civilization, socialist and sexually liberated, where "no longer used as a full-time instrument of labor, the body would be resexualized."

The regression involved in this spread of the libido would first manifest itself in a reactivation of all erotogenic zones, and, consequently in a resurgence of pregenital polymorphous sexuality and in a decline in genital supremacy. . . . This change in the value and scope of libidinal relations would lead to a disintegration of the institutions in which the . . . interpersonal relations have been organized, particularly the monogamic and patriarchal family. . . . The process just outlined involves not simply a release but a transformation of the libido: from sexuality constrained under

genital supremacy to the eroticization of the entire personality. It is
a spread rather than an explosion of the libido.

These theories were outlined in his magnum opus, *Eros and Civili-*
zation, published in 1955. Marcuse did not use the phrase "sexual revolution" (although he was familiar with, if disdainful of, the work of
Wilhelm Reich, a fellow Jewish émigré with overlapping research interests, whose corpus included the 1945 book *The Sexual Revolution*) but
with the publication and popularity of this book he would be forever
associated with it. This tall, dour man, with his pipe and widow's peak
and old-world manners, became the unlikely hero of a whole generation
of student activists, radical intellectuals, and exponents of sexual liberation. In charting the relationship between the economic and the sexual
spheres, Marcuse unleashed a discussion about the political significance
of sexual behavior that reverberated around the Western world. As the
Fifties gave way to the Sixties, Marcuse's reputation as the prophet of
the Sexual Revolution continued to grow. In 1965 he moved to California to teach in the Edenic surroundings U.C. San Diego. There this
unassuming old man with his rich German accent, who could be found
most afternoons smoking a cigar in his La Jolla garden or walking hand-
in-hand with his wife down beneath the cliffs on Torrey Pines Beach,
became the epicenter of the culture wars that wracked the West. Styled
the "angel of the apocalypse" by the *New York Times*, he received death
threats from the Ku Klux Klan, and an offer from the American Legion
to pay his salary on the condition that he never teach again.

His supporters were no less ardent. His books were read from
Oakland to Bonn; student protesters in Paris and Frankfurt marched
with signs that read "Marx, Mao, Marcuse;" he was credited (probably apocryphally) with the slogan "Make Love, Not War"; he counted
Angela Davis, Shulamith Firestone, and Kathy Acker among his disciples;

students flocked to his classes in such numbers that loudspeakers were rigged up to broadcast his words to the crowds gathered outside the lecture hall. When in the summer of 1967, the Summer of Love, he told students in Berlin that "we have to develop the political implications of the moral, intellectual, and sexual rebellion of the youth" he announced himself as the intellectual idol of a whole generation intent on proving that the personal was indeed political.[7] At the heart of this fascination with Marcuse was his passionate insistence on the centrality of sexual questions to political affairs and his original insights into how intimate matters were correlated to economic structures.

One young person whose early life seemed evidence of the radical promise of sexual liberation, was Janine Ceccaldi. Born in colonial Algeria in 1926, Ceccaldi's family was firmly bourgeois. Her father was a prosperous functionary of the Third Republic; her mother an elegant housewife. Despite the conservatism of her surroundings, Janine quickly emerged as a precocious daughter. She was a brilliant student at school, and her intellectual curiosity led her to literature—Dostoevsky and Thomas Mann in particular—and to Marxism. Aged fifteen when Hitler invaded the Soviet Union, Janine's communist sympathies were a rebellion against the stifling circumstances of her upbringing but also an act of individual courage. France was occupied by the Germans, and the Vichy regime actively persecuted left-wing groups. She involved herself in the communist underground in wartime Algiers and got herself excluded from school for a term for calling her anti-Communist philosophy teacher "a lackey of capitalism and colonialism." Janine tested the limits of her society in other ways, too. From her early teens, her parents worried about her apparent sexual permissiveness. She also rebelled against the spiritual norms of a uniformly catholic society by showing an adolescent interest in mysticism and the occult.

Shortly before the war ended, she took her Baccalaureate and looked to attend university. Characteristically, she was drawn to the two degree courses she considered the most masculine: law and medicine. Her parents considered the latter the more appropriate course for a woman and she took up the grueling course of studies, eventually specializing in anesthesiology. All the time, she maintained her communist sympathies, participating in 1944 in the first conference of the Algerian Communist Party after it was formally reconstituted after several years underground. There she marveled at the sight of Jews, Muslims, and Christians, French and Arabs working together and "expressing in many languages the same dream of fraternity." After qualifying as a doctor in 1948 she left Algeria for Slovakia, where she helped "build socialism" as part of a volunteer brigade working on the railroads. Once that project was completed she attended a Communist youth conference in Budapest.

Back in Paris, she found herself at the Gare de l'Est without a job or a home but free to live her life as she wished. She found a job as a medical adviser to the Social Security bureau responsible for working-class districts in suburban Paris. In 1951, while on a trip to the forest of Fontainebleau she met René Thomas, a casual laborer from Clamart, a solidly proletarian neighborhood in southwest Paris. The couple cohabited for two years before moving to the French Alps where René hoped to get a job as a ski guide. They moved around from Chamonix, to Albertville (where they married), before settling in Pralognan-la-Vanoise where she got a job as doctor at a ski station and he found work on the mountains. In 1955, Janine's contract in the mountains expired and she accepted a posting on an anti-tuberculosis project on the island of Réunion in the Indian Ocean. While she waited for her husband to join her she had an affair with a local diver, who she referred to as her "dolphin."

When René arrived a few months later, the afterlife of this affair did little to improve the state of their marriage—already afflicted by the tension between her impassioned bourgeois Communism and his pragmatic working class upward mobility—but she became pregnant shortly afterward and they spent those months awaiting the birth of their child nursing exotic travel plans. They would kayak down the Nile, scale the peaks of Africa, drive from one end of the continent to the other.

When their child, Michel Thomas, was born in February 1956, they decided that they should not let him interfere with their travel plans. Only five months old, Michel was entrusted to his paternal grandmother Henriette in Clamart. At their farewell in Réunion, Janine took a final look at him, said goodbye with a "l'oeil sec" and went off on the long-planned African adventure. At the end of their trip, in 1957, René and Janine separated. Janine returned to Réunion and practiced medicine. Single and working long days at the hospital she decided she could not raise Michel herself, but was uncomfortable with his upbringing in Clamart and insisted that he be transferred to her mother's care in Algiers. Algeria was then in the midst of a brutal insurgency mounted against French colonial rule. For the first few years of his time there, Michel's own life was blissfully unaffected by it. His grandmother lived in an apartment of five or six light-filled rooms, down whose corridors and balconies he rode his tricycle. At a young age he was clearly an intelligent child, reading by the time he was three and inventing elaborate games at the age of four. There was little time to get comfortable in Algiers. He was four and a half when his parents formally divorced—still something of a rarity at that time in France—and only five when his grandfather died of cancer and his father came to Algiers, escorted by two parachutists, to get his son out of a city that was fast becoming a permanent war-zone. Once again he was sent to his grandmother's home on the periphery of Paris. Michel would be raised by Henriette, his loving surrogate mother, with her reliably working class ways and reflexive communist beliefs. He would see his parents on holidays—hiking or skiing with his father in the Alps, the occasional trip to Réunion to see his mother—but otherwise they were absent from his upbringing. His father prospered as a mountain guide, traveling around the world for work, expeditions to the United States, to Chile, to Nepal, two trips to Afghanistan. His mother remained in Réunion but traveled a great deal too, sometimes for work, sometimes for pleasure. As time passed she drifted away from communism and passed through several phases of belief—Hinduism, Islam, Christianity, and New Age—what her son would later disdain as "spiritual channel-hopping."

In his teenage years, Michel also had a spiritual awakening of sorts. Although his childhood was largely happy, thanks to his adoring grandmothers, and the permanent cast of aunts and uncles, his own worldview took a pessimistic turn in his mid-teens. A bright, bookish boy, he read Baudelaire and listened to Pink Floyd. The turning point, in his telling, came during a school trip to Bavaria in 1971, when he was fifteen. There he first read Blaise Pascal's notoriously gloomy *Pensées*. It was a transformative experience. "There must have been some *secret flaw* in me," he later wrote, "that I tumbled, feet together, offering not the least resistance, into the abyss that Pascal opened up beneath my feet." From Pascal it was a natural progression into Nietzsche, The Velvet Underground, Kafka, The Stooges, Dostoyevsky, and Schopenhauer. This anxious philosophical turn took place against the backdrop of the turbulence of France in the Sixties and Seventies. The tremors of 1968 were felt even in his exurban *lycée* and his formative years were played out amid the disintegration of the values of his childhood—the values of his grandmothers. Michel came to believe that his experience of abandonment and family breakdown was somehow symptomatic of the new world born in those decades. "In a sense," he later commented of his parents decision to transfer him out of their care, "this was a precursor of the vast movement towards the dissolution of the family which would follow. I grew up with the clear awareness that a great injustice had been committed towards me." His parents were too old to be *Soixante-Huitards*, but he judged them as the necessary "precursors" to that generation, two canaries in the coal mine of the post-war West. The world he would mature into would be populated almost exclusively by people like them: hyper-mobile, sexually free, and unashamedly individualistic. It was a world defined by unending interpersonal conflict, what he termed *la lutte*, the struggle. The world of the struggle was far removed from what he remembered as the tranquil, loving world of his childhood, of France in the Fifties and early Sixties. Many years later, in his second novel, he would refer to this world as the "Lost Kingdom" whose values were embodied for him in the figures of his grandmothers. In tribute to them, and in homage to that lost world and those lost values, Michel took as his nom-de-plume his grandmother Henriette's maiden name, Houellebecq.

One of Michel Houellebecq's contentions about the post-1968 world is that rampant materialism, consumerism, and individualism, have effectively attenuated experience to the extent that it would be naive to consider individuals as having something so dramatic as a unique biography. Furthermore, the "progressive effacement of human relationships" means that individuals cannot even orientate their lives in relation to those of others. Westerners live within a spiritual and emotional void; as such there is no narrative arc to their existences, simply a period of growth, consumption, and decay lasting several decades.[8] Consequently, outside of the circumstances of his early childhood and the immediate family drama triggered by his wayward parents, Houellebecq's own life sheds little light on the themes of his writing nor on the history of seduction. This is, however, completely in line with his intuition that this crisis in personal history mirrors a larger stalling in Western history—that the societies he has lived in and describes in his writing are simply spinning their wheels. It was appropriate, then, that his literary debut should have occurred in the 1990s, the vaunted decade of the "End of History" as described by American political theorist Francis Fukuyama.

Yet in terms of Houellebecq's own analysis of the cause of this societal crisis, occasioned by the Sexual Revolution, a different idea of Fukuyama's is germane. In 1999 Fukuyama published *The Great Disruption*, an attempt at explaining some of the centripetal social forces he observed at work within the developed world. Fukuyama argued that the trends associated with the Sexual Revolution—the collapse in the fertility rate, the demise of traditional marital norms, the deterioration of the family unit—should be understood not as a consequence of a revolution in values but as the result in a revolution in economic structures. What happened in the 1960s and 1970s, he argued, was a transition in advanced economies away from manufacturing and toward services. Physical labor lost its primacy and was replaced by intellectual labor. This leveled the labor market for men and women. In aggregate, men might enjoy a natural advantage over women in physically demanding jobs in heavy industry. There is no such advantage in service roles that rely on intellectual and interpersonal abilities. The onset of the much-trumpeted "Information Age" effectively ended centuries of male economic advantage. Female labor force participation soared; the wage gap narrowed. A strata of economically independent women sprung into being, their ranks growing with each passing year.[9] [10]

This economic narrative runs counter to the popular narrative that foregrounds the cultural dimension of the Sexual Revolution. John

Updike's couples, frolicking in their "post-pill paradise." Alexander Portnoy's complaints. Isadora Wing traveling from New World to Old in search of the "zipless fuck" in Erica Jong's *Fear of Flying*. Brigitte Bardot—who claimed she was the "first to demonstrate that a woman could very well lead a man's life without being a prostitute"—taking the role of the historically male ur-seducer in *Don Juan (ou Si Don Juan était une femme)* (1973). Serge Gainsbourg and Jane Birkin's "Je t'aime . . . moi non plus." James Bond and the Bond girls. The landmark obscenity cases over *Lolita*, *Howl*, and *Naked Lunch*. Jim Morrison telling reporters "We make concerts sexual politics. The sex starts with me." The list goes on: Twiggy, *Alfie*, *Deep Throat*, Mick Jagger, *Hair*, Hugh Hefner, Helen Gurley Brown, *The Graduate*, Janis Joplin, *Oh, Calcutta!*, *Last Tango in Paris*, *Les Valseuses*, *Emmanuelle*, hippies, Haight-Ashbury, the Latin Quarter, Swinging London, miniskirts.[11]

The cultural map is, however, a poor guide to the terrain of the Sexual Revolution. As entertaining as the output of these years was, and as stark a contrast as it provided to the bland offerings of the 1940s and 1950s, it was not in historical terms a unique explosion of transgressive creative expression. The 1920s were a remarkably fertile period for cultural iconoclasm and was by a number of metrics a more progressive era than the decades that immediately followed it.[12] As discussed in earlier chapters, Venice, London, and Paris had been hotbeds of cultural and sexual experimentation throughout the eighteenth century. (It is telling, on this point, that *Fanny Hill*, or *Memoirs of a Woman of Pleasure*, the text at the center of several obscenity cases on both sides of the Atlantic in the 1960s, had been written in England in 1748, the same year that the first volumes of *Clarissa* were published.) The cultural manifestations of the sexual freedoms of these years were brilliant but they were not new and they were not decisive. By contrast, the transition from a labor-intensive economy to a knowledge economy was without historical precedent.

There are two critiques that might be made of this line of argument. The first is political. Many of the transformations of the 1960s and 1970s occurred because of legislative action. Changes to the law helped liberalize social norms on, for example, divorce, but also had economic implications. In West Germany, for instance, married women could not get jobs outside the home without their husband's permission until the law was changed in 1957; similar laws (the so-called Marriage Bar) persisted in the United States into the 1960s. Likewise, well into the 1970s English women could not get loans or mortgages without a male guarantor on their applications. In Britain these and other economic inequities were not challenged until the passage of the Equal Pay Act (1970) and the Sex Discrimination Act (1975). In other words, the Information Age economic revolution was still constrained by antiquated laws. The fact that these were eventually abolished had less to do with pure economics than it did with the fact that women had been enfranchised earlier in the century and were able to mobilize to bring about legislative reform. In this narrative, it was suffrage, not economics, that sparked the Sexual Revolution.

The second, connected criticism relates to contraception and abortion. The Sixties and Seventies saw a wave of landmark legal rulings and legislative events that transformed women's control over their bodies. The development and popularization of oral contraceptives ("the pill," marketed under the brand-name Enovid) in the 1960s was feted as one of the greatest technological breakthroughs in human history. In the next decade, the incremental successes of the pro-choice movement granted women even greater sexual freedoms. For feminists, it was taken as writ that sexual freedom was born of contraceptive rights. "It is no longer possible to deny that we face the certainty of a sexual revolution," Margaret Drabble wrote in 1971, "and that this revolution, which much affects the institutions of marriage and parenthood, is caused largely by the development of contraceptive techniques." This focus on contraception was a motif of much of the literature of the Sexual Revolution. One of the few things that really shocks Alexander Portnoy is the discovery that the prostitute he sleeps with in Rome has neither diaphragms nor oral contraceptives. Much to her dismay, he gifts his girlfriend's supply of Enovid to her. Likewise, the whole plot of *Fear of Flying* hinges on Isadora's easy access to, and generous use of, contraception.[13]

Taken together the political and the contraceptive cases for the Sexual Revolution constitute potent criticisms of the economic argument outlined above. The shortcoming common to both is the outsized emphasis both place on events within the particular decades of the sixties and seventies. In the United States, for instance, the campaign for contraceptive rights dated back to the 1920s. This scored major successes in the pre-pill era. By 1955 seventy percent of white married women age eighteen to thirty-nine had used some form of contraception at some point in their lives, a figure that had risen to eighty percent by 1960. Furthermore, the uptake in usage of the pill was a lengthier process than is typically allowed for in the more breathless accounts of the Sexual Revolution. Due to state laws, racial and economic disparities, and information deficits, the pill did not become truly widespread in America until the 1970s. The situation was even starker in Europe. In France and England the pill was not totally legalized until the late sixties and not made available through state health services until the seventies. The circumstances surrounding abortion were even more diverse. Sweden legalized abortion in 1938; Ireland legalized abortion in 2018. In America, *Roe v. Wade* has been constantly attacked and circumscribed at a state and national level since 1973.[14] The point is not that contraceptive and abortion rights are peripheral to questions of sexual freedom but that the accumulation of these rights have been far more piecemeal and contingent than is normally articulated in narratives of sexual liberation. Zooming out, it is clear that while the struggle for these rights was integral to the Sexual Revolution, local and national circumstances were paramount in deciding their success. In contrast, the economic story was the same across the West. In the same decades, across a wide variety of countries with a range of social policies, manufacturing as a share of economic activity declined, female participation in the workforce shot up, women flooded into the professions, and female incomes rose. This "Quiet Revolution" in the economy grabbed fewer headlines but underwrote all the other changes that occurred in public and private life.

There is space for a synthesis of these competing yet interconnected arguments. Again, it is the language of economics that comes to the rescue. In 2004 economists Roy Baumeister and Kathleen Vohs published a groundbreaking theory of sexual behavior that they termed "Sexual Economics." For most of history, they argued, women had exchanged sex for male resources. Denied full or fair participation in the economy, and unpaid for domestic and care work, a woman's "value" lay in her sexuality. In contrast, male sexuality had a very low value but men could "trade" non-sexual goods for access to female sexuality:

Men will offer women other resources in exchange for sex, but women will not give men resources for sex (except perhaps in highly unusual circumstances). In any event, the bottom line is that sexual activity by women has exchange value, whereas male sexuality does not. Female virginity, chastity, fidelity, virtuous reputation, and similar indicators will have positive values that will be mostly absent in the male.[15]

At the heart of sexual economics is the notion that female sexuality is a "good" with a "price." For much of history that "price" had been kept very high. Baumeister and Vohs argued that the pressure to keep this price high explained many of tropes and taboos of Western sexual discourse, most notably the double standard which held a promiscuous woman to be worthless but a promiscuous man to be worthy of admiration. Furthermore, they noted that in the absence of alternatives women were incentivized to police sexuality in their own ranks as the collective could not afford to allow the actions of one individual to "lower" the price of all female sexuality.

The language of sexual economics can come across as cold and dehumanizing. Nonetheless, its insights closely correspond to those of the Marxists critics of bourgeois sexuality who had claimed that capitalism had commodified all interpersonal relationships. Socialism, they believed, would liberate woman by allowing them to share equally in the fruits of the economy. As discussed above, this was a recurrent theme in socialist literature. In *News From Nowhere*, William Morris showed how gender roles and sexual expectations would be upturned by the restructuring of the economy under socialism:

> *By far the greater part of these in past days were the result of the laws of private property, which forbade the satisfaction of their natural desires to all but a privileged few, and of the general visible coercion which came of those laws. . . . Again, many violent acts came from the artificial perversion of the sexual passions, which caused overweening jealousy and the like miseries. Now, when you look carefully into these, you will find that what lay at the bottom of them was mostly the idea (a law-made idea) of the woman being the property of the man, whether he were husband, father, brother, or what not. That idea has of course vanished with private property, as well as certain follies about the 'ruin' of women for following their natural desires in an illegal way, which of course was a convention caused by the laws of private property.*

In sexual economic terms, what Morris is saying is that under socialism the "price" of sex would fall. Women would no longer depend on men for resources and would no longer need to suppress their sexual desires in order to maintain their "value." A "low" price for sexuality is indicative of improved gender equality. Women no longer have to depend on men and marriage for survival; they need men, as the feminist quip went, like a fish needs a bicycle. ("We had more in our lives than just men," Isadora Wing declares in *Fear of Flying*, "we had work, travel, friends.") One way of understanding the Sexual Revolution of the twentieth century is to consider it as a sustained decrease in the price of female sexuality brought about by increased economic independence, improved contraceptive rights, and expanded legal protections for women. In this low price sexual economic market, expressions of sexuality proliferated because they were no longer attended to by the same risks as they were in the past. Love did not become free, it became cheap.[16] It was not at all clear what this meant for seduction. Feminist thinkers were split on the issue. In her essay "Seduction and Betrayal" (1973) Elizabeth Hardwick argued that the Sexual Revolution meant the abolition of seduction. "Now the old plot is dead, fallen into obsolescence." She wrote. "You cannot seduce anyone when innocence is not a value. Technology annihilates consequence." Margaret Drabble, writing in 1971, was not so sure. She accepted that the contraceptive revolution had irrevocably altered the morality of sexual relations because "morality is inseparably connected with the notion of responsibility, and an act which *cannot* have the consequence of conception, of producing a new helpless life, cannot be irresponsible *in the same sense* as an act which risks such an event." Still, this did not mean that manipulation and exploitation were no longer possible:

This does not imply that sexual relations that don't risk conception
are unrelated to personal responsibility and morality; clearly

there is still room, in the most technically sterile relationship, for
treachery and loyalty, generosity and abuse.[17]

At the height of the Sexual Revolution the future of seduction was in the balance.

— ⚊◆⚊ —

Marxists are often more certain of capitalism's strengths than capitalists themselves. In the decade after the publication of *Eros and Civilization*, with the American economy still booming, and the Sexual Revolution in full flower, Herbert Marcuse began to have doubts about the imminent arrival of the socialist revolution. Capitalism, he complained, had been too successful. Workers with full fridges, cars, and homes were not primed for revolutionary action. In *One-Dimensional Man* (1964) he struck a pessimistic tone absent from his earlier work, decrying capitalism's infernal ability to absorb and redirect potential challenges to its hegemony.[18] The flourishing of sexual freedoms and the enthusiastic participation of many women in the modern economy were further causes of concern. Under the influence of radical feminist thought, in particular the writings of his graduate student Angela Davis, Marcuse began to develop a theory to explain how capitalism had been able to adapt so readily to women's liberation and the spread of sexual freedoms. His argument foreshadowed Fukuyama's made twenty-five years later. "Under the impact of technological progress, social reproduction depends increasingly less on physical strength and prowess," Marcuse wrote, "either in war or in the material process of production, or in commerce. The result was the enlarged exploitation of women as instruments of labor." The transition toward a knowledge economy more welcoming of women's contributions as well as the success of the Western democracies in meeting women's political demands and contraceptive needs had unleashed a revolution within the capitalist order that did not challenge its basic structure.[19] "These liberating tendencies," he continued,

> *are made part of the reproduction of the established system.*
> *They become exchange values, selling the system, and sold by*
> *the system. The exchange society comes to completion with the*
> *commercialisation of sex.*

The sexual revolution he had prophesied in *Eros and Civilization* had arrived but it was decidedly capitalist in its characteristics.[20] [21]

While Marcuse fretted about the fate of the Sexual Revolution from his sunny perch at La Jolla, a group of French intellectuals in Paris published a series of books that described with eerie prescience the post–Sexual Revolution world. In 1970 Pierre Klossowski published *La Monnaie vivante* (*Living Currency*) a brief, dense work of critical theory in which he described how in advanced industrial economies sexuality, intimacy, and emotion were becoming increasingly commoditized. This ran counter to the predictions of several generations of socialist intellectuals, who having identified "erotic enjoyment" as one of "the most vital human needs . . . decided to extend the 'communization' of all goods to the living objects of voluptuous desire." In reality, Klossowski observed, sex had been privatized, not collectivized, and so it was better to think of modern sexuality in capitalist terms as something that was marketed, bought, and sold, something that circulated like currency within society. Klossowski's ideas were developed by Jean-François Lyotard in his 1974 work, *Libidinal Economy*. Written during a period of disillusionment with Marxism, *Libidinal Economy* was a paean to capitalism's immense energies. Far from depending on the repression of sexuality, Lyotard wrote, capitalism was riven with "libidinal intensities" and was more sexually liberating than socialism.

Jean Baudrillard drew upon the work of both Klossowski and Lyotard in the composition of his 1980 book *Seduction*. Baudrillard, like the others, accepted that the Sexual Revolution had happened but was essentially capitalist in nature. The exercise of one's sexuality, he reasoned, was now conducted along entrepreneurial lines. "As a mode sex takes the form of an individual enterprise based on natural energy, to each his desire and may the best man prevail (in matters of pleasure). It is the selfsame form as capital." What interested Baudrillard was the role seduction would play in this new order. Socialists had imagined that seduction would be abolished along with private property. Now, with the triumph of sexual freedoms alongside the survival of private property, some argued that seduction was anachronism that would vanish in the face of women's liberation and permissive sexual mores. Not so, Baudrillard declared. "Revolutions and liberations are fragile," he wrote, "while seduction is inescapable." The fallacy common to both notions was that sexuality was simply something that could be transacted. In reality this was not the case. "To believe in sex's reality and in the possibility of speaking sex without mediation is a delusion." Outside of prostitution, sex cannot simply be purchased. ("In the last instance, a purely sexual statement, a pure demand for sex, is impossible.") In this respect it is different from other "goods." Sex occurs between individuals after a period of mediation. Seduction is that mediation. Although liberated sexuality behaves in all other ways like any other liberalized market, in this respect it is unique. Sexuality responds not to impersonal market mechanisms but to what Baudrillard calls the "poetry of desire." By unleashing sexual freedom, the Sexual Revolution had greatly multiplied the number of potential sexual encounters occurring between individuals. In the process, far from being abolished, seduction became ever more important to the lives of sexually liberated peoples.[22]

In the early 1980s, Michel Houellebecq got a job in the exemplary profession of the new data-driven economy—he became a computer engineer. He loathed this profession ("Computers make me puke. My entire work as a computer expert . . . has no meaning.") but it did give him an early prospect on the digital revolution and how vast flows of information, enabled by computers, would upend society. More unusually, Houellebecq connected this technological transformation to the Sexual Revolution. In his first published work, a long essay on the horror writer H.P. Lovecraft, Houellebecq wrote scathingly of modern capitalism, in words that recalled Marx and Engels' famous passage in *The Communist Manifesto*:

> *The reach of liberal capitalism has extended over minds; in step and hand with it are mercantilism, publicity, the absurd and sneering cult of economic efficiency, the exclusive and immoderate appetite for material riches. Worse still, liberalism has spread from the domain of economics to the domain of sexuality. Every sentimental fiction has been eradicated. Purity, chastity, fidelity, and decency are ridiculous stigmas. The value of a human being is measured in terms of his economic efficiency and his erotic potential.*[23]

This was to be the philosophical launchpad for his first two novels: *Whatever* (1994, published in French with the more explicitly Houellebecqian title *Extension du domaine de la lutte*) and *Atomized* (1998), two books that by virtue of their subject matter and their bitter, brooding tone, might be considered as the first two novels of the twenty-first century. Both dealt with the condition of men and women in the post–Sexual Revolution era and both considered the primacy of seduction in newly sexually liberalized societies. It is not clear whether Houellebecq was influenced by the works of Klossowski, Lyotard, or Baudrillard. If he was not, then he arrived at startlingly similar conclusions. *Whatever*, which details the miserable existence of its unnamed narrator, an IT technician with a taste for pessimistic philosophizing, contains the canonical passage:

> *In societies like ours sex truly represents a second system of differentiation, completely independent of money; and as a system of differentiation it functions just as mercilessly. The effects of these two systems are, furthermore, strictly equivalent. Just like unrestrained economic liberalism, and for similar reasons, sexual liberalism produces phenomena of absolute pauperization. Some men make love every day; others five or six times in their life, or never. Some make love with dozens of women; others with none. It's what's known as "the law of the market." In an economic system where unfair dismissal is prohibited, every person more or less manages to find their place. In a sexual system where adultery is prohibited, every person more or less manages to find their bed mate. In a totally liberal economic system certain people accumulate considerable fortunes; others stagnate in unemployment and misery. In a totally liberal sexual system certain people have a varied and exciting erotic life; others are reduced to masturbation and solitude. Economic liberalism is the extension of the domain of the struggle, to all ages and all classes of society. Sexual liberalism is likewise an extension of the domain of the struggle, to all ages and all classes of society.*[24]

The Sexual Revolution, in Houellebecq's account, was not a liberating event along the lines that socialists has predicted. Rather it was the triumph of a certain kind of social libertarianism that in the sixties and seventies had been masked by the rhetoric and costume of the hippie movement and other cultural phenomena. By the eighties and nineties, flower power and bell bottoms were long gone, but the permissiveness of the Sexual Revolution had persisted. These were the same decades that saw neo-liberalism triumph on both sides of the Atlantic. For Houelle-becq, this was no coincidence as both valorized selfish individualism. His key insight, however, is that sexuality "represents a second system of differentiation." This is the vital distinction. Houellebecq is not arguing that all capitalist societies will be sexually liberal, or vice versa. There are several examples—most notably in Scandinavia—of social democracies where sexual freedoms are the norm. Houellebecq's observation is that it has proven easier to manage capitalism than it has sexual liberalism. A socially democratic society is readily conceivable but what he terms a "sexual social democracy" is not. This is because although sexuality mimics economics in its fundamental dynamics, it assigns value differ-ently—it is a second system of differentiation. In a society tolerant of unrestrained sexual liberalism, the sexual "economy" recognizes seduc-tion as its only unit of exchange. Market forces, once unleashed, might be reigned in with regulation; sexual liberalism, once unleashed, is much harder—perhaps impossible—to bring under control. In this sense, it is easier to imagine the end of capitalism than the end of seduction. With typical bathos, Houellebecq inserts this insight into a ludicrous conver-sation between Bruno (one of the antiheroes of *Atomized*) and an old hippie at a New Age summer camp Bruno is attending in hope of finding a sexual partner. "You must have a lot of stories about this place when it first opened," Bruno asks, "—the Seventies, sexual liberation . . ." "Liberation my arse," the hippie replies, before going on to disabuse Bruno of the notion that free love meant on-demand sexual pleasure for all. The encounter leaves Bruno with much to consider:

"So, what you're saying," said Bruno thoughtfully, "is that there never was real sexual liberation—just another form of seduction."

"Oh yeah . . ." agreed the hippie, "there's always been a lot of seduction."

This didn't exactly sound promising.[25]

For almost three centuries the seduction narrative described sexual relations in societies where sexuality was still shrouded in custom and taboo. In particular, female chastity was prized highly and scrutinized closely. Seduction narratives drew their drama and their moral power from these high stakes. Indeed, the stakes were so high that seduction narratives tended to focus on the susceptibility of women to confusing passions, momentary impulses, and devastating lapses in judgement. There were also counternarratives, those that argued for the primacy of reason in sexual relations. Hitherto the history of seduction was played out in the rivalry between these two narratives, that of passion and that of reason. Post–Sexual Revolution, reason won. Sexuality was essentially rationalized. Long held in suspicion, seduction now triumphed. The seducer was no longer a villain or a transgressive figure but someone at ease in the new sexual order. Houellebecq is profoundly skeptical of this development. His *oeuvre* and his public utterances are filled with suspicion of seduction, something he sees as impure and inauthentic, something that precludes the possibility of love. His sympathy is with those men and woman who cannot navigate the new sexual marketplace. His books are, in a sense, anti-seduction narratives, tales of sexual failure. Sometimes this sympathy is expressed with feeling, at others with bitter humor. However it is depicted, Houellebecq understands the experience of sexual inadequacy as among the most potent of the post–Sexual Revolution era.

In a shocking episode at the end of *Whatever*, when the narrator encourages his hapless colleague Rafael to kill a young couple whom they have followed to an assignation on a beach, sexual inadequacy is portrayed as the source of a murderous rage. The scene looks forward to the subculture of incels ("involuntary celibates") formed online in the early years of the new millennium. Specifically, it forecasts the rage of Elliot Rodger, the 22-year-old man who in 2014 published a 140-page manifesto entitled "My Twisted World" in which he bemoaned his lack of sexual success shortly before going on a heavily armed rampage at the University of California at Santa Barbara. Rodger's killing spree began with the murder of his male roommates. Shortly before heading to his principle target on campus, the Delta Delta Delta sorority house, he uploaded a video under the tagline "Retribution" in which he explained that he was targeting the sorority house because he considered the sorority sisters (none of whom he knew) as symbols of a world of sexual freedom from which he was excluded. In the event, nobody answered when he knocked on the door and denied access to the object of his loathing he began shooting random passersby. The Isla Vista attack killed seven and wounded fourteen. In the wake of these killings Rodger became a hero in those pestilential corners of the internet where incels congregated. Lauded as the "supreme gentleman" (a term he had used to refer to himself in his video "Retribution") and as the "Saint" of the incel community, his actions inspired a slew of copycat killings. In the years, since dozens of people have been killed in acts of incel-related terrorism. Alek Minassian, the 25-year-old man who drove a van into pedestrians in Toronto in April 2018, praised the "Supreme Gentleman Elliott Rodger" on Facebook shortly before his attack, and claimed in the same post that his actions were the first strike in an "Incel Rebellion." A mass uprising of sexually frustrated men has yet to occur although the threat posed by these men is being taken seriously. In June 2019, slides were leaked from a briefing for airmen at Andrews Air Force Base in Maryland, outlining incel ideology and the risks posed by its adherents.[26]

Houellebecq offers no solutions to the problem of incel rage. From his vantage point, these are merely the inexorable consequences of sexual inequality. This does not go far in explaining the particular pathologies of the incel subculture. Even if one accepts that the phenomenon of sexual loneliness—and indeed, loneliness and isolation of all kinds—has grown in the last fifty years, it cannot be said that this is an experience limited to men. Indeed, feminists were among the first to complain of the coarsening of gender relations as a consequence of sexual liberation in the 1960s and 1970s. Yet only men are doing the killing. It is probably not necessary to over-intellectualize the incel community. It clearly arises out of the intersection of mental illness, social maladjustment, and intense misogyny.[27]

There were those, however, who recognized early on that the male loneliness, frustration, and periodic rage produced by as a byproduct of sexual liberation was the occasion for entrepreneurialism. Among them was Style, who in 2003 took a couple of men to a bar in Belgrade and advised them on how to approach women. One of the group, Sasha ("who was twenty-two, said he had been with one woman, though we suspected he was exaggerating by one") followed his recommendations and approached a girl, spoke to her, and then got her email address. Sasha was so excited that after they left the bar he skipped down the street. Watching him go, Style waxed sociological: *A significant percentage of violent crime, from kidnappings to shooting sprees, is the result of frustrated sexual impulses and desires of males. By socialising guys like Sasha, Mystery and I were making the world a safer place.*

Style was the nom de guerre of Neil Strauss, and in 2005 he would write *The Game.*

One of the more durable concepts developed by the French critical theorists was that of "capital." In 1986, Pierre Bourdieu wrote a landmark paper suggesting that the concept of economic capital could be extended to other, less tangible, forms of wealth. Bourdieu had in mind social capital and cultural capital both of which he identified as "convertible" into material wealth, power, and status. In 2010, sociologist Catherine Hakim extended Bourdieu's idea yet further, suggesting that in addition to these pre-existing categories of capital, individuals also possessed a stock of erotic capital. "In the sexualized culture of affluent modern societies," Hakim wrote,

> *Erotic capital is not only a major asset in mating and marriage markets, but can also be important in labour markets, the media, politics, advertising, sports, the arts, and in everyday social interaction.*

In the post–Sexual Revolution world, seduction was a competence that every individual was incentivized to develop. Unsurprisingly, ever since the early days of the Sexual Revolution men had been seeking to do just that.[28]

In 1965, an NYU graduate named Eric Weber found himself working in Manhattan, toiling in a lowly job in the advertising industry, and struggling to meet women. "The Beatles had just hit, the times were changing, sex was in the air," Weber recalled. "I'd ride the bus home to Englewood and see the kinds of girls I always thought I should marry. But I was shy." In the late 1960s Weber decided to take matters into his own hands. He began systematically seeking out how to improve his chances at meeting women. Part of this involved a series of frank interviews with twenty-five unattached young women from which he tried to derive a set of rules for negotiating the new, unregulated singles scene. What Weber realized in the course of his research was that in his own lifetime the rules for sex, romance, and relationships had radically altered. Sex had been decoupled from marriage. Moreover sex had been decoupled from morality.[29] "Twenty years ago you would have been right in assuming it was almost impossible to strike up a relationship with a strange girl." He wrote. "But . . . that was before the Pill and miniskirts and see-through blouses and the whole sexual revolution type thing." In 1970, Weber wrote up his findings in a book entitled *How To Pick Up Girls!* which he self-published and promoted independently through magazine commercials. Within a decade he had sold 650,000 copies, grossing $5 million.[30]

Weber was the first to realize that post–Sexual Revolution men were desperate to learn how to navigate the currents of sexual liberation. He succeeded in monetizing seduction. He did not, however, succeed in creating what in the fullness of time would be known as the "Seduction Community." That dubious honor belonged to Ross Jeffries, a Californian who in 1992 authored the spectacularly obnoxious and singularly successful seduction manual *How to Get the Women You Desire into Bed.* Operating in the very early days of the internet, Jeffries built an online community of several thousand men who followed his advice and shared their own experiences of putting his teachings into practice. Jeffries very much presented himself as a guru. Whereas Eric Weber had been something of an enthusiastic dilettante, Ross Jeffries presented his work as a coherent system. He brought into his seduction theories other strands of thought, in particular the pseudoscience of neurolinguistic programming (NLP), thus connecting his twentieth century body of seduction theory with the old Victorian anxieties of the seducer as hypnotist, as the bridge between the rational and the irrational worlds of the mind.[31]

The conflict between reason and passion, the rational and the irrational—the debate which has been at the heart of the history of seduction since the Enlightenment—was central to the work of the most influential seduction theorist of the post–Sexual Revolution era. Well into his twenties Erik von Markovik was a luckless, lanky young man failing to find love in Toronto. Markovik did possess a passion and ability for magic and he determined to make a career for himself as an illusionist. Plying his trade in the late 1990s, operating under the pseudonym "Mystery," Markovik began to develop alongside his stage routine a system of seduction that he came to believe was practically infallible. He called it Mystery Method. A synthesis of evolutionary psychology, sales and marketing techniques, stagecraft, and self-help, Mystery Method was the most sustained attempt yet to teach men seduction. Although infamous for popularizing the technique of "negging" and widely mocked for its dependence on magic tricks and New Age–inspired personality "tests," from a historical perspective, it was also a milestone in the rationalization of sexual relations. For Markovik, seduction is a science. He refers variously to the "science of courtship" and the "algorithm for getting women." There is an algebraic quality to his formulations (A1A2A3—>C1C2C3—>S1S2S3) and his scheme is meant to be obeyed, not played around with. "The game is linear," he intones. Markovik propagated his theories in a self-published book and also in costly private seminars.[32]

In 2002, one of the men who handed over $500 to learn the secrets of seduction was writer and journalist Neil Strauss. Taken under Markovik's wing as a promising young student, Strauss later became a master pick-up artist (PUA) in his own right. By the middle of the first decade of the twenty-first century, the seduction community had swelled to tens of thousands of men communing on online forums and in real life at "boot camps" run by a multiplying number of seduction coaches. It was this subculture and his participation in it that Strauss chronicled in his 2005 book *The Game: Penetrating the Secret Society of Pickup Artists*. His book went on to sell over 2.5 million copies worldwide and

propelled Strauss to media celebrity as the face of contemporary seduction. For a brief window between 2005 and 2010, the seduction community enjoyed something of a moment in the sun. There were talk show
appearances, spin-off TV shows, friendly interviews, and fascinated profiles. This period of grudging acceptance was not to last.

If the seduction community was one product of the Sexual Revolution,
then so too was a feminism that was skeptical of the new permissiveness.
Doubts about sexual liberation had been around since the early 1960s.
In 1962, in an otherwise upbeat article on the new sexual freedoms
enjoyed by young women, Gloria Steinem included the proviso that "the
main trouble with sexually liberating women is that there aren't enough
sexually liberated men to go around."[33] By the time Shere Hite came to
publish her epochal feminist survey of female sexuality (*The Hite Report*
[1976]) the mood among radical women had soured. Hite's respondents
described the bleak topography of sexual freedom. "The sexual revolution liberated a vast amount of masculine bestiality and hostility and
exploitativeness" one woman wrote; others described it as "male-ori-
ented and anti-woman," "the biggest farce of the century for females,"
and as "late sixties bullshit. It was about *male* liberation."[34] Everyday
women recounted what feminist commentators saw abroad in Western
culture at large. One feminist study of contemporary film (revealingly
entitled *From Reverence to Rape*) listed the various roles women were
allowed on-screen: "Whores, quasi-whores, jilted mistresses, emotional
cripples, drunks. Daffy ingenues, Lolitas, kooks, sex-starved spinsters,
psychotics. Icebergs, zombies, and ballbreakers."[35]

Throughout the seventies the feminist vanguard identified and
objected to a coarsening of attitudes toward women advanced under the

standard of sexual liberation. The result was a new attitude of suspicion. At the very moment that much of the old apparatus of sexual discipline was being dismantled, radical women were beginning to agitate for the improved regulation of heterosexual relations. Andrew Dworkin and Catherine MacKinnon famously campaigned in favor of anti-pornography ordinances and helped steer feminism back toward an interest in jurisprudence, in particular with respect to the workplace. Both evinced doubts about the very possibility of sexual freedom for women. Dworkin extended this doubt to seduction itself, half-joking that "seduction is often difficult to distinguish from rape. In seduction, the rapist often bothers to buy a bottle of wine." One consequence of this new trend in feminist thought, was a notable attempt to revive the old seduction laws, or some version of them.[36] Jane E. Larson was a Professor of Law at the University of Wisconsin Law School who spent a good part of her career studying the history of sexual legislation, including the development and repeal of state seduction laws. To her mind the repeal of the seduction statutes from the 1930s onward was a consequence of a misplaced faith in sexual liberation. Gains in female educational achievement, economic independence, and reproductive control did not obviate the need for protections in other spheres. Permissiveness, she suggested, did not de-complicate sexual power dynamics:

> *Having gained the right to say yes, women found they had lost some of their previous power to say no. The new sexual liberalism was an attack on sexual repression . . . but it was more specifically an attack on women's control over men's sexuality.*[37]

Larson married this insight to her deep knowledge of the law and proposed a feminist defense of the now-defunct seduction statutes. In civil law, the tort of seduction was part of a larger body of contract law that regulated how individuals deal with one another. In business it was illegal to engage in "intentional misrepresentation," that is to wittingly deceive one's counter-party. It was perverse, Larson argued, to allow this principle to apply to some of the blandest interactions between corporate entities but not extend it to the most intimate relations between individuals. She proposed a modern tort for sexual fraud that would grant this protection to women who consented to sex under false pretenses. The proposed law would provide a way out of a binary view of the sexual landscape that offered women the choice between "Orwellian oppression and the Hobbesian jungle."[38]

In the early 1990s Larson launched a short and ill-fated campaign to introduce these laws. She soon discovered that there was little public appetite for a bold legislative attempt to regulate sex and courtship. In retrospect the nineties constituted a period of ideological and institutional retrenchment, a hiatus between two great waves of feminist activism. Circa 2010, feminism and feminists burst back into public discourse. Rallying around an emergent discourse that identified the existence of "rape culture" on college campuses and in society at large, a new generation of activists began to challenge sexual norms. The activities of the seduction community did not escape their attention. Self-identified pick-up artists were soon enveloped by the new critique and confronted online and in-person. This was a conflict waged largely outside the public eye. Then in 2014 it was thrust into the news cycle.

In November 2014, Julien Blanc was traveling in Australia for business when a hashtag, #TakeDownJulienBlanc, started circulating, first in American activist circles, then across the world. In Melbourne, an event held by his company attracted 900 protesters—some of them violent—and had to be canceled. Under pressure from campaigners, businesses started to refuse to serve him or his associates, websites took down all reference to his events and venues canceled his reservations. On

November 5, barely a week after he had entered the country, an online petition was set up called "Cancel Julien Blanc's Visa." It was addressed to Scott Morrison, an MP and the Minister of Immigration and Border Protection, and sought the immediate withdrawal of Blanc's right to be in the country. The next day the petition's aim was fulfilled. The Australian authorities revoked Blanc's visa and by November 7 he had been flown out of the country. Nor was this the end of Blanc's woes. The tale of his unceremonious eviction from Australia was now a global news story. Activists all over the world sought to prevent him from entering other countries. Similar petitions began to circulate in Japan, Canada, Argentina, Iceland, Ireland, Germany, Denmark, Sweden, and New Zealand. Some of these met with success: Blanc was denied entry to Singapore and the United Kingdom and was told by the Brazilian and South Korean authorities that they would deny him a visa were he to apply for one. In a matter of weeks he had become an international pariah. *Time* magazine asked: "Is Julien Blanc the most hated man in the world?."

Blanc was a seduction "coach" associated with a company named Real Social Dynamics (RSD), which had been referenced in *The Game*, that was part of a new ecosystem of seduction schools that had come into being over the previous decade. RSD was known for its hyperactive tactics and brash methodology which bordered on harassment and assault. The immediate cause of the campaign against Blanc was the circulation of a video of him in Tokyo where he was shown grabbing and pushing women and in one instance violently handling a woman's head. In the same period, Blanc had been bragging on social media about the effectiveness of his aggressive and manipulative techniques. The global media storm surrounding Blanc's Tokyo misdemeanors and subsequent expulsion from Australia was the occasion for the collision between a revitalized feminism and a complacent seduction community. Feminism won. The episode marked the end of the era of the pick-up artists social acceptability. The attitude toward them shifted from tolerance to disgust. Many seduction "professionals" closed their businesses or rebranded as conventional self-help authors, life coaches, and charisma experts. The community's final demise was signaled by Neil Strauss's disavowal of the theory and practice of seduction in a series of interviews given in 2015 to mark the tenth anniversary of the publication of *The Game*. In *The Atlantic*, Strauss characterized the methods of the PUAs, the same methods he had, a decade before, practiced and popularized, as "objectifying and horrifying."[39] In *The Guardian* he further distanced himself from the movement:

> [The Game] *was really a book about scared men who were afraid of women. But then it became a part of the culture. And it became a reason for women to be afraid of guys."* He's sad about that. *"It was never meant to be an advocacy of a lifestyle, even though it's come to symbolise one.*[40]

Ironically, at the very same time as the seduction community was being exiled from polite society another dehumanizing, more Houellebecqian trend in seduction was rising to dominance.

In *Whatever*, Houellebecq had imagined a world where "every human relationship is *reduced* to an exchange of information."[41] A world where humans were reduced to data, managed and studied by computers. In the two decades since his novel's publication this prediction has been vindicated in the growth and social acceptance of online and app-enabled dating. In 1995, only two percent of the couples met online. By 2017 thirty-nine percent of couples were first connected through the

internet and as many as twenty percent of newlyweds had first interacted in cyberspace.[42] Tellingly, the gains made by online dating websites and apps have been made at the expense of more traditional, com-
munitarians ways of finding love. As late as 2000, about a quarter of
couples met through family, neighbors, or in church. A decade later this
number had plunged to ten percent while online dating had soared in
popularity.[43]

Dating apps and websites have created an actual libidinal economy.
They are marketplaces for desire where attractiveness is the dominant
value expressed in a currency of likes, swipes, and messages. Houellebecq had surmised in *Whatever* that unregulated sexual markets would
create huge disparities in sexual outcomes. This is a view that has been
utterly vindicated online. On dating apps and websites inequality is
ubiquitous. Data from the dating app Hinge in 2017, found that the top
1 percent of men on Hinge received 16.4 percent of all messages; the
top 1 percent of women on Hinge received 11.2 percent of all messages.
To put these figures in context consider how they would translate into
economic measures of income inequality, typically measured by a Gini
Coefficient whereby 0 is perfect equality and 1 is perfect inequality. On
this basis, the "economy" of Hinge for women has a Gini Coefficient
of 0.376, and for men a Gini Coefficient of 0.542. In the real world the
Gini Coefficient for OECD-EU nations on average is approximately 0.3.
In other words, at a time of yawning economic inequality, hundreds of
thousands of people are looking for love on online platforms whose
dynamics are even more unequal than those they are subject to in their
everyday lives.[44]

On the surface this looks like men have a harder time online than
women. The data points toward a more complex set of circumstances.
Men and women seem to interact differently online. On Tinder, one study
found that men typically "like" more women but engage less when they

match. In contrast, women on Tinder "like" fewer men but are more likely to engage when they match.[45] Moreover, attractiveness is judged differently by men and women. Data from OkCupid found that women are far harsher on men than vice versa. On a 1 to 5 scale of attractiveness the average man judges the average woman to be a 3.0; the average woman judges the average man to be a 2.0.[46] The obverse of this phenomenon is that female judgements of male attractiveness have less variance whereas male judgements of female attractiveness run the gamut from 0 (perfectly ugly) to 5 (perfectly attractive). This matters because across all dating apps and websites there is evidence that both men and women are aspirational in their pursuit of an attractive partner. On OkCupid it was estimated that the average man sought a partner 17 percent more attractive than himself but the average woman sought a partner only 10 percent more attractive than themselves. Another cross-platform study found that these figures were even higher: 26 percent for men and 23 percent for women.[47] This leads to the perverse outcome whereby at the extremes the most attractive men are getting more messages than the most attractive women, while on average women are more forgiving in terms of looks, and message men they deem to be of below-average attractiveness at far higher levels than they do men who they deem to be of above-average attractiveness. Men act differently, increasing their message flow in proportion to their judgement of the attractiveness of the woman in question.[48]

Furthermore, these inequalities are exacerbated by the relative weight given to visual information on individual profiles. When OkCupid experimented with changing the format of dating profiles such that images of each individual came to dominate the screen—at the expense of non-visual written information—then the most attractive people saw their message inflow increase by up to 75% while the least attractive people saw their already meagre message count decrease by 5-10%. "All those extra pixels allowed the pretty faces to outshine the others all the more," OkCupid founder Christian Rudder wrote of this phenomenon, "the rich got richer."[49]

However the data is interpreted, it is clear that online dating rewards the beautiful and ignores the less desirable. The result is the creation of a Houellebecqian residuum of undesired and uncontacted people, a struggling middle class of middling looking individuals just getting along, and then a minority of ultra-desirable men and women under virtual siege from suitors. In 2014, *New York Magazine* profiled some of these ultra-desirable individuals by reaching out to the four most contacted OkCupid profiles in New York City. The article detailed lives of unimaginable sexual opportunity. The most contacted woman was receiving 245 messages a week. The most contacted man revealed that he was using two different dating apps and that the week before had matched with 890 women on Tinder.[50] This theme of superabundance for an attractive minority replicate across platforms and across studies. A 2018 study of online dating in four major North American cities identified one woman in New York who was receiving messages in such quantity that it amounted to a single message received every half an hour, day and night, for an entire month.[51]

Attractiveness is not the only driver of sexual inequality on online platforms. Age is major determinant of message traffic and acts differently on men and women—with women typically experiencing a drastic reduction of interest from men as they age while interest in men tends to rise into their forties. Race is another factor, with numerous studies showing that online dating has created a racial hierarchy of attractiveness.[52] What is most wretched about the creation of these new, uncomfortable dynamics is that they seem to be a product of the particular experience of being online. Based on the data available, Christian Rudder found that on OkCupid people seemed to be operating from certain assumptions and preferences that did not reflect how they behaved in the real world. "In short," he wrote, "people appear to be heavily preselecting online for something that, once they sit down in person, doesn't seem important to them." If sexual inequality does not describe our past, then given the growing pervasiveness online dating, it likely describes our future.[53]

Yet even this is not the whole story. Increasingly, the unequal dynamics of online dating do not simply resemble the unequal dynamics of advanced economies—they actively feed into one another. This is because the majority of the most popular dating apps are either subscription services, "freemium" services, or some mixture of the two. Raw desirability—what Hakim called erotic capital—is no longer enough. Actual capital—money—is needed to have a hope of finding love online. The pay-to-play aspects of online dating arise out of the simple need for the companies hosting the platform to turn a profit. This is not in itself bad. But the mechanics of *how* they monetize online romance are often overlooked. This is a shame because it reveals a great deal about the workings of modern love. To start with, like much of the tech sector, the online dating world is highly concentrated. One company, Match Group, owns forty-five different platforms, grossing close to two billion dollars in revenues each year. Almost half of those revenues come from a single product: Tinder.[54]

When Tinder shot to popularity in 2014, much of its appeal derived from its democratic architecture: the app was free to download and all the users were simply thrown together and left to choose among themselves who they engaged with. Over the years, Tinder has become noticeably less open. The rise of paid subscription services like Tinder Premium and Tinder Gold as well as the introduction and heavy promotion of in-app purchases to improve the chances of matching have reduced the viability of simply using the app for free. The enhanced user experience given to those who pay for Tinder has come at the expense of those who do not. In the process, what has been revealed is that the algorithms that run Tinder are not intended to be democratic at all. By way of example: one of the most popular products on Tinder is "Boost," a feature that promotes the profile of the person who purchases it. Tinder claims that people who buy Boost will get tenfold exposure for half an hour when there is peak traffic on the app. Boost works because Tinder is essentially a long line of profiles queuing up to meet each other. Customers who use Boost essentially cut in front of other profiles. In 2019, Tinder introduced "Super Boost," a product that would function the same way, allowing users, in the words of the company, to "cut to the front and be seen by up to 100x more potential matches." Tinder boasts that "Super Boost" is "the ultimate Tinder hack," essentially acknowledging that the Tinder "economy" is rigged in favor of those willing to pay to get ahead. The real-world equivalent would be a night club filling up with wealthy individuals bribing the doormen for entry while a long, static queue builds up outside.[55]

The phenomenon is not limited to Tinder. Almost all online dating companies offer products whose workings basically admit to the inequitable premise of the services they provide. The prices of these services vary. Depending on how long a user commits to, a subscription could cost between $10 to $30 per month. Likewise, onetime app purchases can cost between $5 and $30. These are not huge amounts but the target market tends to skew young and hence lower-income. Furthermore, prices can be variable. Age and location (and, it is rumored, attractiveness) can impact the cost of both subscriptions and app purchases. Paradoxically, the increasing popularity of these products is testament not to the merit of any one dating platform but to their failings. However, because they enjoy oligopolistic status, the companies behind the apps can afford to keep pushing paid products while systematically undermining the user experience of those who refuse to buy in. This might matter less if the product being sold by these companies was not love. The financial statements of Match Group are filled with cynicism. Under "Risk Factors" in the annual report, the accountants wring their hands about the possibility of "a meaningful migration of our user base from our higher monetizing dating products to our lower monetizing dating products [which would] adversely affect our business, financial condition and results of operations." Meanwhile, in the quarterly investor presentation the marketing team trumpets the new Hinge brand campaign "resonating with users and the press." Its slogan: "Designed to be Deleted."[56]

Online dating is the logical end result of a Sexual Revolution more informed by liberalism than liberation. Technology has merely better enabled an impulse unleashed many decades ago. Writing in *Seduction*, Baudrillard suggested that

> *The sexual jurisdiction is but a fantastic extension of the commonplace ideal of private-property, where everyone is assigned a certain amount of capital to manage: a psychic capital, a libidinal, sexual or unconscious capital, for which each person will have to answer individually, under the sign of his or her own liberation.*[57]

This seems to capture the reality of contemporary online dating. It is a commonplace to state that dating is now a kind of work, a form of labor. In her 2016 book *Labor of Love: The Invention of Dating*, Moira Weigel suggested that the work of online dating resembled that of the unpaid internship. This, it seems now, does not capture the extent to which online dating requires investment—the investment of time, money, emotion, and erotic capital. The user of a dating app or website is engaged in the work of investment rather than the work of labor and this work is performed "under the sign of his or her own liberation."

In this sense, the hundreds of thousands of online daters engaged in the daily speculation on themselves are a kind of fractal reflection of the entrepreneurial Silicon Valley business culture that gave rise to the dating apps and websites that host them. The Sexual Revolution has turned its grandchildren into startups. And most startups fail.

The general acceptance of online dating stands in stark contrast to the widespread revulsion at the seduction community. An oddity, for both are part of the same post–Sexual Revolution phenomenon of the rationalization of sexual relations. Eric von Markovik dreamt of creating an "algorithm for getting women"; the immensely profitable corporations that own and operate the online dating platforms have in their own way realized that dream, only at the level of populations rather than individuals. If the true legacy of the Sexual Revolution is sexual liberation with capitalist characteristics then OkCupid, Tinder, and all the other dating companies are its true beneficiaries. In the tug-of-war between reason and passion that has been the overriding feature of the history of seduction, reason, for now, seems to have won. Modern Westerners, as Houellebecq recognized earlier than most, live lonely, diminished lives in part because their capacity to forge and sustain human connections enjoys an inverse relationship to their capacity to internalize the logic of liberal capitalism. The decrepitude of the average individual's emotional vocabulary and sentimental universe is a poignant testament to this. "Tenderness is a deeper instinct than seduction," Houellebecq writes in *Atomized*, "which is why it is so difficult to give up hope." Increasingly, this small hope has been surrendered to profit-minded tech companies. The desocialization of Western nations proceeds apace while at the same time hundreds of thousands of lonely people flock to online dating services who treat their dreams of romantic happiness with spectacular venality.

At least such were my own thoughts upon encountering a would-be pick-up artist in the wild. It was in London, one Saturday in the January of 2016, not long after Strauss had renounced the methodology of seduction that he had once been a master of. The day had been gray and dismal. I had been invited to a friend's birthday drinks in Clapham that evening. Shortly before I left it began raining torrentially. It stopped not long before I arrived. Water covered every surface, including the awnings and the tables in the forecourt of the pub where we were meeting, as well as the short, steep, stone steps that led up to its front door. Inside, it was quiet on account of the rain. There were a few couples having dinner and a few small groups of friends. The group I joined was by far the largest and the most boisterous in the place. I went to get a drink. Waiting for my order I noticed a boy, he could not have been much more than twenty-two, standing alone at the bar a few meters down from me. Something about his pose caught my eye. He looked hunted. He held his pint glass close to his chin in between sips, the arm holding it held tight against his chest, the other thrust into his jean pockets. His eyes moved nervously around. Occasionally he would turn to survey the room in a single, sweeping, anxious movement before turning back to the bar. On the other side, two barmen were drying glasses and chatting casually, their relaxed informality a counterpoint to his clearly agitated state. He was of average height, a slight build, his upper half bulked out by a beige fatigue jacket and beneath that a blue jumper. He had dark brown hair in a slightly mussed side parting. He had soft eyes, gentle features. He looked like the kind of boy whose mother worries about him; indeed, it seemed as if his mother no longer dressed him then the ghost of her past purchases still haunted his wardrobe. He was quite good looking, or would have been if he was not in a state of such obvious discomfort. My drink arrived; I returned to the group.

Some time later the party decamped to the beer garden out front so the smokers could smoke. Outside it was dark, cold, and wet. The street-lights made moons on the pools of rainwater that now sat atop all the

tables and all the benches. We huddled at a row of tables that were shel-
tered by an awning and warmed by a single patio heater that deactivated
every couple of minutes. After a period, I went back inside to get another
drink, mindful as I went of the perfectly slick steps at the entrance. I was
at the bar again. The boy was no longer there. I assumed he had left,
as he had arrived, alone. I got my drink and turned and began to walk
the ten meters or so from the bar to the front door. It was then that I
saw him. Just to the right of the door was a low, oblong table with two
velveteen pouffes on either side and two candles in the middle. The light
was particularly dim in this portion of the room and the candlelight
moved atmospherically across his face and across that of the pretty bru-
nette now sat across from him. I can see the tableau in my mind: she
is leaning forward, her right hand resting on her face, her lips apart in
anticipation; there are four cards on the table and his hand is poised over
one of them but his eyes are looking up at her through his lashes with
something like happiness.

I experienced a shock of recognition. This was Mystery Method in
action before me.

My interests being what they are I was now in a heartbreaking position. I was too committed to turn back to the bar and could hardly stop
and stare from the middle of the room. Instead, I decelerated in order
to soak in as much of the scene as possible before I was obliged to exit.
Over at the table his little magic trick was arriving at its conclusion. He
turned over the final card and said something in a low voice. Both hands
flew to her face. She squealed and rocked back with glee. He smiled and
made some modest motion with his hands but I could see that he was
basking in the glow of his success.

I was now only three meters or so from the door. One of the maxims
of Mystery Method is that "seldom will you see women of beauty alone"
in a bar, or anywhere else. It occurred to me at this point that this was

likely true of this girl as well. Not many people go to bars alone on a Saturday night, excepting the guy she was now talking to. Then I noticed at table against the wall just in front of the door a group of three, one blonde girl and two well-built men. One of them had his back to the wall and was staring at the aftermath of card trick with undisguised disdain. His friend was hunched over the table. "It's this thing from a book," he said to the girl, "so you can trick a girl into bed." She looked utterly distraught at the news, one hand covering her mouth in horror. She half stood up in her seat, her eyes searching for her friend's attention.

I stepped outside and went back to my seat beneath the awning. I had a view across the empty beer garden of the front door. Barely a minute later he emerged. Defeat was stamped all over his face. He looked up at the night sky and turned his jacket collar up to the cold. He took a step down. The rain and the smooth stone collaborated in his humiliation. He slipped and collapsed down the steps onto the asphalt. Instinct had saved his face from harm but he had landed hard on his forearms. He was still for a moment on the floor. Then he stood up and checked to see if anyone had seen him fall. Nobody on my table seemed to have noticed. He dusted himself down, put his hands in his jacket pockets, and walked away into the night.

AFTERWORD

This book was commissioned in August 2017. In October of the same year the *New Yorker* and the *New York Times* published a series of articles detailing a long list of sexual assault allegations against film producer Harvey Weinstein. In the wake of the Weinstein revelations survivors of sexual assault began to share their stories on social media under the hashtag #MeToo. This explosion of storytelling about sexual assault—which in most (but not all) cases involved a female accuser and a male culprit—sparked a vigorous transatlantic debate about sexual mores that continues to elicit comment and generate controversy. Although this book was conceived of, planned, and begun before the advent of the #MeToo era, it was largely written and researched within it and will doubtless be read by some against the background of the impassioned debates of the past few years. It is too soon to tell whether the #MeToo era is at its beginning, middle, or end. Nor can we know what its ultimate historical significance will be. Writing this book against the backdrop of blossoming scandal has been a challenge, though still an enjoyable one, but it has had the advantage of proving beyond doubt the basic contention of this book, namely that seduction narratives are very powerful things.

We began with Francis Charteris; we end with Harvey Weinstein. In between we have witnessed Casanova's morally questionable sexual escapades, we have heard denunciations of male rapacity from Laetitia Pilkington, Mary Wollstonecraft, and Claire Clairmont, we have followed the decades-long struggle to secure legal protections for women, we have seen how sexual liberation was challenged by feminists wary of the consequences of unilaterally removing controls on male sexuality. All of this resonates in the #MeToo era. The phrase that has surfaced again and again in my mind as the disclosures and dismissals have come one after the other was uttered by Pamela Andrews, the heroine of Samuel Richardson's classic novel of seduction: "And pray, said I, walking on, how came I to be his Property? What Right has he in me, but such as a thief may plead to stolen Goods?" Pamela's protest has been the protest of the past few years, a protest not only at the abuse that assault survivors have endured but at the presumption and the entitlement of their abusers and assaulters. It is a summons for social and legal intervention as well as a demand for a change in norms and a reformation of male sexual manners.

All of which raises an obvious objection: what does any of this have to do with seduction? What do allegations of abuse, assault, and rape have to do with matters of love, courtship, and consensual sex? The trajectory of the #MeToo era answers its own question. Four months after the allegations against Harvey Weinstein became public, media attention alighted on a very different episode of alleged sexual misconduct. In January 2018, Babe.net published the account of a date that took place the previous September in Manhattan between a 23-year-old woman and celebrity comedian Aziz Ansari. The woman, identified under the pseudonym "Grace" (an incidental echo of the allegorical names favored for the heroines of eighteenth century seduction narratives), painted a lurid account of an innocent evening turned into an ordeal of unwanted advances ending in her weeping in an Uber on the way home. Once public, the episode became a flashpoint in the unrolling #MeToo moment. But whereas the response to the Weinstein allegations was unanimous revulsion and condemnation, the reactions to the allegation against Ansari were divided. For Grace's partisans it was readily apparent that her story belonged in the #MeToo pantheon alongside the criminal allegations made against Weinstein and others. Yet there were a number of prominent dissenting feminist voices arguing that not only was her experience not comparable to serious charges of sexual assault, but that nothing had happened that night with Ansari that could credibly be understood as sexual impropriety. In the febrile atmosphere of the time the two sets of positions were quickly (and crudely) characterized as a conflict between those who were looking to bravely push the nascent #MeToo movement into new territory and those who were arguing that #MeToo had gone too far. What was overlooked was that these two positions conformed to the centuries-old narrative structures discussed in this book. For some, it was obvious that a continuum existed between sexual assault allegations (Weinstein) and a bad date (Ansari). For others, it was equally obvious that these episodes were incomparable. For one group, the distance between Weinstein's accusers and Grace was only the distance between *Pamela* and *Clarissa*. For the other group, Grace and Ansari were both knowing participants in a liberalized sexual marketplace.

This polarity in feminist responses to the #MeToo movement is often described as generational. An older group of feminists associated with the activism, ambitions, and experiences of the sixties, seventies, and eighties is held in uniform and imaginary opposition to a new cohort of millennial feminists shaped by a separate set of circumstances and sharpened by new intellectual influences. This mothers and daughters narrative holds an obvious appeal. By declaring that things were that way then and they will be this way now we can take comfort in the idea that progress is being made. The history of seduction suggests otherwise. The contemporary divide closely mirrors the divide between the flappers and the women of the WCTU. It is the same fissure that we observed within Mary Wollstonecraft's thought. It recalls the literary differences between Samuel Richardson and Henry Fielding in Georgian London.

It is a divide which is larger than #MeToo and predates modern feminism. It is a question grounded in classic Enlightenment debates over the nature of the mind—whether we are moved more by reason or by the passions, whether we are rational agents or creatures vulnerable to error, deceit, and suasion—that have found expression in seduction narratives since the birth of modernity. Zooming out from individual episodes, we can see that the broad outlines of contemporary debates map on to older discussions described in the earlier chapters of this book. This is because the heart of the matter is an irresolvable conflict over first principles. We can allow that progress can occur on a material basis—women are clearly better off in 2020 than they were in 1700—while accepting that progress in manners and mores is altogether harder to observe or even to agree upon. Even the briefest survey of recent history confirms this. It is important to remember that the decade that preceded the #MeToo movement was one that saw *The Game* author Neil Strauss welcomed on late night talk shows and feted at the Oxford Union, his mentor Mystery given his own reality TV show, *The Pickup Artist*, on VH1, *Fifty Shades of Grey* become the standout publishing phenomenon of the 21st century, and films like *Hitch*, *Wedding Crashers*, and *Crazy Stupid Love* become pop culture touchstones. The point is that sexual culture can change very quickly. And there is no reason why it might not change again.

In the meantime, we have to contend with the present. And the present is scathing of the permissive sexual culture of their parents' and grandparents' generation. One area where this is apparent is in the renewed interest in using legal and bureaucratic devices to shape sexual behavior. In the sixties and seventies sexual discipline was fought against by student radicals and activist judges. On campuses on both sides of the Atlantic, female students fought successfully to dismantle systems of sexual control that they regarded as patronizing and coercive.

In America, the once formidable body of seduction law (discussed in Chapter 5) was torn down as courts ruled that they no longer reflected prevailing cultural norms. "The woman of today is not the woman of yesteryear," concluded the judges presiding over *Breece v. Jett*, a seduction suit heard in a Missouri courtroom in 1977:

> *She has a new-found freedom. The modern adult woman is*
> *sophisticated and mature. The former notion that women belong*
> *to the weaker sex has long been abandoned. The modern woman is*
> *not easily "beguiled" and does not easily fall to the "wiles" of man.*
> *Women desire and should be held to a reasonable responsibility.*[1]

This position meets with suspicion in the #MeToo era, in part because some of the more egregious accused have sought to defend themselves by reference to the carefree mores of a bygone era. "I came of age in the 60s and 70s," Harvey Weinstein pleaded in a statement made in response to the allegations against him, "when all the rules about behavior and workplaces were different. That was the culture then." Of course, Weinstein is not the representative figure of the ethos of sexual liberation. But that he believed he could retreat into a *Mad Men*-esque popular conception of that era as an explanation for his behavior is indicative of the ambiguous legacy of the Sexual Revolution. What was once regarded as a period of carefree sexual adventuring is now subjected to revisionist scrutiny. One area where this is apparent is in the discussion surrounding the existence or otherwise of the so-called "sex recession." When in 2019 the *Economist* posited that the decline in sexual activity could be attributed to "economics, technology, and female empowerment" congresswoman Alexandria Ocasio-Cortez shot back that "if you think your 'celibacy' is due to 'female empowerment,' maybe it's because far too many people relied on the disempowerment + silence of women to not be 'celibate' in the first place." A few weeks earlier, a *Guardian* writer reflecting on the connections between her memories of 1960s California and the contemporary discussion of the "sex recession" concluded that "in the 60s, rampant misogyny was dressed up as emancipated 'permissiveness'" and that the current decline in sexual activity might be a good thing for women. Such sentiments have deep wells in feminist thought. They recall the unforgettable slogan of Christabel Pankhurst—"Votes For Women and Chastity For Men"—and the concern expressed by the respondents to the *Hite Report* about the brutal experience of liberation for women on the frontline of sexual reality. It is not surprising that 2019 also saw the rehabilitation of Andrea Dworkin, the most unforgiving critic of the sexual culture of her youth. Indeed, it was feminist activists who fought for laws like those the judges in *Breece v. Jett* challenged. Yet these oppositions conceal a common purpose. First wave feminists were champions of a "Single Standard" of sexual morality that would replace the more famous "Double Standard." The search for such a single standard is implied by the judges' decision in *Breece v. Jett* ("Women desire and should be held to a reasonable responsibility.") to deny the plaintiff protection under (in their view) an archaic law. Whether an equality of sexual experience is best assured through the creation of law or through the reduction of law is a question that the experience of the twentieth century has clearly been unable to answer. The better question for those who might turn to law to combat the abuses of the twenty-first century is whether it is possible to design a body of law to protect women without recourse to infantilizing narratives about female agency that ultimately serve to restrict their liberties rather than expand them.[2]

Strictly speaking, the search for legal solutions predates #MeToo. As we saw in the case of Julien Blanc (discussed in Chapter 7), under pressure from activists some nations have used immigration laws to prevent the entry or expedite the departure of those deemed guilty of sexual misconduct. Another, more popular, legal arena has been consent law. In Chapter 5 we saw how American seduction laws had their origins in foundational campaigns, spearheaded by Frances Willard, to increase the age of sexual consent. Under the Obama administration, activists operating with the rhetorical support of the White House and the bureaucratic support of the Department of Education, sought to change the definition of consent with an end to combatting the widely discussed epidemic of sexual assault on college campuses. Rather than increase the age of consent, recent campaigns have sought to change the standard of consent from "No Means No" to "Yes Means Yes." This shift has been portrayed as one broadly in line with the spirit of sexual liberation— hence the emphasis on "enthusiastic consent" between willing and presumably joyful partners—but the tenor of the campaign has sometimes recalled the fearful language of the WCTU. Writing in support of California's recently passed "Yes Means Yes" law in 2014, left-wing pundit Ezra Klein argued that the American left should support the new law not because it was a good law but because it was a bad one. "If the Yes Means Yes law is taken even remotely seriously," Klein wrote,

It will settle like a cold winter on college campuses, throwing everyday sexual practice into doubt and creating a haze of fear and confusion over what counts as consent. This is the case against it, and also the case for it.[3]

In 2014 Klein welcomed the attempt "to change, through brute legislative force, the most private and intimate of adult acts." Post-2017 many people expected courts to prosecute sexual assault cases energetically. The legal realities suggest that the justice many seek will not come from the courts. The California law praised by Klein only covered the postsecondary schools[4] that were the recipient of state money for student financial aid. Jeannie Suk Gersen, a law professor at Harvard University, has cautioned that many of the legal cases sprouting as a result of #MeToo allegations "will not end in legal vindication" because

> *The alleged behavior doesn't match legal definitions, or because*
> *of statutes of limitations, or insufficient evidence, or questionable*
> *witnesses, or police misconduct, or prosecutorial overreach, or*
> *doubtful juries—in short, for all the reasons that cases can fall*
> *apart when subjected to scrutiny in court.*[5]

Extensive legal innovation is unlikely. We are not going to see contemporary equivalents of the old state seduction laws or the federal Mann Act emerge as a response to #MeToo. However, this does not mean that action is not going to be taken in response to outrage of recent years—simply that it will take a different form. Elsewhere, Jeannie Suk Gersen has chronicled the rise of what she and her co-author Jacob Gersen describe as "the Sex Bureaucracy," a cohort of administrators in American universities whose job it is to regulate sexual conduct on campus and promulgate guidelines for sexual interactions between students. The origins of the sex bureaucracy lie in the 1970s. In 1972 the United States Congress passed Title IX, a federal civil rights law intended to combat gender discrimination in higher education. Title IX has had several consequences, among them the creation of a caste of university employees tasked with ensuring that their institutions do not violate Title IX requirements in their handling (or mishandling) of sexual assault allegations on campus. In the hands of university administrators, who are themselves under pressure to ensure compliance with the most expansive readings of the law, Title IX has morphed into a wide-ranging attempt to police sexual activity on American campuses. There are several historical ironies in play here. The first is that the pressure to create stronger codes of sexual conduct are coming from below, from the student body, rather than from above. As Laura Kipnis has observed: "A previous generation of student activists fought against the in loco parentis policies of universities; today's students are fighting to extend them." The second is that students at American universities now abide by codes of conduct closer in spirit to the seduction legislation that governed the private lives of their great grandparents and great-great grandparents than to the permissive sexual culture of their grandparents and parents. Noting that universities now "regulate conduct traditionally in the domain of morals regulation," Gersen and Suk Gersen go on to write that university consent guidelines "are how-to's for sexual arousal, proposition, and seduction—not just consent or agreement to have sex." The final irony is that these sexual regulations, although originating in federal law, are far more severe than any legal statute on the books at a state or federal level. Consequently, for four years while at college, typically between the ages of eighteen to twenty-two, the American undergraduate will be held to a codified standard of behavior far more stringent than any they will face once they leave campus upon graduation.[6]

That may be changing. #MeToo arose out of allegations about sexual impropriety in the workplace. Inevitably, there has been pressure on corporations—especially those caught up in #MeToo allegations—to introduce new policies designed to tackle sexual harassment and misconduct in their offices. Just as in the university system, these new policies have been created, codified, and promulgated by a sex bureaucracy operating extra-legally but with considerable power over the lives of the employees they oversee. The content of these new policies varies. At the extreme, employers have introduced rules that forbid employees to hug, make eye contact for five-seconds or longer, or to ask for one another's phone numbers. What is striking about these new guidelines is that they are grounded in the assumption that their subjects (adult employees with advanced degrees) are *either* intensely psychologically vulnerable *or* lustful predators and then proceed to assume that all the potential human interactions that arise within the workplace environment can be rationally managed by bureaucratic fiat. This is not to deny that systematic and widespread predation has not been uncovered, much less that it should not be taken extremely seriously. It is simply to observe that there is a paradox present in the overarching narrative—a paradox that recalls the centuries old Enlightenment debate as to whether we are rational or passionate beings.[7]

Support for a more vigorous response to #MeToo allegations and the environments that gave rise to them cuts across political divides. There are those on the left, the right, and in the center, who will find merit in the existence and the activities of the sex bureaucracy. There will also be those who look for the introduction of new legal measures to combat sexual assault in their societies. Ultimately, individuals will have to decide for themselves what legal and bureaucratic innovations—if any—are called for in response to #MeToo. But those who do seek the empowerment of courts and bureaucracies will have to reckon with the long history of racialized policy-making in the realm of sexual conduct. And there are already signs of a renewal of the kind of racial-sexual fears described in chapters 5 and 6 of this book.

In Europe, nationalist populist political parties have used sexual assault allegations against members of immigrant communities to advance their electoral agendas. In Sweden, a country at the forefront of progressive legislation on matters like consent, assault, and harassment, this has led to peculiar dynamics. In 2013, activists successfully sought changes to how the authorities recorded and handled sexual crimes. This led, as had been expected, to a rise in the number of reported sexual crimes. The Swedish Democrats (a nationalist populist party) then claimed that this rise in sexual criminality was due to the influx of immigrants and asylum-seekers during the same period. Their share of the vote rose from five percent in 2010 to seventeen and a half percent in 2018. The Swedish establishment is understandably eager to play down this issue but are caught between campaigning pressure from the activist left for more robust sexual offense laws and the willingness of the populist right to take advantage of the statistical trends that result from the introduction of those same laws. Moreover, because the authorities do not collect racial data in connection with reported sexual offenses there is no way of establishing the truth.[8]

The same risks are present in America. It is an axiom of anti-racist thought and scholarship that systemic racism finds expression in bad law.[9] As discussed in chapter 5, this was true in the nineteenth and twentieth centuries where loosely worded seduction statutes were used as vehicles for racial persecution. It is not hard to see how the sex bureaucracy might well replicate the racial wrongs of the past. This is not a matter of intentions but of consequences. One need not believe that individual university administrators are racist to recognize that the system they preside over might facilitate racist outcomes. The reality is that it already does. Gersen and Suk Gersen write that the sex bureaucracy's real-world functioning "creates a significant risk of precriminalizing minority men." Their concerns have been echoed by civil rights activists.[10] In America, as in Sweden, advocacy is complicated by the nature of the systems in place. The quasi-legal processes set up to rule on cases of sexual assault on American college campuses are notoriously opaque. Ezra Klein may have welcomed the "haze of fear and confusion" generated by "terrible law" but that haze has settled, perhaps predictably, on vulnerable minority students. Similarly, although there is plenty of anecdotal evidence of racial bias at work in the Title IX–mandated sexual regime on American campuses, because they do not report racial data there is no way of knowing the facts. When racial data has been released it has confirmed the worst fears of those skeptical of the workings of the sex bureaucracy. In 2014, Colgate University, a private liberal arts college in upstate New York, made public the relevant data for the academic year of 2013/14. It revealed that although black male students were 4.2 percent of the student body they were accused of 50 percent of the sexual offenses reported to the university.[11]

There are no easy solutions. There are limits, also, to how useful history is as a guide to how to navigate the present. Much about the present has no clear antecedent. Likewise, much about the past no longer applies. When the seduction narrative was born in the eighteenth century, certain things were taken for granted. First, there was a thriving sentimental culture that valorized rich emotional experiences. To be passionate and sensible (in the eighteenth-century meaning of the word) were signs of sophistication and refinement—even of fashion. There were plenty of satires of the culture of sensibility and there was plenty of poor behavior despite of its existence. Still, when we read the writings of Mary Wollstonecraft or Mary Shelley, highly intelligent women who were capable of writing unselfconsciously, lyrically, and at length about their emotional lives, we are getting a glimpse of a portion of the emotional spectrum that is no longer visible to us. This matters because it was self-evident to many Georgians that morality arose out of humans' emotional experiences, not from their reasoning faculties. It was Adam Smith—no swooning ingénue he—who declared it "altogether absurd and unintelligible to suppose that the first perceptions of right and wrong can be derived from Reason." Instead it was "immediate sense and feeling," refined into sentiments, that provided the foundations for morality. #MeToo is many things, but it is surely evidence of a major breakdown in the capacity to empathize, to relate, to feel. We should not, however, hold out too much hope for the renewal of sentimental culture in an age where the median number of characters in a Tinder message sent from a man to a woman is twelve.[12]

Another aspect of eighteenth century living we have lost is the culture of sociability, civility, and conviviality. Mostly for want of alternatives our ancestors spent a great deal of time together in clubs, balls, coffee shops, taverns, churches, recitals, public gardens, readings, ridottos, carnivals, religious processions, gambling houses, the theatre, the opera, the public square. Time spent mingling in public or semi-public spaces was considered vital for fostering goodwill between strangers, polishing manners, and learning how to interact with others. Humans still need this kind of training in social life. Increasingly, we are not getting it. Social scientist Robert Putnam has chronicled in fact what Michel Houellebecq has portrayed in fiction, that we are living isolated, atomized existences, sundered from any kind of larger community. American psychologist Jean Twenge has documented how among the generation raised by smartphones and tablets instances of depression, loneliness, and suicidal tendencies are steadily climbing. This generation will likely know no other romantic experiences other than those mediated by online and mobile dating platforms financially incentivized against their lasting happiness. Absent of change, these desocialized individuals will be essentially illiterate when it comes to reading the kind of subtle, nonverbal cues that abound in courtship scenarios.

If it is mere accident that #MeToo took root amid the wreckage of our social and emotional existences then it is still an informative coincidence. For without a countervailing culture of sentiment mediated by a lively and generous civil society we are left with only a commercial logic to understand human relations. Many commentators have made the connection between #MeToo and the rampant economic inequality at large in Western societies. In the twenty-first century (as it was in the eighteenth) this material disparity has been dramatized by the spectacle of a precariously employed woman at the mercy of a wealthy, powerful, and rapacious male boss. The power of this scenario persists for good reason—as has been abundantly document in the last few years. But it is not the whole truth. One of the underreported stories that has run parallel to the #MeToo era is that we are living in what economist Claudia Goldin has called the "last chapter" of the "grand convergence" in male and female economic outcomes. The same year that saw the Weinstein revelations make global headlines, women in the West overtook men among a number of vital metrics including law school, medical school, and undergraduate admissions.

The trend lines still point toward economic equality. Rather than seeing these facts in opposition to one another, or worse in denial of one another, we might see that they are divergent expressions of the same phenomenon. We are living in a liberal-capitalist monoculture which has brought economic progress on paper while coarsening our social existence. It is understandable why some would react to the logic of the commodification of desire with the logic of brute legislative and bureaucratic force. While tempting, this would not solve the underlying crisis. What we need is a return to equilibrium. Mary Wollstonecraft, like many eighteenth-century thinkers, recognized we needed a balance between logic and sentiment. "The impulse of the senses, passions, if you will," she wrote, "and the conclusions of reason, draw men together." She felt the injustice wrought in her own time by "the fragility, the instability, of reason, and the wild luxuriancy of noxious passions" while also recognizing that permitting an infantilizing sentimental culture to attempt a bureaucratic takeover of our desires would be a disaster, too. We would do well to remember her dictum that "freedom, *even* uncertain freedom — is dear." Likewise, those who would tame the chaos of human desire with bureaucratic logic would do well to remember the words of that other great Georgian, Alexander Pope, in his *Essay On Man*:

> *Alas what wonder! Man's superior part*
> *Uncheck'd may rise, and climb from art to art;*
> *But when his own great work is but begun,*
> *What Reason weaves, by Passion is undone.*

ACKNOWLEDGMENTS

This book was many years in the making, and many people directly and indirectly supported it and contributed toward its completion. Dom Pakenham has been there since the beginning and read some of the earliest and least promising versions of this book. Alex Hunting gave valuable advice on the introduction. Chris Clube provided pointers on Greek vocabulary as well as insights from the classical context. Carlotta Bonafini was the first to read the entire manuscript through and was the source of immeasurable encouragement and solace besides. Josh White was tolerant of the moody writer under his roof these past years. I am grateful to all those at Waterstones, especially Richard Humphreys, who put up with me whilst I ground away at this project. I owe a great debt to the staff of the London Library, where much of that grinding took place. At William Collins, Arabella Pike, my wonderful and indulgent editor, made all of this possible, and Paul Erdpresser was the indispensable man. In America I am grateful for Alison Lewis's hard work on my behalf as well as her close reading of all that I have written. Katie McGuire and Claiborne Hancock at Pegasus have been fantastic to work with. This book would not exist without the mercurial brilliance of my agent Sophie Scard, hers is the kingdom, the power, and the glory.

ENDNOTES

INTRODUCTION

1 Donald G. Nieman, ed., *Black Southerners and the Law, 1865-1900* (Clemson, SC: Clemson University, 1994), 29.

2 Ovid, *Metamorphoses*, trans. David Raeburn (London: Penguin, 2004), 35–37, 67, 89–90, 389.

3 Stephen Greenblatt, *The Rise and Fall of Adam and Eve* (London: Bodley Head, 2017), 90, 106–110, 122–123; and St. Jerome, "On Marriage and Virginity," from "Letter XXII to Eustochium" and the treatise "Against Jovinian."

4 Bernard O'Donoghue, trans, *Sir Gawain and the Green Knight* (London: Penguin, 2013), 75.

5 Lawrence Stone, *The Family, Sex and Marriage in England 1500–1800* (London: Weidenfeld and Nicolson, 1977), 502.

6 Jonathan Rée, *Witcraft: The Invention of Philosophy in English* (London: Allen Lane, 2019), 185. This conflict also has a geographic dimension. It has become something of a trope to contrast the eighteenth-century tradition of skepticism in British philosophy with the cult of reason that reigned in France. George Orwell was nodding at this national stereotype when he remarked (in "The Lion and the Unicorn") that "the English will never develop into a nation of philosophers. They will always prefer instinct to logic and character to intelligence."
For a contemporary iteration of the reason vs. passion debate, see the opposition in Daniel Kahneman's book *Thinking, Fast and Slow* between System 1 thinking and System 2 thinking.

7 Pamela Haag, *Consent: Sexual Rights and the Transformation of American Liberalism* (Ithaca, NY: Cornell University Press, 1999), 33.

8 *The White Slave Traffic* (London: Published at the Offices of "M.A.P.", 17 and 18, Henrietta Street, 1910), 11.

9 Germaine Greer, *The Female Eunuch* (London: MacGibbon & Kee, 1970), 45.

CHAPTER ONE

1 *Some Authentick Memoirs of the Life of Colonel Ch— s, Rape-Master-General of Great Britain. By an Impartial Hand* (London: 1730). See also pp1–2 for the account of the public reaction to Charteris's conviction: "When the News was first spread about the Town, Mankind was amaz'd; People stood aghast, looking at one another like Statues . . . The Demolition of *Ch——s*, and the *Opening* of his Maid's *Port* and *Harbour*, and in what Manner he had raz'd the fortifications of her Vertue, was the Subject on which all Conversation turn'd."

2 Charteris allegedly claimed her escape as one of the greatest losses of his career, lamenting that, "*A Woman that had such a large Share of Courage when on her Heels, must have had a vast deal more when between a Pair of Sheets.*" Ibid, 25.

3 Philogamus [pseud.], *The Present State of Matrimony or the Real Cause of Conjugal Infidelity,* (London: 1739), 25.

4 Some cosmic justice was, on occasion, forthcoming. It is recorded that Charteris's henchman Gourley once identified a particularly attractive and very devout milliner in Westminster. Charteris went to visit her store where he engaged her in a religious discourse and then "inveighed bitterly against the Wickedness of the Age, the licentious Manner in which all Ranks and Conditions of Christians lived; and that the unguarded Actions of the Clergy had been a great Inlet to that Sea of Atheism and Immorality that had poured in upon the Nation." "After this religious Courtship had been carried on some time," we are told, he lured her to an apartment in Golden Square where "the Colonel made a Declaration of his real Principles, professing himself a staunch Whoremaster, and that she must even, *sans Ceremony,* tumble a pillow with him that night." After some fainting fits and other theatrics the

women agreed to do so for money. In the morning she vanished leaving him with a vicious case of the pox and the dawning realization that she had been a prostitute all along. Charteris was obliged to retreat from London for a period to take the painful treatment for such diseases—a hot mercury solution injected into the urethra.

5 Through extensive bribery he had secured a royal pardon for his Scottish rape charge on New Year's Day, 1722.

6 Georgian slang for £100,000.

7 His testament also provided for his pistols to go to the Duke of Argyll and his stable of horses to go the Prime Minister, Sir Robert Walpole.

8 Cesar de Saussure, *A foreign view of England in the reigns of George I and George II: The letters of Monsieur Cesar de Saussure to his family*; trans. and ed. by Madame Van Muyden (London: John Murray, 1902). The original letters were composed 1725–30. De Saussure also provides a more wholesome account of young Londoner's celebrating St. Valentine's Day in the 1720s:
"The 14th of February, or St. Valentine's Day, is a festival day for young people. A young man chooses a maiden to be his valentine; she cannot refuse him unless she is already provided with one. Sometimes young men will draw lots for a favourite valentine. What I think most amusing is that a young man may on that day meet a maiden, and though he has never seen her before, he may if he wills it ask her to be his valentine, and she cannot refuse him unless she already has one. This custom is the cause of many marriages."

9 There were also other benefits to lingering in these quarters: by ancient privileges those residents in houses adjacent to the canal could not be arrested for debt—the nearby Fleet Prison awaited if they strayed—and allowed for marriages to take place "without any licence or publication of banns. Sailors and people of the common sort make great use of this latter privilege, their marriage being blessed in some tavern or pot-house, the priest being paid with half a crown and a bottle of wine." De Saussure, *A Foreign View of England*.

10 Five printers registered as operating in the area in 1750, growing to thirty-two by 1790. One of them belonged to John and Paul Knapton, sons of James Knapton, also a printer, and brother of George Knapton, who painted the members of the Medmenham Abbey "Order" of St. Francis — the rakes Wilkes, Dashwood, et. al. James Knapton moved his business to Samuel Richardson's neighborhood in the mid–1730s so the two men may have been familiar with each other.

11 *The English Malady* (1732), *An Essay on Regimen* (1740), and *The Natural Method of Cureing* (1742) — all published by Richardson.

12 Tells Lady Bradshaigh in 1748 "by first wife I had 5 sons and one daughter; some of them living to be delightful prattlers, with all the appearances of sound health, lovely in their features and promising as to their minds, and the death of one of them, I doubt accelerating from grief, that of the otherwise laudable afflicted mother." "I cherish the memory of my lost wife to this hour." (Letter to Lady Bradshaigh, Dec. 15, 1748.)

13 Critics have noted the similarity between Mr. B— and Colonel Charteris. See Alan Dugald McKillop, *Samuel Richardson: Printer and Novelist* (Chapel Hill, NC: University of North Carolina Press, 1936), 32: "The worst parts of Richardson's plot, Mr. B—'s clumsy and brutal attacks on the heroine, can be paralleled in the exploits of the infamous Colonel Charteris, who lures his victims to his house in town or country, come upon them through trap-doors or disguised in women's clothes, and is aided in his schemes by one Moll Clapham, a Mrs. Jewkes in real life." Much the same point is made in Ian Watt, *The Rise of the Novel* (Berkeley: University of California Press, 1957).

14 Such sham marriages existed. Until the 1753 Marriage Act a variety of loopholes and folk traditions made it possible to mislead someone into believing they had been legitimately married. An example survives in the prison memoir of career criminal James Dalton, hung at Tyburn in May, 1730, in which he recounts his use of this method to attain sex from women other than prostitutes: "With this Money I purchased me a Suit of Clothes, and got acquainted with a Person that procured Husbands for unfortunate young Women. He told me that he had one at that Time, that was a Gentleman's Daughter who lived in very good Repute, and that being big with Child her Friends would not admit her into their Presence without the Sight of a Certificate; and that if I would only take the Trouble to go to Church and marry her, he would give me two Guineas for my Trouble and upon my agreeing with his Desire, he sent for the Gentlewoman, and we went to St. Clement's Church in the Strand and

were there married, my Acquaintance the Procuror performing the Part of the Father : After this we
adjourned to the Tavern, where I was very handsomely entertained; and the Wine getting Influence
over my Brains, I insisted on lying all Night with my Wife : A great many Arguments were made use
of to persuade me to the contrary, but to no purpose upon which a Quarrel ensued, and the Landlord
coming to know the Reason of the Disturbance, I related the whole Affair to him he immediately
quitted the Room, and sent to the Church to know the Truth, which he was soon inform'd of;
wherefore he took my part; and one of his Servants called a Coach, and my Wife and I went to the
Bell-Inn in *West-Smithfield* where we lay together all Night. One Thing made me somewhat uneasy
when I awoke the next Morning sober, and that was, I had the Foul Disease, which I knew must in
all Likelihood be communicated to her, therefore I arose and left her to pay for our Night's Lodging."
Quoted in: Philip Rawlings, *Drunks, Whores and Idle Apprentices: Criminal Biographies of the
Eighteenth Century* (New York: Routledge, 1992), 88–89.

15 Erasmus Jones, *The Man of Manners: Or, Plebeian Polish'd* (1735).

16 *An essay on modern gallantry : address'd to men of honour, men of pleasure, and men of sense: with a
seasonable admonition to the young ladies of Great Britain* (London: Printed for M. Cooper, 1750).

17 Quoted in Faramerz Dabhoiwala, *The Origins of Sex* (Oxford University Press, 2012), 176–177. This
sentiment was echoed in Kitty's verdict on her sister Lydia in Jane Austen's *Pride and Prejudice* (1813):
"Unhappy as the event must be for Lydia, we may draw from it this useful lesson; that loss of virtue in
a female is irretrievable—that one false step involves her in endless ruin—that her reputation is no less
brittle than it is beautiful,—and that she cannot be too much guarded in her behaviour towards the
undeserving of the other sex."

18 See his letter to George Cheyne written August 31, 1741: "In my scheme, I have generally taken
Human Nature as it is; for it is no purpose to suppose it angelic, or to endeavour to make it so. There
is a time of life in which the passions will predominate; and ladies, any more than men, will not be
kept in ignorance; and if we properly mingle instruction with entertainment, so as to make the latter
seemingly the view, while the former is really the end, I imagine it will be doing a good deal."
And also his letter to Aaron Hill on February 1, 1741: "I thought the story, if written in an easy and
natural manner, suitably to the simplicity of it, might possibly introduce a new species of writing,
that might possibly turn young people into a course of reading different from the pomp and parade
of romance-writing, and dismissing the improbable and marvellous, cause of religion and virtue. I
therefore gave way to enlargement: and so Pamela became as you see her."

19 By 1742 a pamphlet entitled "Lettre Sur *Pamela*" was circulating in London. A French response to
the book, it attacked its style and noted derisively of its content that if this was a fair representation
of English morals then that nation was more debauched than had originally been suspected. It is
improbable that Richardson read it as he did not know French; he may well have not known it
existed. He was, however, caught up in a minor contretemps over the translation of *Pamela* into
French after allegations were traded over the conversion of his demotic English into highly mannered
literary French. This episode gave rise to an unabashedly Little Englander tirade in a letter from Aaron
Hill to Richardson in November 1741:
"Manly Decency, and modest Reserves, are the Dress, and Decorums, of Life.—But they who substitute
brisk Insignificance, in the Place of a solid Vivacity, let *Them* still be called French-men—And let *us* be
content to be English *John Bulls:* the only Pity is, that our Horns are no *sharper*."

20 *Pamela* was published in America in 1755 where Richardson found his work in the hands of a
Philadelphia printer by the name of Benjamin Franklin.

21 These were begun but, tragically, never finished and the drafts for them were later lost. In the early
1740s the painter Joseph Highmore did, however, produce a major series of twelve paintings inspired
by episodes from the novel. These survive and are split between the Tate Britain, the Fitzwilliam
Museum, and the National Gallery of Victoria.

22 Samuel Richardson, *Correspondence with Aaron Hill and the Hill family*, ed. Christine Gerrard
(Cambridge University Press, 2013), 105; Hill to Richardson in a letter on July 29, 1741.

23 Anonymous, *Pamela Censur'd* (London: 1741).The author also agreed with Fielding, Haywood, et
al. that Pamela seemed far too worldly for an alleged innocent: "Pamela instead of being artless and
innocent sets out at first with as much Knowledge of the Arts of the Town, as if she had been born and
bred in Covent Garden."

24 Though not enough for Victorian publishers, who heavily redacted *Pamela*.

25 While Matthew succeeded in placing Swift's work in various publications his attempts to ingratiate himself among the literary tastemakers of the capital were less fruitful. Swift engineered a meeting for him with Alexander Pope in his Twickenham retreat. Pope was extremely unimpressed with Matthew, writing to Swift in Ireland that the man he had talked up to him to secure the audience was "a most forward, shallow, conceited fellow" who had bored and disgusted him for three whole days. This damning verdict on his protégé sent Swift into a rage.

26 Romantic marriages were increasingly the norm in England by the second quarter of the eighteenth century. Clarissa's insistence on this practice was linked to her knowledge of the various rights and freedoms she would lose upon wedlock. "Surely, Sir," she writes to her uncle, "a young creature ought not to be obliged to make all these sacrifices but for such a man as she can love."
For more on romantic marriage see: Ian Watt, *Rise of the Novel* (Berkeley: University of California Press, 1957); and Lawrence Stone, *The Family, Sex and Marriage in England, 1500–1800*.

27 Lovelace is well aware that he owes his early success with Clarissa to her family's pig-headedness. "I knew that the whole stupid family were in a combination to do my business for me." He crows to Belford, "I told thee that they were all working for me, like so many ground moles; and still more blind than the moles are said to be, unknowing that they did so. I myself, the director of their principal motions; which falling in with the malice of their little hearts, they took to be all their own." Samuel Richardson, *Clarissa* (London: Penguin Classics, 1985), 387.

28 This "commonly received notion," as Richardson had it, was not without its critics in its own day. No less an authority than Lady Mary Wortley Montagu mocked the prevailing expectations of the time as "barbarous manners . . . well calculated for the establishment of vice and wretchedness." *The Letters of the Right Honourable Lady Mary Wortley Montagu* London: Printed for M. Cooper, (1763).

29 R.F. Brissenden, *Virtue in Distress: Studies in the Novel of Sentiment from Richardson to Sade* (New York: Macmillan, 1974), 22.

30 James Forrester, *The Polite Philosopher: Or, an Essay on that Art which Makes a Man Happy in Himself, and Agreeable to Others* (Edinburgh: Robert Freebairn, 1734). "Books may furnish us with the right ideas, experience may improve our judgement, but it is the acquaintance of the ladies only, which can bestow that easiness of address, whereby the fine gentleman is distinguished from the scholar and the man of business." Quoted in Dabhoiwala, *The Origins of Sex*.

31 See, inter alia, Hume on urbanization as the essential element in civilization advancing and the refinement of social discourse:
"Clubs and societies are everywhere formed. Both sexes meet in and easy and social manner; and the tempers of men, as well as in their behaviour, refine apace. So that beside the improvement which they receive from knowledge and the liberal arts, it is impossible but they must feel an increase of humanity from the very habit of conversing together." David Hume, "Of Refinement in the Arts," quoted in Keith Thomas, *In Pursuit of Civility*, (New Haven: Yale University Press, 2018), 176; See also Samuel Johnson: "man's chief merit consisted in resisting the impulses of nature," quoted in Watt, *The Rise of the Novel*, 157; and Dabhoiwala, *The Origins of Sex*, 180–83.

32 Locke continued with a metaphor that captured the emergent cliché of the women as the "fairer sex" while slyly recognizing the attractions of seduction:
"Eloquence, like the fair sex, has too prevailing beauties in it to suffer itself ever to be spoken against. And it is in vain to find fault with those arts of deceiving, wherein men find pleasure to be deceived."

33 We know Richardson was familiar with Locke's writings as he includes an extensive reflection on Lockean pedagogy in the latter portion of *Pamela*. Locke was, in any case, one of the most widely read philosophers of the period, running through nine editions between publication and 1760. See Roy Porter, *The Enlightenment* (New York: Palgrave, 2001), 67, 70. Whether Richardson had read or knew of Hume's writing is unknown but unlikely.

34 Richardson, *Clarissa*, 262–263

35 Lady Mary Wortley Montagu in 1750: "This Richardson is a strange fellow. I heartily despise him, and eagerly read him, nay, sob over his works in a most scandalous manner. The first two tomes of *Clarissa* touched me, as being very resembling to my maiden days; and I find in pictures of Sir Thomas Grandison and his lady, what I have heard of my mother, and seen in my father." In McKillop, *Samuel Richardson*, McKillop, 134.

36 Sarah Fielding also recorded her impressions in a letter to Richardson of January 8, 1749: "When I read of her, I am all sensation; my heart glows; I am overwhelmed; my only vent is tears; and unless tears could mark my thoughts as legibly as ink I cannot speak half I feel. . . .
In short, Sir, no pen but your's can do justice to Clarissa. Often have I reflected on my own vanity in daring but to touch the hem of her garment." *The Correspondence of Henry and Sarah Fielding*, eds. Martin C. Battestin and Clive T. Probyn (Oxford, Clarendon Press, 1993).

37 Henry Fielding to Richardson October 15, 1748. Fielding reporting his thoughts on reading *Clarissa*, apart from last two volumes, so presumably he had read five of seven volumes at the time of writing. He specifically praised the character of Lovelace: "the Character of Lovelass [sic] is heightened with great Judgement. His former Admirers must lose all Regard for him on his Perseverance, and as this Regard ceases, Compassion for Clarissa rises in the same Proportion. Hence we are admirably prepared for what is to follow—." He describes in detail his reaction to the climactic rape and praises Richardson's artistry and power of sentiment. "Let the Overflowings of a Heart which you have filled brimfull speak for me.' He also joked that the world believes that "We are Rivals for that coy Mrs. Fame" before declaring goes on "I heartily wish you Success. That I sincerely think you in the highest manner deserve it." *The Correspondence of Henry and Sarah Fielding*, eds. Battestin and Probyn), 70–74.

38 T.C. Duncan Eaves and Ben D. Kimpel, *Samuel Richardson: Biography* (Oxford: Clarendon Press, 1971), 183.

39 The Correspondence of Henry and Sarah Fielding, eds. Martin C. Battestin and Clive T. Probyn (Oxford, Clarendon Press, 1993). She continues with a hilarious description of Cibber's hyperbole: "I am not quite sure, whether Mr. Cibber is not so strongly enamoured with her perfections, and touched with her distresses, that, were they exhibited on the stage, he would not, like Don Quixote, rise up in wrath and rescue the lady from the hands of her violater [sic]." Before concluding with an imprecation of her own: "Spare her virgin purity, dear Sir, spare it!"

40 In *The Cambridge Edition of the Correspondence of Samuel Richardson* Volumes 5—7, xv and in a letter from Richardson to Bradshaigh of February 1751.

41 He further alleged that having conferred with "two very delicate Minds of the Sex" he was certain that Clarissa's actions were true to life. Richardson to Hill, October 29, 1746 and Hill to Richardson January 23, 1747; in *Correspondence*, Volume 1.

42 She finished with a threat: "If you disappoint me, attend to my curse:—May the hatred of all the young, beautiful, and virtuous, for ever be your portion! and may your eyes never behold any thing but age and deformity! may you meet with applause only from envious old maids, surly bachelors, and tyrannical parents! may you be doomed to the company of such! and, after death, may their ugly souls haunt you! Now make Lovelace and Clarissa unhappy if you dare." Bradshaigh to Richardson, October 10, 1748, *Correspondence*, Volume 5, 3–5.

43 *Correspondence*, Volume 5, xxxvii. Barbauld on the first meeting of Bradshaigh and Richardson at Birdcage Walk: "No lover ever expected his mistress with greater ardour than the grave Richardson seems to have felt for his *incognita*, when he paced so fruitlessly up and down the Mall, gazing with expectation at every lady he met."

44 Richardson to Bradshaigh, October 26, 1748, *Correspondence*, Volume 5, 7–11.

45 Bradshaigh to Richardson, 1748, *Correspondence*, Volume 5, 20–21.

46 Bradshaigh to Richardson, November 1749, and his response shortly afterward; *Correspondence*, Volume 5, 73–77. Bradshaigh's letter contained a catty remark about Richardson's propensity for pious old women. "You know so many good old maids, Sir," she wrote, "that, perhaps, you may accidentally hear of some one, who would not be having the *dirty impudent baggage sent to Bridewell*." Her allusion to Bridewell seems intended to echo some of the more callous language of Richardson's great villains, Mr. B—, Sir Hargrave Pollexfen, and Lovelace, though such sentiments were widespread. Lady Mary Wortley Montagu stated flatly that any girl "that runs away with a young fellow without intending to marry him should be carry'd to Bridewell or Bedlam the next day." Quoted in Carol Houlihan Flynn, *Samuel Richardson: A Man of Letters* (Princeton University Press, 1982), 108.

47 Richardson affirmed this connection in another letter to Bradshaigh in which, apropos of *Clarissa*, he described his heroine as "a *second Magdalen* in her penitence, and yet not so bad as a *Magdalen* in her faults."

48 See *Correspondence*, Volume 5: Bradshaigh to Richardson, October 29, 1749; Richardson to Bradshaigh, late November 1749; and Bradshaigh to Richardson December 1749.

49 Catherine Talbot to Richardson, March 1750: "They much wish also, that he may have Leisure, Spirits and Inclination to comply with the repeated Requests of his Agreeable Incognita, and shew the World such a Man as would neither have been unworthy of a Clarissa, nor unagreeable to a Miss Howe." *Correspondence*, Volume 10, 7; See also Christian Bernhard Kaiser [translator in Hannover] to Richardson July 10, 1753: "When is Your Sir Charles Grandison to appear? Every body here wishes, soon to see him." *Correspondence*, Volume 10, 97. And Richardson's letters on the new work to Jean Baptiste de Freval in January 1750, and to Alexis Claude Clairaut in July 1753.

50 Eaves and Kimpel, *Samuel Richardson*, 302.

51 Allen Michie, *Richardson and Fielding: The Dynamics of a Critical Rivalry* (Lewisburg, PA: Bucknell University Press, 1999), 39–41.

52 Donald Thomas, *Henry Fielding* (London: Weidenfeld & Nicolson, 1990), 393.

53 Richardson adhered rigorously to his own moral-literary precepts. Hence the critical argument, advanced by Roger Moore, that Richardson was the exemplary female writer of his time, and possibly of all English literature until Austen, who was explicit in her debt to him. "Richardson may be called, in all seriousness, one of our great women." Robert Etheridge Moore, "Dr. Johnson on Fielding and Richardson," *PMLA* 66, No. 2 (March, 1951).

54 Richardson to Sarah Chapone, December 6, 1750; Richardson to Sarah Chapone, January 11, 1751; *Selected Letters of Samuel Richardson*, ed. John Carroll (Oxford: Clarendon Press, 1964), 172–173.

55 Richardson's pusillanimity need hardly be commented on; what is too easily forgotten is how his attitude toward women and literature was to predominate for the next century and a half. English society produced (against its own wishes, in many cases) many great female writers but they were for the most part writers of the private world. There were very few Laetitia Pilkington's in the Victorian era. As Virginia Woolf noted in the late 1920s, the belief that women ought "to confine themselves to making puddings and knitting stockings, to playing on the piano and embroidering bags" meant they suffered "from too rigid a restraint, too absolute a stagnation, precisely as men would suffer" in the same conditions. The miracle of women's writing was that it had achieved so much while constrained to tightly: She knew, no one better, how enormously her genius would have profited if it had not spent itself in solitary visions over distant fields; if experience and intercourse and travel had been granted her. But they were not granted; they were withheld; and we must accept the fact that all those good novels, *Villette*, *Emma*, *Wuthering Heights*, *Middlemarch*, were written by women without more experience of life than could enter the house of a respectable clergyman; written too in the common sitting-room of that respectable house and by women so poor that they could not afford to, buy more than a few quires of paper at a time upon which to write *Wuthering Heights* or *Jane Eyre*. Virginia Woolf, "A Room Of One's Own," (Richmond, UK: Hogarth Press, 1929).

56 And also: "Love, eternal Love, is the subject, the burthen of all your writings; it is the poignant sauce, which so richly seasons Pamela, Clarissa and Grandison, and makes their flimsy nonsense pass so glibly down." Anonymous, *Critical Remarks on Sir Charles Grandison, Clarissa, and Pamela* (1754), with an introduction by Alan Dugald McKillop (Los Angeles: William Andrews Clark Memorial Library, University of California, 1950.

57 This was not a new complaint nor one limited to men. See Lady Mary Wortley Montagu "I am very sorry for the forlorn state of Matrimony, which is as much ridicul'd by our Young Ladys as it us'd to be by young fellows; in short, both Sexes have found the Inconveniencys of it, and the Apellation of Rake is as genteel in a Woman as a Man of Quality." Letter of October 1723, quoted in Flynn, *Samuel Richardson*, 56–57.

58 Anon., *Critical Remarks on Sir Charles Grandison, Clarissa, and Pamela*.

59 Mark Hildesley to Richardson, December 20, 1753, *Correspondence*, Volume 10, 168.

60 Flynn, *Samuel Richardson*, 3.

61 One such cynic was Richardson's client Daniel Defoe who opposed an early campaign to establish the Foundling Hospital for exactly this reason. Such an institution, he believed, would "set up a nursery for lewdness, and encourage fornication . . . Who would be afraid of sinning, if they can so easily get rid of their bastards? We shall soon be over-run with foundlings when there is such an encouragement given to whoredom." Quoted in Dabhoiwala, *The Origins of Sex*, 243.

62 Samuel Johnson, "Properantia's hopes of a year of confusion. The misery of prostitutes." *The Rambler*, No. 107. March 26, 1751. The piece offers a fascinating insight into the world of the gadding literary men about town and their conflicted consciences:

"How frequently have the gay and thoughtless, in their evening frolicks, seen a band of those miserable females, covered with rags, shivering with cold, and pining with hunger; and, without either pitying their calamities, or reflecting upon the cruelty of those who, perhaps, first seduced them by caresses of fondness, or magnificence of promises, go on to reduce others to the same wretchedness by the same means!"

63 *The Gentleman's Magazine*, March, 1751. This belief that seduced women and prostitutes were equivalent would linger in discussion of the Magdalen for some time. An 1810 account of the institution discuss the important function it served for *"young women who have been seduced from their friends under promise of marriage and have been deserted by their seducers.* They have never been in public prostitution, but fly to the Magdalen to avoid it." John Feltham, *The Picture of London for 1810*, 225–228.

See also Reverend William Dodd, *An Account of the Rise, Progress, and Present State of the Magdalen Charity*, (1761), 3–4:

"Poor, young, thoughtless Females, plunged into ruin by those temptations, to which their very youth and personal advantages expose them, no less than those passions implanted in our nature for wise and good ends . . . Surrounded by snares, the most artfully and industriously laid; snares, laid by those endowed with superior faculties, and all the advantages of education and fortune; what virtue can be proof against such formidable seducers? . . . And when once seduced, how soon their golden dreams vanish! Abandoned by the seducer, deserted by their friends, contemned by the world, they are left to struggle with want, despair, and scorn. . . . It is well known, that this is the case with most of the Prostitutes in their several degrees."

64 For example, Astrea and Minerva Hill to Richardson, December 13, 1748: "How fast, if England has such Sanctuary Retreats as Protestant Nunneries, wou'd a Clarissa's Fate contribute to the filling of 'em!" Richardson to Bradshaigh, June 5, 1759: "Your Ladyship makes me a great Compliment, in supposing the Institution owes its beginnings to Hints in Sir Charles Grandison."

65 His reasoning was predicated on the assumptions of the cults of sentiment and sensibility: I have another scheme, my lord, proceeded Sir Charles—An hospital for female penitents; for such unhappy women, as having been once drawn in, and betrayed by the perfidy of men, find themselves, by the cruelty of the world, and principally by that of their own sex, unable to recover the path of virtue, when perhaps (convinced of the wickedness of the men in whose honour they confided) they would willingly make their first departure from it the last.

These, continued he, are the poor creatures who are eminently intitled to our pity, though they seldom meet with it. Good-nature, and credulity the child of good-nature, are generally, as I have the charity to believe, rather than viciousness, the foundation of their crime. Those men who pretend they would not be the first destroyers of a woman's innocence, look upon these as fair prize. (Samuel Richardson, *The History of Sir Charles Grandison* , Vol 4 (1753), 126.) Elsewhere he makes the connection to the models of Catholic convents: "We want to see established in every county, protestant nunneries" and "though a Protestant, I am not an enemy to such foundations in general. I could wish, under proper regulations, that we had nunneries among us I would not, indeed, have the obligation upon nuns be perpetual: let them have liberty, at the end of every two or three years, to renew their vows, or otherwise, by the consent of friends." This is close to what happened in the Magdalen House once it was established.

66 Dubbed "the Macaroni Parson," Dodd's was one of the great Georgian lives. A socially ambitious and sensually profligate young clergyman who had married a domestic servant, he served as the Evening Preacher at the Magdalen chapel from 1759 to 1777 and became an integral part of the services' appeal. He wrote an early history of the Magdalen and a novel, *The Sisters*, on prostitution. (Ostensibly a sentimental narrative, *The Sisters* descended at times into proto-Sadean pornography: "At their commands she was obliged to strip naked as she was born, and thus submit to the hellish purposes of either; and after having been thus abused, each presented a red hot poker, near to every part as possible, made her dance, as they called it, for all their amusements.") Generously

compensated by the charity, he developed ruinously expensive tastes including a town house, a country house in Ealing, a carriage, and spendthrift jaunts to the West End that he could ill afford. He teetered on the edge of disgrace until 1777 when, in financial crisis, he tried to cash a fraudulent check under the name of his sometime tutee, the Earl of Chesterfield. Caught in the act, he was hauled before the Old Bailey, found guilty, and sentenced to hang. His case attracted the intense interest of Samuel Johnson who is said to have written Dodd's final appeal to the Recorder at the Old Bailey and maintained a close correspondence with him as he approached the day of his hanging. Johnson also wrote on his behalf to the King, the Queen, Lord Mansfield, and Lord Chancellor Bathurst. He is even alleged to have written Dodd's sermon delivered to his fellow convicts at Newgate Prison. (Johnson would later deny to Boswell that he wrote Dodd's sermon, memorably quipping "Depend upon it, Sir, when a man knows he is to be hanged in a fortnight, it concentrates his mind wonderfully.") The day before his execution he wrote a consoling letter to Dodd, telling him "Be comforted: your crime, morally or religiously considered, has no very deep dye of turpitude. It corrupted no man's principles; it attacked no man's life. It involves only a temporary and reparable injury." Despite the best efforts of his friends to try and bribe the judge, the jailers, and the hangman, Dodd was hanged the next day on June 27, 1777. Their strenuous efforts led to persistent rumors that Dodd had escaped his fate at Tyburn and was living pleasantly in Provence. His wife died in seclusion in England in 1784.

S.B.P. Pearce, *An Ideal in the Working: The Magdalen Hospital 1758–1958* (London: privately printed, 1958); Gerald Howson, *The Macaroni Parson: The Life of the Unfortunate Doctor Dodd* (London: Hutchinson, 1973); and James Boswell, *The Life of Samuel Johnson* (1791).

67 Bradshaigh to Richardson May 22, 1759, *Correspondence*, Volume 5, 752–56; see also Richardson to Bradshaigh, June 5, 1759: he praises her going and agrees that "I could not have stood it."

68 Furthermore, one of the roles of the Magdalen House was to re-induct women into the cult of sensibility. So much of the Magdalen's work, in the minds of its managers, was to make the women ready for a life of domesticity after a period of perilous misadventure in the streets. The ultimate aim was that the penitents find a new husband, or, at least, a new and Christian home where they could devote themselves to suitably feminine work. Prayer, simple living, and honest work would repair their damaged delicacy and pave the way for marriage. Marriage was considered a self-fulfilling prophecy as childrearing and home keeping would ensure a woman's loyalty to the code of domesticity. As Richardson put it in the *Familiar Letters*, "Childbed *matronizes* the giddiest Spirits." The governors of the Magdalen claimed a ten to fifteen percent success rate in finding penitents husbands, and that two thirds of all women who passed through their doors left satisfactorily reformed. Dabhoiwala, *The Origins of Sex*, 249–250; and Feltham, *The Picture of London for 1810*, 225–228.

69 Horace Walpole, *Letters*, Volume III, Letter 11 to George Montagu, Esq., January 28, 1760.

70 Early in his courtship Lovelace scandalizes the Harlowes by turning up in their church in order to catch a glimpse of Clarissa. She has been safely stowed at home but she guesses why he came: "Did he come for my sake; and, by behaving in such a manner to those present of my family, imagine he was doing me either service or pleasure?" Richardson, *Clarissa*, Letter XXX.

71 Dodd was known for his suggestive preaching style. For example, an extract from a sermon he included in his *An Account of the Rise*, 92: "You, who have known the fatal pleasings of passion, can more easily pity them, whom those pleadings have seduced and destroyed. And you, who are possessed of all the sweetness and delicacies of the tender mind, and happier state, can more easily guess the extreme misery which must arise to a female heart, from the foulness and horror of promiscuous prostitution."

72 Dabhoiwala, *The Origins of Sex*, 261–264.

73 *Gentleman's Magazine*, LXXVI, 1816 Vol 1, 577–578.

CHAPTER TWO

1 James Boswell, *Boswell on the grand tour: Italy, Corsica, and France, 1765–1766*, eds. Frank Brady and Frederick A. Pottle (London: Heinemann, 1955); The notion that climate informed behavior was widespread. Montesquieu's *The Spirit of Laws* (1748) was the foundational text for the claim that climate and geography shaped morals but the idea was commonly held in the decades before its publication. See, for example, Daniel Defoe's "True-Born Englishman" (1701):

> *Lust chose the torrid zone of Italy*
> *Where blood ferments in rapes and sodomy.*
> *Where swelling veins o'erflow with livid streams,*
> *With heat impregnate from Vesuvian flames:*
> *Whose flowing sulphur forms infernal lakes,*
> *And human body of the soil partakes.*
> *There nature ever burns with hot desires.*

In, Maurice Andrieux, *Daily Life in Venice at the Time of Casanova* (London: Allen and Unwin, 1972), 126.

2 John Murray was no relation to the line of John Murrays of London that published Byron. However, through marriage, Casanova's Murray did have a connection to the Byron story: Murray's wife, Bridget Milbanke, whom he married in 1748, was the only daughter of Sir Ralph Milbanke, 4th Baronet of Halnaby Hall in North Yorkshire. Murray may have lived at Halnaby Hall for a time before going to Venice, in which case he inhabited the rooms that housed Byron during his disastrous "Treacle-Moon" with Anna Milbanke (1792–1860), who was the only daughter of Sir Ralph Milbanke, 6th Baronet, nephew of John Murray's wife Bridget. See Christine Laidlaw, *The British in the Levant* (London: I.B. Tauris, 2010), 53.

3 Laidlaw, *British in the Levant*, 58.

4 Andrieux, *Daily Life in Venice at the Time of Casanova*, 164.

5 Carlo Goldoni, *Memoirs of Carlo Goldoni*, (London: Alfred A. Knopf, 1926), 154.

6 Giacomo Casanova, *History of My Life*, Vol 1. 92.

7 Her father was Joseph Imer the impresario behind a touring acting troupe of which Zanetta Farussi was a member. Imer and Farussi had a longstanding and furious relationship that is said to have inspired some of Goldoni's plays.

8 There is a poignant passage in Volume 6 of Casanova's memoirs in which he alludes, meta-referentially, to the conditions of his memoir's composition: "I have been writing memoirs for the last seven years, and though I repent of having begun, I have sworn to go on to the end. However, I write in the hope that my Memoirs may never see the light of day; in the first place the censure would not allow them to be printed, and in the second I hope I shall be strong-minded enough, when my last illness comes, to have all my papers burnt before my eyes. If that be not the case I count on the indulgence of my readers, who should remember that I have only written my story to prevent my going mad in the midst of all the petty insults and disagreeables which I have to bear day by day from the envious rascals who live with me in this castle of Count Waldstein, or Wallenstein, at Dux. I write ten or twelve hours a day, and so keep black melancholy at bay. My readers shall hear more of my sufferings later on, if I do not die before I write them down."

9 Casanova, *History of My Life*, Vol 2, 106.

10 Casanova, *History of My Life*, Vol 2, 101.

11 Sharpe also provides an enchanting account of seeing the ladies of Venice rowed up and down beside the *giardini* of the Giudecca by their respective *cicisbei* at dusk "as in former days, our gentry in England frequented the Ring in Hyde-Park."

12 The count did at one point try to expel Byron and rein in his wayward wife but was met with a scorn that speaks volumes about the entrenched status of *cicisbeismo* in this period. "It is hard," Teresa informed her husband, "that I should be the only woman in Romagna who is not to have her *Amico*." Society censured jealous husbands more than it did wandering wives; Byron stayed in their lives. Iris Origo, *The Last Attachment* (London: Jonathan Cape and John Murray, 1949), 205.

13 Byron to Hobhouse, from Bologna, August 23, 1819.

14 Goldoni, *Memoirs*, 246.

15 See Origo, *The Last Attachment*, 82: "the essence of *Serventismo*, as he was to realize later, was that the lady should *stay* with her husband."

16 Origo, *The Last Attachment*, 151.

17 Casanova, *History of My Life*, Vol 2, 183.

18 See Jan Morris, *Venice* (London: Faber & Faber, 1960), 47. Rialto is home to the Venetian banks and the Casteletto, at one end, the most storied brothel in Europe, sanctioned and monitored by the state. Prostitutes operating there had to display red lights on the prow of their gondolas. At the end of the

16th century there were said to be 2889 patrician ladies, 2508 nuns, and 1936 middle class wives—but 11,654 prostitutes!!

19 Peter Ackroyd, *Venice: Pure City* (New York: Vintage, 2009), 96.

20 Andrieux, *Daily Life in Venice*, 136–37.

21 William Alexander, *The History of Women* (1796), 137.

22 Roberto Bizzocchi, *A Lady's Man: The Cicisbei, Private Morals and National Identity in Italy*, (London: Palgrave Macmillan, 2014), 14–21. Compare with David Hume in "The Rise of Arts and Sciences," 1742: "Gallantry is not less compatible with wisdom and prudence, than with nature and generosity; and when under proper regulations, contributes more than any other invention, to the entertainment and improvement of the youth of both sexes. Among every species of animals, nature has founded on the love between the sexes their sweetest and best enjoyment. But the satisfaction of the bodily appetite is not alone sufficient to gratify the mind; and even among brute-creatures, we find, that their play and dalliance, and other expressions of fondness, form the greatest part of the entertainment. In rational beings, we must certainly admit the mind for a considerable share. Were we to rob the feast of all its garniture of reason, discourse, sympathy, friendship, and gaiety, what remains would scarcely be worth acceptance, in the judgment of the truly elegant and luxurious."

23 See Bizzocchi, *A Lady's Man*, 191–92; Beccaria on adultery in *Dei delitti e delle pene*: "When the interest or pride of families, or paternal authority, not the inclination of the parties, unite the sexes, gallantry soon breaks the slender ties, in spite of common moralists, who exclaim against the effect, whilst they pardon the cause."

24 Charles Burney, *The present state of music in France and Italy* (1771), 150–52.

25 Casanova, *History of My Life*, Vol 2, VIII, 202.

26 This made a problem for Carlo Goldoni when he had to adapt Samuel Richardson's *Pamela* for the Italian stage: nobody would believe that an Italian nobleman would ever marry their maid, however virtuous. "For some time the novel of 'Pamela' had been the delight of the Italians, and my friends urged me strongly to turn it into a comedy. I was acquainted with the work, and felt no difficulty in seizing the spirit of it, and approximating the objects; but the moral aim of the English author was not reconcileable with the manners and laws of my country. A nobleman in London does not derogate from his nobility in marrying a peasant; but at Venice, a patrician who should marry a plebeian would deprive his children of the patrician nobility, and they would lose their right to the sovereignty. Comedy, which is, or ought to be, a school for propriety, should only expose human weaknesses for the sake of correcting them; and it would be unjustifiable to hazard the sacrifice of an unfortunate posterity under the pretext of recompensing virtue. . . . I did not, however, begin the work till I had invented a denouement which, instead of being dangerous, might serve as a model to virtuous lovers, and render the catastrophe both more agreeable and more interesting." Goldoni, *Memoirs*, 255–56.

27 He would boast in his memoirs that he returned to Venice having "become the superior of several of my equals in respect to experience and to knowledge of the laws of honour and good manners." Casanova, *History of My Life*, Vol III, Chapter XIII, 235.

28 "The infamous supper" described in Volume III, 260.

29 Ackroyd, *Venice*, 343–45

30 *Selections from the Letters of De Brosses*, trans. Lord Ronald Sutherland Gower, (London: Kegan Paul, Trench, Trubner, & Co., 1897), 30, 53.

31 Abraham Nicolas Amelot de la Houssaye, *The history of the government of Venice wherein the policies, councils, magistrates, and laws of that state are fully related, and the use of the balloting box exactly described: written in the year 1675* (London: Printed by H.C. for John Starkey, 1677).

32 "The nuns take nothing but ready money," Carlo Goldoni grumbled apropos of the costs entailed with properly educating his niece. Goldoni, *Memoirs*, 455.

33 Giuseppe Marco Antonio Baretti, *An account of the manners and customs of Italy*, Vol 2, (1768), 17.

34 Casanova, *History of My Life*, Vol III, 281.

35 Either the San Giacomo di Galizzia or the Santa Maria Degli Angeli.

36 Casanova, *History of My Life*, Vol IV, 9–10. She writes that he has become "the puzzle of the entire convent" after five or six such attendances. "The old nuns said that I must have some sorrow from which my only hope of being relieved was the protection of their Holy Virgin, in whom it was clear

that I must have perfect trust; and the young ones said that I must be suffering from melancholia, a misanthrope who shunned the great world."

37 Casanova, *History of My Life*, Vol IV, 17.

38 "They included all that the wisest philosophers have written against religion and all that the most voluptuous pens have written on the subject which is the sole aim of love. Seductive books, whose incendiary style drives the reader to seek the reality, which alone can quench the fire he feels running through his veins. Besides the books there were folios containing only lascivious engravings." Casanova, History of My Life, Vol IV, 34.

39 This resulted in the First Treaty of Versailles in 1756 and, indirectly, to the outbreak of the Seven Years War (1756–1763).

40 It was in early 1755 that Casanova began to spend time with John Murray, the English resident in Venice, so for much of 1754 and the first half of 1755 he was indeed consorting with high-ranking foreign diplomats. In the same period he also moved out of the Palazzo Bragadin into private apartments, possibly to protect his sponsors from lethal allegations of fraternizing with diplomats.

41 J. Rives Childs, *Casanova: A New Perspective*, (London: Constable, 1989), 71–72.

42 Rives Childs, *Casanova*, 71–72.

43 See Peter Ackroyd on the significance of his imprisonment in the Piombi: "It is perhaps no wonder that his story of the his imprisonment in the dungeons of the ducal palace, and of his subsequent escape, is a central text in Venetian social history; he was in the prison of his unreflecting self. It is in any case rare to find, in Venetian literature, any attempt at analysis or self-criticism. There is just no interest in the subject, the fruit of a culture in which individualism of any kind was discouraged." Ackroyd, *Venice*, 272.

44 Casanova's description of this book is excellent: "I read everything that the extravagance of the heated imagination of an extremely devout Spanish virgin, given to melancholy, shut up in a convent, and guided by ignorant and flattering confessors, could bring forth. All these chimerical and monstrous visions were adorned with the name of revelations."

45 The Lisbon earthquake of 1755 inspired Voltaire's famous attack on Catholic doctrine. How was it, Voltaire asked, that pious Lisbon was destroyed while more sinful cities were untouched?

> *Was then more vice in fallen Lisbon found,*
> *Than Paris, where voluptuous joys abound?*
> *Was less debauchery to London known,*
> *Where opulence luxurious holds her throne?*
> *Earth Lisbon swallows; the light sons of France*
> *Protract the feast, or lead the sprightly dance.*

Voltaire, "Poème sur le désastre de Lisbonne" (1756).

46 Casanova gives its length both as two feet and as twenty inches long. In any case, a sizeable device for digging through plaster and bashing through rotten wooden paneling.

47 "Nature commanded me to escape, and religion could not forbid me to do it." Casanova, *History of My Life*, Vol IV, 293.

48 "Seingalt" is a perfect anagram of "genitals," not likely a coincidence given Casanova cabala-inspired fascination with hidden meaning, word games, and substitution. The Chevalier's implicit libidinism was signaled by the richness of his dress. Here is Casanova in 1763: "I wore a suit of grey velvet, trimmed with gold and silver lace; my point lace shirt was worth at least fifty louis; and my diamonds, my watches, my chains, my sword of the finest English steel, my snuff-box set with brilliants, my cross set with diamonds, my buckles set with the same stones, were altogether worth more than fifty thousand crowns."

49 "But Rousseau, great man though he was, was totally deficient in humour." There is no mystery to the lack of connection between the two men—Rousseau's sexual politics were famously austere and his attitude toward female emancipation conservative in the extreme. See: Joel Schwartz, *The Sexual Politics of Jean Jacques Rousseau* (University of Chicago Press, 1984).

50 Casanova did not speak and did not seriously try to learn English. His movements around London were facilitated by a black manservant named Jarbe whom he hired upon arrival and "who spoke English, French, and Italian with equal facility." Despite this barrier, there were plenty of Italians in the Covent Garden area he could speak to and he also found that many well-born Englishmen and women spoke passable French. The relative ease with which he moved through London without

the native language is testament to the cosmopolitan nature of the city in this period but also to the insignificance of English as a transnational language: a veteran traveler like Casanova needed only French to make his way around the world.

51 John Hawkesworth, *An account of the voyages undertaken by the order of His present Majesty: for making discoveries in the Southern Hemisphere* (London, 1773), 480–482.

52 *The Pacific Journal of Louis-Antoine de Bougainville 1767–68*, ed. and trans. John Dunmore (London, The Hakluyt Society, 2002), 63.

53 Patricia Fara, *Sex, Botany, and Empire*, (London: Icon, 2003), 114.

54 Such associations would persist for some time. Fascinated by what he heard of Tahiti, James Boswell asked Captain Cook at dinner whether he might join the next expedition to the island. This did not happen but he later defended Tahitian mores to a skeptical Samuel Johnson. Erasmus Darwin, in his *The Loves of the Plants* (1789), describes Tahiti as the home of the Adonis plant, with a hundred male stamens and a hundred female pistils within a single flower—a botanical metaphor for Pacific polygamy and free love. Claire Clairmont, the unhappy sometime lover of Lord Byron, described the Shelley-Byron circle as "tribe of the Otaheite philosopher's [sic]," a joke that played on the widespread assumption that the group were practitioners of free love. Byron's grandfather, the sailor John Byron, had conducted expeditions in the South Pacific in the 1760s and had command of the *Dolphin* before it was handed over to his deputy, Samuel Wallis.

55 Denis Diderot, *Political Writings,* eds. John Hope Mason and Robert Wokler (Cambridge University Press, 1992), 68, 69, 73.

56 Casanova, *History of My Life*, Vol V, Chapter V, 101.

57 George Gordon Byron [Lord Byron] to Douglas Kinnaird Venice, October 26, 1819.

58 Compare Byron telling Teresa Guiccioli in a letter from 1819 "I am a citizen of the world—all countries are alike to me." (Origo, *Last Attachment*, 170) with Casanova's oft-proclaimed cosmopolitan status; for example, Albert Haller's account of him: "He tells me he is a free man, a citizen of the world." (Ian Kelly, *Casanova*, (London: Hodder & Stoughton, 2008) 237.

59 Ah! pieta Signori miei, 2:10b:

> Ah, be not so hard upon me,
> Give me leave, good friends, to speak!
> Wrongs like yours surely had undone me.
> But, believe me, I am not he you seek.
> I will tell you how my master, did from bad to worse descend.
> Donna Elvira, do you tell them,
> By what arts he gains his end;
> As for thee, I've not a notion what befell thee;
> As this lady here can tell thee,
> For I met her, with him philand'ring,
> Well I knew how all would end;
> And to your lordship, I will admit it,
> I've acted wrongly, not as befitted . . .
> I know I've trespas'd, I ask your pardon,
> Lost in the darkness, I entered the garden,
> Not thought t'offend. 'Twas a blunder;
> Greatly I wonder, how all was known!
> Masters, I would now with speed be gone.

accessed from http://www.opera-arias.com/mozart/don-giovanni/ah-pieta-signori-miei.

60 See Kelly, *Casanova*, 335; and "Don Giovanni," Dyneley Hussey, *Music & Letters* 8, No. 4 (Oct., 1927), 470–472; Thomas Forrest Kelly, *First Nights at the Opera* (New Haven: Yale University Press, 2004), 78–87; *Memoirs of Lorenzo Da Ponte*, trans. Elisabeth Abbott (Philadelphia: J.B. Lippincott Company, 1929), 237, 439; and Goldoni, *Memoirs of Carlo Goldoni*, who writes on page 173: "everybody knows the wretched Spanish play which the Italians call "Il Convitato di Pietre," the French "La Festin de Pierre," and the English "Don Juan." In Italy I always considered it with horror, and I could not conceive how such farce could for so long a time draw crowds together, and prove the delight of a polished people." Nonetheless, it was a great success for Goldoni in the 1730s.

CHAPTER THREE

1 Michel Foucault, *Discipline and Punish: The Birth of the Prison*, trans. Alan Sheridan (London: Penguin Books, 1991), 3–5.

2 Giacomo Casanova, *History of My Life*, Volume V, (1822) 56–58.

3 On her travels through Scandinavia she comments unfavorably on local drinking habits and *Maria, or The Wrongs of Women* contains this brilliant description of a hungover libertine: "The squeamishness of stomach alone, produced by the last night's intemperance, which he took no pains to conceal, destroyed my appetite. I think I now see him lolling in an arm-chair, in a dirty powdering gown, soiled linen, ungartered stockings, and tangled hair, yawning and stretching himself."

4 Mary Wollstonecraft, *The Collected Letters of Mary Wollstonecraft*, ed. Janet Todd (New York: Columbia University Press, 2003), 1–3.

5 See William Godwin, *Memoirs of the Author of a Vindication of the Rights of Woman*, (1798) Chapter 3, 214–15: "Mary was now arrived at the twenty-fourth year of her age. Her project, five years before, had been personal independence; it was now usefulness."

6 Shortly before she left for Ireland she had another formative pedagogical experience. That October she visited Eton College and recorded her appalled impressions in a letter to her sister. "I could not live the life they lead at Eton—nothing but dress and ridicule going forward—and I really believe their fondness for ridicule tends to make them affected . . . for witlings abound—and puns fly about like crackers . . . So much company without socibility [sic], would be to me an unsuportable fatigue . . . Vanity in one shape or other reigns triumphant—and has banished love in all its modifications — and without it what is society? A false kind of politeness throws a varnish over every character— neither the heart nor sentiments appear in their true colours. . . . I am in a melting mood." Mary Wollstonecraft to Everina Wollstonecraft from Eton, Sunday, October 9, 1786. Wollstonecraft, *Collected Letters*, 79.

7 See Arthur Young, *The Autobiography of Arthur Young: With Selections from His Correspondence*, (London: Smith, Elder, & Co., 1898), 79–80.

8 Mary Wollstonecraft to Everina Wollstonecraft from Castle Mitchelstown, October 30, 1786, *Collected Letters*, 84–86.

9 Wollstonecraft, *Collected Letters*, 88.

10 For the quotes see p. 291 of the Oxford World Classics edition of the *Vindication of the Rights of Women*, which includes her history of the French Revolution and contains this quote; the second comes from the *Vindication* itself, Chapter 3. Wollstonecraft's own unhappy peripatetic childhood in the countryside and the later success she achieved in London and Paris likely contributed to her skepticism of Rousseau's pastoralism. In Norway she described one particularly isolated community as being "bastilled by nature—shut out from all that opens the understanding, or enlarges the heart" and while she shared in the general belief that cities were hotbeds of vice and corruption, she also saw them as places of progress, writing in her *Historical and Moral View*, that "it has been one of the advantages of the large cities of Europe, to light up the sparks of reason, and to extend the principles of truth." (359)

11 Mary Wollstonecraft to Everina Wollstonecraft from Dublin, March 24, 1787. *Collected Letters*, 114–115. She reaffirms this attitude of admiration in a review of the second part of his *Confessions* for the *Analytical Review*: "The writer of this article will venture to say, that he should never expect to see that man do a generous action, who could ridicule Rousseau's interesting account of his feelings and reveries—who could, in all the pride of wisdom, falsely so called, despise such a heart when naked before him." *The Works of Mary Wollstonecraft*, Volume 7, eds. Janet Todd and Marilyn Butler (London, William Pickering, 1989) 228.

12 *The Works of Mary Wollstonecraft*; also see Wollstonecraft on Lady Kingsborough, whom she judged to be "devoid of sensibility . . . *vanity only* inspires her immoderate love of praise—and *selfishness* her *traffick* of civility." Janet Todd, *Wollstonecraft: A Revolutionary Life* (London: Weidenfeld & Nicolson, 2000), 105.

13 For the Magdalen House, see Chapter 1. There is a passing but pointed allusion to the Magdalen in a *Vindication of the Rights of Woman*: "Many innocent girls become the dupes of a sincere affectionate heart, and still more are, as it may emphatically be termed, RUINED before they know the difference between virtue and vice: and thus prepared by their education for infamy, they become infamous.

Asylums and Magdalens are not the proper remedies for these abuses. It is justice, not charity, that is wanting in the world!" (143)

14 John Knowles, *The Life and Writings of Henry Fuseli* (London: H. Colburn and R. Bentley, 1831), 163–64. A cultivated disregard of fashion had been pioneered by Rousseau and remained in vogue throughout the pre-revolutionary period. During the revolution itself, Helen Maria Williams observed that: "The greatest simplicity in dress is observed, and is sometimes carried even to negligence. Every man seems at pains to shew that he has wasted as few moments as it was possible at his toilette, and that his mind is bent on higher cares than the embellishment of his person." *Helen* Deborah Kennedy, *Maria Williams and the Age of Revolution*, (Lewisburg, PA: Bucknell University Press, 2002), 85–85.

15 Her first recorded review, in June 1788, of *Edward and Harriet, or the Happy Recovery, a Sentimental Novel. By a Lady*, was typically combative: "The Happy Recovery is an heterogeneous mass of folly, affectation, and improbability. Metaphors and vulgarisms abound. The countess, 'wrapt up in the sable and all-encircling mantle of despair, is seized with a violent puking of blood.' An analysis of novels will seldom be expected, nor can the *cant* of sensibility be tried by any criterion of reason; ridicule should direct its shafts against this fair game, and, if possible, deter the thoughtless from imbibing the wildest notions, the most pernicious prejudices, prejudices which influence the conduct and spread insipidity over social converse." *The Works of Mary Wollstonecraft*: Volume 7, 19.

16 Godwin, *Memoirs*, 226.

17 Jenny Uglow, *In These Times: Living in Britain Through Napoleon's Wars 1793-1815* (London: Faber and Faber, 2014), 14.

18 Richard Price, "A Discourse on the Love of Our Country," 1789.

19 In Isaac Cruikshank's 1790 cartoon "The doctor indulged with his favorite scene," Dr. Price is shown watching the *poissardes'* National Guard henchmen ransack Marie-Antoinette's bedroom during the nights of October 5–6 through a peephole, with a little black demon for company. Price watches the scene kneeling, his hands in prayer. A speech bubble says: "Lord now lettest thou thy Servant depart in peace for mine Eyes have Seen." This is a line lifted from his lecture "A Discourse on the Love of Our Country."

20 Edmund Burke, *Reflections on the Revolution in France*, (Oxford University Press, 1993), 14, 72, 76, 77.

21 Kennedy, *Helen Maria Williams*, 80.

22 Godwin's diary quoted in Nicholas Roe, *Wordsworth and Coleridge: The Radical Years*, (Oxford: Clarendon Press, 1990), 42.

23 *Women in Revolutionary Paris, 1789–1795*, eds. Darline Gay Levy, Harriet Branson Applewhite, Mary Durham Johnson, (Champaign, IL: University of Illinois Press, 1978), 76–77.

24 Todd, *Mary Wollstonecraft*, 179.

25 *Women in Revolutionary Paris*, 89–93.

26 Wollstonecraft, *Vindication*, 65.

27 Wollstonecraft, *Vindication*, 66.

28 Wollstonecraft, *Vindication*, 106; Shortly afterward she takes an amusing potshot at Rousseau's proposed system of education for girls: "The mother, who wishes to give true dignity of character to her daughter, must, regardless of the sneers of ignorance, proceed on a plan diametrically opposite to that which Rousseau has recommended with all the deluding charms of eloquence and philosophical sophistry." (108)

29 Wollstonecraft, *Vindication*, 71.

30 Wollstonecraft, *Vindication*, 93. Wollstonecraft perceived and decried the notion that a woman would under-educate herself to appear unthreatening to a potential partner as "quitting a substance for a shadow." (99)

31 Wollstonecraft, *Vindication*, 196.

32 Wollstonecraft, *Vindication*, 219. "I have before observed, that men ought to maintain the women whom they have seduced."

33 Wollstonecraft, *Vindication*, 113.

34 Wollstonecraft to Joseph Johnson, London, October 1792. *Letters*, 205,

35 Rachel Hewitt, *A Revolution of Feeling: The Decade That Forged the Modern Mind*, (London: Granta Books, 2017), 192–193.

36 For Tahiti see Chapter 2. Southey even considered traveling to Tahiti, writing that "Otaheitii [had] independent of its women had many inducements, not only for the sailor but the philosopher." This came to nothing and the pantisocratic scheme was also abandoned, but not before notions of free love were preemptively abandoned, too. "I am for Liberty & Long Petticoats," Southey decided in the end. For a brilliant survey of the pantisocracy, free love, and a critique of the self-serving male aspects of the imagined sexual utopias, see chapters 7 and 8 of Hewitt, *A Revolution of Feeling*.

37 William Godwin, *Enquiry Concerning Political Justice*, (1793), Volume 2, Chapter VI.
   Godwin also seemed to believe that in this exulted state of liberty individuals would cease to be the "slave of sensuality and selfishness" and that their interest in sex would become almost purely functional:
"Reasonable men then will propagate their species, not because a certain sensible pleasure is annexed to this action, but because it is right the species should be propagated; and the manner in which they exercise this function will be regulated by the dictates of reason and duty."
It should be noted that Godwin also argued that in a world of perfect freedom the mind would conquer matter and then mortality. "In a word, why may not man be one day immortal?" He wrote. A crucial step on the path to immortality was the abolition of sleep: "before death can be banished, we must banish sleep, death's image." (Chapter VII)

38 Mary Wollstonecraft to William Roscoe, January 3, 1792 in *The Collected English Letters of Henry Fuseli*, ed. David H. Weinglass, (Millwood, NY: Kraus International Publications, 1982), 79.

39 Knowles, *The Life and Writings of Henry Fuseli*, 165.

40 Wollstonecraft, *Letters*, 204–05.

41 Note that by this point Wollstonecraft has, in the eyes of the conservatives, joined the ranks of the Francophile radical vanguard. See: Horace Walpole to Hannah More, August 21, 1792: "But it is better to thank Providence for the tranquility and happiness we enjoy in this country, in spite of the philosophising serpents we have in our bosom, the Paines, the Tookes, and the Woollstoncrofts [sic]. I am glad you have not read the tract of the last-mentioned writer. I would not look at it, though assured it contains neither metaphysics or politics; but as she entered the lists on the latter, and borrowed her title from the demon's book, which aimed at spreading the *wrongs* of men, she is excommunicated from the pale of my library."

42 Knowles, *The Life and Writings of Henry Fuseli*, 167–68.

43 David Andress, *The Terror*, (London: Abacus, 2006), 114.

44 Kennedy, *Helen Maria Williams*, 91.

45 To William Roscoe, November 12, 1792, Wollstonecraft, *Letters*, 206–208,

46 To Joseph Johnson, December 26, 1792, Wollstonecraft, *Letter*, 216–217.

47 Mary Wollstonecraft, "Letter on the Present Character of the French Nation," Paris, February 15, 1793; also see John Hardman, *The Life of Louis XVI*, (New Haven: Yale University Press, 2016), 438–440.

48 Helen Maria Williams Letter V p77, see also Kennedy, *Helen Maria Williams*, 94.

49 Kennedy, *Helen Maria Williams*, 63; and HMW Letter V p77.

50 Her obituary in the *Gentleman's Magazine* in 1828, where Williams was damned as "among the violent female devotees of the French revolution," was also home to some choice words for Stone. Writing apropos of her later disavowal of the Revolution, the *Magazine* declared that "she thus showed that her democratic consistency equalled the republican morality she had previously exhibited by living 'under the protection' (as the phrase is) of the quondam Rev. Mr. Stone,—one of those singularly black sheep, which even the liberal politics of modern ecclesiastical government cannot tolerate." Kennedy, *Helen Maria Williams*, 240–41.

51 Todd, *Mary Wollstonecraft*, 211.

52 Todd, *Mary Wollstonecraft*, 236.

53 For a concise survey of the themes of *The Emigrants*, see John Seelye, "The Jacobin Mode in Early American Fiction: Gilbert Imlay's *The Emigrants*," *Early American Literature*, 22, No. 2, Politics as Art, Art as Politics: Literature of the Early Republic, 1760–1820 (Fall, 1987), 204–212.

54 Virginia Woolf wrote of Imlay's courtship of Wollstonecraft, that "tickling minnows he had hooked a dolphin," a view that captures the persisting view that Imlay was a romantic chancer and a human mediocrity, who ran amok in the emotional world of one Europe's greatest female writers and thinkers

with little care or concern for the disastrous consequences of his coquetry. This view is anchored in an oblivion of literary evidence. We have none of Imlay's letters and consequently only Wollstonecraft's side of the story. For an evenhanded treatment of the Imlay-Wollstonecraft connection see Richard Holmes's essay, "The Feminist and the Philosopher: A Love Story (1987)," in *Sidetracks* (London: HarperCollins, 2000).

55 Andrew Cayton, *Love in the Time of Revolution: Transatlantic Literary Radicalism and Historical Change, 1793–1818*, (Chapel Hill, University of North Carolina Press, 2013), 56.

56 Godwin, *Memoirs*, 241–42.

57 Wollstonecraft to Imlay August, 1793, Wollstonecraft, *Letters*, 228; Todd, 216; Andress, 155–70.

58 Wollstonecraft to Imlay September, 1793, Wollstonecraft, *Letters*, 231; Imlay, November, 1793, 232.

59 Wollstonecraft to Imlay January 1, 1794, Wollstonecraft, *Letters*, 238.

60 Cecilia Lucy Brightwell, *Memorials of the Life of Amelia Opie*, (Lomdon: Longman, Brown, & Co., 1854), 58–59.

61 Rousseau argued that by installing women in the house they would become the true rulers of France. His model was Sparta, which he argued was nominally run by men but whose controlling influence were Spartan wives and mothers. See, "Dedication to the Republic of Geneva," the preface to the Discourse on Inequality: I must not forget that precious half of the Republic, which makes the happiness of the other; and whose sweetness and prudence preserve its tranquillity and virtue. Amiable and virtuous daughters of Geneva, it will be always the lot of your sex to govern ours. Happy are we, so long as your chaste influence, solely exercised within the limits of conjugal union, is exerted only for the glory of the State and the happiness of the public. It was thus the female sex commanded at Sparta; and thus you deserve to command at Geneva." See also: Joan B. Landes, *Women and the Public Sphere in the Age of Revolution* (Ithaca: NY Cornell University Press, 1988), 70–75.

62 Dorinda Outram, *The Body and the French Revolution: Sex, Class, and Political Culture* (New Haven: Yale University Press, 1989), 126.

63 *Women in Revolutionary Paris*, 1789–1795, 180.

64 Helen Maria Williams recorded that even among hardened Jacobins the masturbation slander was regarded as needlessly overblown: "When, Hebert accusing Antoinette of having committed the most shocking crime, she turned with dignity towards the audience, and said, 'I appeal to the conscience and feelings of every mother present, to declare if there be one amongst them who does not shudder at the idea of such horrors.' Robespierre, struck with this answer as by an electrical shock, broke his plate with this fork. 'That blockhead Hebert!' cried he, 'as if it were not enough that she was really a Messaline, he must make her an Aggripina also, and furnish her with a triumph of exciting the sympathy of the public in her last moments." Helen Maria Williams, *Letters Written in France in 1790*, eds. Neil Fraistat and Susan S. Lanser (Peterborough, ON: Broadview Literary Texts, 2001), 172–173.

65 *Women in Revolutionary Paris*, 1789–1795, 213–216.

66 See Simon Schama, *Citizens*: A Chronicle of the French Revolution (New York: Random House, 1989) 637, 653, 686, and Joan B. Landes, *Visualizing the Nation* (Ithaca, NY: Cornell University Press, 2003), 112, 126.

67 Wollstonecraft would consistently refer to herself as Mrs. Imlay until 1796 and it was widely believed that she was legally married to him until she married William Godwin.

68 To Imlay, p253-54; to Ruth Barlow May 20th Wollstonecraft, *Letters*,

69 To Imlay, September 22, 1794. Wollstonecraft, *Letters*, 263–64.

70 To Imlay, Friday June 12, 1795. Wollstonecraft, *Letters*, 297.

71 Wollstonecraft, *Letters*, 130.

72 Holmes, "The Feminist and the Philosopher," *Sidetracks*.

73 To Imlay, September 27, 1795. Wollstonecraft, *Letters*, 322.

74 Godwin, *Memoirs*, 258–259.

75 Knowles, *The Life and Writings of Henry Fuseli*, 170.

76 Wollstonecraft, *Maria*, 102.

77 Wollstonecraft, *Maria*, 137.

78 For a full treatment of seduction laws in England and America see chapters 4 and 5.

79 Wollstonecraft, *Maria*, 170–171.

80 Godwin, *Memoirs*, 256.

81 Holmes, *Sidetracks*, 210.

82 Purely by coincidence, Godwin's memoir was published at the same time as another scandal broke whose particulars were skewed to defame the late Mary Wollstonecraft. Shortly after she died, her former student Mary King was at the epicenter of a salacious affair seemingly lifted from the pages of *Clarissa*. In October 1797, Mary eloped with her cousin, Henry Gerard Fitzgerald. She was retrieved from London and sent back to Castle Mitchelstown. Her brother, Colonel Robert Edward King, fought a duel with Fitzgerald in Hyde Park on the morning of October 1. This was inconclusive, so they agreed to meet again the next day. They were arrested under the orders of the Duke of York before they could do so. Shortly before Christmas, Fitzgerald was spotted lurking about Castle Mitchelstown in disguise. Robert found out which inn Fitzgerald was staying in, went to his room and shot him dead "on the account of [him] seducing his sister." In between his duel in Hyde Park and this murder in County Cork, Lord Kingsborough had died, and Robert had inherited the title. Consequently, he was permitted to request a trial in the House of Lords where he was unanimously acquitted in May 1798. In the run up to the trial, the press began to pick up on the connection between Mary King and her (very briefly) governess Mary Wollstonecraft. The unhappy events in the King household were subsequently held to have been part of the perverse legacy of Wollstonecraft's "detestable system" of morality and education.
See, *Dictionary of National Biography*, 1885–1900, Volume 31, King, Robert (1754–1799); and N. F. Lowe, "Mary Wollstonecraft and the Kingsborough Scandal," *Eighteenth-Century Ireland* 9 (1994), 44–56.

83 *The Anti-Jacobin review and magazine.* v. 1 (July–Dec. 1798), 98 and Index; and William Stafford, *English Feminists and Their Opponents in the 1790s: Unsex'd and Proper Females*, (Manchester University Press, 2002) 13–16, 28.

84 William Hazlitt, *The Spirit of the Age*, 1825.

CHAPTER FOUR

1 Shelley, for his part, believed the whole phenomenon of "seduction" was a product of a corrupt and oppressive moral order, a view he delineated in a letter to Sir James Lawrence in August 1812: "Love seems inclined to stay in the prison, and my only the reason for putting him in chains, whilst convinced of the unholiness of the act, was a knowledge that, in the present state of society, if love is not thus villainously treated, shew who is the most loved will be treated worse by a misjudging world. In short, seduction, which term could have no meaning in a rational society, has now a most tremendous one; the fictitious merit attached to chastity has made that a forerunner to the most terrible ruins which in Malabar would be a pledge of honour and homage. If there is any enormous and desolating crime of which I should shudder to be accused of it is seduction. I need not say how I admire "Love"; and, as a British public seems to appreciate its merit, in not permitting it to emerge from a first edition, it is with satisfaction I find that justice had conceded abroad what bigotry has denied at home.'
Percy Shelley to Sir James Lawrence, August 17, 1812, dated Lymouth, Barnstaple, Devon.

2 H Shelley to C Nugent, November 20, 1814, *A Shelley Library, A Catalogue of Printed Books, Manuscripts, and Autograph Letters*, ed. Thomas James Wise, (London: Privately Printed, 1924).

3 Letter from MWS to Unknown, Geneva, June 1, 1816.

4 This disastrous sojourn was later dubbed their "treacle-moon" by Byron.

5 "Lord Byron took every pains to convince his wife of improper relations subsisting between himself and his sister." Harriet Beecher Stowe, *Vindication of Lady Byron*.

6 Marguerite Gardiner, Countess of Blessington, *Conversations of Lord Byron with the Countess of Blessington* (1834), 142.

7 This was at first part of her appeal to him. In one (pre-nuptial) encomium Byron described her as "a poetess, a mathematician, a metaphysician; yet, withal, very kind, generous, and gentle, with very little pretension." Later he would parody these same traits in *Don Juan*:
Her favourite science was the mathematical,
. . .

> Her thoughts were theorems, her words a problem,
> As if she deem'd that mystery would ennoble 'em.

The notion that Lady Byron was especially "cold and mathematical" would become something of a trope among Byron's partisans. One defender in the *Atlantic Monthly* wrote that "finding that she could not reduce him to the mathematical proprieties and conventional rules of her own mode of life, [she] suddenly, and without warning, abandoned him in the most cruel and inexplicable manner."

8 Leslie A. Marchand, *Byron: A Portrait*, (London: Pimlico, 1993), 211–12.

9 In her 1830 testimony, Lady Byron described her flight from her husband in January 1816:

> The facts are, I left London for Kirkby Mallory, the residence of my father and mother, on the 15th of January, 1816. Lord Byron had signified to me in writing, Jan. 6, his absolute desire that I should leave London on the earliest day that I could conveniently fix. It was not safe for me to encounter the fatigues of a journey sooner than the 15th. Previously to my departure, it had been strongly impressed on my mind that Lord Byron was under the influence of insanity.
> This opinion was in a great measure derived from the communications made to me by his nearest relatives and personal attendant.

Harriet Beecher Stowe, *Lady Byron Vindicated* (1870), 108.

10 Fewer than 350 such divorces had been approved by this method in all English history.

11 Medora Leigh herself believed she was Byron's daughter and said as much in her memoir. There is no genetic evidence available to confirm or deny the allegation.

12 "From the time Mrs L— came to Bennet St. in the year 1813—Lord B—had given her various intimations of a criminal intercourse between them," Marchand, *Byron*, 229–30

13 "The English women are the only good-looking women in Brussels; though, with true English Bullism, they vest *here* a complete Anglomanian costume, preserving their French fashions for the English winds to waft." Polidori, *Diary*, 58.

14 Moore records a hilarious dialogue between Polidori and his employer that took place as they traveled from France to Switzerland: *A dialogue which Lord Byron himself used to mention as having taken place between them during their journey on the Rhine, is amusingly characteristic of both the persons concerned. "After all," said the physician, "what is there you can do that I cannot?" "Why, since you force me to say," answered the other, "I think there are three things I can do which you cannot." Polidori deigned him to name them. "I can," said Lord Byron, "swim across that river and I can snuff out that candle with a pistol-shot at the distance of twenty paces and I have written a poem of which 14,000 copies were sold in one day."*
Moore, *Life of Byron*, Vol III.

15 Polidori, *Diary*, 97.

16 Polidori, *Diary*, 98. On the way to Dover they had visited the grave of Charles Churchill (1732–1764) a poet, satirist, and legendary rake. This lay-by produced a poem "Churchill's Grave": "I stood beside the grave of him who blazed / The Comet of a season"

17 Marchand, *Byron*, 288. Robert Southey had observed them in Geneva and spread rumors back in England about the Byron-Shelley-Godwin-Clairmont group, leading Byron to rage in an 1820 letter to Hobhouse: "The son of a bitch on his return from Switzerland, two years ago, said that Shelley and I 'had formed a League of Incest, and practised our precepts with, &c.' He lied like a rascal, for they *were not sisters* . . . he lied in another sense, for there was no promiscuous intercourse, my commerce being limited to the carnal knowledge of Miss C." He later took his revenge on Southey, a radical turned conservative, in the bitter dedication to *Don Juan*:

> Bob Southey! You're a poet—Poet-laureate,
>   And representative of all the race;
> Although 'tis true that you turn'd out a Tory at
>   Last—yours has lately been a common case;
>
> . . .
>
> Europe has slaves—allies—kings—armies still,
> And Southey lives to sing them very ill.

18 Moore, *Life of Byron*, 279.

19 The very first reference Polidori made to Mary and Claire is revealing. Shelley, he recorded, "keeps the two daughters of Godwin who practise his theories [free love]." Leaving aside his clear ignorance of

the stepsisters actual relations (he was not alone in either his confusion or his indifference to clearing it up) it suggests a certain presumption on his part: perhaps Mary might practice Godwin's theories on him?

20 Giovanni Aldini, *An account of the late improvements in galvanism* (1803), 216. Accessed at: https://wellcomelibrary.org/item/b20595256#?c=0&m=0&s=0&cv=210&z=-0.0666%2C0.3626%2C1.1478%2C0.6168.

21 *Don Juan*, Canto I, CXXX, 35.
The full quote makes the allusion to Aldini's Newgate experiments even more explicit:
And galvanism has set some corpses grinning,
  But has not answer'd like the apparatus
  Of the Humane Society's beginning
  By which men are unsuffocated gratis
The Humane Society had collaborated with Aldini in his 1803 experiments.
  Richard Holmes notes that Shelley had been passionately interested in electricity since his Oxford days when he had kept an "electrical apparatus" in his room and spoke "with vehemence of the marvellous powers of electricity, of thunder and lightning" while he tinkered with it. (Richard Holmes, *Shelley: The Pursuit* (New York: HarperCollins, 1994) 44.

22 The same point is made in Sandra Gilbert and Susan Gubar's *The Madwoman in the Attic: The Woman Writer and the Nineteenth-Century Literary Imagination* (1979): *At the same time, just as surely as Eve's moral deformity is symbolized by the monster's physical malformation, the monster's physical ugliness represents his social illegitimacy, his bastardy, his namelessness. . . . Mary Shelley's monster has also been "got" in a "dark and vicious place." Indeed, in his vile illegitimacy he seems to incarnate that bestial "'unnameable' place" And significantly, he is himself as nameless as a woman is in patriarchal society, as nameless as unmarried, illegitimately pregnant Mary Wollstonecraft Godwin may have felt herself to be at the time she wrote* Frankenstein. *"This nameless mode of naming the unnameable is rather good," Mary commented when she learned that it was the custom at early dramatizations of* Frankenstein *to place a blank line next to the name of the actor who played the part of the monster. But her pleased surprise was disingenuous, for the problem of names and their connection with social legitimacy had been forced into her consciousness all her life.*

23 And to her estranged husband: *My dear Bysshe let me conjure you by the remembrance of our days of happiness to grant my last wish—do not take your innocent child from Eliza who has been more than I have, who has watched over her with such unceasing care.—Do not refuse my last request—I never could refuse you & if you had never left me I might have lived but as it is, I freely forgive you & may you enjoy that happiness which you have deprived me of.*
Accessed at: http://shelleysghost.bodleian.ox.ac.uk/harriet-shelleys-suicide-letter#Transcript.

24 The Shelleys also tried, more gently, to dissuade him. In a letter from Pisa, dated October 21, 1821, Percy offered to take Allegra into his own household: *The Countess tells me that you think of leaving Allegra for the present at the convent. Do as you think best; but I can pledge myself to find a situation for her here such as you would approve in case you change your mind.* Wise, *A Shelley Library*, 66.

25 Mary Shelley to Claire Clairmont, May 11, 1821, *My Best Mary: The Selected Letters of Mary Wollstonecraft Shelley*, ed. Muriel Spark, (London: Allan Wingate, 1953).

26 This is now known to history as "A Fragment of a Novel." It is only a few pages long and contains no reference to vampires or vampirism.

27 *The Vampyre* was quickly translated into French and German and was wildly popular in both countries. In France it also became the basis for the popular plays *Lord Ruthann ou les Vampires*, by Cyprien Bérard (1820); *The Bride of the Isles, a Tale*, by J.R. Planché (1820); and *Le Vampire*, by Charles Nodier (1820); and *La Guzla* by Prosper Mérimée. Many of *The Vampyre*'s knock-offs claimed to have been written by Byron himself, and for many in Europe it was the first piece of Byron they ever read. Goethe famously, and hilariously, described it as "the English poet's finest work." (See Chapter 2 of Christopher Frayling's, *Vampyres*.)

28 Confusingly, "Oneirodynia" is now the technical term for nightmares but in the early 19th century the word was used to refer to sleepwalking, or somnambulism.

29 The connection of sleep with the disabling of man's reasoning faculties was widespread. Describing her sister in a delirious fever, Mary Wollstonecraft had compared her condition to "something like strange

dreams when judgement sleeps and fancy sports at a fine rate." (See Todd, *Wollstonecraft*, 45.)

30 Anthelme Richerand and John Howell, *Elements of physiology* (Bristol Royal Infirmary, 1815).

31 Joseph Deleuze, Francis, *A critical history of animal magnetism* (University of Leeds, 1816).

32 Tim Fulford, "Conducting the Vital Fluid: The Politics and Poetics of Mesmerism in the 1790s," *Studies in Romanticism* 43, No. 1, Romanticism and the Sciences of Life, Spring, 2004.

33 Deleuze *A Critical History of Animal Magnetism,* 1816.

34 Dr. John Bell, *The General and Particular Principles of Animal Electricity and Magnetism* (1792), 65–70; See also *The Skeptic* (1800), accessed on British Library http://explore.bl.uk/primo_library/libweb/action/display.
l&frbrVersion=1610&frbg=&&vl(488279563UI0)=any&dscnt=0&scp.the%20skeptic%201800&dstmp=1512332185264.

35 Richard Holmes, *Age of Wonder*, 273, and Anonymous, *The Skeptic* (1800), British Library, Digital Store Cup.407.gg.37. DRT

36 "The apples and the horse-turds; or, Buonaparte among the golden pippins," James Gillray, 1800 British Museum, Museum number 1851,0901.1018

37 Review of *Du Fluide-Universel, de son Activite et de l'Utilite de ses Modifications, &c.*, *Anti-Jacobin Review* (1806).

38 Louis Odier (1748–1817) a Swiss doctor whose research was, typical to his era, diverse, encompassing pediatrics, vaccinations, laughing gas, and animal magnetism. Intriguingly, in the aforementioned *Anti-Jacobin Review* article on universal fluid, the author notes that somnambulism is associated with the doctors of Lyons and Geneva but not Paris, who hold it "in just contempt."

39 Polidori, *Diary*, 119–22.

40 *New Monthly Magazine*, Volume 31, 180–85.

41 Byron may well have approved of the comparison for he was a huge fan of her grandfather's work both on the stage and in Parliament, and had, off course, sat on the board of the Sheridan family's Drury Lane Theatre. The great man died in July 1816, and Byron composed his elegy "On the Death of Richard Brinsley Sheridan" while staying in the Villa Diodati.

42 Thornton Butterworth, *The Journal of Henry Edward Fox* (London, 1923), 292.

43 There is scholarly debate as to whether the story was Mary's or Claire Clairmont's. See: Bradford A. Booth, "The Pole: A Story by Clare Clairmont?," *ELH*, 5, No. 1 (March, 1938), 67–70.

44 From *The Diary of Benjamin Robert Haydon*, Vol. 4, ed. Willard Bissell Pope (Cambridge, Harvard University Press, 1960–63), 110-11.

45 During the same period Haydon records a conversation he had with Edward Ellice, an acquaintance of Byron and a minister in Lord Grey's cabinet, on the subject of Byron's wife that is revealing of contemporary male sexual attitudes: "I said, 'She was a prig—she married him to reform him.' 'Yes,' said Mr. Ellice, 'not only to *reform* him but to *refuse* him.'" Haydon confides in his diary that if Lady Byron should have actually "checked his [Byron's] natural appetites" then he should have "prostrated her by force!—at any rate a man can't be hung for a rape on his wife." *Diary of Benjamin Robert Haydon*, 99–100.

46 Following his participation in the Greek War of Independence, Trelawney had proposed marriage to both Claire Clairmont and Mary Shelley. The latter rejected him in brutal fashion, with a wonderfully backhanded compliment thrown in for good measure:
My name will never be Trelawney. I am not so young as I was when you first knew me, but I am as proud. I must have the entire affection, devotion, &, above all, the solicitous protection of any one who would win me. You belong to womankind in general, & Mary Shelley will never be yours. Muriel Spark, *Mary Shelley: A Biography* (London: Constable, 1993), 122.

47 Under Breach of Promise to Marry, plaintiffs could seek damages on the grounds of seduction—that is, if the promise of marriage led to sex—but even in the absence of that were secure in claiming compensation for the psychic, emotional, reputational distress sustained by the unexpected and undesired end to their nuptial plans. The results could be ridiculous but also fortuitous at a time when social mobility was limited and women's life prospects were particularly tightly constrained. In 1828, the 58-year-old Sally Simpson was overjoyed to discover that an obviously humorous offer of marriage made nineteen years earlier by a local landlord resulted in a court-ordered payout of £350. Nonetheless, leading English jurists took the suit seriously. Referring to the survival of "contract

marriage" in Scotland, Lord Brougham observed in 1849: "the promise [of marriage] is made secretly, in the course of a seduction, and is parcel of the act of seducing the female. Then the difficulty is for the female to prove it."

See: Denise Bates, *Breach of Promise to Marry: A History of How Jilted Brides Settled Scores* (Barnsley, UK: Pen & Sword, 2014); and Lawrence Stone, *Road to Divorce: England 1530–1987* (Oxford University Press, 1990), 80–81.

48 Fluke had been castrated by shrapnel at the battle of Waterloo and thereafter was taken into the household service of the Nortons, one of whom was his commanding officer in the Lowlands.

49 Much like the lawyers and jurists in nineteenth-century Crim. Con. cases, contemporary historians have probed the historical record for conclusive evidence as to whether Melbourne and Norton were, in fact, intimate. The closest to a smoking gun is a letter Melbourne's brother sent to their sister five days after the trial: *Quel triomphe ! J'ai ta letter du 23 . . . Don't let Wm think himself invulnerable for having got off again this time; no man's luck can go further.*

The "again" refers to Lord Brandon's Crim. Con. suit that Melbourne had rid himself of earlier in the decade. The affair was common knowledge at the time. Lord Malmesbury, hearing of Melbourne's acquittal, joked that to accept the court's ruling one would have to believe that "Melbourne had had more opportunities than any man ever had before, and made no use of them." Quoted in: *The Letters of Caroline Norton to Lord Melbourne*, eds. James O. Huge and Clarke Olney (Columbus: Ohio State University Press, 1974); Stone, *Road to Divorce*, 280.

50 For an account of the trial see: Diane Atkinson, *The Criminal Conversations of Mrs Norton* (London: Preface Publishing, 2012), 8–22.

51 Letter from Caroline Norton to Mary Shelley, June 25, 1836, quoted in Jane Gray Perkins, *Life of Mrs. Norton* (London: John Murray, 1910), 95.

52 Letter to John Murray, 1838, quoted in Perkins, *Life of Mrs. Norton*, 151.

53 BROTHELS, &C. SUPPRESSION BILL., House of Lords Debate, June 14, 1844 vol. 75 cc877-91.

54 See Hansard, House of Commons Debate, June 23, 1847 vol. 93 cc811-4.

55 *The Spectator*, for example, praised the Bill: *Such a law would entail responsibility on another; it would operate as a check on seducers, and a powerful one—for all deceivers of women are mean men. The prospect of having to pay heavily for their "successes" would convert many a Don Juan into Scipios.* Scipio was the Roman general known for his temperance and moral rectitude. In *Littell's Living Age*, Vol. 14, July–September, 1847.

56 *Married Women and the Law*, Eds. Tim Stretton and Krista J. Kesselring, (Montreal: McGill-Queen's University Press, 2013), 7.

57 THE HON. G. C. NORTON AND THE HON. MRS NORTON, *The Morning Post* (London, England), Friday, August 19, 1853.

58 Caroline Norton, "English Laws For Women in the Nineteenth Century," 1854.

59 Allen Horstman, *Victorian Divorce*, (London: Croom Helm, 1985), 77.

60 These clauses were:

> 21 — Protects earnings of a wife deserted by her husband
>
> 24 — Court could direct payment of separate maintenance to a wife or to her trustee
>
> 25 — A wife can inherit and bequeath property like a single woman
>
> 26 — A Separated wife was given power of contract and suing, and being sued, in any civil proceeding

61 Sybil Wolfram, "Divorce in England 1700–1857," *Oxford Journal of Legal Studies* 5, No. 2, (Summer, 1985), 155–86.

CHAPTER FIVE

1 Jack Johnson, *My Life In the Ring and Out* (New York: Dover, 2018), 48.

2 Ida B. Wells, *The Red Record*, (1895), Chapter 3, "Lynching Imbeciles."

3 As opposed to the English tradition which required that fathers or guardians bring them on behalf of their daughters using the fiction of a putative "loss of services" from their seduced daughters. See Chapter 4 for an overview of the English actions.

4 These were Alabama, Alaska, California, Georgia, Idaho, Indiana, Iowa, Kentucky, Michigan,

Mississippi, Montana, Nevada, Oregon, South Dakota, Tennessee, Utah, Virginia, and West Virginia. Washington, D.C. also enacted the reform. All but Alabama eliminate the lost services clause; five states (Georgia, Kentucky, Michigan, Virginia, West Virginia) did not extend the right to sue to woman on her own behalf. The rest enacted both reforms simultaneously.

5 M. B. W. Sinclair, "Seduction and the Myth of the Ideal Woman," *Law & Inequality* 5, no. 1 (1987), 57, 64.

   Note how closely the language of the law ("priceless. jewel") mimics that of sentimental literature, such as Richardson's *Pamela*: "that jewel, your virtue, which no riches, nor favour, nor any thing in this life, can make up to you."

6 Larry Whiteaker, *Seduction, Prostitution, and Moral Reform in New York, 1830–1860*, 143.

7 H. W. Humble, "Seduction as a Crime," *Columbia Law Review* 21, no. 2 (Feb. 1921).

8 As absurd and condescending as these ideas now seem, they do not devalue the NYFMRS's attempt to introduce seduction legislation. The attempt to introduce these laws cannot be understood without a proper understanding of the legal and political landscape that these women were operating within. Nineteenth-century American women had very few sexual rights. The age of consent was ten years in the majority of states, and as low as seven in some. Rape convictions were very hard to come by as the law assumed that any failure to actively resist at any point in an assault was evidence of consent. The threat or use of violence by men to extract sexual compliance was not automatically considered rape. The demonstrative injustices posed by the rape laws filtered into other aspects of sexual existence. Identifying genuine sexual consent in such a deeply unequal, deeply patriarchal society was very hard. Furthermore, women were punished in the marriage market for any extramarital sexual encounters they may have had, consensual or otherwise, damaging their prospects for long-term financial and physical security. Finally, women could not vote and were not expected to involve themselves in politics in any way. They were locked out of the only institutions that could have improved their position. In such an environment, the fact that the NYFMRS proved themselves capable of mobilizing women activists to generate popular support for improved sexual protection and extract such protections from an all-male legislature was no small feat.

9 Mary Frances Berry, "Judging Morality: Sexual Behavior and Legal Consequences in the Late Nineteenth-Century South," in *Black Southerners and the Law: 1865–1900*, ed. Donald G. Nieman; See, for instance, the case of Emmett Till and his accuser Carolyn Bryant who later admitted that her allegation was completely fictitious; Timothy B. Tyson, *The Blood of Emmett Till*, 2017. Lynching was a wedge issue within the feminist cause, with black women reformers constantly at odds with their white allies over the issue. Black women recognized that the uncompromising rhetoric of the WCTU and similar organizations on matters of sexual discipline endangered black lives. When white reformer Mrs. Ormison Chant voted against an anti-lynching resolution at the National Conference of Unitarian Churches in 1894, black reformer Florida Ruffin Ridley wrote an open letter declaring "We here solemnly deny that the black men are the foul fiends they are pictured; we demand that until at least one crime is proved upon them, judgement be suspended." Frances Willard was famously silent on the subject of lynching—she wished not to antagonize her Southern allies—leading to a public spat with Ida B. Wells, who dedicated a whole chapter of *The Red Record* to criticizing Willard and the WCTU for their policy toward lynching. The upshot of these internal tensions was that black women stayed out of the age of consent campaign. Mary E. Odem, *Delinquent Daughters: Protecting and Policing Adolescent Female Sexuality in the United States, 1885–1920* (Chapel Hill: University of North Carolina Press, 1995), 29–33. (It is important to note that policing sexuality was not the only motivating factor for lynch mobs. The desire to appropriate the property of a new class of black landowners was often a material factor in designating the victim. See: https://features.propublica.org/black-land-loss/heirs_property-rights-why-black-families-lose-land-south/. "Ray Winbush, the director of the Institute for Urban Research, at Morgan State University, told me, 'There is this idea that most blacks were lynched because they did something untoward to a young woman. That's not true. Most black men were lynched between 1890 and 1920 because whites wanted their land.'")

10 Johnson, *In the Ring and Out*, 33–35.

11 Johnson, *In the Ring and Out*, 38.

12 Johnson, 37–39.

13 Ada "Bricktop" Smith would later write of Johnson's smile: "There were reasons why his smile was

so famous. It reflected the real champion, the warm generous, impulsive, wonderful, loveable man. That smile gave him the handsomeness his looks didn't really deserve." *Bricktop*, Bricktop with James Haskins (New York: Atheneum, 1983), 43.

14 Indeed, Johnson experienced the global sporting scene as his travels, celebrity, and legal misadventures took him across the world. "I had opportunities to observe denizens of the underworld in nearly every country of the world," he wrote in his memoirs, "I have witnessed scenes among them that have no parallel even in the most imaginative fiction of melodramatic writers." Johnson, *In the Ring and Out*, 112; Bricktop would later describe him as "this champion of the world, driver of fast cars, escorter of beautiful women, symbol of the wild, irresponsible sporting man," *Bricktop*, 46.

15 Johnson, 63–65, and Geoffrey C. Ward, *Unforgivable Blackness: The Rise and Fall of Jack Johnson*, (London, Yellow Jersey Press, 2015), 77.

16 Johnson, *In the Ring and Out*, 65.

17 *Bricktop*, 185.

18 Ward, *Unforgivable* Blackness, 44.

19 Johnson, *In the Ring and Out*, 52.

20 Johnson, 66.

21 "He made Chicago his home. I can understand why—it was big and sprawling, full of vitality and excitement, just like Jack." *Bricktop*, 43.

22 The Ketchel fight was one of Johnson's more gruesome encounters. Ketchel, a former bouncer, was a brutal puncher but was 49lbs/22kgs lighter than the champion. Johnson quite literally carried Ketchel around the ring for 11 rounds. In the 12th, Ketchel launched a blistering attack that sent Johnson to the ground and sent the almost entirely white crowd to their feet. An enraged Johnson got to his feet and threw a brawling right hand with such conviction that it carried him over Ketchel and onto his knees on the other side of the ring. Ketchel was out for a minute and a half, a starfish in center ring. Even in the grainy black and white film Johnson can be clearly seen picking out three of Ketchel's teeth from his glove, and letting them sprinkle down onto the canvas. Then he leans back with one arm across the rope to admire his work.

23 Johnson had no illusions about Jeffries motivations. In his memoirs he describes him as "a one-time champion . . . had been coaxed back to contend for the title in order to satisfy jealousy, hatred, and prejudice." He also recalled with some bitterness how Jeffries had diminished his victory over Tommy Burns by attacking "Burns for fighting me, saying that he was money-mad and that he had sold his pride and the pride of the Caucasian race by fighting me." Johnson, *In the Ring and Out*, 134.

24 Ward, *Unforgivable Blackness*, 197; This "bull fiddle" was in fact a bass viol that Johnson had learned to play with some skill during his nomadic youth. The bass viol is essentially the largest type of viola. It is not as big as a cello but is played in the same way, that is, seated. It is not clear when Johnson learned to play or why he chose this particular type of viol, though it is possible that this was simply the type best-suited to his size. Full string sections were common in the better sort of clubs and bars that Johnson frequented at this time and one of his party tricks was to join in with these bands when the fancy took him. As a voracious reader, it might have pleased Johnson to know that the bass viol had a Shakespearean pedigree. The instrument was popular among sixteenth- and seventeenth-century players and is referenced on occasion in Shakespeare's plays. One allusion, from *A Comedy of Errors*, is especially fistic: in Act 4, Scene 3, Dromio describes Adam, the sergeant of the guard, as "he that goes in the calf's skin . . . he that went, like a bass-viol, in a case of leather."

25 Ward, *Unforgivable Blackness*, 198

26 Examples are all taken from Al-Tony Gilmore, *Bad Nigger* (Port Washington, NY: Kennikat Press, 1975) 60–66.

27 Louis Armstrong, *Satchmo: My Life in New Orleans*, Da Capo Press, 1986, 36.

28 In a striking example of how anti-Johnson feeling ran concurrent with progressive sentiment, Thetus Sims of Tennessee was a passionate supporter of women's suffrage. In the official history of the suffrage movement he is named alongside the eponymous champion of the Mann Act as one of those who went above and beyond to ensure the passage of a suffrage bill in the house in 1918: "Republican Leader Mann of Illinois at much personal risk came from a hospital in Baltimore. He had not been present in Congress for months and his arrival shortly before five o'clock caused great excitement in the chamber. Representative Sims of Tennessee, who had broken his shoulder two days before, refused

to have it set until after the suffrage vote and against the advice of his physician was on the floor for the discussion and the vote. Representative Barnhart of Indiana was taken from his bed in a hospital in Washington and stayed at the Capitol just long enough to cast his vote. One of the New York Representatives came immediately after the death of his wife, who had been an ardent suffragist, and returned on the next train." *The History of Woman Suffrage*, Volume V, ed. Ida Husted Harper.

29 Gilmore, *Bad Nigger*, 90.

30 "Women Denounce Vice." *New York Tribune*, 1901; as early as 1885—amid the campaign for the age of consent laws—Willard had called for the "punishing with extreme penalties such men as inflict upon women atrocities compared with which death would be infinitely welcome." The same logic was at work in her subsequent campaign against the White Slave Trade. See Odem, *Delinquent Daughters*, 19.

31 Chapter 30, *Fighting the Traffic in Young Girls, or War on the White Slave Trade*, ed. Ernest A. Bell (1910).

32 In his memoirs, Johnson mentions in passing that the Café de Champion's art collection included "a few real Rembrandts which I had obtained in Europe." This is a casual and quite transparent lie, but if reflected his interest in being taken seriously as a man of the world with refined tastes. Through his travels, notably his recent trip to Paris and London, Johnson had "had gained a comprehensive idea of decorative effects; I had viewed some of the most notable amusements centers of the world, both as to their exterior and interior arrangements. I also had collected many fine works of art, curios, and novelties." He wanted his club to be a showcase for his cultivation/discernment. Johnson, *In the Ring and Out*, 59.

33 Johnson, *In the Ring and Out*, 68.

34 Suicide seems to have dominated the *Times*' columns that September. Excluding the coverage of Etta Duryea's death, the *Times* ran no fewer than twenty-two stories on, or closely related to, suicide, including the incredible:

SHOOTS HIMSELF; WINS GIRL.; Rejected for Another, Young Georgian Sways Her by Trying Suicide.

35 Ward, *Unforgivable Blackness*, 301.

36 Ward, *Unforgivable Blackness*, 302–303.

37 Ward, *Unforgivable Blackness*, 302–312.

38 Al-Tony Gilmore, "Jack Johnson and White Women: The National Impact," *The Journal of Negro History* 58, no. 1, (January 1973).

39 Al-Tony Gilmore, *Bad Nigger*, 97.

40 *Chicago Defender*, October 26, 1912.

41 Lucille "begged me to marry her," Johnson wrote in his memoirs, "declaring that not only had she been ruined in the eyes of the world, but that furthermore her mother was making her the object of abuse and nagging which she could not bear." Johnson, *In the Ring and Out*, 70.

42 Al-Tony Gilmore, *Bad Nigger*, 107.

43 See *New York Times*, December, 1912. It should be noted that these declarations were widely condemned by politicians and by commentators in the press. The *Times* joked that Blease "Out-Tillmans Tillman in South Carolina and elsewhere." Benjamin Tillman was a notorious racial demagogue, rabid Redeemer, and South Carolina Senator. In 1928 Blease would have the dubious distinction of being the last American legislator to agitate for a constitutional amendment that would have outlawed interracial marriage.

44 Al-Tony Gilmore, *Bad Nigger*, 108.

45 In the same December 1912 conference, Blease cited a "higher law" than the constitution in defense of lynching. This was an exact duplication of abolitionist William Seward's famous statement that there was a "higher law" than the constitution which justified resistance to slavery. Abolitionists, like lynchers, were disdainful of the constitution which they called a "covenant with death" because of its codifying of slavery.

46 Al-Tony Gilmore, *Bad Nigger*, 122.

47 Al-Tony Gilmore, *Bad Nigger*, 125.

48 Johnson, *In the Ring and Out*, 72.

49 http://montrealgazette.com/news/local-news/second-draft-champion-boxer-jack-johnson-got-under-white-peoples-skins.

Also Ward, *Unforgivable Blackness*, 344–49

50 Jessica R. Piley, *Policing Sexuality: The Mann Act and the Making of the FBI* (Cambridge: Harvard University Press, 2014), 101.

51 For more on how women with interracial lovers and/or johns were treated in court, see the example of Ray Vernon discussed in Sharon R. Ullman, *Sex Seen: The Emergence of Modern Sexuality in America*, 131–35.

52 David J. Langum, *Crossing over the Line: Legislating Morality and the Mann Act.*

53 Piley, *Policing Sexuality*, 107–13.

54 Piley, *Policing Sexuality*, 112–13.

55 All quotes from *Caminetti v. U.S.*, (1917), no. 139
    http://caselaw.findlaw.com/us-supreme-court/242/470.html.

56 Additional biographical material is available in: *100 Americans Making Constitutional History: A Biographical History*, ed. Melvin I. Urofsky.

57 Both men were out within a year and there was a happy ending to this story for Maury Diggs, at least. Maury and Marsha married in San Francisco in 1915 and remained married until his death in 1953 in St. Helena, California. After his release from prison Diggs resumed his career as an architect and became a specialist in design and construction of horse race tracks. He was responsible for the designing some of the largest in the state, including Golden Gate Fields in Albany, San Francisco.

58 Three justices dissented. Justice McKenna wrote the minority opinion in which he attacked the "immoral purposes" clause as imprecise but also argued that in the context of the law's specific mission to erase the threat of White Slavery the "immoral purposes" could only reasonably be applied to "commercialized vice, immoralities having a mercenary purpose." McKenna then went further and challenged the assumptions underlying both the law itself and the majority opinion of the court: *There is much in the present case to tempt to a violation of the rule. Any measure that protects the purity of women from assault or enticement to degradation finds an instant advocate in our best emotions; but the judicial function cannot yield to emotion—it must, with poise of mind, consider and decide. It should not shut its eyes to the facts of the world and assume not to know what everybody else knows. And everybody knows that there is a difference between the occasional immoralities of men and women and that systematized and mercenary immorality epitomized in the statute's graphic phrase "white slave traffic." And it was such immorality that was in the legislative mind, and not the other.* McKenna also concurred with the *Times* that the law's naive view of prevailing social and sexual morality opened the door to abuses, blackmail in particular: *There is danger in extending a statute beyond its purpose, even if justified by a strict adherence to its words. . . . The present case warns against ascribing such improvidence to the statute under review. Blackmailers of both sexes have arisen, using the terrors of the construction now sanctioned by this court as a help—indeed, the means—for their brigandage. The result is grave and should give us pause. It certainly will not be denied that legal authority justifies the rejection of a construction which leads to mischievous consequences, if the statute be susceptible of another construction.*

59 Johnson, *In the Ring and Out*, 76–80.

60 Ward, *Unforgivable Blackness*, 379–81.

61 Johnson, *In the Ring and Out*, Johnson, 115.

62 There is a long and revealing passage in his memoirs where he describes an indigenous tribe his party encountered during their travels in Mexico:
    "We discovered that it was not uninhabited, but that it was the camping place of a tribe of Indians, the name of which I never learned. Perhaps they had never acquired any designation for they were without doubt the lowest in the human scale that I had ever seen. They had human forms but other than that they were animals. They were even worse than animals so unclean and lazy as they were. They were naked and their skins were filthy with slime. They lay about in camps like vermin, men, women and babies piled up together with dogs who had the same privileges as the others—privileges which permitted them to nurse at the breasts of the human mothers who lolled listlessly about, a suckling babe on one side, a dog on the other."
    Even Johnson, who knew all there was to know about racial prejudice, was not free of the racist assumptions of his time. Johnson, *In the Ring and Out*, 95.

63 Johnson, *In the Ring and Out*, 98.

64 Zelda made it clear to her friends, at least, that her acceptance of his proposal was contingent on his acceptance by a publisher. A friend of both F. Scott and Zelda recalled the latter's attitude as: "If Scott sells the book, I'll marry the man, because he is sweet." But sweetness was no substitute for financial security. In the event, Zelda became Mrs. F. Scott Fitzgerald a mere eight days after the publication of *This Side of Paradise*. This was a book that contained the observation (from Rosalind, a Zelda avatar) that "given a decent start any girl can beat a man nowadays." David S. Brown, *Paradise Lost: A Life of F. Scott Fitzgerald* (Cambridge: Belknap Press, 2017), 75, 90.

65 Paula S. Fass, *The Damned and The Beautiful: American Youth in the 1920's* (Oxford University Press, 1977), 22–23.

66 Ward, *Unforgivable Blackness*, 425.

67 All Fitzgerald quotes are taken from F. Scott Fitzgerald, *The Best Early Stories of F. Scott Fitzgerald* (New York: Modern Library, 2005).

68 *Recent Social Trends in the United States; Report of the President's Research Committee on Social Trends* (1933), 417–419

69 Sinclair, "Seduction and the Myth of the Ideal Woman."

70 Pippa Holloway, *Sexuality, Politics, and Social Control in Virginia, 1920–1945* (Chapel Hill: University of North Carolina Press, 2006), 40–46.

71 Piley, *Policing Sexuality*, 132.

72 Angus McLaren, *Sexual Blackmail: A Modern History* (Cambridge: Harvard University Press, 2002), 87–88, 93, 95–97.

73 Anita Loos, *Gentlemen Prefer Blondes and But Gentlemen Marry Brunettes* (New York: Penguin, 1998); McLaren, *Sexual Blackmail*, 172.

74 This interpretation continued to baffle her long into her life: "The thing that was so amazing and truly surprising to me was that it was widely interpreted as giving free rein to predatory males to take advantage of chaste maidens which, of course, was diametrically opposed to what my conception was. I thought—and I still think—that it was an early blow for women's liberation."

75 The seven states that passed anti-heart balm legislation in 1935 were Indiana, Illinois, Alabama, New Jersey, New York, Michigan, and Pennsylvania. California, Colorado, and Massachusetts followed over the next five years. Florida abolished these actions in 1945.

Arizona, Connecticut, Idaho, Maryland, Minnesota, Missouri, Nebraska, North Carolina, Oklahoma, Oregon, Rhode Island, Texas, Washington, Wisconsin, Ohio tried and failed in 1935 to pass similar legislation.

76 Among them was Illinois. A state which had searched the law books for any pretext to hold Jack Johnson for the crime of seducing a very willing white woman now described the heart balms as "action conducive to extortion and blackmail" and abolished them.

77 Sinclair, "Seduction and the Myth of the Ideal Woman"; for all details relating to Roberta West Nicholson, refer to the Roberta West Nicholson Oral History transcript at the Indiana State Library Digital Collections: http://cdm16066.contentdm.oclc.org/cdm/ref/collection/p16066coll40/id/77.

78 Sinclair, "Seduction and the Myth of the Ideal Woman."

CHAPTER SIX

1 Daniel Pick, *Svengali's Web: The Alien Enchanter in Modern Culture* (London: Yale University Press, 2000), 66.

2 Irving knew exactly what he was doing to the impressionable Stoker. "The effects of his recitation upon Stoker was all that Irving had hoped," Irving's son, Laurence, would later write, "—as welcome as the effects of the 'Murder of Gonzago' on his uncle were to Hamlet."

Laurence Irving, *Henry Irving: The Actor and His World* (London: Faber and Faber, 1951), 279.

3 Du Maurier would later state that Florence Stoker was among the three most beautiful women he had ever met. *Punch*, September 11, 1886, "Filial Reproof"; *The Times*, March 6, 1934 (ON THE ONE HUNDREDTH ANNIVERSARY OF DU MAURIER'S BIRTH), citing E.V. Lucas's *The Creator of Trilby*.

4 Oscar Wilde, in contrast, praised Irving effusively for resisting the lure of public favor and staying true to his artistic visions: "With his marvellous and vivid personality, with a style that has really a true

colour-element in it, with his extraordinary power, not over mere mimicry but over imaginative and intellectual creation, Mr Irving, had his sole object been to give the public what it wanted, could have produced the commonest plays in the commonest manner, and made as much success and money as a man could possibly desire. But his object was not that. His object was to realize his own perfection as an artist, under certain conditions, and in certain forms of Art."
Oscar Wilde, *In Praise of Disobedience: The Soul of Man Under Socialism and Other Writings*, (New York: Verso, 2018), 28.

5 The Lyceum became one of the few places where the two men could be found together. By the 1880s Gladstone was going blind and had to be given a special seat in the prompt corner so he could follow the action. A very old and very frail Disraeli remained mischievous, however. When he came to see *The Corsican Brothers* in 1880, his companion Corry asked Stoker as they left the performance whether "we could have supper somewhere and ask some of the Coryphées to join us, as we used to do in Paris in the fifties?"
"Stoker hastened to explain that the ballet dancers at the Lyceum would be deeply shocked at such a suggestion and that Loveday had been driven frantic in trying to persuade them to overcome their suburban primness in the abandon of the bal masqué. . . . The Conservatives would be slow to change their view of the theatre as an Arcadia populated with captivating and warm-hearted nymphs who could be lured into 'cabinets particuliers' where their slippers, brimming with champagne, could be raised to Love, Life and Laughter."
Laurence Irving, *Henry Irving*, 363–64.

6 Horace Wyndham, *The Nineteen Hundreds* (London, 1922), 118.

7 The 1882 House of Lords select committee recorded the causes of mass juvenile prostitution: "A vicious demand for young girls; overcrowding in dwellings, and immorality arising therefrom; want of parental control, and in many cases parental example, profligacy, and immoral treatment; residence, in some cases, in brothels; the example and encouragement of other girls slightly older, and the sight of dress and money which their immoral habits have enabled them to obtain; the state of the streets in which little girls are allowed to run about, and become accustomed to the sight of open profligacy; and sometimes the contamination with vicious girls in schools."

8 *The Pall Mall Gazette*, Tuesday, July 28, 1885.

9 Josephine Butler was later one of the vice-presidents (the president was the Duke of Westminster) of the National Vigilance Association (NVA), an organization created to ensure the enforcement of the 1885 Criminal Law Amendment Act and the preeminent combatant of the white slave trade in the United Kingdom. The offices of the NVA were on 267 Strand—a short walk from the Lyceum.

10 Susan Kingsley Kent, *Sex and Suffrage in Britain, 1860–1914*, (Princeton University Press, 1987), 10, 120.

11 W.T. Stead, *If Christ came to Chicago!* (Review of Reviews, London, 1894), 262; John D'Emilio and Estelle B. Freedman, *Intimate Matters: A History of Sexuality in America* (University of Chicago Press, 1997), 152–53.

12 See also Oscar Wilde's criticism of sentimental philanthropy in "The Soul of Man Under Socialism": "Charity they feel to be a ridiculously inadequate mode of partial restitution, or a sentimental dole, usually accompanied by some impertinent attempt on the part of the sentimentalist to tyrannise over their private lives."
The bill was certainly regarded as a seduction statute by its most vigorous supporters. In response to an 1899 survey of European and North American seduction laws conducted by the International Congress on the White Slave Trade, the British delegation declared that the 1885 Criminal Law Amendment Act was the governing British law on such matters and "has been used to punish married men who have seduced girls under promise of marriage." Indeed, the successful campaign by Butler and Stead to introduce and enforce the 1885 law was the inspiration for Frances Willard and the WCTU in their campaign to increase the age of consent in American states discussed in Chapter 5. See: *The White Slave Trade: Transactions of the International Congress on the White Slave Trade*, (London: Office of the National Vigilance Association, 1899), 19, 60.

13 On of the prominent victims of the law in its early years was Captain Verney, MP, who *The Times* described as "conspicuous for his zeal in the 'purity movement' and for the unction of his language in discussing questions of morality, while he was leading a double life and methodically employing

a procuress in the service of his profligacy. . . . His evil practices were deliberate, systematic, and apparently long continued. His punishment is heavy, and the 12 months imprisonment is, perhaps, the lightest part of it. As Sir Charles Russell said:—'His position is lost, his rank in the Navy is gone, his honoured name has departed from him.'" "CAPTAIN VERNEY, M.P., pleaded guilty yesterday." *The Times*, Thursday, May 7, 1891.

14 Ironically, Stead was charged with abduction of a minor and tried under the new legal procedures stipulated in the Criminal Law Amendment Act of 1885. See: *The Times*, Wednesday, November 11, 1885. High-profile campaigns to release Stead were launched, including a direct appeal by Josephine Butler to the Home Secretary (see *The Times*, Friday, November 13, 1885), but Stead served his full six month sentence, the majority of it at Holloway Prison whence he continued to edit the *Pall Mall Gazette*. He took some pride in his imprisonment and each year would pose for photos in his old prison uniform to commemorate the day of his conviction.

15 Letter from Dighton Macnaughten Probyn to Henry Irving, July 4, 1885. Irving's own antipathy toward evangelical Christianity was shaped by his mother, an unbending Methodist, whodisowned her son for his decision to work in the theatre.

16 For Stead, as places of entertainment theatres were scenes of seduction; as places of business they were scenes of debauchment. For example, in the "Maiden Tribute" series: "It is said that at a certain notorious theatre no girl ever kept her virtue more than three months."

17 Through Watts, Terry met all the major figures in this circle: Millais, Rossetti (who was John Polidori's nephew; see Chapter 4), Hunt, and Leighton. She married Watts not long after the most famous Pre-Raphaelite muse, Elizabeth Siddal, died of a laudanum overdose. Siddal was most famous for being the model of Ophelia in Millais's famous painting. Despite her own immense success, Terry lived in the shadow of Siddal's legend and her own breakout performance was of Ophelia in Irving's *Hamlet*, the first play run at the Lyceum in 1878. Terry and Siddal's portraits (posing as Lady Macbeth and Ophelia respectively) can now be found on the same wall at the Tate Britain.

18 Nina Auerbach, *Ellen Terry: Player in Her Time* (London: Phoenix House 1987), 116–17.

19 "Strange Case Of Dr. Jekyll And Mr. Hyde," *The Times*, Monday, January 25, 1886; 13.

20 From the outset Lankester made it clear that he saw this law at work on human society:

"Any new set of conditions occurring to an animal which render its food and safety very easily attained, seem to lead as a rule to Degeneration ; just as an active healthy man sometimes degenerates when he becomes suddenly possessed of a fortune; or as Rome degenerated when possessed of the riches of the ancient world. The habit of parasitism clearly acts upon animal organisation in this way. Let the parasitic life once be secured, and away go legs, jaws, eyes, and ears; the active, highly-gifted crab, insect, or annelid may become a mere sac, absorbing nourishment and laying eggs." Edwin Lankester, *Degeneration: A Chapter in Darwinism*, (London: 1880).

21 TATTOOING IN FRANCE, *The Pall Mall Gazette*, Tuesday, October 25, 1881.

22 THE SCIENCE OF CRIME, *The Pall Mall Gazette*, Monday, October 10, 1887.

23 Letter in the British Museum. https://www.bl.uk/collection-items/anonymous-letter-to-city-of-london-police-about-jack-the-ripper. Also says: "I thought it Strange this Play Should have Commenced before the Murders for it is Really Something after the Same Stile. The Murders take place on Saturday nights Mr M never has A Performance on Saturday. The Murders Once Took Place on Friday & once Mr M Was to ill to Perform at the Saturday Morning Performance."

24 *Daily Telegraph*, Friday, October 12, 1888, Dramatic and Musical.

25 Stoker also knew another man suspected of being the murderer: his great friend Hall Caine's acquaintance Francis Tumblety.

26 *The Spectator*, October 6, 1888.

27 Laurence Irving, *Henry Irving*, 333–34.

28 *The Pall Mall Gazette*, September 8, 1888.

29 Neil R. Davison, "'The Jew' as Homme/Femme-Fatale: Jewish (Art)ifice, 'Trilby,' and Dreyfus," *Jewish Social Studies*, New Series, 8, No. 2/3 (Winter–Spring, 2002), 73–111.

"'The Jew' remained subversive, powerful yet morally inferior, and degeneratively feminized throughout the decade and beyond."

30 Lombroso, *Criminal Man*, 140; also see the Austrian delegation's comment on the white slave trade made in 1899: "The agents [of the white slave trade] themselves are invariably Jews. The victims are

not sent directly to Constantinople. . . . But they at length arrive in that city. From thence some are forwarded to Cairo, some to Trezibond: none of them ever come back to their native country." *The White Slave Trade*, 83.

31 "Is It Not Time?," *The Pall Mall Gazette*, October 16, 1883. See also: Willian Henry Wilkins, *The Alien Invasion*, Chapter 3, "Jewish Immigration." (London: 1892).

32 *Anti-Semitism in British Society: 1876–1939*, Colin Holmes, (New York: Holmes & Meier Publishers, 1979). For specific association with Ripper case, see *Jewish Chronicle*, October 12, 1888. Accessible one: http://www.casebook.org/press_reports/jewish_chronicle/jc881012.html.

33 See Anthony S. Wohl, "Dizzi-Ben-Dizzi": Disraeli as Alien, *Journal of British Studies*, 34, no. 3, Victorian Subjects (July, 1995), 375–411; Pick, *Svengali's Web*, 130–31: Carlyle on Disraeli: "a superlative Hebrew conjurer, spellbinding all the great Lords, great parties, great interests of England."

34 Christopher J. Probst, *Demonizing the Jews: Luther and the Protestant Church in Nazi Germany*, (Bloomington, IN: Indiana University Press, 2012), 48–49; Luther called the Jews "a whoring and murderous people," "bloodthirsty bloodhounds and murderers of all Christendom," witches and magicians capable of "conjuring signs, figures, and the tetragrammaton of the name, that is, with idolatry, envy and conceit."

35 The epicenter of late-Victorian discourse on hyponosis was the Parisian hospital of Salpêtrière, where Jean-Martin Charcot conducted his famous experiments on "hysterical" women. In 1885 Sigmund Freud was one of his students. The fissure within the field of hypnosis was between the "Parisian school" led by Charcot and the "Nancy school" led by Hippolyte Bernheim. The latter argued that all women were susceptible to the power of suggestion and hypnosis, not just hysterics. This debate was followed in England and was the subject of debate at the Second International Congress of Psychology in London in 1892. Pick, *Svengali's Web*, 66–67.
  Charcot is directly referred to in *Dracula* during a conversation between Seward and Van Helsing: *"Yes," I said. "Charcot has proved that pretty well." He smiled as he went on: "Then you are satisfied as to it. Yes? And of course then you understand how it act, and can follow the mind of the great Charcot—alas that he is no more!—into the very soul of the patient that he influence. No? Then, friend John, am I to take it that you simply accept fact, and are satisfied to let from premise to conclusion be a blank? No? Then tell me—for I am student of the brain—how you accept the hypnotism and reject the thought reading. Let me tell you, my friend, that there are things done to-day in electrical science which would have been deemed unholy by the very men who discovered electricity—who would themselves not so long before have been burned as wizards. There are always mysteries in life."* See also: Ralph M. Leck, *Vita Sexualis* (Champaign: Illinois University Press, 2016). Jean-Martin Charcot's 1882 *Inversion du sens génital et autres Perversions sexuelles* was one of the first books to link degeneration with sexual deviance, which becomes a trope in French medical and scientific discourse in the last decade of the nineteenth century.

36 The geographic reach and temporal endurance of this canard is remarkable. When Olga Ivinskaya was questioned about her romantic association with the poet Boris Pasternak in Moscow's Lubyanka prison in 1949, her interrogator expressed disbelief that a Russian woman could be attracted to a Jewish man: "I can't believe that a Russian woman like you could really be in love with this old Jew—there must be some ulterior motive here! I've seen him myself. You can't love him. He's just mesmerised you, or something." Anne Pasternak, *Lara*, (London: William Collins, 2016), 98.

37 Hypnotism was also posited as an explanation for the Ripper killings, either as a tool for the murderer to use on his victims or as a device used to compel the murderer to kill. See, for example, *The Evening News*, October 16, 1888: HAS THE MISCREANT BEEN HYPNOTISED? and the *Daily Chronicle*: "Hypnotism and Crime." For the connection made between hypnotism and crime see: Ruth Harris, "Murder Under Hypnosis," in *The Anatomy of Madness*, Vol. 2, ed. W. F. Bynum, R. Porter, and M. Shepherd (London: Tavistock, 1985); for a contemporary account of the connection between seduction and hypnosis see Ernest Mesnet, *Outrages Against Modesty* (1890).

38 "Svengali's vanity, treacherousness, selfishness, personal uncleanliness and so forth," George Orwell observed, "are constantly connected with the fact that he is a Jew." *As I Please*, George Orwell, *Tribune*, December 6, 1946.

39 Jonathan Freedman, *The Temple of Culture: Assimilation and Anti-Semitism in Literary Anglo-America* (Oxford University Press, 2000), 91–92.

40 Jeannette L. and Joseph B. *Gilder, eds., Trilbyana: The rise and progress of a popular novel* (New York: The Critic, 1895), 8.

41 "No such magnificent or seductive apparition has ever been seen before or since on any stage or platform—not even Miss Ellen Terry as the priestess of Artemis in the late Laureate's play, *The Cup*." Trilby, p209 Nina Auerbach argues that Terry was in fact the inspiration for Trilby. When she was newly wed to artist George Watts in the 1860s, Du Maurier had been a visitor to her husband's home at Little Holland House and had been scathing of the pretentious old artists who gathered there and the women who fawned over them. Whether this image of the teenage Terry—then Nelly Watts—as the beautiful plaything of older, bohemian men survived the thirty year interval between his visits and the publication of *Trilby* is hard to know, but alluring nonetheless. See: Auerbach, *Ellen Terry*, 109.

42 *The Times*, Friday, May 28, 1897.

43 Rossetti had himself indulged in some pretty ghoulish antics in his time. In 1860 Rossetti had married Elizabeth Siddal, the Pre-Raphaelite muse and model. In 1862 Siddal had died of a laudanum overdose and Rossetti had buried her with a notebook of his unpublished poetry, much of which concerned his love for her, nestled amid her golden hair. In 1869 he decided he wanted the notebook back and had her corpse exhumed by the light of an enormous fire lit by her grave in Highgate Cemetery. According to Hall Caine, her body had not decomposed and they found her as beautiful as ever, the volume of poetry still in her hair. This was retrieved, the body returned to the ground and the verses returned to Rossetti. It is not clear whether Stoker knew about this story, though given Cain's role in recording the event for posterity, and given that Rossetti was long dead by the time *Dracula* was written, it is plausible that he told Stoker at some point during the writing process or before. He could also have heard it from Ellen Terry who was a part of the Pre-Raphaelite circle as a young woman. William Michael Rossetti, *Dante Gabriel Rossetti; his family-letters, with a memoir* (1895), 274–75.

44 "With his left hand he held both Mrs. Harker's hands, keeping them away with her arms at full tension; his right hand gripped her by the back of the neck, forcing her face down on his bosom. Her white nightdress was smeared with blood, and a thin stream trickled down the man's bare breast which was shown by his torn-open dress. The attitude of the two had a terrible resemblance to a child forcing a kitten's nose into a saucer of milk to compel it to drink." For a critical discussion of this scene and others see: Dejan Kuzmanovic, "Vampiric Seduction and Vicissitudes of Masculine Identity in Bram Stoker's *Dracula*," *Victorian Literature and Culture*, 37, no. 2 (2009), 411–25.

45 Stoker had a personal connection with the region through his brother, George, who had served as a doctor there during the Russo-Turkish war and published a book recounting the experience. David J Skal, *Something in the Blood: The Untold Story of Bram Stoker*, (New York: Liveright, 2016), 109.

46 *Spectator*, November 10, 1888, "Transylvania" book review. Interest in the region was piqued in this period by the "Eastern Question," a slow-moving geopolitical crisis generated by the decline of the Ottoman Empire. The English public's concern with the Eastern Question helped stoke mainstream anti-Semitism, partially because Disraeli was largely indifferent to the matter, which his more scurrilous critics, Gladstone included, alleged reflected his Jewish indifference to the suffering of Christians in the Ottoman domains. See: Anthony Julius, *Trials of the Diaspora: A History of Anti-Semitism in England* (Oxford University Press, 2010), 264–65.

47 Dracula: "a tall thin man, with a beaky nose and black moustache and pointed beard"; Svengali: "bold, brilliant, black eyes, with long heavy lids, a thin, sallow face, and a beard of burnt-up black, which grew almost from under his eyelids; and over it his moustache, a shade lighter, fell in two long spiral twists." See: Bram Dijkstra, *Idols of Perversity* (Oxford University Press, 1986), 343.

48 Stoker had used anti-Semitic tropes in his other novels. *The Watter's Mou'* (1895) features the wicked German-Jewish money lender Solomon Mendoza, an "elderly man with a bald head, keen eyes, a ragged grey beard, a hooked nose, and an evil smile."

49 Historian Anthony Julius notes that anti-Semitic discourse in 1890s England attached itself to the Boer War, which was allegedly orchestrated by and for Jewish "gold bugs" intent on securing the mineral wealth of the Transvaal. See: Julius, *Trials of the Diaspora*, 271.

50 There is an interesting if somewhat opaque allusion to Dracula's Jewishness in his ability to turn into a wolf. Jews had long been associated with magical powers, including the ability to assume animal form. "The Discoverie of Witchcraft," a 1584 treatise on witches includes a description of "one Bajanus a Jew, being the sonne of Simeon, which could, when list, turne himselfe into a wolf." It is of course

highly improbable that Stoker would have been familiar with this obscure text, but he did know *The Merchant of Venice* and may have absorbed, by osmosis if nothing else, Gratiano's attack on Shylock in from Act IV, Scene I:

> *O, be thou damn'd, inexecrable dog!*
> *And for thy life let justice be accused.*
> *Thou almost makest me waver in my faith*
> *To hold opinion with Pythagoras,*
> *That souls of animals infuse themselves*
> *Into the trunks of men: thy currish spirit*
> *Govern'd a wolf, who, hang'd for human slaughter,*
> *Even from the gallows did his fell soul fleet,*
> *And, whilst thou lay'st in thy unhallow'd dam,*
> *Infused itself in thee; for thy desires*
> *Are wolvish, bloody, starved and ravenous.*

51 Max Nordau, German-Jewish author whose best-known work, *Degeneration,* was published in England in 1895. Stoker would not have to had read Nordau to be familiar with the broad contours of his theory of cultural and metaphysical decay. It includes a sustained attack on Ibsen along lines illustrative of what many contemporaries found objectionable in the playwright's work. Nordau saw in Ibsen's plays "such unqualified approval of all feminine depravities, was bound to secure the applause of those women who in the viragoes of Ibsen's drama—hysterical, nymphomaniacal, perverted in maternal instinct—recognise either their own portrait or the ideal of development of their degenerate imagination." He also considered the proliferation of ghost stories that include themes of "hypnotism, telepathy, somnambulism" a hallmark of the collapse of high culture—ironic, given the positive allusion to him in *Dracula.* George Bernard Shaw's *The Quintessence of Ibsenism* (1891) made the robust case for the connection between Ibsen and "the woman question." For a more balanced, modern take on the relationship between Ibsen and late-nineteenth century feminism see: Joan Templeton, "The Doll House Backlash: Criticism, Feminism, and Ibsen," *PMLA* 104, no. 1 (January, 1989), 28–40.

52 "In some faculties of mind he has been, and is, only a child," and also "The criminal always work at one crime—that is the true criminal who seems predestinate to crime, and who will of none other. This criminal has not full man-brain. He is clever and cunning and resourceful; but he be not of man-stature as to brain. He be of child-brain in much. Now this criminal of ours is predestinate to crime also; he, too, have child-brain, and it is of the child to do what he have done. The little bird, the little fish, the little animal learn not by principle, but empirically; and when he learn to do, then there is to him the ground to start from to do more."

53 Pick, *Svengali's Web,* 63–66, and Harris, "Murder Under Hypnosis, 207, 217–18; the latter contains an account of the 1878 rape trial of a French Jewish doctor, Paul Lévy, who allegedly used hypnosis to molest a young, gentile girl. He received ten years imprisonment. The case was referred to in the more famous Bompard trial of 1890 in which the defendant, Gabrielle Bompard, alleged she had been hypnotized by her lover, Michel Eyraud, and made an accessory to the murder of Toussaint-Augustin Gouffé while the powerless tool of Eyraud.

54 As defined by Thomas Hardy the New Woman was:
"The woman who was coming into notice in her thousands every year—the woman of the feminist movement—the slight, pale "bachelor" girl—the intellectualized, emancipated bundle of nerves that modern conditions were producing, mainly in cities as yet; who does not recognize the necessity for most of her sex to follow marriage as a profession, and boast themselves as superior people because they are licensed to be loved on the premises." Thomas Hardy, postscript to *Jude the Obscure,* first edition 1895.

55 There were inevitable comparisons made with the French Revolution. See the *Quarterly Review* on the "New Woman" in 1894: "she advances, with drums beating and colours flying, to the sound also of the Phrygian flute, a disordered array, but nowise daunted, resolute in her determination to end what she is pleased to define as the slavery of one-half the human race."
Quarterly Review (1894) 179, quoted in, Elaine Showalter, *Sexual Anarchy*, (London: Bloomsbury, 1991), 39.

56 The New Woman, and Other Emancipated Woman Plays, (Oxford University Press, 1998).

57 DRAMA AT ROYAL ACADEMY, *The Era*, Saturday, May 18, 1895.

58 Edy helped radicalize her mother, who by 1914 was boasting to Australian journalists "Of course you know I'm a suffragette. Of course I am and so is my daughter Edith Craig." From 1909 Edy was involved with the Actresses' Franchise League and directed *A Pageant of Great Women* which opened on November 12, 1909 featuring Ellen Terry as eighteenth-century Drury Lane actress Nance Oldfield. See: Michael Holroyd, *A Strange and Eventful History: The Dramatic Lives of Ellen Terry, Henry Irving, and their Remarkable Families* (London: Chatto & Windus, 2008), 426, 432.

59 "Woman, however, if physically and mentally normal, and properly educated, has but little sensual desire. If it were otherwise, marriage and family life would be empty words. As yet the man who avoids women, and the woman who seeks men are sheer anomalies."
Psychopathia sexualis, Dr. R. v. Krafft-Ebing; only authorized English adaptation of the twelfth German edition by F. J. Rebman,1893.

60 In *Man and Superman* John Tanner, the Don Juan stand-in, accuses Ann Whitefield of being a vampire in the play's final line.

61 In Chapter VIII: "We had a capital 'severe tea' at Robin Hood's Bay in a sweet little old-fashioned inn, with a bow-window right over the seaweed-covered rocks of the strand. I believe we should have shocked the "New Woman" with our appetites. Men are more tolerant, bless them! Then we walked home with some, or rather many, stoppages to rest, and with our hearts full of a constant dread of wild bulls. Lucy was really tired, and we intended to creep off to bed as soon as we could. The young curate came in, however, and Mrs. Westenra asked him to stay for supper. Lucy and I had both a fight for it with the dusty miller; I know it was a hard fight on my part, and I am quite heroic. I think that some day the bishops must get together and see about breeding up a new class of curates, who don't take supper, no matter how they may be pressed to, and who will know when girls are tired. Lucy is asleep and breathing softly. She has more colour in her cheeks than usual, and looks, oh, so sweet. If Mr. Holmwood fell in love with her seeing her only in the drawing-room, I wonder what he would say if he saw her now. Some of the "New Women" writers will some day start an idea that men and women should be allowed to see each other asleep before proposing or accepting. But I suppose the New Woman won't condescend in future to accept; she will do the proposing herself."

62 After Marie Stopes published *Married Love*, a celebration of female sexuality, in 1918 she received an angry letter from an anonymous aristocrat enraged at her proselytization of the joys of sex. "Once you give women a taste for these things," he wrote, "they become vampires, and you have let loose vampires into decent men's homes." Quoted in Carol Dyhouse, *Heartthrobs* (Oxford University Press, 2017). William J. Robinson of Bronx hospital in his *Married Life and Happiness* (1922) describes wives who want sex every two weeks/ten days as normal but:
"there is the opposite type of woman, who is a great danger to the health and even the very life of her husband. I refer to the hypersensual woman, to the wife with an excessive sexuality. It is to her that the name vampire can be applied in its literal sense. Just as the vampire sucks the blood of its victims in their sleep while they are alive, so does the woman vampire suck the life blood and exhaust the vitality of her male partner—or victim. And some of them—the pronounced type—are utterly without pity or consideration." Dijkstra, *Idols of Perversity*, 344.

63 One prominent male ally of the women's movement was W.T. Stead who voiced his support in an article entitled "The Novel of the Modern Woman" (*Review of Reviews,* 10, 1894). The New Woman was only claiming "rights, privileges, and responsibilities of a human being," he wrote, "[she] is not going back to her old position. Through whatever stormy seas and across no matter what burning desert marked by the skeletons and haunted by the ghosts of those who have fallen by the way, she will press on, fleeing from monogamic prostitution of loveless marriage and the hideous outrage of enforced maternity." A.L. Ardis, *New Women, New Novels* (New Brunswick, NJ: Rutgers University Press, 1990), 21–22.

64 Ruth Brandon, *The New Woman And The Old Men: Love, Sex and The Woman Question*, (London: Secker & Warburg, 1990), 197.

65 Sheila Rowbotham, *Dreamers of a New Day* (London: Verso, 2010), 61.

66 Charlotte Despard, *Woman in the New Era* (The Suffrage Shop, 1910), 32–33.

67 *The New Womanhood*, Winnifred Harper Cooley, 1904

68 Rowbotham, Dreamers, 65.

69 Christabel Pankhurst, *The Great Scourge and How To End It*, (1913).

70 See Sir T.S. Clouston: "The ideals which would exalt culture above motherhood are suicidal and should be abandoned. It will not do to say that women should have a choice either to take up culture and intellectual work, whether it has a lessened capacity for motherhood or not, or to select domestic life. Mothers of high brain power are as much needed for an advancing race as fathers—rather more so, in fact."
Quoted in: Carol Dyhouse, *Girls Growing Up in Late Victorian and Edwardian England*, 154.

71 David J. Skal, *Hollywood Gothic* (New York: W.W. Norton & Company, 1990), 43–44, 54–55; of course, at least one copy survived this purge and the film remains in circulation.

72 Ewers would later become an in-house novelist for the Nazi elite, writing, in one instance, a hagiographic portrayal of Nazi martyr Horst Wessel at Hitler's request. See Eric Kurlander, *Hitler's Monsters: A Supernatural History of the Third Reich*, (New Haven: Yale University Press, 2016), 79.

73 Siegfried Kracauer, *From Caligari to Hitler* (London: Dennis Dobson, 1947), 77–79.

74 See Kurlander, *Hitler's Monsters*, chapters 1 & 2.

75 Adolf Leschnitzer, *The Magic Background of Modern Anti-Semitism* (International Universities Press, 1956), 144. Leschnitzer notes that this magical conception of Jews allowed for the suspension of certain logical precepts—clear causation, consistency of argument, generalization of behaviour to large, inchoate groups—which allowed for aggression toward an out-group without recourse to reality.

76 Kurlander, *Hitler's Monsters*, 42.

77 One of Hitler's favorite rhetorical turns was to describe Jews as "*Schadlinge am Volkskorper*," "Parasites on the Body Politic." The German *Volkskorper* better captures the anthropomorphic imagery. Combined with the near constant equation of Jewish men with sexual predation the listener's thoughts are practically led to the image of the vampire feasting on a sleeping women's arteries. Robert Gellately, *The Gestapo and German Society* (Oxford University Press, 1990), 92.

78 The assumption that Jews ran the white slave trade in Central Europe was, by the 1920s, several decades old. "The majority of unfortunate girls who form the prostitutes of the larger towns have fallen through Jewish depravity," Theodor Fritsch wrote in *Antisemiten-Katechismus* (1893), "the notorious 'girl commerce' will soon be carried on exclusively by the Jews."

79 Dennis E. Showalter, *Little Man, What Now?: Der Sturmer in the Weimar Republic* (Hamden, CT: Archon Books, 1982), 100.

80 Theodor Fritsch *The Riddle Of The Jews' Success* (1927), 191.

81 Fritsch, *Riddle Of The Jews' Success*, 260.

82 This had been a recurring theme of *Der Sturmer*'s depiction of Jews as constantly seeking to entrap German women into sex through ostentatious displays of wealth. Such encounters always resulted in the ruin of the Gentile woman. See for instance "The Talmudist" in which a brutish Jewish lothario dresses himself while an Aryan swoons in post-coital shame in a soiled hotel bed. Alcohol lies around the room. The caption says: "The Goy's Temple is Our Toilet." (Showalter, *Little Man, What Now?* 89.) Another cartoon shows "The Beginning"—a Weimar flapper with a bob, professional clothes, and a clutch, hopping into a sleek car driven by a Jew—and "The End"— the same woman shivering on the street, now a prostitute with her Jewish pimp leering over her shoulder. http://research.calvin.edu/german-propaganda-archive/images/sturmer/sturm06.jpg.

83 James Q. Whitman, *Hitler's American Model* (Princeton University Press, 2017).

84 Coincidentally, in the same year as the Prussian Memorandum was published, an anti-Semitic forgery now known as the "Franklin Prophecy" appeared in a pro-Nazi paper in the United States. It purported to be an extract from a "lost" speech given by Benjamin Franklin in 1787 and contained the following description of Jews:
"*They are vampires and vampires cannot live on other vampires—they cannot live among themselves. They must live among Christians and others who do not belong to their race.*"

85 One of the priorities of the exclusionary campaign was to exclude Jews from the practice of medicine. This had a clear sexual subtext as anti-Semitic propagandists believed that the Jewish monopoly on medical practice was a ruse to access Aryan bodies for sexual purposes. "Now we know why the Jew uses every artifice of seduction in order to ravish German girls at as early an age as possible," Julius

Streicher had written in *Der Sturmer*'s New Year's issue of 1935, "while the Jewish doctor rapes his patient while they are under anaesthetic. He wants the German girl and the German woman to absorb the alien sperm of a Jew." Louis W. Bondy, *Racketeers of Hatred* (London: Newman Wolsey, 1946), 48.

Nazi's also believed that Jewish doctors were responsible for the undermining of the Aryan race through the provision of abortions. "The racial hatred Jews had for their Aryan host people extended to the growing life in a mother's womb. Jewish scoundrels made this part of the programs of political parties. How many millions of unborn children and how many hundreds of thousands of mothers fell prey to the greed and racial hatred of Jewish doctors?"

Hanns Oberlindober, Ein Vaterland, das allen gehört! Briefe an Zeitgenossen aus zwölf Kampfjahren (Munich: Zentralverlag der NSDAP, 1940), 152–67; The "Decent" Jew: A Letter to an Englishman, 1937.

86 See in connection with this Daniel Goldhagen on anti-Jewish legislation and social death. Daniel Goldhagen, *Hitler's Willing Executioners*, 1996.

87 Kurlander, *Hitler's Monsters*, 81–83.

CHAPTER SEVEN

1 See: *The Communist Manifesto*: "Our bourgeois, not content with having the wives and daughters of their proletarians at their disposal, not to speak of common prostitutes, take the greatest pleasure in seducing each other's wives."

2 Quoted in Kristen Ghodsee, *Why Women Have Better Sex Under Socialism*, (London: Vintage, 2018), 116.

3 Bellamy saw a eugenic benefit in allowing women to be the arbiters of the sexual marketplace under socialism: "You were speaking, a day or two ago, of the physical superiority of our people to your contemporaries. Perhaps more important than any of the causes I mentioned then as tending to race purification has been the effect of untrammeled sexual selection upon the quality of two or three successive generations. I believe that when you have made a fuller study of our people you will find in them not only a physical, but a mental and moral improvement. It would be strange if it were not so, for not only is one of the great laws of nature now freely working out the salvation of the race, but a profound moral sentiment has come to its support. Individualism, which in your day was the animating idea of society, not only was fatal to any vital sentiment of brotherhood and common interest among living men, but equally to any realization of the responsibility of the living for the generation to follow. To-day this sense of responsibility, practically unrecognized in all previous ages, has become one of the great ethical ideas of the race, reinforcing, with an intense conviction of duty, the natural impulse to seek in marriage the best and noblest of the other sex. The result is, that not all the encouragements and incentives of every sort which we have provided to develop industry, talent, genius, excellence of whatever kind, are comparable in their effect on our young men with the fact that our women sit aloft as judges of the race and reserve themselves to reward the winners. . . . Our women have risen to the full height of their responsibility as the wardens of the world to come, to whose keeping the keys of the future are confided. Their feeling of duty in this respect amounts to a sense of religious consecration. It is a cult in which they educate their daughters from childhood."

4 Ghodsee, *Why Women*, 118–19. It was this "communist morality" Yevgeny Zamyatin was satirizing in his great dystopian novel *We* (1921), in which the citizens ("ciphers") of the One State have free sexual access to one another through the state distribution of pink tickets:

"Having subjugated Hunger . . . the One State began an offensive against the other master of the world—against Love. Finally, even this natural force was also conquered, i.e., organized and mathematicised, and around three hundred years ago, our historical *Lex Sexualis* was proclaimed: 'Each cipher has the right to any other cipher as a sexual product.'" *We*, Yevgeny Zamyatin, (London: Vintage, 2007), 21.

5 Herbert Marcuse, *Eros and Civilization: A Philosophical Inquiry into Freud* (Boston: Beacon Press, 1955), 202.

6 Marcuse, *Eros and Civilization*, 198.

7 Marcuse always deftly denied that he was in anyway the intellectual leader of the New Left, though he

did coyly admit on at least one occasion that "it would have been better to call me not the father, but the grandfather of the New Left." His influence on the student movement has likely been overstated even if his theories were taken seriously by the intellectual elite of the new left-wing and radical movements of the sixties and seventies. He was in any case, an odd choice of hero for the *Easy Rider* generation, this man who once described the motorcycle as "a fascist invention which equates speed and power with virility and besides it makes such a dreadful noise and pollutes terribly." See: Tom Bourne, "Herbert Marcuse: Grandfather of the New Left" *Change* 11, no. 6 (Sep., 1979); and Herbert Marcuse, *Philosophy, Psychoanalysis and Emancipation, Collected Papers of Herbert Marcuse*, Volume 5, eds. Douglas Kellner and Clayton Prince (Abingdon: Routledge, 2011), 201–05.

8 See Michel Houellebecq, *Whatever* (London: Serpent's Tail ,1998), 40: "This progressive effacement of human relationships is not without certain problems for the novel. How, in point of fact, would one handle the narration of those unbridled passions, stretching over many years, and at times making their effect felt on several generations? We're a long way from *Wuthering Heights*, to say the least. The novel form is not conceived for depicting indifference or nothingness; a flatter, more terse and dreary discourse would need to be invented."

9 Francis Fukuyama, *Great Disruption: Human Nature and the Reconstitution of Social Order*, (New York: The Free Press, 1999.) "The changing nature of work tended to substitute mental for physical labor, thereby propelling millions of women into the workplace and undermining the traditional understandings on which the family had been based. . . . [B]roadly speaking, the technological change that brings about what economist Joseph Schumpeter called 'creative destruction' in the marketplace caused similar disruption in the world of social relationships." (5–6)

10 Shere Hite argued for the primacy of economic factors to the success or failure of the sexual revolution. "It is important to remember that *you cannot decree women to be 'sexually free' when they are not economically free*; to do so is to put them into a more vulnerable position that ever." See: Shere Hite, *The Hite Report: A Nationwide Study on Female Sexuality* (London: Talmy Franklin, 1977), 305. This was anticipated by Kate Millet in 1970:
"The goal of revolution would be a permissive single standard of sexual freedom, and one uncorrupted by the crass exploitative economic bases of traditional sexual alliances." Quoted in: David Allyn, *Make Love Not War: The Sexual Revolution: An Unfettered History* (Boston: Little, Brown, 2000.), 104. A similar point is made at the end of Alix Kates Shulman's best-selling 1972 novel *Memoirs of An Ex-Prom Queen* when Sasha, the female protagonist, complains: "To find myself at thirty locked under a dryer eagerly studying ads in magazines while I worry about the sitter and my husband is away on a business trip; now, after my schemes and triumphs, my visions and dares, to be, without income or skill, dependent on a man and a fading skin—it can only be the fulfilment of a curse!" *Memoirs of An Ex-Prom Queen,* Alix Kates Shulman, (London: Serpent's Tail, 2019), 249.

11 See, Véronique Mortaigne, *Je T'Aime: The Legendary Love Story of Jane Birkin and Serge Gainsbourg*, (London: Icon, 2019). For a contemporaneous perspective on the cultural influences of the sexual revolution see the brilliant scene in John Updike's *Couples* in which the adulterous Piet surveys his lover's husband's bookshelf:
"Curiously he would finger and skim through Thorne's bedside shelf—Henry Miller in tattered Paris editions, Sigmund Freud in Modern Library. *Our Lady of the Flowers* and *Memoirs of a Woman of Pleasure* fresh from Grove Press, inspirational psychology by the Menningers, a dove-grey handbook on hypnosis, *Psychopathia Sexualis* in textbook format, a delicately tinted and stiff-paged album smuggled from Kyoto, the poems of Sappho as published by Peter Pauper, the unexpurgated Arabian Nights in two boxed volumes, works by Theodor Reik and Wilhelm Reich, various tawdry paperbacks." John Updike, *Couples* (London: Penguin, 1969), 63–64.

12 See Kate Millett, *Sexual Politics* (London: Rupert Hart-Davis, 1971), 63. "Save for [the pill], the 'New Woman' of the twenties was as well off, and possibly better provided with sexual freedom, than the woman of the fifties."

13 Perhaps not unrelated to the foregrounding of Enovid in the high cultural discourse of the sexual revolution was the high rates of uptake among the demographic consuming and producing such literature. By 1965 more than 80 percent of unmarried, white, non-Catholic college graduates, age 20 to 24 had used oral contraceptives. See: Elizabeth Siegel Watkins, *On the Pill: A Social History of Oral Contraceptives 1950–1970*, (Baltimore, Johns Hopkins University Press, 1998), 34.

14 There is a comparable trend in divorce, which was not legalized in Italy until 1970, Spain until 1981, Ireland until 1985, and Malta until 2011. See: https://ec.europa.eu/eurostat/statistics-explained/pdfscache/6790.pdf.

15 Roy Baumeister and Kathleen Vohs, "Sexual Economics: Sex as Female Resource for Social Exchange in Heterosexual Interactions," *Personality and Social Psychology Review* 8, No. 4 (2004), 339–63.

16 In Nora Ephron's 1983 novel *Heartburn,* Nora Samstat's verdict on the sexual revolution makes much the same point in pithier terms: "Their wives went out into the world, free at last, single again, and discovered the horrible truth: that they were sellers in a buyer's market, and that the major concrete achievement of the women's movement in the 1970s was the Dutch treat."
Nora Ephron, *Heartburn* (London: Virago, 2018), 81.

17 Margaret Drabble, "The Sexual Revolution," *The Guardian,* October 11, 1967; Elizabeth Hardwick, "Seduction and Betrayal," originally published in the *New York Review of Books,* May and June 1973.

18 Stuart Jeffries describes Marcuse speaking in the summer of 1964 at a conference on the island of Korcula in Croatia:
"Why should the overthrow of the existing order be of vital necessity for people who own, or can hope to own, good clothes, a well-stocked larder, a TV set, a car, a house and so on, all within the existing order?" and quotes him in *One-Dimensional Man* (1964):
"Here, the so-called equalization of class distinctions reveals its ideological function. If the worker and his boss enjoy the same television program and visit the same resort places, if the typist is as attractively made up as the daughter of her employer, if the Negro owns a Cadillac, if they all read the same newspaper, then this assimilation indicates not the disappearance of classes, but the extent to which the needs and satisfactions that serve the preservation of the Establishment are shared by the underlying population." Stuart Jeffries, *Hotel Abyss: The Lives of the Frankfurt School,* (London: Verso, 2016), 303, 305.

19 The factors he lists, which are those Angela Davis had identified in "Women and Capitalism" (1971), are the: alleviation of heavy physical labor, the reduction of labor time, the production of pleasant and cheap clothing, the liberalization of sexual morality, birth control, general education.

20 See "Marxism and Feminism" (1974); Marcuse pinned his hopes on the revolutionary potential of feminism as a political movement: "Feminism is a revolt against decaying capitalism, against the historical obsolescence of the capitalist mode of production. This is the precarious link between Utopia and reality: the social ground for the movement as a potentially radical and revolutionary force is there; this is the hard core of the dream. But capitalism is still capable of keeping it a dream, of suppressing the transcending forces which strive for the subversion of the inhuman values of our civilization."

21 This was the same argument Shulamith Firestone made in *The Dialectic of Sex* (1970) where she decried the "pseudo-liberation" of Western women: "They were told then as we still are now, 'You've got civil rights, short skirts and sexual liberty. You've won your revolution. What more do you want?' But the 'revolution' had been won within a system organized around the patriarchal nuclear family. And as Herbert Marcuse in *Eros and Civilisation* shows, within such a repressive structure only a more sophisticated repression can result ('repressive de-sublimation')."

22 Pierre Klossowski, *Living Currency,* trans. Jordan Levinson; Jean-Francois Lyotard, *The Libidinal Economy,* trans. Iain Hamilton Grant (Bloomington: Indiana University Press, 1993); Jean Baudrillard, *Seduction,* trans. Bryan Singer (New World Perspectives, 1990).

23 Michel Houellebecq, *H.P. Lovecraft: Against the World, Against Life* (London: Weidenfeld & Nicolson, 2006), 115–16.

24 Houellebecq, *Whatever,* 99.

25 Michel Houellebecq, *Atomized* (London: Vintage, 2001), 161–62.

26 https://www.vox.com/world/2018/4/25/17277496/incel-toronto-attack-alek-minassian.; https://edition.cnn.com/2014/05/24/us/elliot-rodger-video-transcript/index.html.; https://nypost.com/2019/06/21/air-force-warns-about-nationwide-threat-of-incels/.; https://www.vox.com/platform/amp/the-highlight/2019/4/16/18287446/incel-definition-reddit.

27 Houellebecq, *Whatever,* 148. "No civilization, no epoch has been capable of developing such a quantity of bitterness in its subjects. In that sense we are living through unprecedented times."

See also: https://www.theatlantic.com/ideas/archive/2019/04/happiness-recession-causing-sex-depression/586405/; https://www.theatlantic.com/magazine/archive/2018/12/the-sex-recession/573949/.

28 Pierre Bourdieu, "The Forms of Capital," in *Handbook of Theory and Research for the Sociology of Education* ed. J. Richardson (Westport, CT: Greenwood, 1986), 241–58; Catherine Hakim, "Erotic Capital," *European Sociological Review* 26, no. 5 (2010).

29 Weber's own methods were unabashedly amoral and casually misogynistic. They also relied heavily on the cultural tropes of his day. For example: "March in a peace demonstration, even if you're secretly for war. I've heard countless stories of guys who've picked up fantastic broads at peace demonstrations." (163); "One of the best ways to compliment a woman is to tell her you dig something about her she had no idea was particularly digable." (60); "What else will make you look sexy? Experiment. When you find something that works you'll know it from the way chicks start looking at you. Try on some of the new wild clothes. Bell bottoms and English boots and wide ties. Wear a body shirt or leather dungarees or a groovy vest. Be dramatic. Leave the top button on your shirt open. Wear shades or those new rimless glasses. *Think* sexy. Think, I am a virile male animal." (p43); "Now you know damn well that the way these girls would like you to feel is not necessarily the way you're going to feel. Half the time you want to pick up a girl it's because she's got a set of breasts that makes you dizzy. Or the face of a movie star. Or the hips of a belly dancer. Not because she has some magnetic inner quality. . . . But you can't let them know that. You've got to pretend otherwise." (53)

30 Randall Rothenber, "Copywriter's Foray Into Book Writing," *New York Times*, May 15, 1990; Eric Weber, *How To Pick Up Girls!* (New York: Bantam Books, 1977), 17; Suzanne Chazin, "Some Women Would Tell Eric Weber to Buzz Off, but Men Are Buying His Line on Picking Up Girls," *People*, August 17, 1981.

31 Neil Strauss, "He Aims! He Shoots! Yes!!" *New York Times*, January 25, 2004.

32 The counterpoint to this mathematical attitude is a profound distrust of emotion (what Locke and Hume would have called the passions). See *The Game*, 22: "All your emotions are going to try to fuck you up," Mystery continued. "They are there to try to confuse you, so know right now that they cannot be trusted at all. You will feel shy sometimes, and self-conscious, and you must deal with it like you deal with a pebble in your shoe. It's uncomfortable, but you ignore it. It's not part of the equation." This was an attitude adopted by Mystery's successors. In its promotional material Real Social Dynamics promised to "Make girls beg to sleep with you after short-circuiting their emotional and logical mind."

33 Gloria Steinem, "The Moral Disarmament of Betty Coed," *Esquire*, September, 1962; interestingly Eric Weber made much the same point in his landmark seduction manual: "Women have come a long way recently. They're learning they have the same right to sexual freedom that men have. In fact I think it's going to be harder for men to adjust to the sexual revolution than it is for women." *How to Pick Up Women!*, 22.

34 Hite, *The Hite Report*, 311, 319, 320.

35 Molly Haskell, *From Reverence to Rape: The Treatment of Women in the Movies* (London: New English Library, 1975), 327–28

36 See Chapter 5

37 Linda R. Hirshman and Jane E. Larson, *Hard Bargains: The Politics of Sex*, 165.

38 Jane E. Larson, "'Women Understand so Little, They Call My Good Nature "Deceit"': A Feminist Rethinking of Seduction," *Columbia Law Review* 93, no. 2 (Mar., 1993), 374–472.

39 https://www.theatlantic.com/entertainment/archive/2015/10/neil-strauss-the-game/409789/.

40 https://www.theguardian.com/lifeandstyle/2015/oct/10/neil-strauss-the-game-book-truth.

41 Houellebecq, *Whatever*, 41.

42 This is for heterosexual couples; the figure for same-sex couples is 60 percent. See: How Couples Meet and Stay Together survey data, managed by Michael Rosenfeld at Stanford University. For wedding data see https://www.bustle.com/p/how-do-most-couples-meet-these-days-online-is-the-top-way-people-are-finding-their-spouses-today-survey-finds-3344742. Numbers vary widely on both how many couples and marriages originate online. The only certainty is that is has increased a great deal and continues to rise.

43 See the chart in Rosenfeld et al., "Disintermediating Your Friends," 2019: https://web.stanford.
edu/~mrosenfe/Rosenfeld_et_al_Disintermediating_Friends.pdf.

44 https://hingeirl.com/hinge-reports/whats-the-biggest-challenge-men-face-on-dating-apps-a-qa-with-aviv-
goldgeier-junior-growth-engineer/.; https://qz.com/1051462/these-statistics-show-why-its-so-hard-to-
be-an-average-man-on-dating-apps/. This is data for straight men and straight women. The country
data for Gini Coefficeints comes in this instance from the CIA World Factbook. The OECD-EU figures
comes from "Understanding the Socio-economic Divide in Europe: Background Report," January 26,
2017. (7) https://www.oecd.org/els/soc/cope-divide-europe-2017-background-report.pdf.

45 http://www.eecs.qmul.ac.uk/~tysong/files/Tinder.pdf. (4)

46 See: Christian Rudder in *Dataclysm*: "Translate this plot to IQ, and you have a world where the
women think 58% of men are brain damaged." Christian Rudder, *Dataclysm: What Our Online
Selves Tell Us About Our Offline Selves*, (London: Fourth Estate, 2016), 23–24.

47 https://theblog.okcupid.com/a-womans-advantage-82d5074dde2d.
Elizabeth E. Bruch and M. E. J. Newman, "Aspirational pursuit of mates in online dating markets,"
Science Advances 4, no. 8 (August, 8 2018).

48 Rudder, *Dataclysm*, 98.

49 Rudder, *Dataclysm*, 133. Given the lack of data, one can only speculate, but it seems likely that
Tinder's format, which consists of single images and very little written information, would tend to
exaggerate this effect.

50 https://www.thecut.com/2014/02/okcupid-most-desired-people-in-new-york.html.

51 Elizabeth E. Bruch and M. E. J. Newman, "Aspirational pursuit."
This is not to suggest that this is not necessarily an enjoyable situation to be in. Many women on
online dating platforms experience harassment and obscene and objectifying proposals. However,
one of the false intuitions about the dynamics of online dating is that the sheer quantity of messages
(crude, polite, or otherwise) that women are receiving is dampening their enthusiasm to participate
equally in contacting potential partners. Heterosexual women are 3.5 times less likely to send the first
message than men but curiously this holds stable whether the women are deemed attractive or not *and*
whether they are receiving a huge volume of messages or very few. https://theblog.okcupid.com/a-
womans-advantage-82d5074dde2d.

52 https://theblog.okcupid.com/race-and-attraction-2009-2014-107dcbb4f060. Jevan Hutson, Jessie
G. Taft, Solon Barocas, and Karen Levy. "Debiasing Desire: Addressing Bias & Discrimination on
Intimate Platforms, *Proceedings of the ACM on Human-Computer Interaction* , CSCW 2, Article 73
(November 2018). https://doi.org/10.1145/3274342.

53 Rudder, *Dataclysm*, 98.

54 Kaitlyn Tiffany, "Nearly all of the big dating apps are now owned by the same company," (February
11, 2019). https://www.vox.com/the-goods/2019/2/11/18220425/hinge-explained-match-group-tinder-
dating-apps.

55 Tinder Boost, https://www.help.tinder.com/hc/en-us/articles/360029087891-Super-Boost.

56 Rebecca Jennings, "Dating apps like Tinder and Bumble are free. But people say paying for them is
worth the money," (September 19, 2018). https://www.vox.com/the-goods/2018/9/19/17856860/
tinder-plus-gold-bumble-boost-okcupid-a-list-dating-apps-premium. "Match Group, Inc. Report on
Form 10-K for the Fiscal Year ended December 31, 2018." Match Group annual financials available
on: https://ir.mtch.com/financials/sec-filings/default.aspx. "Q1 2019 Investor Presentation—May 7,
2019" Quarterly Investor Presentation available on: https://ir.mtch.com/news-and-events/quarterly-
results/default.aspx.

57 Baudrillard, *Seduction*, 39.

AFTERWORD

1 Sinclair, "Seduction and the Myth of the Ideal Woman."

2 Weinstein was quoted in Caroline Frankie, "Deciphering Harvey Weinstein's bizarre defense
against sexual harassment claims," vox.com, (October 5, 2017). https://www.vox.com/
culture/2017/10/5/16432006/harvey-weinstein-statement-sexual-harassment. Chantal Da Silva,
"ALEXANDRIA OCASIO-CORTEZ: IF YOU THINK U.S. SPIKE IN CELIBACY IS DUE TO

'FEMALE EMPOWERMENT,' YOU'RE MISSING THE POINT," (May 13 2019). https://www.newsweek.com/alexandria-ocasio-cortez-if-you-think-us-spike-celibacy-due-female-1423889. Yvonne Roberts, "The sex revolution of my youth wasn't so great. Maybe today's celibacy is a sign of progress," (April 7, 2019). https://www.theguardian.com/commentisfree/2019/apr/07/sex-revolution-my-youth-wasnt-great-maybe-celibacy-sign-progress.

3 Ezra Klein, "'Yes Means Yes' is a terrible law, and I completely support it," vox.com, (October 13, 2014). https://www.vox.com/2014/10/13/6966847/yes-means-yes-is-a-terrible-bill-and-i-completely-support-it.

4 The California State University and University of California systems backed the legislation having already adopted similar consent standards that year.; https://abc7chicago.com/news/yes-means-yes-california-sb-967-sex-assault-bill-signed/328741/.

5 https://www.newyorker.com/news/our-columnists/unpopular-speech-in-a-cold-climate.

6 Laura Kipnis, *Unwanted Advances: Sexual Paranoia Comes to Campus,* (New York: Verso, 2018), 76; Jacob Gersen and Jeannie Suk, *The Sex Bureaucracy,* 104; Calif. L. Rev. 881 (2016).
For a general overview of the state of Title IX, the growing backlash against its execution, and a profile of Jeannie Suk Gersen, see Wesley Yang, "The Revolt of the Feminist Law Profs," *The Chronicle of Higher Education,* (August 7, 2019).

7 See: "Netflix film crews 'banned from looking at each other for longer than five seconds' in #metoo crackdown," *The Independent,* (Wednesday, June, 13 2018). https://www.independent.co.uk/arts-entertainment/tv/news/netflix-sexual-harassment-training-rules-me-too-flirting-on-set-a8396431.html?amp.
For a comprehensive code of conduct that reflects the substance of progressive modern thought on sexual harassment in the workplace see the Code of Conduct of the International Faculty and Staff Sexual Misconduct Conference (FASSM) available at: https://facultysexualmisconduct.com/code-of-conduct.

8 "Reality Check: Is Malmo the 'rape capital' of Europe?," BBC News, February 24, 2017. https://www.bbc.co.uk/news/uk-politics-39056786.

9 See Bryan Stevenson:
"The explicit use of race to codify different kinds of offenses and punishments was challenged as unconstitutional, and criminal statutes were modified to avoid direct racial references, but the enforcement of the law didn't change. Black people were routinely charged with a wide range of 'offenses,' some of which whites were never charged with."
http://www.nybooks.com/articles/2017/07/13/presumption-of-guilt/

10 See "The Sex Bureaucracy," and https://reason.com/2017/09/14/we-need-to-talk-about-black-students-bei/.

11 Emily Yoffe, "The Question of Race in Campus Sexual-Assault Cases," *The Atlantic,* (September 11, 2017). https://www.theatlantic.com/education/archive/2017/09/the-question-of-race-in-campus-sexual-assault-cases/539361/.
This article also notes a serious disparity in between the proportion of Asian students at Colgate (3 percent) and the number of Asian students accused of sexual assault (13 percent).

12 Adam Smith in *The Theory of Moral Sentiments* (1759), quoted in Dennis C. Rasmussen, *The Infidel and the Professor: David Hume, Adam Smith, and the Friendship that Shaped Modern Thought,* (Princeton University Press, 2017), 89.
Gareth Tyson, Claudiu Perta, Hamed Haddadi, and Michael Seto. "A First Look at User Activity on Tinder." In 8th IEEE/ACM International Conference on Advances in Social Networks Analysis and Mining (ASONAM), San Francisco, CA (2016). Accessed from http://www.eecs.qmul.ac.uk/~tysong/#selectedpublications. The same report notes that 25 percent of messages from men to women are 6 characters or less.

INDEX

A

abortion, 386, 387
Acquaviva, Cardinal, 91–92, 93
Act of Toleration, 24
actresses, 343–344, 363–364
Adair, Robert, 45
Addison, Joseph, 7
Adorno, Theodor, 374
adultery, 43–44, 100, 193, 236–237, 247–249
Advocate, The, 259
African American migration, 279
Age of Reason, 7. *See also* Enlightenment
Alabama, 260–261
Aldini, Giovanni, 213–214
alienation of affection, 236, 256, 312
Amar, André, 182
Amelia (Fielding), 67
American Revolution, 156
Analytical Review, 154, 175
Ancilla, 82
Anglo-Saxon Clubs of America (ASCOA), 310, 311
animal magnetism, 224–229
Ansari, Aziz, 419–420
anti-heart balm legislation, 316–319
Anti-Pamela; or Feign'd Innocence Detected (Haywood), 39
anti-Semitism, 351–357, 360, 368–373
app-enabled dating, 407–417
apprentices, 27–29, 32
Apprentice's Vade Mecum, The (Richardson), 32–33
Armstrong, Eliza, 342
Armstrong, Louis, 276, 309
Ascension Day, 113, 114
Atomized (Houellebecq), 394–397, 414
attractiveness, 409–410
Augustine, St., 4
Austen, Mary, 266, 268

B

Balbi, Marin, 129–132
Balcombe, Florence. *See* Stoker, Florence
Bankes, William, 201
Banks, Ada, 282, 286
Banks, Joseph, 135
Barbaro, Marco, 102–103, 111
Bardot, Brigitte, 385
Barlow, Joel, 175, 177
Barlow, Ruth, 175
bastard children, 215, 216, 230, 240, 245
Baudrillard, Jean, 393, 413
Baumeister, Eric, 388–389
Baxter, William, 197
Bebel, August, 375–376
Bell, John, 227
Bellamy, Edward, 376
Benson, Edward White, 339–340
Bertati, Giovanni, 141–142
Bill of Rights, 24
Blake, William, 165–166, 168
Blanc, Julien, 405–406, 423
Blavatsky, Madame, 320
Blease, Cole, 290–291
Blood, Fanny, 146–147, 148
Bonaparte, Napoleon, 228, 302
Bond, Anne, 13, 22, 23
Boswell, James, 20, 72, 80, 134
Bourdieu, Pierre, 400
boxing, 261–266, 268–275, 302–303
Bradshaigh, Lady Dorothy, 59–64, 66, 75–76, 77
Bradshaigh, Sir Roger, 59
Bragadin, Matteo Giovanni, 101–104, 111, 112, 113, 117, 127, 129
Breece v. Jett, 422, 423
Bryant, William, 267
Bulwer-Lytton, Edward, 259
Bureau of Investigation, 281, 288–289
Burgh, James, 147
Burgh, Mrs., 147, 148, 149
Burke, Edmund, 155–159, 162, 197, 322
Burne-Jones, Edward, 365
Burney, Charles, 109
Burns, Tommy, 269–271
Butler, Josephine, 334–335, 338–339
Byron, Ada, 205
Byron, Annabella Milbanke, 201–206, 207
Byron, Clara Allegra (Alba), 217–220

Byron, Lord George Gordon, 10, 85, 152, 229–230, 237, 249–250, 259; affairs of, 202–203; Casanova and, 137–138; *Childe Harold's Pilgrimage*, 201; *cicisbeismo and*, 98–100; Claire Clairmont and, 207, 210, 217–222; marriage to Annabella, 201–206; Polidori and, 207–210, 211–212; scandal surrounding, 206–207; Shelleys and, 210–214, 217–222

C

Café de Champion, 282–283, 288, 309
Café de Luxe, 308–309
Cagliostro, Alessandro, 226
Caine, Hall, 357, 358
Callisto, 3
Cameron, Archibald, 72
Cameron, Lucille, 282, 284–286, 288–291, 300, 314
Cameron-Falconet, Mrs. F., 284–286, 290
Caminetti, Anthony, 297
Caminetti, Drew, 296–300
Caminetti v. United States, 299–300
Canterbury Tales, The (Chaucer), 5
capital, 400
capitalism, 36, 320, 375, 376, 391–394, 396, 414, 431
Capretta, Caterina, 115–120, 122, 126
Capretta, Pietro, 115–117
Captive of the Castle of Sennaar, The (Cumberland), 165–166
Carpentier, Georges, 301, 302
Caruso, Enrico, 312
Casanova, Gaetano, 83–84
Casanova, Giacomo, 10, 80–142; affairs of, 92–101, 112, 115–127, 134, 137–138; arrest, imprisonment, and escape of, 127–132; Byron and, 137–138; death of, 142; Don Giovanni and, 138–142; in France, 143–144; love children of, 93, 116; travels by, 111–113, 132–138; in Venetian society, 101–132; youth of, 83–93
Casanova, Zannetta, 83–84, 89–90
Catiglione, Baldassare, 5–6
Ceccaldi, Janine, 379–381
Chapman, Annie, 348
Chapone, Sarah, 49, 69
charitable institutions, 73–74
Charles II, 14
Charteris, Francis, 13–16, 21–24
Charteris, Janet, 14–15, 22–23
chastity, 4, 36, 48, 194, 259, 318, 335, 397
Chaucer, 5
Cheyne, George, 31, 53
Chicago, 279–280, 282

Childe Harold's Pilgrimage (Byron), 201
Chivers, Emma, 1–2, 11, 12
Choynski, Joe, 264–265, 274
Christianity, 4–5, 360, 382
Christie, Thomas, 175
Churchill, Charles, 27
Cibber, Colley, 46, 58–59
cicisbeismo, 96–101, 108
Civilization and Its Discontents (Freud), 376–377
Clairmont, Claire, 10, 199–201, 207, 210–214, 216–220, 249–250
Clairmont, Mary Jane. *See* Clairmont, Claire
Clarissa: or, the History of a Young Lady (Richardson), 9, 50–64, 68, 385
Coleridge, Samuel, 166
Collier, Jane, 49
Colonda, Maria, 115–117
Commerce Clause, 276–277, 280
Communist Manifesto, The (Marx and Engels), 375, 394
Compagnoni, Giuseppe, 107–108
Condulmer, Antonio, 127
consent, 8–9, 11, 206, 257, 424, 426, 427
consent law, 277, 335, 340, 424
Constantinople, 93
consumerism, 383
Contagious Diseases Act, 338
contraception, 386–387, 390–391
convents, 117–119
Cook, Captain, 135
Coram, Thomas, 73
Corday, Charlotte, 181
Corfu, 93–96
Cornelys, Teresa, 133
Cotton Club, 309
Council of Three, 110–111
court culture, 107
courtesans, 20–21
courtliness, 5–6
coverture, 244–245, 247, 248
Craig, Edy, 363–364
Cranston, Isabella, 21–22
Cravan, Arthur, 304
criminal conversation, 236–237, 239, 256
Criminal Law Amendment Act, 337, 338, 340–342, 357, 367
criminals, 345–347
Critical Remarks on Sir Charles Grandison, Clarissa, and Pamela (anonymous), 70–71
Cruel Intentions (film), 9
Cumberland, George, 165–166
Curley, Jack, 302
Custody of Infants Act, 240, 242–243

D

Damian, St. Peter, 4–5
Dandolo, Marco, 102–103, 111
d'Antoni Vallati, Anna Maria, 92–93
Darwin, Charles, 344–345, 348
Darwin, Erasmus, 213, 215
dating apps, 407–417
Davis, Angela, 391
Davy, Humphry, 227
de Bernardis, Bernardo, 90–91
de Bernis, François-Joachim de Pierre, 126,
    132–133
de Bougainville, Louis-Antoine, 135
Declaration of the Rights of Woman (de Gouges),
    161, 182
Defoe, Daniel, 31
degeneration, 345
de Genlis, Madame, 176, 182
de Gouges, Olympe, 161, 181, 182
de la Houssaye, Abraham Nicolas Amelot, 118
Delany, Patrick, 42
Deleuze, Joseph, 226
Dennigan, William P., 317
de Pizan, Christine, 4
de Ponte, Lorenzo, 139, 141
Depsey, Jack, 312, 314
Descent of Man, The (Darwin), 344, 348
Diderot, Denis, 136
Diggs, Maury, 296–300
digital revolution, 394
Disraeli, Benjamin, 355
divorce, 44, 45, 160, 161, 172, 177, 193,
    205–207, 243, 247–249, 386
Dodd, William, 75
Dohrn, Anton, 345
Don Giovanni (Mozart), 138–142
Don Juan character, 138–139
Don Juan (Byron), 137, 214
Don Juan (film), 385
double standards, 44, 248, 312–313, 339, 389, 423
Doyle, Arthur Conan, 328, 357
Drabble, Margaret, 386–387, 390–391
Dracula (Stoker), 358–368
Dr. Jekyll and Mr. Hyde (Stevenson), 344–350
Ducal Palace, 127–130
Du Maurier, George, 326, 355–357
d'Urfé, Madame, 133
Duryea, Etta. *See* Johnson, Etta Duryea
Dworkin, Andrea, 404, 423
Dyer, Alfred, 334

E

economic capital, 400
economic inequality, 386, 408, 430–431

Eddowes, Catherine, 348
education, female, 149–152, 160–161, 163–164,
    182
Edwards, Thomas, 67–68
Elements of Physiology (Richerand), 225
Eller v. Lord, 258
Ellington, Duke, 309
embryology, 345
Emigrants, The (Imlay), 177
Émile, or On Education (Rousseau), 151–152
Engels, Friedrich, 375, 394
Enlightenment, 6–10, 12, 49, 53, 83, 106–107,
    112, 123, 134, 240, 421
Eros and Civilization (Marcuse), 378, 391
erotic capital, 400, 411
Essay Concerning Human Understanding, An
    (Locke), 53–54
Essay On Man (Pope), 432
Europa, 3
European civilization, 106–108
European Slave Trade in English Girls, The
    (Dyer), 334
Eve, 4–5
evolutionary theory, 344–345
extramarital sex, 309–310. *See also* adultery

F

false morality, 193–194
family dissolution, 382–383
Fanny Hill, or Memoirs of a Woman of Pleasure
    (Cleland), 385
Fasussi, Zannetta. *See* Casanova, Zannetta
Fear of Flying (Jong), 385, 387, 390
Federal Bureau of Investigation (FBI), 281,
    311–312
female education, 149–152, 160–161, 163–164,
    182
Female Eunuch, The (Greer), 12
Female Quixote, The (Lennox), 49
female sexuality, 388–390, 403
Female Spectator, The, 48–49
female writers, 47–50, 69. *See also specific writers.*
feminism, 6, 366–367, 386, 391, 403–407,
    420–421
Fenton, Lavinia, 20
Fielding, Henry, 10, 37, 39, 58, 66–67, 133
Fielding, Sarah, 49, 68, 69
Fifty Shades of Grey (James), 2, 421
film, 368–369, 373, 403
Final Solution, 373
Fisher, Kitty, 21
Fitzgerald, F. Scott, 306, 309
Fitzgerald, Zelda, 306
flappers, 306–307, 308, 420

Fluke, John, 239
Foundling Hospital, 73–74
Frankenstein (Shelley), 214–216, 220, 229
Free Love, 10, 12, 165–173, 194, 196, 199, 200, 212, 230, 250
Freisler, Roland, 370–371
French Revolution, 154–161, 168, 170–185, 196
Freud, Sigmund, 375, 376–377
Fritsch, Theodor, 370
Fukuyama, Francis, 384, 391
Fuseli, Henri, 168–171, 190, 195, 365

G
Galvani, Luigi, 213–214
Galvanism, 213–214
Galveston, Texas, 253, 261–262, 272
Game, The (Strauss), 399, 402–403, 406, 407, 421
Ganymede, 3
Gardiner, Marguerite (Countess Blessington), 220
Gentlemen Prefer Blondes (Loos), 313
George II, 22
Germany, 319, 368–376, 386
Gersen, Jacob, 425, 426, 428
Gilray, James, 228
Gimbel, Frederick, 312
Girondins, 178, 180
Glenarvon (Lamb), 220–221
Glorious Revolution, 24, 25, 155, 156
Godwin, Mary. *See* Shelley, Mary
Godwin, William, 158, 166–167, 170, 188–191, 194–199, 228, 235
Goethe, Johann Wolfgang von, 108–109
"gold digger," 313
Goldin, Claudia, 431
Goldoni, Carlo, 84, 99, 141
Gourley, John, 16
Gover v. Dill, 257
Graham, Catherine Macaulay, 158
Graham, David, 67
Grand Tour, 80
Grau, Fritz, 371–372
Great Disruption, The (Fukuyama), 384
Great Reform Act, 238, 242
Great White Flight, 270
Greer, Germaine, 12
Grimani, Alvisi, 84–85
Grundy, Sydney, 362–363
Guiccioli, Teresa, 98–99, 100

H
Haeckel, Ernst, 345
Hakim, Catherine, 400, 411
Hammond, William, 44–45

happiness, pursuit of, 123
Hardwick, Elizabeth, 390
Harlem Renaissance, 309
Harlot's Progress, The (Hogarth), 23
Hart, Marvin, 269
Haydon, Benjamin, 233
Haygood, Bishop, 253–254
Hays, Mary, 189
Haywood, Eliza, 39, 48–49
Hazlitt, William, 196
heart balm acts, 257, 316–319
hedonism, 12
Hell-Fire Club, 44
"Heroic" seduction narrative, 10
Hewlett, John, 148, 149
Highmore, Joseph, 76–77
Hill, Aaron, 31, 39, 59, 67
Hinge, 408
History of Sir Charles Grandison, The (Richardson), 64–69, 70, 74–75
Hite, Shere, 403
Hite Report, The (Hite), 403
Hitler, Adolf, 369–370, 371, 374, 379
Hobhouse, John, 203, 223
Hogarth, William, 23, 28
Hoppner, Richard, 219
Horkheimer, Max, 374
Houellebecq, Michel, 381–384, 394–399, 407, 414, 430
How to Get the Women You Desire into Bed (Jeffries), 401
How To Pick Up Girls! (Weber), 401
Hume, David, 8, 54
Hunt, Leigh, 229
hypnotism, 225, 355, 361–362
hypnosis metaphor, 11

I
Ilive, Jacob, 20
illegitimate children, 215, 216, 230, 240, 245
Imer, Teresa, 88, 89, 116, 133
Imlay, Fanny, 183–184, 191, 216
Imlay, Gilbert, 177–180, 183–186, 188, 190, 195, 216
immigration, 279, 367
incels (involuntary celibates), 398–399
individualism, 383, 396
Industry and Idleness (Hogwarth), 28
Information age, 384, 386
Inquisition, 126–127
interpersonal conflict, 383
interracial relations, 260–261, 271–273, 284, 290–291, 294, 296, 310–311, 319
Io, 3

Irving, Henry, 323–325, 329–331, 343, 344, 351–352, 356, 357

J

Jack the Ripper, 348–351, 353–354
Jacobins, 159, 178, 180–184, 196
James II, 24, 25
jazz, 307–308
Jazz Age, 308–314
Jeffries, Jim, 268–269, 273–276
Jeffries, Ross, 401
Jenkins, Nettie, 295–296
Jerome, St., 4, 5
Jews, anti-Semitism and, 351–357, 360, 368–373
Johnson, Etta Duryea, 272–274, 282–284, 287, 319
Johnson, Jack (John Arthur), 251–277, 314; boxing career of, 261–275; decline of, 314–315, 318–319; in exile in Europe, 300–305; heavyweight championship and, 268–271, 274–276, 302–303; Mann Act and, 281–295; return to U.S. by, 305, 308–309; white women and, 268, 271–273, 282, 284–286, 290–291, 314
Johnson, Joseph, 152, 154, 157, 165, 169, 175, 189, 195
Johnson, Lucille. *See* Cameron, Lucille
Johnson, Samuel, 17, 49–50, 72, 74, 148
Johnson, Sol C., 294
Jong, Erica, 385, 387, 390
Joseph Andrews (Fielding), 66
Journal of a Voyage to Lisbon (Fielding), 67–68

K

Kelly, Mary, 348–349
kerdaelophron, 132
Kerr, Clara, 266–268
Ketchel, Stanley, 272
Kingsborough, Lord and Lady, 150–152
Kipnis, Laura, 426
Klein, Ezra, 424, 428
Klossowski, Pierre, 392–393
knowledge economy, 385, 391–392
Kollontai, Alexandra, 376
Ku Klux Klan, 315, 378

L

Labor of Love (Weigel), 413–414
Ladies National Association (LNA), 334–335, 338
Lamb, Lady Caroline, 201, 202–203, 207, 220–221, 237
Lamb, William (Lord Melbourne), 236, 237–239
Langford, Sam, 301
Lankester, Ray, 345
Larson, Jane E., 404–405

laughing gas, 227, 228
La Valeur, 94–96
Lawrence, William, 212–213, 215
Leake, Elizabeth, 32
Leather Apron, 353, 360
Leigh, Augusta, 202, 204, 206–207
Lennox, Charlotte, 49
Letters Written in France (Williams), 158
Letters Written in Sweden, Norway, and Denmark (Wollstonecraft), 186–189
liberalism, 6
libertinism, 24–25, 106, 110
Libidinal Economy (Lyotard), 392–393
Living Currency (Klossowski), 392
Locke, John, 53–54
logic, 7–8
Lombroso, Cesare, 345–347, 354
London: Casanova in, 133; City of, 25–26; early eighteenth century, 16–21, 27–30; fog, 328–329; seventeenth century, 25–27; Victorian era, 327–344; Wollstonecraft in, 153
London, a poem (Johnson), 17
London, Jack, 271
loneliness, 399
Looking Backward (Bellamy), 376
Loos, Anita, 313
Louis, Joe, 318–319
Louis XIV, 107
Louis XV, 143, 144
Louis XVI, 144–145, 159, 173–175
Lovecraft, H. P., 394
Loving v. Virginia, 319
Lyceum Theatre, 327–332, 343–344, 349–350, 356, 364
lynchings, 254–256, 261, 268, 287, 291, 297
Lyotard, Jean-François, 392–393

M

MacKinnon, Catherine, 404
madness, 225
Magdalen House, 75–77, 153
male sexuality, 388
Malipiero, Alvise, 87–89
Malleus Maleficarum, 5
Man, The (Stoker), 363
Man and Superman (Shaw), 364
Mann, James Robert, 280–281
Mann Act, 277–300, 311–313, 319
Man of Feeling, The (Mackenzie), 10–11
Mansfield, Richard, 344, 348–350
Manuzzi, Giovanni Battista, 126–127
Marat, Jean-Paul, 181
Marcuse, Herbert, 374–379, 391–392
Maria: or, The Wrongs of Woman (Wollstonecraft), 191–194

Maria Teresa, 113
Marie-Antoinette, 181–182
Markovik, Erik von, 402, 414
marriage, 7, 108, 166–167, 216, 244–245,
    247–249; interracial, 261, 291, 294, 310–311,
    319; reformation of, 366–367. *See also* divorce
Marriage Bar, 386
Marx, Karl, 375, 394
Marxism, 374–377, 379, 389, 391
Mary, A Fiction (Wollstonecraft), 152, 154
Mary Magdalen, 63
Mary Stuart, 24, 26
Match Group, 411, 413
materialism, 6, 7–8, 383
Maxwell-Stirling, Sir William, 249
Mazeppa (Byron), 222
McClay, Hattie, 271–274, 282
McIntosh, Hugh D., 270–271
McMillan, Margaret, 367
Mein Kampf (Hitler), 369–370
Melbourne, Lady. *See* Lamb, Lady Caroline
Melbourne, Lord. *See* Lamb, William (Lord
    Melbourne)
Memmo, Lucia, 127
memoirs, 47–49
Memoirs of Laetitia Pilkington, The (Pilkington),
    47–48
*Memoirs of the Author of A Vindication of the
    Rights of Woman* (Godwin), 195–196
Merchant of Venice, The (Shakespeare), 352
mesmerism, 355
Metamorphoses (Ovid), 3–4
#MeToo movement, 418–432
Milbanke, Annabella. *See* Byron, Annabella
    Milbanke
Millar, Andrew, 30
Minassian, Alek, 398
miscegenation, 260–261, 272, 291, 319
misogyny, 4–5, 6, 423
modernity, 2, 3, 79, 278, 279, 320
Montagu, Lady Mary Wortley, 58, 81
Moral Essays (Pope), 21, 23
morality, 36, 38–39, 69–70, 192–194, 247, 340,
    390–391, 429
moral panic, 73, 292–293
Moran, Frank, 301
Morisson, Fynes, 104
Morris, William, 376, 389–390
Morrison, Jim, 385
mothers, rights of, 240–241
Mount Tambora, 210
Mozart, Wolfgang Amadeus, 138–142
Murnau, F. W., 368, 373
Murray, Fanny, 20

Murray, John, 81–82, 208
Mystery Method, 402, 416–417

N
natural rights, 240–241, 247
natural selection, 320, 344–345
Nazis, 319, 369–375
negging, 402
neo-liberalism, 396
New Man, 366–367
News From Nowhere (Morris), 376, 389–390
New Woman, 320, 343–344, 362–368
New Woman, The (Grundy), 362–363
New York Female Moral Reform Society
    (NYFMRS), 259
Nichols, Mary Ann, 348
Nicholson, Roberta West, 315–318
Nootbaar, Max, 286
Norris, Lola, 297
Norton, Caroline, 230–249
Norton, George, 231, 237–238, 242, 244–247,
    249
Norton v. Viscount Melbourne, 238–240
Nosferatu, 368, 373
Notorious Mrs Ebbsmith, The (Pinero), 363
Nuremberg Laws, 372

O
O'Brien, Nellie, 271–272
Ocasio-Cortez, Alexandria, 422–423
OkCupid, 409–411, 414
One-Dimensional Man (Marcuse), 391
online dating, 407–417
On the Origin of Species (Darwin), 344–345
Osborn, John, 30
Osborne, Walter, 363
Ovid, 3–4, 5, 66
Oxford, Lady, 202

P
Padua, 85–86, 113
Paine, Thomas, 158, 175, 228
Pall Mall Gazette, 333, 334, 335, 337–338, 343,
    346–347
Palm, Etta, 160
Pamela Censur'd (anonymous), 39–40
Pamela; or, Virtue Rewarded (Richardson), 2,
    34–41, 49–51, 58, 66, 419
Pankhurst, Christabel, 423
Pantisocracy, 166
parental authority, 312
Pascal, Blaise, 382
passion, 7–8, 10–11, 54, 55, 57, 83, 164–165,
    401–402, 421

philanthropy, 73–74
Philipps, Constantia, 69
pick-up artists, 402, 405–407, 414–417
Pilkington, Laetitia, 42–48, 69
Pilkington, Matthew, 42–45
"pill, the," 386–387
Pineau, Irene Marie, 314
Pinero, Arthur Wing, 363
Pitt the Younger, 154–155
pleasure, 123–124
Plecker, Walter, 311
Polidori, John William, 207–209, 211–214,
    222–224, 228–229
Political Justice (Godwin), 166–167, 199
Polwhele, Richard, 195
Pope, Alexander, 21, 23, 432
Portugal, 148
post-Sexual Revolution, 392–403, 414
Powell, John, 311
Price, Richard, 147, 156
Priestley, Joseph, 228
Printing Act, 24
printing industry, 27–31
prizefighting, 261–266, 268–275, 302–303
Prohibition, 305, 312
property rights, 240–241, 243
prositition, 19–20, 63, 74–75, 108, 243, 278,
    281, 288, 293, 336–338, 340, 343, 354
Prussian Memorandum, 370–371
Public Assemblages Act, 311
public spaces, 430
Punch, 326, 329, 349, 355
Pushkin, Alexander, 77
Putnam, Robert, 430
Puységur, Marquis de, 225, 226

Q
Queen Mab (Shelley), 216

R
race relations, 252
race theory, 320
race treason, 371
racial laws, 260–261
racial violence, 275–277. See also lynchings
racism, 294, 428–429
rake culture, 13–79
rape, 8, 13, 35, 51, 404
rape culture, 405
rationality, 12
Real Social Dynamics (RSD), 406
reason, 7–11, 54, 55, 57, 83, 123, 149–150, 158,
    164–165, 397, 401–402, 421, 429
Reconstruction, 252, 253, 292

Reflections on the Revolution in France (Burke),
    157, 158
Reich, Wihelm, 378
Reign of Terror, 180–184
Religious Courtship (Defoe), 31
religious freedom, 24–25
repression, 376–377
Richardson, Martha, 29, 31–32
Richardson, Samuel, 24–79, 419; *Apprentice's
    Vade Mecum, The*, 32–33; biography of,
    24–34, 71–79; *Clarissa: or, the History of
    a Young Lady*, 50–64, 68; criticism of, 39,
    70–71, 77–78; Fielding and, 39, 66–68;
    History of Sir Charles Grandison, The, 64–69,
    70, 74–75; influence of, 77–78; moral values
    of, 69–70; *Pamela; or, Virtue Rewarded*, 2,
    34–41, 49–51, 58, 66; Pilkington and, 46–48;
    wealth of, 41–42, 47
Richardson, Thomas Verren, 32
Richerand, Anthelme, 225
Rivington, Charles, 30
Robespierre, Maximilien, 171, 178, 180, 228
Roddenbery, Seaborn, 277, 291
Rodger, Elliot, 398
Roe, Clifford G., 280
Roebuck, John Arthur, 244
Roe v. Wade, 387
Roland, Madame, 182–183
Romantics, 10, 12
Roscoe, William, 169, 172–173
Rossetti, Dante Gabriel, 358
Rousseau, Jean-Jacques, 132, 151–152, 161, 180, 223
Rudder, Christian, 410
Russia, 376

S
Salieri, Antonio, 141
Salisbury Court, 29–30
Schreiber, Belle, 272, 273, 274, 282, 289–290,
    293, 296
Schwartz-Bostunitsch, Gregor, 372–373
Scott, Benjamin, 334, 335
Sebottendorf, Rudolf von, 369
seducers, 8–9, 10, 397
seduction: definition of, 258–259; end of, 376,
    393, 396; legal dimension of, 2, 8–12, 236–
    239, 243–244, 256–261, 404–405; literary
    history of, 2–6; Sexual Revolution and, 393,
    396–397; as social issue, 2–3
Seduction (Baudrillard), 393, 413
seduction community, 401–403, 405–407, 414
seduction narrative, 1–12, 397, 429; classical,
    99–100; *Pamela* as first, 34–51; sexual
    ideology and, 49–50

seductress, 20–21
segregation, 311, 371–372
sensibility, 53–54, 56, 73
September Massacres, 171–172
Seward, Anne, 49
Seward, Thomas, 49
sex bureaucracy, 425–429
sex recession, 422–423
sex trafficking, 334–337. *See also* white slave
    trade
sexual assault allegations, 418–432
sexual culture, 421–422
sexual economics, 384–393, 396
sexual experience, 6
sexual fraud, 405
sexual freedom, 10, 12, 105, 108, 165–173, 199,
    245, 312, 366, 386–387, 391, 393
sexual harassment, 426–427
sexual ideology, 39, 69–70
sexual liberation, 12, 165, 167, 366, 378, 379,
    387, 396–397, 402–403, 414, 424. *See also*
    sexual freedom; Sexual Revolution
sexual morality, 6, 309–310
Sexual Revolution, 12, 309–312, 378, 384–396,
    422
sexual virtue, 196
sex workers, 19–20, 74–75, 281, 354. *See also*
    prostitution
Shakespeare, William, 6
Shamela (Fielding), 39, 66
Sharpe, Samuel, 97
Shaw, George Bernard, 323, 324–325, 330, 357,
    364
Shelley, Clara, 217, 218–219
Shelley, Harriet, 197–198, 199, 217
Shelley, Mary, 10, 11, 194, 196, 197–250,
    429; Byron and, 210–214; Caroline Norton
    and, 230–236, 239–242; death of, 249;
    Frankenstein, 214–216, 220, 229; Free
    Love and, 230; Percy Shelley and, 197–201,
    217–219, 229; tragic sensibility of, 200
Shelley, Percy, 10, 197–201, 207, 210–214,
    216–219, 229, 249–250
Shelley, William (Wilmouse), 200, 216, 218, 230
Sheridan, Caroline. *See* Norton, Caroline
Sheridan, Richard Brinsley, 231, 322
Shylock character, 352
Sidney, Philip, 5–6
Signora F., 94, 96, 100
Sims, Edwin W., 280
Sims Act, 277
Sir Gawain and the Green Knight, 5
Sixties, 378–379, 382, 385, 386, 423
slavery, 252

Smith, Adam, 429
Smith, Alfred E., 312
Smith, Henry, 254–256, 275
Smollett, Tobias, 99
sociability, 106–107, 108, 110
social democracy, 396
social interactions, 430
socialism, 375–376, 389–390, 393
social mobility, 20–21
Society for the Reformation of Manners, 26
sodomy, 207–208
somnambulism, 224–229
Sorrows of Rosalie, The (Norton), 231
Southey, George, 166
Southey, Robert, 195
sporting culture, 266, 308
Stanley, Edward Lyulph, 341
"Statues, The" (Pilkington), 46
Stead, William Thomas, 333–344, 354, 368
Steinem, Gloria, 403
sterilization acts, 311
Sterne, Laurence, 27
Stevenson, Robert Louis, 344–350
Stoker, Bram, 11, 320–368; biography of,
    320–323; career of, 357–358; death of, 368;
    Dracula, 358–368; Henry Irving and, 323–325,
    329–330, 357; Lyceum Theatre and, 327–332,
    350, 356, 357; *The Man*, 363; marriage of,
    325–327; W.T. Stead and, 343
Stoker, Florence, 325–327, 363, 365, 368
Stoker, Irving Noel Thornley, 326
Stone, John Hurford, 176
Strauss, Neil, 399, 402–403, 407, 415, 421
Streicher, Julius, 370
Stride, Elizabeth, 348
Suk Gersen, Jeannie, 425, 426, 428
surplus-repression, 377
Svengali character, 355–356
Sweden, 427–428
Swift, Jonathan, 23, 27, 42, 43

T
Tahiti, 134–136, 166
Talfourd, Sir Thomas, 241
Talleyrand, Charles-Maurice, 160–161
telepathy, 355
Tellez, Gabriel, 138–139
Terry, Ellen, 343–344
Tertullian, 4, 5
Thelwall, John, 224, 228
This Side of Paradise (Fitzgerald), 306
Thomas, Michel. *See* Houellebecq, Michel
Thomas, René, 380–382
Thoughts on the Education of Daughters

(Wollstonecraft), 149–150
Thule Society, 369
Tillman, Ben, 297
Tinder, 410, 411–412, 414, 430
Tinger, 408–409
Titanic, 368
Title IX, 425–426, 428–429
Tom Jones (Fielding), 66–68
Torbillon, Robert A., 312
Tower of London, 25
Treatise of Human Nature, A (Hume), 54
Tree, Herbert Beerbohm, 356
Trelawney, Edward, 229, 233–235
Trilby (Du Maurier), 355–357
Tunney, Gene, 312
Twenge, Jean, 430
Twenties, 306–314

U
United States v. John Arthur Johnson, 292–295,
   297, 300
university consent guidelines, 425–426
"Unsex'd Females, The" (Polwhele), 195–196
"unsexed," 338–339
Updike, John, 384–385

V
Vampire, The (Burne-Jones), 365
vampires, 358–370
Vampyre, The (Polidori), 220–224, 229
Vance, Myrtle, 253–254
Vanderbilt, Cornelius, 312
Vane, Lady Frances, 69
Venice, 80–82, 85, 97, 101–132, 136, 142;
   convents of, 117–119; Enlightenment in,
   106–107; society of, 108–111; women in,
   104–106, 117–119
Venus, 135
Victoria (queen), 239
Victorian era, 69–70, 320, 327–344, 361–368
Vienna, 113
villainous seduction narrative, 8–12
Vindication of the Rights of Men, A
   (Wollstonecraft), 157–159
Vindication of the Rights of Woman
   (Wollstonecraft), 161–165
virtue, 36–37, 51, 71, 196
Vohs, Kathleen, 388–389
Volstead Act, 305
Voltaire, 10, 133
von Schlabrendorf, Gustav, 176–177
W
Walcott, Joe, 264
Wallis, Samuel, 134–135

Walpole, Horace, 37, 76
Warrington, Marsha, 297
Washington, Booker T., 286–287
Watts, George, 343
Webb, Beatrice, 366
Weber, Eric, 400–401
Webster, Sir Richard, 341
Weigel, Moira, 413–414
Weimar Republic, 368–369
Weinstein, Harvey, 418–422, 431
Wells, Ida, 254
Westbrook, Harriet. *See* Shelley, Harriet
Whatever (Houellebecq), 394–395, 397–398,
   407, 408
White, Arnold, 355
White Cross League, 340
whiteness, 311
white slave trade, 277–281, 291–292, 334–347,
   372
White-Slave Traffic Act. *See* Mann Act
white supremacists, 252
whores, 20
"Wife of Bath's Tale, The" (Chaucer), 5
Wilberforce, William, 73
Wilde, Oscar, 325, 329, 357
Willard, Frances, 277, 424
Willard, Jess, 302–303
William of Orange, 24
Williams, Helen Maria, 158, 171–172, 176, 182
Wing, Isadora, 385
witches, 5, 320
Wollstonecraft, Mary, 10, 145–198, 338, 429,
   431; biography of, 145–154; death of, 194;
   in France, 173–185, 196; Free Love and,
   165–173, 194; *Letters Written in Sweden,
   Norway, and Denmark*, 186–189; *Maria: or,
   The Wrongs of Woman*, 191–194; marriage to
   Godwin of, 189–191; *Mary, A Fiction*, 152,
   154; *Thoughts on the Education of Daughters*,
   149–150; *Vindication of the Rights of Men, A*,
   157–159; *Vindication of the Rights of Woman*,
   161–165
womanhood, ideal of, 69
"woman question," 6
women: early eighteenth century, 19–21;
   education of, 149–152, 160–161, 163–164,
   182; Enlightenment view of, 53–54; European,
   107; exploitation of, 63; flappers, 306–307,
   308, 420; in French Revolution, 155–161,
   180–183; Mann Act and, 295–296, 298–299,
   312–313; marriage and, 244–245; rights of,
   159–164, 240–243, 245–249, 257–258, 362;
   sexual economics and, 384–391; sexuality
   of, 388–390; sexual rights of, 338; Venetian,

104–106, 117–119; Victorian era, 338–340,
    361–368; vilification of, 4–5
Women and Socialism (Bebel), 375–376
Women's Christian Temperance Union (WCTU),
    277, 310
Women's March, 155, 156
Wood, Myron, 1–2
Woolf, Virginia, 168
World War I, 301–305
World War II, 319, 374–375, 379
Worsdale, James, 43–44
Wyndham, Horace, 331, 332

Y
"Yes Means Yes," 424
Yorke, Henry Galgacus Redhead, 243
Young, Arthur, 150
Young, Edward, 58
youth culture, 308, 312

Z
Zeus, 3